SURVIVAL
OF THE FITTEST

A NATURAL HISTORY OF THE EXMOOR PONY

SUE BAKER

LINE DRAWINGS BY STEPHANIE POULTER

EXMOOR BOOKS

Notice: I, Susan Elizabeth Baker, hereby assert and give notice
of my right under section 77 of the Copyright, Designs and
Patents Act 1988 to be identified as the author of this book.

Extract from "Alaska" © 1988 by James Michener, reprinted by
permission of Martin Secker and Warburg Limited.

First published 1993

Exmoor Books
Dulverton, Somerset

Trade sales enquiries
Westcountry Books
Chinon Court
Lower Moor Way
Tiverton EX16 6SS

Tel: (0884) 243242
Fax: (0884) 243325

Exmoor Books in partnership between
The Exmoor Press and Exmoor National Park

British Library Cataloguing in Publication Data

A CIP Catalogue Record for this book is available from the
British Library

ISBN 0-86183-220-5

Designed for Exmoor Books
Topics Visual Information
397 Topsham Road
Exeter EX2 6HD

Telephone: (0392) 876800

Typeset by Exe Valley Dataset Ltd, Exeter
Printed in Great Britain by The Bath Press

FOREWORD

Sue Baker has described the Exmoor Pony as a National Treasure. This may sound like an extravagant claim, but it is not, as this book will soon convince you.

What is so special about the Exmoor is that it is much more than just another local breed of pony, fashioned by man with generations of selective breeding. This fascinating equine was fashioned, not by human breeders but by nature itself. It has roamed the countryside of the British Isles for perhaps tens of thousands of years. Amazingly hardy and able to stand up to even the harshest of our winters, it is in all probability a surviving prehistoric horse. If you look at it when it is wearing its winter coat, it is remarkably similar to the images of small horses you find on the painted cave walls of France and Spain. It seems to have changed little over the millennia and today its characteristics are so firmly fixed that no colour variations ever occur. Its beautiful markings are present in every single animal.

As the most ancient of British equines, the Exmoor Pony should be of great importance to us as a nation and yet, sadly, its numbers are dangerously low. Only about 140 free-living ponies still survive on Exmoor itself. Worldwide their number totals less than 800 and it is not surprising that it has been placed on the critical list of the Rare Breeds Survival Trust.

The Exmoor clearly needs all the friends it can get and, in Dr Baker, it certainly has one of its very best friends. Her fascination for the breed – she would prefer to call it a race, giving it the status of a variety of wild equine – has become a personal crusade, a fierce passion to promote and protect the animal she admires so much. But make no mistake, hers is not merely an emotional attachment. It goes far beyond that, and is also an erudite and scientific defence of this wonderful member of the equine family. I hope her new book will be as widely read as it deserves to be and that it will ensure a far less "critical" status for the Exmoor Pony in the years to come.

Desmond Morris, Oxford 1992.

PREFACE

Writing a book has been likened to producing a child. If that is true, then I have undergone a very long pregnancy! As soon as I finished my thesis back in 1979, I knew I had to write a book about the Exmoor Pony. There was so much of interest to relate and no one book which told the full story of these fascinating animals. I embarked upon researching their origins and history to add to what I had learnt of their way of life out on the moors. I little realised at the time that it would be twelve years before I wrote the last page.

This is a "Natural History" in all senses, exploring the ancestry of the Exmoor Pony, its place in recorded history and its ecology or relationship to its environment on Exmoor today. I have chosen to start the story far back in time and very distant from Exmoor. This is not only to provide the context of how horses evolved in the first place but to make later comparisons involving the Exmoor Pony meaningful.

This is not an academic text-book but there are some measurements quoted. I apologise to those who have been educated according to the metric system for I have used the traditional British measurements, which seem natural to me. Thus sizes of enclosures are given in acres and distances in miles etc. Also, heights of ponies are quoted in "hands" e.g. 12.2 hands meaning 12 hands and 2 inches. A conversion table of all the statistics is included in "Author's Notes" at the end of the book. In approaching the subject as a zoologist, there may be some terms which are unfamiliar to readers, so I have also included a Glossary of Scientific Terms.

I have provided a full Bibliography and must register my debt to all those writers whose work has been invaluable to me. My thanks to all those who have generously allowed me to quote their words.

There are so many people who have contributed to this book in various ways. I would like to thank them individually but a full list would go on for pages! So many members of the Exmoor Pony Society have helped me that I can perhaps convey my gratitude by thanking the whole Society. There are, of course, a few people who I must single out for recognition.

I was fortunate enough to meet and talk at length with the late James Speed who was, without doubt, an inspiration to me. I also had the good fortune to live at Knighton Farm with Bob and Creenagh Mitchell whilst studying the Exmoor Ponies; I thank them for both their practical help and unstinting encouragement then and ever since. Thankyou too to David and Sandra Mansell, who have not only helped me enormously in their Exmoor Pony Society secretarial capacity but have been so generous with their friendship and support. I am greatly indebted to Stephanie Poulter for her wonderful drawings; her talent is matched by her infinite patience with me.

Thanks are due to my husband, mother and friends, Jane and Kevin Andreoli, for checking the manuscript and helping me with the index. Finally, I owe an incalculable debt to my whole family. No-one has escaped helping out in some way; my husband Ian, my parents Marjorie and Sam Gates and my sister Di Freeman have contributed so much. Without them there would have been no doctorate and no book. I cannot adequately convey my love and thanks to them.

"He's been impossible since he heard he was a wild horse!"

CONTENTS

FOREWORD   BY DESMOND MORRIS   iii

PREFACE   INTRODUCTORY NOTES   v

CHAPTER 1   WILD ABOUT PONIES   1
The fascination of Exmoor Ponies – Wildness and domesticity – Scientific confusion.

CHAPTER 2   IN THE BEGINNING   5
The Dawn Horse – Evolution of the horse family – Natural selection and survival of the fittest – The spread of wild horses – Emergence of types – Horses of steppe and tundra – Horses of hot climates – Horses of forest and marshland – Horses of hills and mountains.

CHAPTER 3   THE BRITISH HILL PONY   23
The Age of Ice – Primitive hunters and ponies – Extinction or survival? – The birth of the British Hill Pony – A portrait of the British Hill Pony.

CHAPTER 4   THE LAST SURVIVORS   36
Echoes of British Hill Pony in the pony breeds – The Faroe Pony – Final decline of the British Hill Pony type – Survival in the Exmoor Pony – Description of the Exmoor Pony – White Exmoors? – Studies of bones and blood – Fanciful ideas – Expert opinions.

CHAPTER 5   THE PONIES OF THE ROYAL FOREST OF EXMOOR   58
Domesday records – Henry VIII and his horse laws – The Free Suitors of Exmoor – The Exmoor courts – The 1600s – The 1700s – The 1800s – The sale of the Royal Forest.

CHAPTER 6   DISPERSAL, DECLINE AND CONSERVATION   76
The Acland herd of Exmoor Ponies – The Knight Ponies – The Exmoor
breeders – Daniel Evans – The Westcott family – The Milton family – The
Thorne family – The Crockford and Western families – The birth of the
Exmoor Pony Society – The Second World War – Mary Etherington and James
Speed – Are the Exmoors the last of the British Hill Ponies?

CHAPTER 7   HOMES, HERDS AND HABITATS   104
Winsford Hill and the Acland/Anchor herd – Withypool Common and Nos. 23
and H8 herds – Molland Moor and herd No. 99 – Codsend Moor and herd No.
12 – The Forest of Exmoor and herd No. H52 – Brendon Common and herd
No. H67 – Haddon Hill and herd No. H42 – Helman Tor, Cornwall – Cumbria
and herds 14 and 37 – Scoraig, Scotland and herd No. 21 – The island of Taero,
Denmark – Population size – Home ranges – Are Exmoors territorial? –
Favourite Places – Moving round the range – Keeping away from people.

CHAPTER 8   SURVIVING   140
Exmoor winters – Adaptations to climate – The moorland menu – Diet –
Feeding adaptations – Teeth – Competition – Parasites – Predators – Death.

CHAPTER 9   BREEDING   167
The breeding cycle – The foaling season – The Exmoor foal – Reproductive life
– Herd Productivity – Natural versus unnatural influences – Exmoor Pony
genetics – Bloodlines – Inbreeding – The breeding balance.

CHAPTER 10   EXMOOR PONIES AND MAN   188
Gathering ponies – Inspecting and marking – Pony sales – Selection of
stallions – The Exmoor Pony on the wild to domestic spectrum –
Domesticating Exmoors – Driving and charioteering – Use in Agriculture –
Riding – Showing – Ponies as food – Ponies as conservationists – Public
relations work – Scientific studies – Exmoors abroad – The Exmoor Pony
Society – The Stallion Parade – The annual show.

CHAPTER 11   FIT FOR THE FUTURE?   218
Habitat conservation – Hill farming – Exmoor traditions – Security measures –
Conserving wildness – Worming and feeding – Selecting ponies –
Development of two types of Exmoor Pony – Bloodline management – The
effect of Europe – The conservation challenge.

GLOSSARY OF SCIENTIFIC TERMS 235

BIBLIOGRAPHY 239

AUTHOR'S NOTES 244
Measurement conversions.

INDEX 246

USEFUL ADDRESSES

Mr David Mansell,
Secretary, Exmoor Pony Society,
Glen Fern,
Waddicombe,
Dulverton,
Somerset,
TA22 9RY.
Telephone: 03984-490

Rare Breeds Survival Trust,
National Agricultural Centre,
Kenilworth,
Warwickshire,
CV8 2LG.
Telephone: 0202-696551 Fax: 0203-696706

Exmoor National Park Authority,
Exmoor House,
Dulverton, Somerset,
TA22 9HL.
Telephone: 0398-23665

National Pony Society,
Willingdon House,
102, High Street,
Alton,
Hampshire.
Telephone: 0420-88333

ACKNOWLEDGEMENTS

I am most grateful to all those who have kindly allowed me to reproduce their words or pictures within this book and acknowledge the considerable contribution they have made.

PHOTOGRAPHS AND DRAWINGS
Ian Baker (Plates 32, 42, 51, 58, 61, 62 & 98)
M.G. Best (Plates 7, 37 & 38)*
Merethe Bock (Plate 66)
Yvonne Campbell (Plate 50)
Debbie Davy (Plates 13 & 65)
Peter Dean (Plate 64)
Annie Dent (Plate 128)
Neville Dent (Plate 46)
Professor J. Cossar Ewart (Plates 16 & 17)*
Field Museum of Natural History, Chicago, U.S.A. (Plates 3, 4 & 5, Neg # GEO-82365, Neg # GEO-82367 & Neg # GEO-82366). Plates reproduced by courtesy of the Museum authorities.
Des & Gill Girdler (Plate 63)
Richard Hancock (Plates 131 & 133)
Captain M.H. Hayes (Plates 15 & 40)*
Bill Johnson (Plate 129)*
John Keene (Plates 18, 19, 39, 41, 57, 59, 67, 73, 74, 75, 76, 81, 82, 83, 89, 97, 99, 100, 101, 105, 109, 110, 111, 112, 113, 114, 117, 118, 132, 137)

John Knowles (Plate 9)
Roly Langdon (Plate 60)
Inez MacDonald (Plate 123)
David & Sandra Mansell (Plates 6, 72, 104, 138)
Colonel John Mennel (Plate 124)
Creenagh Mitchell (Plates 56, 85 & 91)
G. Halling Nielsen (Plate 84)**
Frances O'Connell (Plates 92, 93 & 94)
Evelyn March Phillips (Plates 34 & 35)*
Polo Pony Society Stud Books (Plates 14 & 36)
Stephanie Poulter (Cartoon, chapter heading & ending drawings; Plates 1, 10, 11 & 88; Figures 4.02, 5.01, 7.01, 8.01 & 8.02)
Royal Albert Memorial Museum, Exeter (Plates 23 & 27)
C. Reid (Plate 30)*
Gaye Sinclair (Plate 136)
James & Mary Speed (Plates 8, 12, 20, 21, 22, 24, 31, 43, 45, 47, 48, 49, 102, 103, 121, 122, 125, 126, 127, 130 & 134)*
The National Trust, Killerton House (Plate 33)
Alfred Vowles (courtesy of Joan Snarey Astell) (Plates 44 & 119)*

All remaining plates and figures by the author.
 * indicates original photographer deceased.
** unable to trace this photographer, would welcome his contact.

QUOTATIONS

The full list of credits to authors and publishers is given in Bibliography A. I regret that I have been unable to trace the copyright holders of quotations from the following to obtain permission to use them. I would therefore welcome knowledge of who owns any copyright still applying to the following:

A Book of Exmoor by F.J. Snell 1903
Prehistoric Communities of the British Isles by G. Childe 1947

Thoroughbreds and Other Ponies by Sir Walter Gilbey 1903
Ponies Past & Present by Sir Walter Gilbey 1900
Current Excavations in Cranborne Chase by A.H.L. Pitt Rivers 1888
The Parish of Selworthy by F. Hancock 1897
The Little Horses of Exmoor by M.G.S. Best & M.G. Etherington 1947

Plate 1 *Moonlight experience*

CHAPTER 1

WILD ABOUT PONIES

The Land Rover took us part way out across the hilltop. Then on foot we approached the herd of Exmoor Ponies and looked to see if the mare was there. We called her name but there was no response. By the time we reached the second herd across the river, the light was fading, making it even harder to distinguish one pony from another, with their uniform markings and so little difference between individuals. Yet this time when we called, a pair of small ears pricked up and though a year had passed since she had seen us, there was no mistaking the mutual recognition. She surrendered her freedom and walked out of the herd to us and was haltered. As we set off to walk back to the farm another mare joined us, unwilling to be parted from her companion, but she would not come too close and followed on behind.

We crossed the bridge just as the moon rose above the hill which loomed black against the night sky. As we headed towards the farm up a track which was no more than a dryish water course, the moon's reflection glistened on the sparse puddles and illuminated the way ahead. Two ponies, two people and a scene that could have been two thousand years ago or yesterday. Apart from the sound of their hooves upon the stones and the ponies' gentle breathing, all was still and as we walked, the sweet, grassy smell of the mares accompanied us. It was a night to be recalled with wonder,

almost a spiritual experience out of time. Walking in the moonlight with these beautiful ponies something very special happened; the Exmoor Ponies, already the focus of my scientific interest, captivated my heart.

Extract from Author's Diary, April 1976

Seventeen years later, that magical walk taking a friend's mare from the open moorland back to her home farm is as fresh in the memory as ever. It perhaps explains why an academic study was transformed into a labour of love, continuing over many years and finally culminating in the writing of this book. My fascination with Exmoor Ponies began with my very first sight of one of the herds living free on Exmoor and the realisation that here was something very different and very special.

The ponies have cast their spell on scientists and artists alike. Back in the 1940s, the renowned artist Sir Alfred Munnings lived and worked at Withypool. He wrote:

Ponies on the moor – I always wanted to paint them. Wild ponies wandering free over thousands of acres of wide, undulating expanse . . . . standing there alone, two or three suspicious mares would stare at me, ready to trot off, whilst I pretended to look the other way, and walked nearer

Plate 2 *My moonlight companion coming to introduce her 1991 foal*

to them backwards . . . . brushes in hand I would wait awhile. At last the mothers, seeing I was harmless, resumed grazing, whilst I stood up, crept nearer and began work . . . . hours fled by; the foals resting or playing, the herd keeping to the same spot. If I wake in another life, wherever it may be, I shall look back with regret upon those days with the ponies on the moor, far from anywhere, out of sight and sound of anyone.[1]

These two reminiscences reveal why the Exmoor Pony is such a fascinating animal and so enigmatic. Here we have ponies which live out on the moorlands of Exmoor independent of Man though managed by owners. Here are ponies equipped by Nature to survive all of its challenges yet also blessed with a temperament which allows them to be tamed and become partners to Man. The mare we walked home that April night was remarkable and unusual for she had been tamed when young and then returned to the free life within a herd. She faced the hardships of the natural life without help but would freely associate with humans she came to know and trust. Normally of course, the Exmoor Ponies living free are not tame, although they do all have owners. The ponies are suspicious of people and have to be approached quietly. They do however have the potential

for being domesticated and most of the foals born into the herds are destined for a life with people.

The beauty of Exmoors may inspire artists but often eludes their skills. Few have painted the ponies to good effect, finding that eyes attuned to painting horses distort the very different lines of the pony form. Only those who live with Exmoor Ponies or who have observed their natural way of life, seem to be able to capture their essence; Stephanie Poulter's wonderful drawings within this book reveal a great love and understanding of the ponies.

Yet as with all things "beauty is in the eye of the beholder"; in the early 1800s, W. Youatt wrote:

> *The Exmoor Ponies, although ugly enough, are hardy and useful.*[2]

F.J. Snell however found them far from ugly, writing in 1903:

> *It is scarce possible, in the animal world, to behold anything prettier than a drove of Exmoor Ponies.*[3]

Opinions regarding beauty may differ but the Exmoor Ponies will usually command great respect from all those who come to know them, for they thrive in an environment which is harsh and unsympathetic. They intrigue the scientific community because they present a real problem in finding a word that describes their status. The traditional labels of "wild" or "domestic" just don't fit. If we are to understand Exmoor Ponies we need to appreciate just why they are neither wild nor domesticated.

Wild animals live their lives subject only to the laws of Nature. Their characteristics and way of life are shaped by Nature so that they are adapted to their natural environments. Being wild means obtaining food, water and shelter independently, without assistance from Man, and having social structures and breeding behaviour which naturally favour the selection of the most suitable animals to breed successfully. There is no element of dependence upon people. Human activity as we know can affect wild animals in many ways but independence is the key to wildness. Wild animals can become used to

Man's presence but if there is no dependence involved and no interference in the animals' breeding, then this is tameness not domestication.

In contrast, domestic animals are not so much adapted to environments, but more to some humanly-determined purpose. Their characteristics have been selected artificially by people utilising husbandry skills to suit the animals to some function. Their survival is ensured by providing a suitable environment for them. Thus, Man removes the need for natural survival capabilities and often breeds them out of domestic animals. Owners of domestic stock provide food, water, shelter, veterinary treatment and protection from threats; in return they channel the domestic animal's energy into work or the offspring become a "crop". Perhaps the Thoroughbred Racehorse offers us the ultimate example of a domesticated animal, so changed from its wild relatives, so utterly dependent on Man and so perfectly designed by Man for its purpose.

Although domestic animals may instinctively retain some degree of natural social organisation, they are rarely allowed to express it as the structure of most groups is designed by Man to maximise productivity or efficiency. This usually involves artificial selection of breeding animals, with judgements often influenced more by outward appearance than genetic merit. Thus domestication invariably brings fairly drastic genetic changes to a breed and alters it considerably from its wild ancestors.

As we explore the natural history of the Exmoor Ponies throughout this book, it becomes obvious that they fit neither of these outlines of wild or domesticated. We will discover a way of life out on Exmoor in which they find their own food, water and shelter unaided by their owners, living out on the moorland all year independently. As we come to know the ponies, their adaptations to the natural environment reveal themselves and we will find no trace of human design in their characteristics. We will see herds on Exmoor with a breeding season still governed by Nature and not altered to suit their owners' convenience. All this will speak of wildness.

However, we will also encounter the management of the ponies where their owners interfere with the natural social organisation and population dynamics. We will find people selecting which stallions should sire the foals rather than Nature favouring the strongest and fittest; similarly, we will see that the owners choose which filly foals should remain to become breeding mares. All these aspects relate to domestic influence.

The Exmoor Ponies can be understood best if we think of a spectrum ranging from wild to domestic, rather than two unrelated states. The spectrum is made up of three main factors; firstly it ranges from total independence to total dependence in terms of ecology (which is the animal's relations to its surroundings) and survival in its environment. Secondly, the spectrum ranges from being a wild race, with features adapted solely to natural influences, to a humanly designed breed. Finally, at one extreme, wildness implies no human management of the animal's reproduction while full domestication involves complete control over breeding. Figure 1.01 illustrates this wild to domestic spectrum.

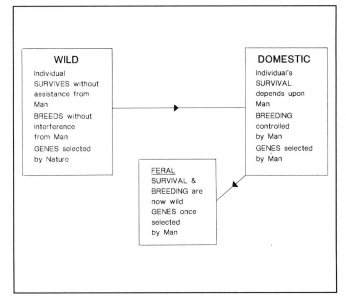

Figure 1.01 *The wild to domestic spectrum*

If we are to place the Exmoor Pony on this wild to domestic progression, then we must examine whether it represents a natural race or a breed. We have to assess whether at any stage in its background Man has superimposed his requirements over those of Nature and shaped the Exmoor to some artificial design. We will therefore investigate the ponies' origins and history to find out whether Man has been a more significant factor than he is today. For if in their history the ponies have ever been domesticated fully, only to resume their free life later, then we would class them as "feral" animals such as the Mustangs of North America. Feral is used for animals which are domesticated at some time but by accident or design return to living in a truly wild state.

The Exmoor Pony is a perplexing animal and hopefully the journeys we will make into the past and our visits to its present home on Exmoor will clarify the status of this remarkable animal, which now lives out a compromise between wildness and domesticity close to the wild end of our spectrum.

Perhaps too, we will be able to establish whether or not this pony really is a zoological treasure, the survivor of an ancient race of ponies. No absolute certainty exists as to which theory of origins applies because there is, as yet, insufficient evidence to be totally sure one way or the other. However, many zoological authors are reluctant to consider the possibility of anything other than domestic origin. The attitude seems to be that it is impossible to envisage how ponies could have survived during the prehistoric period and it is more probable that they were reintroduced later. How dangerous it is to dismiss an idea just because it is difficult to believe.

With Exmoor Ponies much of the uncertainty about their origins and status may perhaps be overcome if we take a look at their natural history as a whole, and at Exmoor and its people as much as the ponies themselves. We have to explore the ponies' past with care, carefully distinguishing fact from theory and making it quite clear when we are speculating. Where more than one interpretation exists, we must examine them all: where personal opinion is given this will be made evident.

The Exmoor Pony will undoubtedly emerge as fascinating, important and worthy of our efforts at conservation, whatever the final conclusions as to its exact zoological significance. For the people of Exmoor and owners of Exmoor Ponies throughout the country, the pages which follow may just confirm their knowledge of, and high regard for, these animals. Nonetheless, it is hoped that this book will add to their understanding of the importance of their ponies. Perhaps others, particularly those who live on Exmoor but who take the few herds for granted, will see their local pony in a new light and decide to help in safeguarding its future.

For anyone who meets the Exmoor Ponies for the first time within this book, no words or pictures can substitute for the excitement of a walk out across the moorland and seeing these marvellous animals for the first time, set against the stunning Exmoor scenery. So go to Exmoor, visit the ponies and you will surely come away the richer.

For now, join us in an expedition as we set off to explore the origins, history and natural history of the Exmoor Pony. Perhaps surprisingly, our starting point is not upon Exmoor, or even in Britain; our story really does begin with:

Once upon a time in a far off land . . . . .

CHAPTER 2

IN THE BEGINNING

It is dawn, somewhere in northern Wyoming, and the first rays of the sun break through the thick vegetation around us. The forest plants which hide us are strange for this is a dawn some fifty million years ago. We have travelled through time to search for the ancestor of the horse.

A rustling in the undergrowth heralds the arrival of our quarry and gradually it emerges into the clearing. Before us is the creature whose ultimate evolutionary destiny would be as the noble partner and friend of Man. Yet this is such a surprise. Could this unexpected little animal really be the founder of a great and successful lineage?

For this is *Eohippus*, which means "Dawn Horse" and there are only a few hints of equine character. It is a small animal with a curved back and hind-quarters rather higher than its shoulders. It has a long, thick tail and its head has more of a snout than a muzzle. Although there are small hoof-like structures at the end of its toes (four on the front feet and three on the hind), *Eohippus* still walks with its weight on dog-like pads. Our Dawn Horse is very small, just two and a half hands high but there are other species of *Eohippus* in this ancient world which are larger, although even the largest is only the size of a big dog in modern-day terms.

Eohippus has not been difficult for us to find as it is abundant here and in other parts of North America at this time. We have followed its distinctive multiple-toed tracks in the soft muddy earth of the forest. Its home is among the thick vegetation where it browses on soft leaves and fruits. It can only eat such soft plants because it has small teeth with low crowns but already its teeth show the beginnings of differentiating into front teeth for cropping vegetation and cheek teeth for crushing the food. *Eohippus* has a small undeveloped brain and it depends upon concealment to avoid predators. The animal before us becomes unsettled, perhaps detecting our presence and it seems to melt away into the darkness beneath the bushes. We must leave this surprising little ancestor and continue our journey through time.

Of course, in truth, we have no such miraculous time machine but we are able to make this imaginary visit thanks to the skills of those zoologists who search for fossils and those who interpret the bones, providing us with vivid pictures of what the animals must have been like. Fossils of *Eohippus* have mostly been found in North America, but a few, and indeed the oldest, were discovered in gravels in the south of England. These British finds were confusingly given a different name, *Hyracotherium*, but the consensus is that they too repre-

Using the results of these studies, we can continue our visits to the past in our time machine at intervals throughout the last fifty million years. We can see a succession of animals starting with our Dawn Horse gradually developing differences and becoming more and more horse-like. The changes occur so slowly in our human appreciation of time but evolution is a process which counts time in thousands of years as barely a moment.

Mesohippus

Our search for *Eohippus* took us to a landscape of thick vegetation in Wyoming. Our second visit is again to forest but this time in South Dakota and we have advanced some sixteen million years; we are now some thirty-eight million years before present. *Eohippus* is long-gone but its descendants are here and much changed. The animals we see now really look like small horses and are called *Mesohippus*. They are about 6 hands high and while their backs are still slightly arched, their bodies are longer and more slender. Their faces too are slender and now show a muzzle similar to modern-day horses.

Plate 4 *Painting of Mesohippus in South Dakota by John Conrad Hansen*

Plate 3 *Painting of Eohippus by Maidi Wiebe*

sent the Dawn Horse. It seems though that life was too tough for these populations, for they died out and the story of the evolution of the horse continued solely in North America.

Eohippus to Equus

When Charles Darwin wrote his *Origin of the Species* outlining the theory of evolution, he could scarcely have dreamt of some of the supporting evidence that would subsequently be presented. Fortunately for us, one of the best examples of tracing evolution through changes in bones has been with regard to the horse.

These sixteen million years have been a period of major evolution of their brains and this is a much more intelligent animal than the Dawn Horse.

As we watch them, one similarity to *Eohippus* is striking though – these animals still live in the forest and are browsers, eating leaves and soft vegetation. However, if we later study their bones, we find further development of the cheek teeth towards the equine system of grinding molars. Back beneath the trees, we are once again not quiet enough and are detected but this allows us to recognise a further change; their increased height comes from legs that are longer below the knee joint and all the feet have just three toes. *Mesohippus* is a good runner and they have crossed the glade and disappeared in a few moments.

Merychippus

Our next trip forwards in time covers twelve million years to a geological age called the Miocene. To find the descendants of *Mesohippus* we must now visit a new habitat. Before us is an open vista and the most important reason for the true horse evolving at all – grass. These miles of rolling grasslands are not immediately impressive and it is perhaps hard to realise how much is owed to this rather mundane family of plants. Yet, once such grassland habitat had developed, it presented animal life with a great opportunity, a vast food resource to be exploited.

Evolution led to many different horse-like grazing animals which took advantage of this opportunity. Many existed simultaneously and some spread across Asia and Europe, which were of course still joined to North America. Yet for reasons little understood, most of these evolutionary experiments were ultimately unsuccessful and the lines died out. In North America, there was one successful line and here, some twenty-six million years before present, are herds of *Merychippus* grazing in the distance. It is difficult to get close to them for they are alert and nervous.

While the unending supply of freely available grass is a fabulous opportunity, there has been a price to pay. For animals which have become adapted to grazing out on the grassland have had to leave the safety of the undergrowth. Concealment is no longer possible; venturing out, they have had to evolve a new strategy for avoiding predators. Nature's answer to this problem has been to further adapt their bodies for escaping. The ability to run, and run faster than their predators, has become the key to survival. *Merychippus* has successfully adapted further to running with a rebalancing so that their weight rests mainly upon the middle of the three hoofed toes on each foot; the pads have been lost. Another strategy for avoiding danger is their formation of herds out on the grassland, whereby any individual stands a better chance than alone and they can cooperate in defending against attack.

This time then we need some twentieth century assistance in the form of binoculars. We can then see clearly that *Merychippus* has continued some of the changes we last saw. They are yet again somewhat bigger, around ten hands, with a straighter back, longer legs and an elongated muzzle. They are very equine in appearance. If we also look at their bones, we find that the bones in the feet have become fixed and much stronger, and some of the leg bones have fused into more robust arrangements. The jaws are deeper to accommodate much larger high-crowned teeth which, with their ability now to move the lower jaw sideways, allows *Merychippus* to efficiently grind the tough grass. Their eyes are also set further back in the face as they need to be able to observe far around them in their vigilance for predators.

Merychippus then is a very successful animal. In fact so successful and abundant that many different species of it are widely distributed. Our visit has shown us clearly how far the equine characteristics have developed over these thirty million years but because our time travel is imaginary, we cannot answer one intriguing question. Did *Merychippus* or any of its descendants before the zebras have stripes? We will never know!

Pliohippus

Our penultimate visit is to the Pliocene period just seven million years before present and again to the open grasslands of North America. The herds we now observe

Plate 5 *Painting of Pliohippus in Nebraska by John Conrad Hansen*

in the distance are of animals which are almost indistinguishable at first sight from real horses. *Pliohippus* is the last stage of evolution between the Dawn Horse and *Equus* the true horse and represents the last major change; if we look closely we see that in *Pliohippus* the side toes have finally been reduced to mere vestiges or lost altogether. Thus, here is an animal in which the development of the single toe with its immensely strong hoof is finally complete. These animals are even more efficient grazers than their near ancestors because their

teeth have continued evolving, becoming larger with higher crowns, all adaptations to dealing efficiently with the abrasive silica content of their food.

Equus

Finally, we move forwards in time to just four million years before present, to the end of the Pliocene era. Here at last we find the horse, the immediate ancestor of today's equids, recognisable as *Equus*. Our expedition must now travel widely to see these early horses for they are highly successful and are widespread. They have migrated beyond the bounds of North America into Eurasia, and are already diverging into different types as they adapt to varying habitats. These earliest equids have refined the changes seen in *Pliohippus* rather than making drastic alterations. Although larger, they look little different to their immediate ancestors and we must return to the present to study their bones to see that their grinding cheek teeth have now become straight rather than curved, achieving the ultimate grazing efficiency.

Our evolutionary tour comes to its end now; we can no longer use our time machine, not because we are up to date but because the picture we derive from fossil remains begins to lose its clarity. The bone record from *Eohippus* to the earliest *Equus* has been good enough to give us these impressive insights into how evolution gradually perfected its design for equids, adapting them superbly for the grazing way of life. Yet from this point onwards the story of how the many species of *Equus* evolved is complicated and the scientists who have been our guides so far have many different theories. We must now attempt to chart the most likely evolutionary path through the last four million years, accepting that we simply don't know all the details. What a miracle a real time machine would be to those zoologists who have attempted to unravel the next chapters in the story of the horse.

Family Divisions

The evolution of *Eohippus* to *Equus* is so well charted in the fossil bone record that it is a classic example often used in the teaching of evolutionary theory. Ironically, the evidence relating to the subsequent development of the horse family is inadequate and subject to various interpretations. Thus, controversy exists as to the origins of the living equids and their relationships to one another.

However, it does seem agreed that three distinct lines emerged from a common equine ancestor and these we see today as the true horses, the asses and the zebras. Scientists have tried to determine from fossil bones just

exactly how each line developed, in what order and at what time but this has proved very difficult, hence the many theories. In recent years a wholly new approach has shed light upon this enigma.

Studies of DNA, the genetic material which constitutes chromosomes, have shown the degree of differences between living species and thus the closeness of relationships. It was even possible to include a now extinct type of zebra, the Quagga, as the techniques worked on some material from an old skin. Also, as the rate at which changes occur in DNA has been determined, the times at which changes took place have at last been estimated more reliably.

These studies suggest that there was a common ancestor to all the horses, asses and zebras present around 3.9 million years before present. The divergence into those distinct lines took place gradually, as with all evolution, over the following half million years. This DNA analysis is beginning to clarify the relationships between the living species so perhaps before too long an agreed classification of the *Equus* family will emerge. Yet no doubt some intriguing questions will remain. We still do not know which of today's animals the common ancestor most resembled; did it lose its stripes when horses and asses evolved or did it develop stripes to form the zebras?

From this point onwards we must leave the asses and zebras and concentrate upon the true horses. We are faced with a difficult story to unravel. Conflicting theories and disagreements upon the number of species and what scientific names they should be given make it confusing even for the zoologist. Perhaps we can find our way through this equine maze if we take a simpler path and to do this we must equip ourselves with a little understanding of how evolution works.

Natural Selection and Survival of the Fittest

Regular viewers of *Star Trek* will be familiar with Starfleet's "Prime Directive", an over-riding law to which the Captain and his crew are always subject. Nature has a constant prime directive for every living organism which seems to be the fundamental purpose of all life. This is to reproduce itself and contribute its genetic material to the future through its offspring.

Thus the life of any individual is directed towards surviving until old enough to reproduce and then doing so successfully. On its way to that appointment with destiny it must cope with the challenges of finding enough food and water, finding shelter, coping with parasites and avoiding ending up as some other animal's dinner. Once mature enough it must locate and attract a suitable partner, mate successfully and rear its offspring.

All this must take place in a world where competition for all those resources is ruthless and uncompromising. In the natural world countless failures accompany every success. If it were not so there would be population explosions and chaos. So life is a struggle for existence and for posterity.

In such an arena, any characteristic which gives an individual an advantage over its rivals may enhance its chances of success. It may be a longer beak to extract insects from bark or a thicker coat to withstand severe cold. It may be higher resistance to the effects of worms in the gut or better camouflage so that the animal is less likely to be seen by its predator. Equally, it could be a more spectacular display to attract a female or greater skills in protecting the young.

When such an advantageous characteristic arises, perhaps by spontaneous changes in the genetic material called mutations, it is more likely that the individual concerned will survive and breed so contributing its genes to the next generation. If the feature is still advantageous, these offspring are more likely to survive and breed than others and thus the successful genes become an increasing proportion of the whole population. This is the principle of "natural selection" which Charles Darwin explained in his theory of evolution.

Natural selection therefore favours any feature which adapts an animal better to the environment in which it is living and in which it must breed. It is a force which selects against the weak and favours the strong. Its ultimate result is the "survival of the fittest".

So if populations of an animal encounter changes or new environments that require different characteristics or skills to ensure survival and breeding, natural selection operates continuously over thousands of years and keeps on favouring animals which are best adapted to the new conditions. This process of evolution therefore gradually adapts the population of animals to the environment in which they live. It is a process which never ceases and operates callously upon all, from the simplest bacterium to the sophisticated Mountain Gorilla and even, much as we like to deny it, upon ourselves.

Throughout this book then we need to retain this idea that only the fittest survive and that being fit means being adapted well to all aspects of the environment.

The Spread of Wild Horses

The formation of new types and ultimately new species is then triggered by populations encountering new circumstances. The wider an animal population disperses itself, the more new challenges it encounters and the more likely it is that its species will split up into a number of varieties or ecotypes (a type adapted to a particular ecosystem or habitat). If the differences between geographically separated ecotypes intensify, then they may become recognisable sub-species and, ultimately, the genetic basis for their differences may be so great that they diverge into totally separate species.

We left the original true horses having become distinct from the asses and zebras; this was the culmination of the processes of natural selection outlined above. Eventually, they became so different, adapting to diverse habitats, they ceased to interact with each other and formed separate lines.

As movement into new locations is a stimulus to this process, it is not surprising that *Equus* radiated out into so many separate lines each with a richness of different types. The wonderfully designed equine legs so perfected for escaping predators also made the horses, asses and zebras great travellers. Just as some of their pre-equid ancestors had done, they spread out across North America and beyond to Asia and Europe.

The route for these equine explorers was across the Alaskan corridor and the land bridge later submerged beneath the Bering Straits; here Asia and America were joined. James Michener in yet another meticulously researched novel, *Alaska*, eloquently visualises the scene:

The movement of animals across the bridge was by no means always in one direction, for although it is true that the more spectacular beasts – mastodon, sabre-tooth, rhinoceros – came out of Asia to enrich the new world, other animals like the camel originated in America and carried their wonderful capacities into Asia. And the inter-continental exchange which had the most remarkable consequences also moved westwards across the bridge and into Asia.

One morning as Mastodon browsed among cotton- wood trees near the edge of a swamp in central Alaska, he saw approaching from the south a line of animals much smaller than he had ever seen before. Like him they walked on four feet; but unlike him, they had no tusks, no heavy covering of hair, no massive head or ponderous feet. They were sleek creatures, swift of movement, alert of eye, and he watched with ordinary animal interest and inspection as they approached. Not a single gesture, not one movement gave him any indication that they might be dangerous, so he allowed them to come near, stop, stare at him and pass on.

They were horses, the new world's beautiful gift to the old, and they were on their wandering way into Asia, from where their descendants, thousands of years later, would fan out miraculously to all parts of Europe. How exquisite they were that morning as they passed Mastodon, pressing their way into the heartland of Alaska, where they would find a halting place on their long pilgrimage.

Nowhere else could the subtle relationships of nature be so intimately observed. Ice high, oceans low. Bridge open, passageway closed. The ponderous mastodon lumbering toward North America, the delicate horse moving toward Asia. Mastodon lurching toward inescapable extinction. The horse galloping to an enlarged life in France and Arabia. Alaska, in its extremities girt in ice, served as a way station for all the travellers, regardless of the direction in which they were headed. Its broad valleys free of ice and

its invigorating climate provided a hospital resting place. It really was an ice castle, and life within its frozen walls could be pleasant though demanding.[4]

The bones of these ancient animals lie along the route between the continents and their excavation has yielded the data which forms such marvellous material for scientists and novelists alike.

As James Michener describes, the connection between Asia and America was not continuously open for it depended upon the extent of the ice-cap. When the ice-cap was thick and extensive, its use of water was considerable and the sea-level fell. This exposed the land-bridge for a time, until it was obstructed by the ice itself. When climatic changes brought rising temperature, the ice retreated and the melt-water raised the sea-level covering parts of the land. Thus the route for wandering animals was periodically blocked by either ice or water and the migrations into and out of North America occurred in phases. Sometimes when the ice increased and moved south it formed barriers around Alaska, which remained an oasis within the frozen desert.

Plate 6 *Isolated by inhospitable conditions a different type of wild horse had to evolve*

For animals spreading out into new lands this meant that they might experience new environments in two ways; as they moved into new geographic areas they would encounter a variety of habitats but also, climatic changes could transform a once warm and pleasant location into inhospitable tundra. Such changes were probably not rapid; if there were some fast transitions then the animals involved would have been casualties. In normal circumstances, the timescales must have allowed animals to change in response to the trends in their habitat, to evolve into different forms reflecting the demands of their new home. Populations which became trapped in Alaska during periods it was cut off by ice barriers would have had to adapt or perish and this probably accounts for one of the early major divisions within the true horses. These climatic waves would have led to the emergence of two very different ecotypes, one adapted to warm conditions and a relatively rich food supply, the other shaped by the cold and an impoverished diet.

Hermann Ebhardt, who studied the evolution of the true horses in the 1950s, wrote his interpretation of the horse's Alaskan experience in an article in 1975:

> On their migration to Europe they were trapped in Alaska by glacial ice. The large enclave in Alaska which remained free of ice, had caught many different kinds of animals, among them the main enemy of the ponies, the cavern hyena. Another hardship for the ponies was the fact that inside the enclave the summer lasted only for a few months. During the long winter months the ponies had to depend entirely on tough grass and bushes. Such hard conditions brought about an especially vigorous selection among the individual ponies. This is shown by fossilised bones unearthed in the mining district of Alaska.[5]

Thus, it would seem, the early prototype horse split into two forms adapted to very different ways of life. If this is indeed how the adaptive radiation of the horses began, it is easy to understand how upon reaching Asia, the two differing types sought out different locations and further diverged.

If we were now to list out all the finds of equine bones from the many sites across Asia and Europe, we would find that they have been interpreted by scientists in a bewildering number of ways. The array of Latin names attributed to the ancient equids makes understanding the overall picture of the horse's history very difficult. Also, there is as yet no agreement on just how many basic types of horses arose, although the idea that today's horses have multiple origins rather than all stemming from just one of the fossil types is generally accepted.

For our purpose, such an encounter with the intricate detail of bone studies would probably confuse rather than aid in our understanding of the story of how the ancestors of British horses spread westwards to Britain. Also, to adequately and objectively review all the research findings would in itself take up a whole book. Our purpose here is to gain an overall impression of horse evolution which allows us to understand our main theme, the natural history of British Ponies.

So an alternative approach is to continue the theme of animals adapting to different habitats and try to deduce, using the principles of Nature, how the early horses might have responded when they reached Eurasia. These wandering colonisers would have encountered grazing lands or "steppes", thick swampy forests, deserts, tundra, vast open birch forests and hill pastures rising to the snowline on mountains. Each habitat would have presented its own set of challenges and required its own adaptations to conditions. If we are right that there were already differing types adapted to warm or cold conditions then they would no doubt have sought out contrasting environments, so isolating populations from each other and accentuating the processes of divergence. Also, with vast populations of horses competing for resources, it would have been advantageous for any subgroup to adapt to a way of life which others of its own race could not exploit.

The Emergence of Types

Using the idea of populations encountering fresh environments and adapting to them, we can build up a picture of how the horses might have developed. We can then examine how the scientific data relates to such a theory.

Firstly, let us consider the exodus of the North American prototype which was adapted to warm conditions and perhaps more importantly to vegetation which was less coarse. These were the animals which passed through Alaska freely without an icy experience. When such animals reached Asia, they and the following generations would surely have sought out the conditions for which they were best suited and thus headed southwards to warmer climates. Perhaps these early explorers found their way ultimately to Arabia and northern Africa and founded the lineage of eastern horses which resulted in the romantic Arab Horse.

At other times, as we have hypothesised, the prototype horse experienced drastically different conditions on its way to Asia and had to adapt to cold, impoverished life. The horses which emerged from this imprisonment would have been unlike the southern emigrants. For them, a natural home would have been the vast expanses of tundra at the edges of the Eurasian ice-cap and we might think of these horses turning northwards and westwards to find this environment. Yet as they travelled, there were kinder habitats available too. The enormous central Asian steppes were grasslands offering horses an ideal home; though still demanding the abilities to cope with intense cold in winter, the steppe environment provided a far richer food supply and longer summer than the tundra to the north of the open plains. Then as these places were colonised, the horses would have found yet another habitat bordering the grasslands where open land gave way to light forest.

The cold-adapted prototype could have exploited these three major habitat types, tundra, steppe and open forest, without it leading to major divergence and so we might theorise that the resulting populations in these places were fairly similar. It seems likely that these horses were the ancestors of the various extinct forms of Tarpan; also the surviving Przewalski's Horse of Mongolia might well be a specialised form of this type.

Plate 7 *Przewalski's horse*

As the herds moved westwards into Europe there were other environments which offered opportunities. Whilst the fairly open forest edging steppe-lands could be utilised without requiring particular specialisations, the dense, swampy forests of central Europe were another matter. These presented a home which could only be colonised by horses which could browse more than graze and which would once again rely on concealment rather than flight from predators. In order to move into such terrain, natural selection would have had to operate over a long period and produced an equid notably different from the types which were living in the open environments. Perhaps this ecotype gave rise to the heavy horses of Europe.

As the horse invaded Asia and Europe it discovered another ecosystem on its travels; as well as the lowlands so far considered, there were of course the hills and mountains. The cold-adapted prototype was already prepared for some aspects of upland dwelling but would have been presented with a significant new challenge, far higher rainfall. Also, the physical demands of outrunning predators on open hillsides are very different to galloping across flat country, so mountain living would have required adaptations in leg structure just as high rainfall would have created selection pressure for different coat formation. The end result of moving upwards and adapting to the "high life" seems to have been the pony.

We have to try to imagine such a process over hundreds of thousands of years, involving vast numbers of herds travelling great distances. As areas were occupied, competition between herds would always have acted as a spur to moving on yet further and those at the fringes of a habitat would have to try to subsist in the bordering transitional conditions. As their descendants became better adapted to the different country, they would have been able to gradually occupy the land beyond and continue adapting. Eventually those animals at the extremes of the distribution in contrasting habitats would have developed distinctive features. Where geographical barriers kept groups well apart, different ecotypes or even sub-species would have resulted.

Such a view of horse history may be speculation but it is based upon the fundamental processes of biology and it therefore has a logical basis. In arriving at this scenario, we have followed in the footsteps of James Speed, who was a comparative anatomist working at the Royal Dick Veterinary College, Edinburgh back in the nineteen-fifties. He postulated horse prototypes as the reflection of basic types of environment building upon, but advancing more soundly, the ideas of J. Cossar Ewart presented in 1904.

The sequence of adaptive changes would have generated a number of different forms of horse during the last million years of their story as they colonised the continents of Asia and Europe. We can suggest that four basic forms emerged but as the process of divergence described would continue as long as there were new habitats to exploit, it would seem likely that each of those four prototypes would have further produced variants. This would mean that even before Man interfered and through crossing and selective breeding created a chaos of relationships for the hippologist to

Plate 8 *James Grant Speed*

unravel, the horse family had quite naturally fanned out into a myriad of forms.

The horses were one of Nature's masterpieces for the genetic material was so incredibly flexible, able to adapt to so many diverse environments. Remember too, that as well as all the successful lines that radiated out from those first primitive American emigrants, there were many unsuccessful experiments; the fossil record shows us numerous forms which lived for a time but then failed.

One other remarkable aspect of this evolution of horses was that despite adapting to such differing habitats, the changes needed for survival were not gross. The fundamental design of the horse was so good that in diverging into ecotypes to exploit differing food or survive varying weather conditions, the changes Nature wrought in the genetic structure did not lead to the emergence of a large number of species as happens with many other animal families. Today, amidst the dazzling array of horses which Nature and Man have jointly produced, there are traditionally thought to be just two species; one is the Przewalski's Horse, *Equus przewalskii* and all other horses are classified as *Equus caballus*. However, there is also support for the idea that despite having different chromosome numbers (*E. przewalskii* has 66 and *E. caballus* has 64), they are all variants of a single species with no agreement yet on a Latin name.

Now we have this theoretical picture of natural processes producing a number of basic horse types at various times during the last million years (or the Pleistocene period as it is termed geologically), we are ready to delve a little into the scientific discoveries regarding fossil and living horses.

Horses of Steppe, Tundra and Open Forest

In 1878 Colonel N.M. Przewalsky returned from an expedition to Mongolia bringing with him a skull and hide of a wild equid which he gave to the Saint Petersburg Zoological Museum. After extensive study, zoologists concluded that this was no wild ass such as were common to the region but truly a wild horse and in his honour they named it *Equus przewalskii*. The bones and skin were not of some long extinct form but remarkably were from an animal which Przewalsky could confirm was still living in small numbers in the remotest parts of Mongolia.

Dr Sandor Bokonyi explains in his book *The Przevalsky Horse* that Colonel Przewalsky had made a number of visits to Central Asia and seen the wild horses. The Colonel recalled in describing his third expedition:

During my whole stay there I met only two herds of horses. My escort and I shot at the herds, but in vain. With its tail raised high and its neck arched, the stallion whizzed away, the whole herd following it. We could not follow them because we lost trace immediately. On another occasion we succeeded in stalking them from the side, but suddenly one of the animals noticed me. At once they galloped away at the top of their speed and vanished from my sight.[6]

It is perhaps horrifying to us today to realise that explorers of that era would readily kill an animal, whether rare or common, in order to return with a specimen for display in a museum. However Colonel Przewalsky was unsuccessful and the skull and hide he brought back were given to him.

The Mongolian wild horse was indeed a rarity even then and was restricted to very remote and inhospitable parts of Mongolia and bordering areas of China. When it was rediscovered in 1966 and more information emerged, its habitat was described as salty steppe and semi-desert to which the horses had retreated to escape contact with man. Today it is thought that it is totally extinct in the wild, surviving only in zoos and reserves. There are about 950 living in captivity and a project for returning them to the wild in Mongolia is well-advanced. In Britain, we can visit Marwell or Whipsnade zoos and see captive herds of this fascinating animal.

Przewalski's Horse is a robust, stocky animal of around 13 to 14 hands high with a large head and broad forehead. All individuals are essentially the same colour but in shade it ranges from a yellowish dun to a sandy bay. The belly is lighter coloured and the muzzle is almost white with the same colouring ringing the eyes. A black dorsal stripe goes from mane to tail. The mane is short and erect normally although occasionally an individual may show a longer, slightly floppy mane; there is almost no forelock. The colouring of the mane is sandy at the roots and then black. The black tail looks part ass part horse with short hair on the upper part and long flowing hair lower down. Each limb bears a chestnut callosity. As with any wild animal, the

Plate 9 *Przewalski horses at Marwell Zoo, Hampshire*

individuals are virtually identical in appearance with a range of subtle variations in most characteristics.

Looking at the Mongolian wild horse we are perhaps seeing one of the forms of steppe horse which resulted from the early prototype adapting to the various habitats of Asia. There seems no reason to believe that Przewalski's Horse is anything but a fully wild animal; it has probably had an unbroken history in Central Asia. It is then a wild species adapted to the harsher steppe-lands and even semi-deserts and its features reflect those environments. So although, miraculously we have still living an ecotype of the wild steppe horse we must be careful not to assume that it is unchanged from the ancestral type. Przewalski's Horse was driven off the richer terrain and was able to cling to wild existence for a time by coping with the environmental extremes in wilderness areas where water was scarce, food coarse and salty. It is not certain whether its extinction in the wild was from failure to adapt adequately to the conditions or due to Man's occupation of the water-holes and killing of stallions which raided the herds of domestic horses to steal mares. Man seems the more likely culprit.

At one time, scientists thought that Przewalski's Horse represented the ancestor of all other horses as it was apparently the only race of wild horse left in existence. It was often argued that because the Mongolian wild horse had an upright mane, no horse with a floppy mane could possibly be a wild race. Today, there is a greater consideration of ecology and we realise that the mane like any other feature will be shaped by its habitat and an upright mane is simply the best design for living in a place which has hot, dry extremes. Also, as fossil horse bones have been studied more rigorously, a picture is emerging which supports the idea of Przewalski's Horse being just one of many forms which developed from the primitive unspecialised ancestors which left North America. Its great distinction is that it survived for so long as a truly wild species.

Evidence suggesting that Przewalski's Horse has

changed very little from its ancient ancestors comes from several sources. Apart from comparisons of bones, prehistoric art provides convincing information. Palaeolithic Man painted horses on cave walls over ten thousand years ago and their handiwork has been found in many places ranging from Russia to France. There are many different styles of artwork involved and great care has to be taken in interpreting them in relation to types of living horses but undoubtedly the Przewalski's Horse resembles some of the depicted animals very closely.

The studies of horse bones from many locations and dated at various times throughout the Pleistocene era confirm that early Man did indeed see and hunt horses much like Przewalski's Horse. Recent interpretations of bone material from Alaska to France seem to confirm the idea that rather than one fixed type, which was virtually the Przewalski's Horse per se, there were various forms of steppe horse in different locations and of different sizes. Perhaps the most spectacular find of bones was made at Solutré in France where it has been estimated that forty thousand individual horses of a form which Przewalski's Horse resembles were the victims of the Stone Age hunters.

Other forms of steppe horse are thought to have survived until relatively recently and these are referred to as Tarpans. There is by no means universal agreement as to whether Tarpans were truly wild races as there is so little evidence to study, but it does seem likely. According to Dr Sandor Bokonyi, there were wild horse populations on the Russian steppes at the time Przewalski's Horse was discovered but sadly none remain today and just a single skeleton was preserved for posterity. Steppe Tarpans were apparently mouse-coloured with a greyish belly and black points. The mane has been described as "short and frizzy" which might be interpreted as upright but Colin Groves refers to a Tarpan which died in Moscow Zoo in 1887 which had a short mane which fell to one side. Again, thinking ecologically, this feature may have varied depending upon location and habitat.

Groves also relates how Cossack soldiers told the traveller Colonel Hamilton Smith in 1814 that Tarpans of eastern Europe were mainly grey and had interbred with domestic horses. There were however true wild horses near Lake Karakorum, on the Syr Darya river and in Mongolia and these were tan or mouse-coloured. This would tend to confirm the idea that the Tarpans and the Przewalski's Horse were variants of the same species. There were also Tarpans which lived in the forests and it is believed that the Polish Konik Ponies of today are closely related to these animals, which like the steppe Tarpans were driven to extinction around the beginning of this century.

The Tundra dwelling types are known from fossil finds in Alaska and the Yukon and others from northern Siberia, from which the Yakut Horses of today are thought to be descended. In 1969, miners in Yakutia made a remarkable discovery: the carcass of a horse which had been preserved in the permafrost. It became known as Tscherski's Horse and was dated as originating from the upper Pleistocene period. It seems to have been a larger form than existed on the steppe-lands.

We have spent some considerable time looking at the steppe horses because the existence of Przewalski's Horse makes this type particularly fascinating and we will make reference to it at other times. However, this exploration of what is known about the steppe horses is in academic terms both brief and inadequate; the bone evidence and the interpretations of just what forms lived at which times is so very complex and has to be left for zoological papers. Readers who wish to delve further are referred to the bibliography.

Horses of the Hot Climates

As the horse left North America and settled in Asia and Europe, it found in the open grasslands an environment which it could exploit with enormous success. It was adaptable enough to continue that success as it colonised tundra and open forest. It had probably been pre-programmed for such development by emerging from Alaska equipped to cope with an impoverished, coarse food supply. Yet in hotter climates the horse achieved no such dominant position to judge by the sparse fossil material which has been examined.

Perhaps the emigrants from America which were not shaped by isolation over generations in tundra conditions could not exploit the Central Asian habitats and moved southwards in search of lusher, softer vegetation. Certainly horse fossils have been discovered in India. However, although in the history of domesticated horses there can be no story to rival that of the Arab Horse, as yet, there seems to be no clear picture of the ancestor of this and the other horses of Arabia and North Africa. No prototype has been identified from bones in these regions and we have to speculate whether today's breeds had an ancient ancestor specific to their region or whether given the intensity of trade routes, the domestic breeds originated from a mixture of introductions. At present it is difficult to pass an opinion.

There are though a few clues if we look at the dentition of the Arab. The lower jaw is shallow, giving little room for the implantation of teeth and so the teeth are short and relatively inefficient. James Speed commented in an article on the natural history of horses in the 1950s that such dental features could be seen in the Indian fossil horses and this might be a clue to the ancestral path.

For now we can simply recognise that the original dispersal of the horse seems to have included some movement southwards and the environments encountered were far more challenging to the horse. Some may have succeeded but in no way on the same scale as was occurring in Central Asia and Europe. Whether any such prototype persisted and contributed to the modern breeds is uncertain.

Horses of Forest and Marshland

Whilst many millions of years of evolution had perfected the horse for living in open habitats where it was primarily a grazing animal which escaped its predators by running away, its remarkable flexibility permitted adaptation to a very different habitat. In central Europe there were areas of thick forest and swampy terrain which offered a home to animals.

Perhaps due to the intensity of competition on the open grasslands, horses may have moved into this seemingly alien environment.

In order to successfully live in such conditions, yet again the horse had to adapt and in this case, quite considerably. The small, compact hooves so essential for speed and the wide span of vision vital for detecting threats in the open would have conferred no advantage deep in amongst the trees and where the ground was soft. Fossils of horses have been found, particularly in Germany and these have been put forward as the probable ancestors of the heavy horse breeds of Europe.

By looking at both the characteristics of the fossils and at the features of living heavy breeds, James Speed suggested a possible portrait of these early forest/marsh horses. He interpreted their forward-projecting incisor teeth as adaptations to a lush diet which was easily obtained and their long, parallel cheek teeth indicating that their food supply was soft and did not require the harsh grinding that grass demanded. Larger hooves were in his opinion an adaptation to moving on softer ground and the abandonment of running as an escape mechanism. Speed suggested that in colonising this environment, the horse became slow-moving and relied on concealment amongst the trees and vegetation, much as its smaller pre-equid browsing ancestors had done. He identified a narrow range of vision from the position of the eye sockets and related this to the life amongst thick vegetation. He further theorised that for camouflage purposes this type of horse would have been dark brown to black and probably resumed living in very small groups or even a fairly solitary life as the herd system would be inappropriate for a forest dweller.

So if such ideas are sound, we can think of evolution acting upon the horse of open country quite dramatically, changing size, shape, feeding, social life, techniques for avoiding predators, vision, movement and so on. A revolutionary change but one needed if such areas of marsh and forest were to be colonised. It would be easy to understand that the resultant forest/marsh form would eventually have little contact with its cousins on the steppes and recognisably separate types emerged.

Horses of Hills and Mountains

Our final major environment to consider is that of the high country, the upland areas of hills and mountainside pastures. Again, essentially open country but presenting its own challenges and demanding certain adaptations. Whilst lowland grassland was perhaps the habitat which suppported the largest numbers of horses, the uplands represented a home with many advantages. James Speed wrote:

> Finally there was that great highway and home for horses, the mountain ranges. Wherever there are hills you will find horses. The reason is simple, for a mountain is a miniature hemisphere and if there is a snow-cap on the top of it, the sweetest bite of grass is just short of the snowline, and horses know that. Also by moving up or down or round the hill according to the seasonal or climatic changes, suitable conditions can always be found. It is therefore only what we would expect that the great backbone of Asia, the Altai Mountains, has evidently been a main road for horse migrations, and the byways from the Altai spread into the Shan Hills of Burma, the Anatolian highlands, the Indo-China hills, the Korean Islands and Indonesia, while the beginning of the main road seems to have been in Alaska and its end in Britain.[7]

At last we come to some perspective which relates to Britain and our main story. In exploring this upland horse type we are starting along the path leading to our final destination.

As the horse moved upwards onto the hills it seems to have evolved into the pony. Today in the equestrian world, horse and pony are differentiated simply by a height delineation but in terms of natural history, the pony is most definitely a distinct type from the horse, both in the fossil record and in living races and breeds. So what did Nature demand for living on mountains and what adaptations did that produce?

Firstly, movement on upward-sloping land is a very different proposition to flat terrain; an upland horse has to be sure-footed and have good balance. As it must still flee from its predators, being in open pasture, it must be agile and retain the efficient, small, hard hoof. Natural selection thus worked to favour any changes in the limbs which conferred these abilities. Both James Speed and Hermann Ebhardt recognised limbs shaped for hill horses amongst both fossil bones and in living pony races. James Speed developed a picture of the Mountain Ponies from a mixture of bone evidence, observation of today's animals and conjecture:

> Their range and distribution were the most extensive of all of our four main types, and for that matter a census of the horse population of the world today would probably place these ponies and their descendants, pure or cross-bred, at the top of the list for numbers and ubiquity. Although never attaining at any one time to the vast numbers of the horses of the Steppes and Tundra, the mountain ponies maintained their numbers more steadily over a longer period. It has to be taken into account their habit of living in small family groups rather than in large herds, and their choice of rough ground and mountains as a habitat would make them less vulnerable to the accidents which resulted in such large numbers of the bones of bison and Steppe horses being found in pitfalls and other natural traps, or in caves whence they had been carried by Man or other carnivores.
>
> They were and are unspecialised and adaptable to almost any environment. Their teeth, although of not quite the degree of hypsodonty of the Steppe and Tundra horses, being nevertheless suitable for thirty years of efficient grazing on poor rough grass. The curvature of their jaw ensures that even in old age the incisors form a cup and are able to bite cleanly. Their limbs are adapted for activity on rough ground, the scapula and humerus having the same degree of inclination which ensures balance, agility and sure-footedness, qualities so necessary on mountains. In the hind limbs the femur slopes downward and forward from the hip in the same degree of inclination as the tibia slopes backward to the hock. This means that the hindquarters, although rounded and muscular, appear short. The sacrum continues the line of the lumbar vertebrae and therefore the tail is low-set. The chest is wide with well sprung ribs. All these characteristics are essential for an animal living on high, rough ground where really fast bursts of speed either up or downhill may be necessary.

The position of the tail is the natural one for the circumstances where protection of the dock and inside of the thighs in bad weather is essential. In this matter too the arrangement of the coat is important, and in these ponies a weather proof protection is obtained by an insulating undercoat of wool and an outer coat of coarser, but not long, hair which acts as a watershed. The typical coat remains for eight or nine months of the year and is replaced by the short summer coat only during late May, June, July and early August.[7]

James Speed considered the environment of the uplands and realised that high rainfall was one of the most potent pressures for change upon the original colonisers. Although they were adapted to withstand cold and presumably had the effective insulation, driving, relentless rain would have tested them to the limits and natural selection would have favoured the evolution of features for protection from water and water dispersal. Thus these Mountain Ponies were perhaps the first equids to develop a long, floppy mane with forelock and a fully haired tail. Presumably too, given the colouring of their habitats, they probably darkened to brown shadings of coat colour.

The horses which took to the hills and became the ponies had made a good move for their upland habitats had a significant advantage over the lowlands; when Man came on the scene, he preferred living on lowlands rather than mountains. Thus as Man spread first as hunter, then as farmer, it was the Steppe and Forest Horses which came under pressure far more than Hill and Mountain Ponies. If indeed most of todays horses and ponies are of this mountain origin, it would not be inconsistent with the idea of populations surviving more readily on high ground, while their lowland cousins were hunted or taken into domestication.

Thus it would seem that the pony holds its head up high despite its smaller size compared to many modern domestic breeds of horse. This occupation of hills and mountains was a development that took the wild horse away from environments in which it would eventually face its ultimate threat; this was competition from Man,

and failure meant extinction or domestication with its loss of its natural identity. On the hills, ponies were not in direct competition with human settlement.

If we accept James Speed's view of the spread of the Mountain Ponies along upland ranges throughout Asia and Europe, we begin to visualise this type of prototype horse reaching ever further westwards, eventually arriving at the outpost of the European continent, Britain. Pleistocene horse bones appear in the British fossil record from around 130,000 years ago and so we can envisage the processes of evolving types and their spread across from Alaska as having spanned most of the last million years. Before looking more closely at how the British story unfolds, it is worth just considering what we have proposed as the natural history of the horse to this point.

A Logical Hypothesis

Students of horse evolution in the Pleistocene period have a difficult task. Although fossil bones have been discovered over a huge geographical range, much of it is only now coming under adequate scrutiny. Radiocarbon dating is only a relatively modern technique and so even the simple aspect of dating bones accurately is in its infancy and much of the material excavated many decades ago remains to be analysed. Also, interpreting bone structures is no simple task; comparing measurements and deciding when similarities mean variants of the same type or lack of consistency means separate types is complex. Also, researchers are limited to bone studies. The finding of a preserved horse frozen in Siberia was an astounding exception. Generally, the scientists have to work on sparse collections of bones and rarely even a whole skeleton.

No wonder then that even in the 1990s it is impossible to present the story of horse evolution during the last million years backed up with sound confirming evidence that would satisfy the rigorous and correct demands of the academic. Yet we cannot simply ignore this major proportion of the horse's history. We can however turn to our understanding of the evolutionary processes themselves and using this logic, present a reconstruction of what might have happened, recognising that some but not all of it is supported by scientific findings. We have then more of an artist's impression rather than a technical picture and we must await yet further scientific study in order to judge how sound the ideas are.

The horse has emerged from this as a remarkable animal even before Man so creatively shaped it to numerous forms and purposes. Leaving its North American birthplace, it began its wanderings across continents and through time. Of course North America was not totally deserted by all horses on some appointed emigration date; it developed there too throughout the Pleistocene era into various forms but eventually and inexplicably, all of these became extinct.

The horse's colonisation of widely differing environments in Asia and Europe is a tremendous success story. Its early evolution had equipped it with adaptive abilities which allowed it to exploit natural opportunities in almost all types of habitat, from incredibly harsh sub-arctic conditions to the arid deserts. As the horse adapted, natural selection shaped its teeth for different diets and its limbs for varying terrain and predation challenges. Its colouring became varied to aid camouflage with lighter shadings in semi-desert, greyish hues set against the tree trunks of open forest, increasingly darker colour to match upland vegetation and perhaps black for the depths of the forest. In the selection for fitness, the coat structure, the mane and tail became tailored to either dry or wet conditions, to cold or heat. Nature also selected differing behaviour and social patterns to confer advantage for different ways of life.

By understanding these processes we come to appreciate how so many forms of wild horse evolved. It really doesn't matter if there were three, four or more basic types as different scientists have proposed. The horse's secret of success was that it had evolved into a superbly efficient grazing animal with enough genetic flexibility to take advantage of pastures new and to complete a journey from North America to Britain. Now we must focus in upon how the story progressed once horses reached this far-flung land which was to become the British Isles.

Plate 10 *The first British wild horses lived alongside mammoths*

CHAPTER 3

THE BRITISH HILL PONY

The Age of Ice

It is perhaps only when we see pictures of a volcanic eruption or a hurricane that we can begin to appreciate the immense power of natural forces. For us in Britain, natural phenomena are relatively mild and it is the effects of the human population which are now generating selection pressures upon the plants and animals of our islands. However, for many hundreds of thousands of years up until about twenty thousand years before present, the flora and fauna of Britain and indeed most of the northern hemisphere was subject to the influence of an awesome natural architect, ice. The Pleistocene period was the era of ice-ages; although reference is often made to "the" ice-age, there were in fact many. The arctic ice-cap went through a sequence of expansions and retreats which presented contrasting phases of glacial and inter-glacial conditions right around the northern world.

Imagine the utter desolation of a world of ice. Scenes from travel films of the North or South Pole show us that such places are frozen deserts offering a survivable habitat only along their edge for animals which can obtain resources from the sea. The ice-fields themselves provide no food or shelter and their water is inaccessible in its frozen state. Even when Man equips himself with supplies and mobile shelter it is still a cruel environment that has claimed the lives of many explorers. So ice is perhaps the one environment which presents an insurmountable challenge for all but the simplest bacteria.

At the onset of the age of ice movements, temperatures fell to such an extent in the northern hemisphere that ever more water was drawn from the seas to fuel the growing mass of the arctic ice-cap. The ice moved southwards, grinding its way over the northern continents, cutting its U-shaped valleys, literally almost moving mountains. Its force was incredible, its effect devastating. Yet, the advances of ice were at a rate which allowed populations of animals to respond and move south. Once the ice began to retreat, and as their normal environments were re-established, the animals returned home. So we can imagine these waves of ebb and flow of the ice-sheet, then south of that the Tundra and south of that again, the more temperate habitats; their movements were matched by migrations of the animals for this was vital for survival. With animals adapted to particular habitats, they had to seek out the homes to which they were suited; to stay put as the arctic conditions intensified was to perish.

Such a pattern affected the land from North America to Western Europe and Britain was of course still connected to the European mainland. As we take up the story of the horse as it reached Britain, we find it is one dominated by presence during interglacials and movement south when the ice covered much of what is now the British Isles. The horse was a highly successful member of the sub-arctic fauna, occupying tundra-like conditions, perhaps one of the last to leave and first to return. As we have already seen, different types were adapted to various ecosystems but an early development had been a range of features for coping with cold and a coarse, poor diet.

The ice invasions were extensive but did not cover Britain totally; the south and south-west of England escaped and it is from the south that the evidence of the first British horses comes. The gouging effects of the weight of the ice-sheet would have so reformed the landscape over which it passed that it is not surprising that the bones of interglacial animals did not survive in areas that had been ice-covered. In the cliffs near Brighton, in what is known as Coombe rock, the bones of animals from about 130,000 BP (before present) have been discovered. Some of these are in the Mantell Collection in the British Museum of Natural History and they can tell us what that early sub-arctic fauna was like. At least two individual horses are represented. These horses had some dramatic companions for at the same time there were mammoth, bison, deer and woolly rhinoceros.

After the Ice Ages

Perhaps the best picture of the interglacial fauna comes from a much later period after the ice had retreated northwards for the last time, around 12,000 BP and from the area of Somerset called the Mendip Hills. This has proved to be a rich source of bone material because of its many caves; these were occupied by various prehistoric carnivores and eventually Stone Age Man. Their remains, plus those of their various meals, tell the story of the animals. Also, there are bones which were probably washed down into the caves.

One cave is known as Hyena Den and appears to have been just that. H.E. Balch excavated many of the Mendip caves in the late 1940s and wrote about them in *Mendip – its Swallet Caves and Rock Shelters*. He wrote of Hyena Den:

> To summarise our finds in terms of identified specimens we have of Mammoth 6, of Woolly Rhinoceros 16, of Hyena 60, of Cave and Brown Bear 60, of Wild Horse 35, of an unnamed little horse 35, of Red and Roe Deer 40, of Reindeer 22, of Wild Boar 10, of Bison 12, with a very large number of the smaller creatures of the wild, Polecats, Voles, Hares, Mice, Cave Pika, Hedgehog etc.[8]

Hyena Den was also home at some time to early Man for fragments of human bones were found; these people apparently hunted the wild horses amongst other animals for Balch continues:

> The Wild Horse was eaten, for the cuts made by flint knives are seen on a bone of that animal.

For us it is perhaps most interesting that two distinct types of horse were found. This was also the case at Gough's Cavern on Mendip, again from around the same date. James Speed recorded in *A Survey of the Evolution of Horses in Britain* that horses were present, sometimes abundantly, in 21 of the 27 known excavation sites; he observed that the smaller type was present from the early to the latest strata, whilst the larger type occurred only in the later levels, a pattern mirrored by finds in the Dordogne region of France. He suggested that these two forms were the small mountain pony and its larger cousin, the steppe horse.

It would seem from the numbers and frequency of finds in the Mendip area and elsewhere that these wild horses were abundant prey for the hyenas, sabre-toothed tigers and man. Speed explored just why equids were so successful in his article on the natural history of the horse:

> Zoogeographically therefore we find even in Britain such astonishing things as the elephant and hippopotamus sandwiched in between grizzly bears, musk oxen and arctic fox, but all the time and everywhere the horse. Why did the

horse maintain his hold in spite of climatic and geographical changes? The hippopotamus thrived in the warm inter-glacial spells and disappeared in the sub-arctic conditions. The arctic animals did the opposite. These were of course specialised animals. The horse too is specialised, but for one thing only and that is eating grass. The rest of his talents and attributes depend upon or contribute to his ability to eat grass successfully. This is then the secret of the horse's success during the last million years, the epoch which is called the Pleistocene or Recent.[9]

With the flexibility to cope with extreme cold and the ability to live on both sub-arctic tundra or the grasslands when warmer times prevailed, horses were constant colonisers of land as soon as the ice surrendered. Their travelling habits allowed them to take up new locations quickly and their efficient grazing made them most effective competitors.

Spanning the vast period between the horses found at Brighton, from about 130,000 BP and the Mendip horses of about 12,000 BP, we have then successive ice-ages and interglacial periods; some interglacials were warmer, others only attained sub-arctic conditions. Into this Britain came Man, a primitive creature who depended upon hunting and gathering and who found here, as in the rest of Europe, a world full of both opportunity and threat. There were populations of mammoths, bison, wild cattle and horses and various types of deer which would yield meat, fat, hides, antlers, a multitude of resources to both feed him and allow his culture to develop. Yet waiting to prey upon the humans as well as these grazing animals were the large carnivores, the cave lions and hyenas, the sabre-tooth.

John Evans in *The Environment of Early Man in the British Isles* clearly presents the view that the horse played a vital role in the economy of the first human colonisers:

The tundra vegetation, on which low temperatures and a short growing season were limiting factors, was not directly exploitable for food on a large scale by man, although seeds and berries were doubtless eaten. But the reindeer and the horse were ideally suited to it and it was

Plate 11 *Early human settlers in Britain hunted the wild horses*

through these animals that man's livelihood was largely gained. The enormous quantities of bone and antler, and implements made from them, which occur on British and European sites bear witness to the importance of these animals in the life of Upper Palaeolithic man.[10]

Yet we must not imagine that southern Britain around 12,000 BP was inhabited by large numbers of people slaughtering multitudes of unfortunate horses and deer; that was not the case. Professor Gordon Childe wrote in 1948 in *Prehistoric Communities of the British Isles* of the human colonisers of that period and what they encountered:

On their arrival they still found a few mammoth, woolly rhinoceros, bison and reindeer as well as plenty of horses and wild oxen in Britain. But the climate soon – i.e. in the next two or three thousand years – began to grow milder. First the rhinoceros and the mammoth died out, and at last the reindeer vanished even from Derbyshire. One's general impression is that during the closing phases of the last Ice Age southern Britain was occupied by a very sparse and far from prosperous population of hunters and collectors, living for the most part in caves, but also camping on the open plains in East Anglia and Lincolnshire. None of the caves, save Paviland, seems to have been occupied at all intensively nor for long continuous periods. The population must have been very small; Clark's estimate for the winter months of a total of 250 is not extravagantly low.[11]

The French historian, François Bordes summed up the situation as:

A human desert swarming with game.

These views of what is termed the Upper Palaeolithic period, when speaking of human culture, still prevail. The idea of very small human populations of early Man in Britain is also confirmed by what we will learn of later cultures in the Mesolithic period. With regard to the changes in the fauna, John Evans comments in his book that towards the end of the Palaeolithic period, mammoth, woolly rhinoceros, hyena and lion had disappeared; this was probably a response to the warming of the climate.

Let us return to the findings that two races of horse

DATE BEFORE PRESENT (BP)	HUMAN CULTURE	CLIMATE TYPE	VEGETATION PERIOD (Main upland Features)	EVENTS
Present Day				
2,000		Oceanic Cold and Wet	Sub-Atlantic = Spread of Peat Bogs	
3,000	Bronze Age	Continental Warm and Dry	Sub-Boreal = Elm Decline and Forest Clearance	
4,000				
5,000	Neolithic Period			
6,000		Oceanic Warm and Wet	Atlantic = Forests and Bogs	
7,000	Mesolithic Period			< Channel forms – Britain becomes an island
8,000		Warmer and Drier	= Boreal Forests	
9,000				
10,000				< Rapid rise in temperature
11,000				
12,000	Late or Upper Palaeolithic Period	Sub-Arctic	Pre-Boreal (before trees)	
13,000				
32,000				

Figure 3.01 *Timescales and periods of climate, vegetation and human culture*

Plate 12 *James Speed (left) and H.E. Balch excavating in Badger Hole, one of the Mendip caves*

were present in the Mendip caves from this Upper Palaeolithic time of around 12,000 years ago, for it is highly significant to our story. James Speed visited H.E. Balch at the excavations and studied the Mendip finds extensively. He noted that there was no evidence from the fossils that the two types interbred with each other; no intermediate forms were found. Thus we can suggest that these were indeed independent travellers which had followed a separate destiny for some considerable time; this blends in with the idea that races evolved quite early in their spread across Asia and Europe.

Speed believed that the larger type of horse had been part of what zoologists call the Siberian migration, reaching Europe along a route to the north of the Caspian Sea. He viewed the small race as part of the "Oriental Migration" travelling to Europe via Asia

Minor and the Mediterranean via land bridges. The latter wave of colonisation appears to have been the earlier and the more successful for animals.

The larger wild horse represented in the Mendip caves has been likened to the type of animal whose bones were found in such large numbers at Solutré in France, essentially a steppe horse similar to Przewalski's Horse. A decorated horse jaw bone was found at Kendrick's Cavern near Llandudno in 1880 and it has been suggested that this is from a Przewalski-like Horse; unfortunately its date is not certain. If the larger British wild horse was a steppe race then it probably inhabited the lower parts of Britain. Like the smaller race, it reached Britain before the ice-ages ended and Speed observed that it was represented in fossils at the British Museum of Natural History dated from 60,000 BP. It was not however found as widely as the smaller race.

It is uncertain whether this larger wild horse persisted as long as the smaller race or whether it died out; the latter seems more likely. Thinking again of environmental pressures, perhaps it could not tolerate the increasingly wet climate that developed later. Although Przewalski's Horse lives in Britain today, it is in zoos with food and shelter provided and we do not know how it would fare exposed to our wet winters unaided. Alternatively, it has been suggested that the ancestry of the Fell/Dales Ponies might owe something to this steppe horse; there is no hard evidence to substantiate this but equally this aspect has not apparently been studied.

The earlier coloniser of Britain was the small wild horse which Speed suggested was the mountain pony type. The path it had followed emerged when the Mendip bones were compared to other fossil bones. Placed side by side, leg bones from the small Mendip pony of around 12,000 BP, from the Dordogne in France dated at about 32,000 BP, from 130,000 year-old Brighton and from Alaska at around 27,000 years old, were of the same dimensions. Otto Geist who excavated the Alaskan material thought that the bones were perhaps half a million years old but one has now been carbon-dated at about 27,000 BP. These comparisons strongly suggest

that across this vast geographical range and span of time, it was essentially the same race of animal and different from the larger steppe horse. There are many bones from the Mendip excavations in museums at Wells, Taunton and the British Museum of Natural History awaiting further work to reveal more about the Palaeolithic wild horses.

H.E. Balch founded the Wells Museum and was its curator from 1893 to 1954. Professor D.T. Donovan recalls that Balch

> used to talk to one at length about his "little horses" as he called them. I think he thought that the horses he had excavated in the caves were the ancestors of our present moorland ponies.[12]

This is obviously a theme we are going to explore further but for now we must continue with how these British wild ponies fared as Man became an ever-more dominant figure in their environment.

Human prehistory is divided up into periods which are characterised by different ways of life. So far, we have been looking at the Palaeolithic, a time when Man was still highly primitive and his hunting could only support a limited population. The subsequent period is known as the Mesolithic and began about 10,000 years ago, lasting for nearly 5,000 years. For our story, the most relevant aspect of human development was that Mesolithic Man became a much more efficient hunter.

The Mesolithic Puzzle

The Mesolithic period is a crucial one in the history of British horses; it provides us with a picture open to two very different interpretations which divide the zoological community. The cause of this dissension is that there are very few undisputed and clearly documented finds of horse bones from this period and the early part of the following Neolithic era. This apparent "gap" in the bone record may be interpreted in different ways. There is a widely-held theory that no form of wild horse survived the Mesolithic period and that horses were re-introduced later. Others hypothesise that there is an ecological explanation for the absence of finds and that the horse has been present continuously.

The exponents of the extinction theory suggest that this happened during the Mesolithic period because Man so perfected his hunting skills that he totally exterminated the wild horse population throughout Britain. Anthony Dent, author of a number of books on horses and ponies, has written on this subject and he explained his argument to me in a letter back in 1975:

As to killing out by hunters, I base my attitude partly on the relatively small percentage of bones in Neolithic sites, compared to other remains, in a period which is certainly earlier than the domestication of the horse in these islands.

We have to remember that the most worthwhile Cervidae (deer) from the hunter's point of view, the Elk and the Reindeer, migrated out of Britain before the North Sea dried up anyway. Also during the Mesolithic Age which was the great period of the purely hunting culture, the one in which the bow was invented and in which the dog became fully domesticated and developed into a trained and active aid in the hunt, there was an escalating game crisis in these islands. The size of prey animals found on Mesolithic sites gets smaller as time goes on, down to the point where we find a great quantity of such mammals as Squirrels and Water Voles. The Fallow Deer was not indigenous to Britain which left the hunters with only wild Boar, the Red Deer and the Roe Deer; this last does not seem to have been evenly distributed throughout the islands and the same is true of the Aurochs (the original wild cattle).

Whilst the Cervidae, especially the Red Deer, yielded important non-meat material such as the antlers (and the Reindeer while it lasted), which could be worked into pick-axes for example, it may be that the seasonal migration routes of the wild horse were more predictable and made them more vulnerable to ambushes (such as that which appears to have been repeated year after year at Solutré in France) than any Deer except the Reindeer.

We should remember that in the hunting culture the hardest thing to come by in worthwhile quantities is Fat, all year round. This is needed not only for food but for lamps, for lubrication, for waterproofing for . . . you name it. The only time to get it is in the Autumn when animals have a season's grazing behind them and have deposited a layer of tallow under the skin. Especially foals. Ponies not only have a higher killing-out proportion than any Deer but, taken at the right season, a higher proportion of fat to lean. That alone would lead to selective hunting. We think of lard and pigs but then we are thinking of domesticated pigs which run to more fat than the European wild swine. Only among marine mammals could the hunter find a better yielder of fat than the wild horse and if he did not happen to live on the coast the option was not open.[13]

Interpretations such as this, of the apparent rarity of the horse in the Mesolithic period, have convinced many people for a long time that the horse succumbed to intensive hunting and only returned later as a domesticated animal. Whilst much of the concept of the value of the horse as prey to the Mesolithic hunter is fully acceptable, the idea that he hunted the wild horses to extinction seems more doubtful.

Firstly, listen to any documentary about primitive hunting cultures which persist in some exotic corner of the world and the same story is told, of hunters totally in tune with the natural world, who understand the balance of Nature far better than we "civilised" naturalists. Such people fully appreciate the need to take only a proportion of each species and to allow their prey to reproduce and maintain stocks. It is apparently only modern Man who drives species to extinction through ignorance.

However, the aspect of this killing-out theory which remains most suspect is that it must assume a very high number of horses killed each year. Professor Stuart Piggott has studied the Mesolithic extensively and wrote about an excavation of the hunters' lake-village at Star Carr in the Vale of Pickering, Yorkshire in his book *Ancient Europe*:

The lake-side site was occupied repeatedly from late Autumn to early Spring for some twenty seasons by a group of four to five family groups, totalling not more than

25 persons of whom about five would be adult men who could effectively hunt big game. On analogy from North American conditions before the European invasions, one can assume a likely population density of not more than 13 persons to 100 square miles, so the Star Carr population would have ranged over two hundred square miles. If we average this out for Britain we arrive at a total population around 7,500 BC of about 10,000 persons.

Now their (the Star Carr group) main protein diet was provided by Red Deer meat and they would have obtained their minimum necessary calorie intake from the venison of 50 beasts a year, so since the likely Red Deer population in natural conditions would amount to about 3,400 Deer to 200 square miles, they could have gorged themselves on meat without coming anywhere near the full exploitation of the game potential. And of course we have ignored other animals and said nothing of vegetable food.[14]

What a different picture this gives us. It certainly makes the idea of hunting to extinction of any animal by the Mesolithic hunters seem very doubtful, for the people themselves seem to have been few and far between. The fact that these particular hunters concentrated on deer at Star Carr does not mean that they did not utilise the horse; just as Anthony Dent describes, there was much to be gained from equine prey, but presumably horses were not in their immediate locality and anyway, were just one of the resources they might exploit. For the extinction theory to be sound, one would have to accept the concept of a much denser population of people, with an obsessive fixation upon killing horses alone. In my opinion the evidence cannot support this view.

So now we come to the second of the two interpretations of the low numbers of bones found from this period. It seems probable that natural factors of climate and vegetation provide a more credible explanation than the hunting theme. Prior to our modern era, it is generally the ruthlessness of natural selection through food and the elements that usually dominates in the story of changes to species.

The wild horses of Palaeolithic times lived in a cold climate of sub-Arctic conditions and botanists classify this period as the Pre-Boreal phase (i.e. before trees). They were well adapted to grazing on the open hills, steppe and tundra, given the ancestry we have seen earlier. However, early in the Mesolithic period, around 9,600 BP, the climate changed in Britain, becoming warmer and drier and the vegetation responded. The Boreal Phase began and trees spread rapidly forming forests on the lowland areas and gradually invading upland areas to heights of up to 2,500 feet above sea level. This restricted open habitat to the mountains of Scotland and Wales, the Pennines and just a few areas of Dartmoor and perhaps Exmoor.

The forest represented a very different environment for horses. Their natural home was the open country and their style primarily grazing. Their social structure of herding and all their avoidance of predation was based upon living in open terrain. Within the forests they would have been easier prey to predators and indeed the Mesolithic hunters would have found them easier to trap. However, it also seems likely that they would have adapted to some degree to the more open woodland habitat, on the edges of the remaining grazing land. This dramatic shrinking of the extent of open habitat must surely have led to a comparable reduction in the size of horse population in Britain. Also, with the persisting open habitat being on high hills and mountains, it would have been the smaller hill pony race which would have survived, albeit in small numbers; the larger steppe horse might well have become extinct at this time. Up to now, in talking of wild horses in Britain, we have been referring collectively to the mountain/hill pony and the steppe horse; from this point onward we will concentrate on the hill pony and thus change over to speaking of wild ponies.

This environmental crisis would have both reduced the total population of Hill Ponies in Britain and also isolated sub-populations upon the mountains and moorlands. Is it purely coincidence that our surviving pony breeds are still found in these few surviving areas of semi-wilderness? Not only would there have been far fewer ponies in Britain but they would have no longer been as widespread or so readily available as prey.

The Mesolithic hunters would surely have recognised this change and known that there were ponies isolated on the uplands. When living in their winter camps such as at Star Carr, the Red Deer which were abundant in the forests would have been the more likely food source. Perhaps, as would be logical, the hunters moved to the uplands in summer and hunted the wild ponies from temporary summer camps. Such seasonal occupation on the uplands might show few traces and leave little to attract the archaeologist's attention. The bones of the Mesolithic wild ponies would thus lie undiscovered, buried in the anonymity of hillsides.

This interpretation of the Mesolithic, incorporating the environmental effects of major climatic changes, makes the rarity of pony bones from sites of human occupation quite logical and understandable. In the absence of adequate evidence for either this or the extinction theory, readers must make their own judgements, accepting that either might be proved right in the future or we may never know.

The Birth of the British Hill Pony

About 7,500 BP the climate changed again becoming a warm, and primarily wet, oceanic climate in what is termed the Atlantic Phase. This brought about another change in the vegetation, the development of huge areas of blanket bog which replaced forest on sloping ground and created open, if challenging, terrain from about 1,000 feet above sea level. This began the development of the moorland habitat we know today and was perhaps an opportunity for the exiled wild ponies to increase a little.

The continued warming since around 9,600 BP had produced a gradual melt of the ice-cap and a consequent rise in sea-level, drowning some low-lying areas of land. This eventually created the English Channel and gave Britain its island status somewhere between 7,000 and 8,000 years ago. Until then, the story of the wild ponies had been just part of a much wider picture of the spread and development of the two equid races in Europe. At this point, when the waters finally met and cut off the western tip of the continent, the British Hill Pony was born. No longer could populations of grazing animals move freely in and out of Britain; after the formation of the Channel, any emigration or immigration would be dependent upon human development.

Taking the viewpoint that the British Hill Pony was not exterminated by Mesolithic Man, we can picture these beginnings for our island race of wild ponies. High on the mountains and hills, in places too inhospitable for Man to live all year round, wild ponies would have drawn upon their adaptations to cold, wet winters and a meagre diet, which had been shaped by Nature so long ago. There would probably have been some degree of interchange between the fragmented population at first, but this would have meant crossing forested, low ground. As Man spread and his numbers increased, this would have become increasingly hazardous; once Man became a farmer and enclosed land it must have eventually become physically impossible. We can only speculate at what point these pockets of wild pony population finally became completely isolated from each other but it might well have been fairly recent, within historical times.

Plate 13 *Hill ponies of today inhabit several upland areas, their populations isolated from one another*

The Re-introduction Theory

Returning to the alternative theory, that wild ponies became extinct in the Mesolithic period, this demands a companion theory that they were re-introduced at a later stage; it must be so to explain the long recorded history of ponies in Britain. Generally, the view taken is that such a re-introduction occurred after the Neolithic Period. Anthony Dent and Daphne Machin Goodall pointed this out in *The Foals of Epona*:

But once the land-bridge between England and the Continent had sunk under the sea, they could only be re-introduced in ships and no Neolithic boat could transport horses alive.[15]

This interpretation has led to the view that the pony was a Celtic re-introduction in the Bronze Age, which began about 3,700 years ago and lasted until approximately 2,650 BP. The sheer physical demands of transporting large stock across the Channel in primitive boats must have meant that the animals introduced were tame, if not fully domestic stock. Thus advocates of the extinction and re-introduction theories consider that all free-living populations of ponies in Britain have a domestic origin from which they have returned to an essentially wild life. Juliet Clutton-Brock wrote in *A Natural History of Domesticated Animals*:

It seems more probable that these ponies constitute populations of feral animals, perhaps of very ancient origin.[16]

As we saw earlier, feral means animals living in the wild which were domesticated at some point in their history.

Undoubtedly, the Celts brought equids to Britain. However, by that time, the birth of farming which characterised the Neolithic period had matured into sophisticated stock rearing and domestication. Cross-breeding between equine races had apparently begun. Bronze Age pony remains were found in Read's Cavern in the Mendips and H.E. Balch described them as smaller than the Palaeolithic animals, perhaps just eleven hands.

James Speed believed that the Celts imported ponies which were mongrelised and rejected the idea that they were founders of feral populations:

The Celts imported a small ten hands pony but it does not appear to have been pure-bred, because it had some of the characters of the western small pony and some of the characters of the southern horses. It is found buried in the graves of the Celtic settlements and was a domestic horse, but it obviously did not succeed in establishing itself in a wild state here, and its bones show evidence of diseases.[17]

Yet this is not the whole story for in graves of Celtic date at Blewburton, two types of animal were found, the bones of which are in Reading Museum. One was apparently a slender stallion of about 11 hands while the other was identified by Speed as the original British pony type. Did the Celts return the same mountain pony type, now tamed, to Britain as part of their introductions? Alternatively, had they captured such an animal from wild herds which were still inhabiting the uplands of Bronze Age Britain?

Perhaps the Celtic settlers came to Britain where they found the British Hill Pony living on the mountains and moorlands, presenting them with a ready food source. The Celtic people still ate horses and continued to do so for a considerable time. Such herds would have also provided a ready supply of young animals for domestication. At first though, the settlers would probably have wished to import the horses they had succeeded in domesticating and had bred to their own design. Is this the explanation for the British Hill Pony and crossed animals beginning to share the British Isles? Once again, we cannot be sure.

The Celts began the practise of importing animals to the British Isles and in the case of horses and ponies, it was to continue throughout history. Man quickly found that the genetic flexibility which had served the horse family so well in its natural history provided a wonderful basis for animal husbandry. Today, we can see the incredible range of end-products which centuries of selective and cross-breeding have produced. However, the newly evolved skills and the equine products of the

Celtic animal breeders presented a distinct threat to the British Hill Pony. Up to then, in its island kingdom, the British pony was isolated from the blending of horse races which was being practised on mainland Europe.

We have, of course, no recorded history of how the Celtic settlers proceeded with their horse-breeding in Britain. We can suggest that they would have captured individuals from free-living British Hill Pony herds if they were still present. Yet would their imported animals have had any effect on wild populations up on the hills and mountains? It seems fairly unlikely. If the Celts themselves re-introduced the mountain pony to a Britain devoid of horses, it would surely have been this type and not their cross-bred animals which would have been able to re-colonise the mountains and moorlands. So whichever theory we favour, I believe we may legitimately consider that the British Hill Pony probably entered the Iron Age unaltered.

Historical Chaos

It would be so satisfying to be able to continue tracing the story of the British Hill Pony down through the centuries since the Bronze Age ended but this proves impossible. Once again, we have the problem that historians and archaeologists are primarily interested in our own species and because of this, any information about horses and ponies in Britain is about those animals in the service of Man. As breeders were importing and mixing at an accelerating rate throughout historical times, the resultant equine picture becomes totally chaotic. Anthony Dent and Daphne Machin Goodall created some order out of the confusion by intricate research of historical texts, language and art which they presented in the remarkable book *The Foals of Epona*. Yet amidst all of Man's relationship with the horse in domesticity, what was happening in the remote upland areas to the free-living herds of British Hill Pony? We really do need that time-machine!

We are faced then with a question: did Man's desire to create animals suited to his purposes lead to the disappearance of the original ponies, by placing them in the melting pot of cross-breeding? Alternatively, did this ancient survivor evade such an unnatural destiny? We must look at what little is recorded of the history of today's Mountain and Moorland Ponies and see if there are glimpses of the British Hill Pony to be found. Before we search for such clues, we need to have perhaps a clearer picture of the animal itself. From the evidence available, we need to construct an identikit of the British Hill Pony.

A Portrait of the British Hill Pony

So far we have talked about what may have happened to the British Hill Pony but not about the animal itself. If we are to follow its trail further into modern times, we must have an animal of substance not merely a shadowy form. To create a useful picture of our quarry, we must interpret a number of clues.

The only parts of prehistoric animals which have survived in Britain are their bones; it is only in intensively frozen conditions such as in Siberia or in deep lowland peat-bogs that tissues are preserved. So we must look again at the skeletal remains and see what can be deduced. Firstly, bones can convey the height of the pony.

As far back as 1888, scientists were establishing from studying living horses, and subsequently their skeletons, that there are fairly constant relationships between the length of bones and the ultimate height of the horse. Most of this work was done in Germany and studies in 1955 and 1974 confirmed the principles which Keisewalter first proposed. Thus, today we have a series of multiplication factors which we can apply to bones to estimate the size of the animal. Similarly, on the assumption that this height-bone length relationship was true for ancient horses too, we can look at the fossil bones and calculate the dimension of height at withers.

We will see later from the Speed photographs of bone comparisons that the Alaskan, Brighton, and Mendip (smaller type) leg bones are of matching size. Some of the Alaskan material is in my possession. When measured, and the multiplication factors used, the withers height of this ancestral animal is 12.3 hands. Hermann Ebhardt wrote that he had only found one size of what he viewed as the ancestral pony type (which he called Pony Type 1) and this with a withers height of 11.3 to 12.3 hands. We have to remember though that the actual number of individual animals involved in all the research has been very small.

However, it does present us with the view that our British Hill Pony was probably around 12 hands. We cannot be sure of the extremes of the natural height range because we do not have sufficient numbers or spread of ages and sexes in the bone material.

The various bones from our British Hill Pony and its immediate ancestors can tell us other things about the animals. The teeth are very large and arranged in a distinctive pattern; Hermann Ebhardt X-rayed many lower jaw bones and described the pony arrangement:

> The pre-molars as well as the molars swing through to the front with their lower ends growing until all the molars are stretched forwards regularly. If one lengthens the high axis of all the molars upwards, they meet all in one place, in fact 16-18 cm above the chewing surface. All the molars are placed so regularly in a wheel-radius form that it is immediately obvious in the x-ray photos. Harder food in the cold areas required a high chewing pressure which was and is passed on with the growth of the molars onto a much bigger bone length.[18]

This means that the British Hill Pony must have had deep lower jaw-bones to allow room for the large cheek teeth. In turn this must imply that it had a fairly long and deep head. Ebhardt also studied the leg bones and concluded that the structure of the limbs would have produced a fairly even action of front and back legs with a trot involving small steps. He suggested this action had evolved for rapid movement on hillsides and perhaps icy surfaces as opposed to the different alignment of limb bones in other types related to running on flat, hard ground.

Anatomically then, we can envisage a robust pony with immensely strong legs and feet, with a sizeable head to accommodate its efficient teeth. Without a training in anatomy, it is hard to envisage an animal's appearance even with some detail of its skeleton. We need to put some flesh on these bones and to do this we must use deductive reasoning and a few clues.

Firstly, what colour was our British Hill Pony? Given the colouring of Przewalski's Horse and the colours of horses depicted by the palaeolithic cave artists, we can reasonably assume it was some shade of brown. Given the vegetation of north-west Europe, including Britain, we can hypothesise that a fairly dark shade of brown would have been necessary if the wild steppe horses and Mountain Ponies were to blend in with their background. If their colour had not provided some degree of camouflage, they would not have thrived and been such dominant grazers. So our British Hill Pony was probably quite a rich, darkish brown colour, given the colours of moorland grass and heather. Perhaps its shading varied geographically to fit different surroundings. The longer hair of the mane and tail were probably darker brown or black if we look to Przewalski's Horse as a model.

Large, wild, grazing mammals tend towards a natural pattern of brown coat with markings on the head, often a light-coloured muzzle and ring around the eye. This is not only true of wild asses and Przewalski's Horse but can be seen in primitive cattle and in antelope species. Again, the cave painters indicated there was a distinctive muzzle shown by the prehistoric equids. It would seem reasonable then to suppose that the British Hill Pony had a light-coloured muzzle and eye-ring.

Why should such a striking pattern of facial markings be so important to wild grazing animals? We cannot be absolutely certain, but perhaps the key factor in selecting this appearance is that the animals involved are prey for carnivorous predators. At dusk, when hunting animals are seeking food, anything that breaks up the outline of an animal aids in its camouflage. The large, grazing mammals can feed with their bodies virtually still but will lift their heads regularly to look around and check for danger. So the contrast of dark face and light muzzle and eye may make the head less easy for predators to focus upon and thus aid the prey in blending in with its environment. It must be a highly successful feature as it is so widespread in grazing species.

As to other external features, we can suggest logical attributes but have of course no evidence to confirm them. The British Hill Pony existed in a cold and often very wet place. The element of high rainfall must have shaped these animals, as it had their ancestors, providing ways of coping with water. We might then visualise the British Hill Pony as having a long, floppy mane with a well-developed forelock to ensure water-dispersal from the head and shoulders. Similarly, the tail must have been fully haired and long to channel water to the ground. The outer hair of the coat must have been water-proofed, perhaps by being greasy, or the race would have perished in the wet climate. To cope with cold, the winter coat must have provided insulation beneath its water-proofing. The combination of cold and wet in winter demands that animals' body openings are kept small and well-protected, so we can theorise that the British Hill Pony had small ears and its tail would have hung low and close to the body. As summers were warmer though still wet, presumably the coat grew in two phases, the insulation being lost in the summer period.

The other significant factor of appearance we can be sure of is that being a wild race, all individual British Hill Ponies would have been essentially identical in appearance. So now we can close our eyes and think of the hills and mountains of Britain in prehistoric times. There on the hillsides graze small herds of ponies, each the image of its fellows. They are small, stocky, brown ponies with light muzzles and eye-rings. Their coat, here in winter, is thick and after the rain is showing many paths where water has been shed from it. The mane, forelock and tail are very dark and thickly haired. This then is our identikit for a British Hill Pony and we must carry it in our minds as we set out to find if this natural blueprint persisted until recently, or even still endures, amongst the modern Mountain and Moorland Ponies of Britain.

CHAPTER 4

THE LAST SURVIVORS

Britain is renowned internationally for its wealth of breeds of native ponies, for such a diversity is found nowhere else in the world. Visit most major agricultural shows in the British Isles and you will find classes for showing "Mountain and Moorland" ponies. These Mountain and Moorland breeds represent a marvellous variety of ponies which cannot fail to impress those interested in horse-breeding. Each type is named after the geographical area from which it originates, so we have the Shetland, the Highland, the Eriskay, the Fell, the Dales, the Welsh Mountain, the Connemara, the New Forest, the Dartmoor and the Exmoor. Within the Highland there is further variety of types associated with different locations, i.e. the main-land Highland and the Western Isles type. The size of these ponies ranges from the diminutive Shetland at a maximum of 10.2 hands up to the Dales and Highland which can reach 14.2 hands. The colouring and marking within most of the breeds is quite varied too as is the build and conformation.

We cannot explore the history of each of these breeds in detail, for each warrants a book in its own right. If we take a brief look into what has been documented about them, we find that the diversity of types has arisen from differing breeding programmes, some by chance but mostly as deliberate policy. Just as a wine maker uses his skill to mix the different varieties of wine into what he judges to be the perfect end-result, so it has been with pony-breeders in creating many of the localised breeds. In all cases though, there was the common ingredient of the true native animal, the British Hill Pony. The various recipes which yielded the breeds have utilised ingredients such as the Friesian Horse in Roman times, Norwegian Ponies, brought over with the Vikings, and later on, Thoroughbred, Arab, Clydesdale and Hackney. In addition, some of the breeds as we see them today are the result of mixing several of the Mountain and Moorland breeds themselves.

The emergence of these breeds from a foundation of British Hill Pony stock must have taken place at different times in the various locations. However, the populations on the widely separated mountains, moorlands, heathlands and islands would have been virtually the same before introductions began, if the British Hill Pony theory is valid. To find out whether this was so and to discover just when their common characteristics were submerged into the breeds, we have to search amongst the pages of old books and locate the earliest photographs. It sounds a dry and dusty task yet proves to be exciting for quite surprisingly we can find glimpses of the British Hill Pony in a number of places far more recently than might have been expected. We find the words of well-respected and knowledgeable horsemen confirm that the original native pony is only a recent loss in historical terms in locations where a quite altered breed exists today.

We cannot trace the sequence of events thoroughly because for most of the centuries people were insufficiently educated to record information. Even in the later centuries when records could have been kept, those in remote places were usually too concerned with basic subsistence to find the time to write about their animals. Only within the last two hundred years, and mainly since the mid 1800s have writers left us with glimpses of our quarry.

Echoes of the British Hill Pony

The first reference to the various pony populations in Britain, and one which introduces the theme of similarity between them, seems to come from William Marshall who wrote *The Rural Economy of the West of England* in 1796. In the section on horses in West Devonshire he stated:

> The native breed, which are still seen on the mountains that overlook this District, are very small: much resembling the Welsh and Highland breeds; and like them are valuable for particular purposes.[19]

As we will see in the following chapter, the word "pony" was not in usage in the south of Britain until several decades after Marshall gave his fascinating account of all aspects of rural life.

A hundred years later, native ponies began to attract considerable attention in terms of the contribution they could make to pony breeding programmes, designed to produce riding and particularly Polo Ponies. In 1899, sections for registering native breeds were included in the Polo Pony Stud Book and the objective was stated thus:

> By registering such of them as are likely to breed riding ponies, and by periodically going back to this fountain-head of all ponies, we may be able to regulate the size of our high-class riding ponies to the desired limit, while at the same time we shall infuse into their blood the hardiness of constitution and endurance combined with a fiery yet even temper so pre-eminently characteristic of the British native breeds.[20]

That same 1899 volume yields a statement specifically noting the common features of native breeds. This was by Lord Arthur Cecil, who was a founder member of the Polo Pony Society Council and he wrote:

> Personally I am of the opinion that the one great recommendation should be the power of the animal to live and thrive in winter time without any adventitious sustenance, while there are many characteristics which all these possess in common, notably the clean-cut head, small ears, bright full eye and well-curved nostrils together with a strong predisposition to the brown colour, with light tan or mealy points, which we see running through as a common attribute of them all.[21]

Thus even as late as 1899, the British Hill Pony type was still frequently seen within many of the breeds of native ponies. This was confirmed just a few years later when Thomas Dykes published a book on the Highland Pony. In it he explored the variety of types which were being developed by introducing non-native blood but he also referred to a pony called Staffa, saying:

> Bred wild on Rhum. The true brown with mealy nose and belly so often seen in native ponies of all breeds.[22]

We can conclude from these statements that the breeds were emerging and differentiating at different rates but that the blueprint of the British Hill Pony had not yet been totally overwhelmed by introduced blood.

The 1900–01 Polo Pony Stud Book contains some very interesting pictures, relevant to this aspect. There are two photographs showing a group of North Wales Ponies belonging to Mr J. Marshall Dugdale. The

Plate 14 *Group of North Wales ponies belonging to Mr J. Marshall Dugdale (Reproduced from the Polo Pony Stud Book 1900–1901)*

Plate 15 *An "unimproved" Welsh Mountain pony (reproduced from* Points of the Horse *1904)*

group is a mixture of animals showing obvious signs of cross-breeding but a number of individuals still show the British Hill Pony characteristics. The illustration of a Welsh Mountain Pony from *Points of the Horse* published by Captain Hayes in 1904 shows a pony with many signs of the British Hill Pony blueprint, a far cry from the Welsh Ponies of today.

A similar type was also still to be seen on other Hebridean islands as well as on Rhum. A photograph from Thomas Dykes' book, again reprinted here, was entitled "Barra Stallion" and Dykes described it:

A pure-bred Barra stallion, 3-year-old and 12 hands in height, shows all the characteristics of the unmixed pony breeds and is specially interesting in view of future well-arranged combinations. He is a dark brown with black points (no white), has the best of feet and well-turned joints.

Plate 16 *Barra Stallion (reproduced from* The Multiple Origin of Horses and Ponies *1904)*

The same photograph had appeared in J. Cossar Ewart's "The Multiple Origin of Horses and Ponies" in 1904 and he had described the animal as:

a member of the all but extinct old Hebridean race of ponies.[23]

In 1903, in "Thoroughbreds and other Ponies", Sir Walter Gilbey quoted Munro MacKenzie as saying:

After long study and observation I have come to the conclusion that the original Highland Pony was a small animal from 12.2hh to 13.2hh, such as is now seen on the island of Barra.[24]

Lord Arthur Cecil also tells us from the item he wrote for Captain Hayes' book *Points of the Horse* in 1904 that the New Forest Pony had shown the characteristics of the original British pony type until the early eighteen hundreds: he explains that visiting the New Forest in 1890, he found that:

As far as I could ascertain few if any stallions of the old true breed had been kept.[25]

He goes on to say that as far as he could determine, the original breed had shown:

a wonderfully sharp outlook, clean head and bright eyes and also, singularly enough, the tanned muzzle and flanks.

These intriguing references to the native breeds and the pony "wild-type" come from real people who were intimately involved with pony breeding or the traditional way of life. They do not offer us theories or ideas but simply record their own observations and are thus of great value. Their information allows us to conclude that the British Hill Pony type has only faded comparatively recently from some of the breeds. Also we realise that at the beginning of this century, the distinction between the so-called improved ponies and the "old true breed" was readily recognised.

The Faroe Link

Returning to the Barra stallion illustrated in Cossar Ewart's pioneering article, we can start to unravel another fascinating thread in the story. Cossar Ewart described the stallion as closely resembling the dark brown Faroe Pony. The Faroe Islands are about half way between Shetland and Iceland and are officially part of Denmark. The islands are home to a small nation of

Photo. by]   [C. Reid.

Plate 17 *9 month-old Faroe colt (reproduced from* The Multiple Origin of Horses and Ponies *1904)*

just 44,000 people and most of the islands are used for the grazing of animals, mainly sheep. Like Iceland, the Faroe Islands were settled in the ninth century by Celtic emigrants from Scotland and their animals, including ponies. Norsemen also colonised these places around that time but it is uncertain whether they took their ponies to the Faroe Islands.

It is interesting to explore just why the people left Scotland at this time. James Speed, whose research into British pony ancestry we have referred to already and will return to again, wrote an article entitled "The Iceland Connection" and in it explained:

> In the year 850 AD, the MacAlpine dynasty was established in Scotland and the Columban church was given precedence over the older Celtic church. An edict, that the eating of wild horses was forbidden, was a great blow to the pastoral economy of North Scotland, which depended greatly on its wild-living pony herds, and in consequence there was an exodus with their animals; dogs, sheep, ponies and cattle . . . they sailed north and colonised Iceland. The record of this is in the Sagas preserved in Copenhagen Museum. So began the Icelandic Pony.[26]

James Speed believed that these Celtic outcasts colonised the Faroe Islands on their way to Iceland. Scandinavian settlers were also making these isolated places their new home and perhaps they too were responding to the attitudes and laws of the Christian movement. Gunnar Bjarnason has studied the Icelandic Horse since the 1950s. He lectured in Bergen, Norway in 1958 on the horse in the Sagas:

> Scandinavians, at least in Iceland, had the greatest difficulty in submitting to the Christian attitude to the holiness of horses, to the ban on eating horse-flesh . . . As related in the Sagas the adoption of Christianity in Iceland was carried out in a remarkable and peaceful manner. The Saga "Islendingabok" gives this account – "Then it was stipulated in law that all men should be Christians and be baptised but as regard to the eating of horse-flesh the old laws should be in effect". From reading the Sagas and the laws we almost get the idea that the fight for Christianity here in the north is in a way a fight about the horse, against its worship and against eating horse-flesh.[27]

The Scandinavians certainly took horse stock to Iceland and the Icelandic Horse is probably a blend of Norwegian and British Hill Pony. It is interesting to note this is a similar ancestry to that theorised for the Shetland Pony and in many ways, apart from the size of modern Shetlands, the two breeds seem very similar. However, Norwegian stock may not have been taken on to the Faroe Islands at this early time. Trondur Leivsson is vice-chairman of the Breeders of Faroe Ponies and he writes:

> When the founders of this society began their work back in the sixties, they were able to track the ancestors of a handful of ponies back through most of this century. By this, they knew that their breeding stock have had little or no intermix with imported ponies from Iceland and Norway, a practice which began around the beginning of this century.
>
> In the seventies we got in contact with Dr Kaj Sandberg, of the Agricultural University of Sweden, who is a world-wide acknowledged scientist in equine gene-mapping. He offered to test all our ponies at that time and this has continued since. Dr Sandberg's preliminary conclusion was, that the Faroe Ponies did not particularly resemble any of the Scandinavian or the Icelandic breeds.[28]

The Faroese society also contacted the Danish Society of Horse Breeders and Mr Henning Rasmussen made a study of about 20 of the 30 Faroe Ponies which now exist (they came even closer to extinction some decades ago). Mr Rasmussen concluded that the Faroese Ponies more strongly resembled certain British Ponies than any of the Nordic breeds. Just which ponies we will come to shortly. This tends to confirm the idea that the Scots founded the population of ponies on the Faroes and that these surviving 30 ponies have a high proportion of the British Hill Pony in their breeding. Work continues to further clarify the relationships.

The Final Decline

We can find echoes of the British Hill Pony in many places at varying times and surprisingly recently. Whilst the idea of a common foundation for the British breeds has long been accepted, the original native pony has often been portrayed as merely a shadowy form without substance or definition. Yet the evidence is there for the sort of pony we have deduced the British Hill Pony to be. It seems probable that with further blood-typing studies, the relationships between different breeds will emerge more clearly.

Back in the early 1900s, there were lingering traces of this common ancestral type in individuals, as we have seen, but most of the native breeds were well along the path of developing their now distinctive features. By 1920, the process of breed differentiation was virtually complete for the concept of "improvement" had found eager support. In that year, the Ministry of Agriculture, Fisheries and Food, in a study of ponies, commented that although there were common characteristics found with the breeds, they were distinct, differing considerably in size and appearance.

In some cases, the drive to produce an "improved" pony was catastrophic to localised pony populations. In "An Aspect of the Evolution of British Horses", James Speed and Mary Etherington wrote:

Whole races of hill and moorland ponies have been disposed of in Britain by the simple process of turning Arab or Hackney stallions into the herds to replace the native stallions. The Manx, the Cushendal, the Tiree, the Long Mynd, the famous Galloways, the Goonhillys and many others have been exterminated by this means, because the offspring of such crossings were so valuable that they were quickly sold out but further crossings produced animals which were no longer able to fend for themselves as native Northern grazing horses.[29]

In other cases, new breeds were produced which retained enough of their natural ancestry to cope with a continuing free existence, given some assistance from Man. This creation of the Mountain and Moorland breeds was not in itself undesirable; many of the resulting animals have proved to be marvellous additions to the range of horses and ponies used by Man. The problem was that in the enthusiasm for change and so-called improvement, no thought was given to conserving the precious raw material, the British Hill Pony prototype. In creating their works of art, the breeders used up their essential basic ingredient and, without fuss, the British Hill Pony faded quietly away – but not completely.

The Last Survivors

It has surely not escaped the reader's notice that throughout this assessment of the native pony breeds, one has been conspicuously ignored thus far, and that is the Exmoor Pony. Immediately we look at the Exmoor, we find that it represents a unique exception within the story of the breeds and is perhaps not a breed at all. Whilst we have found traces of the British Hill Pony in other localities, on Exmoor alone we are faced even today with a population in which every individual fits our concept of the original wild-type. The ancestral form may have disappeared in the other breeds but it appears to be alive and well, living in relative obscurity in the West Country. So now we must take a very close look at the Exmoor and determine whether this is truly the British Hill Pony which, remarkably, has survived.

The first striking point about Exmoor Ponies is that, apart from subtle variations, they are all identical. While variation is the norm within many of the native breeds, Exmoors conform to a fixed pattern which makes them immediately recognisable. Become familiar with one Exmoor Pony and you know them all. Exmoors have just a single coat colour, brown with black points, although various shadings are seen ranging from "bay" which is a rich, sandy brown through to very dark brown. The Exmoor Pony Society recognises bay, brown and dun as the variants; Exmoor dun seems to be a smokey brown. The mane and tail can range through the various shades of brown to black.

The most notable feature of an Exmoor is its distinctive facial marking. It has a mealy muzzle and the same buff colour rings the eyes and colours the under-belly

Plate 18 *All Exmoor ponies are essentially identical (the Acland/Anchor herd on its way to Old Ashway Farm)*

and the inside of the flanks. The facial markings are very striking, with the contrast of mealy and brown colouring. Although individuals very occasionally appear where the markings are less distinct, Exmoors normally conform to this pattern which of course matches the British Hill Pony blueprint we deduced from the markings of Przewalski's Horse and from cave paintings. The mealy markings are to an Exmoor what the white stripes are to a badger, an inherent part of its identity. A single coat colour with various shadings and the light muzzle and eye-ring are also seen in Przewalski's Horses. So the markings themselves and the uniformity speak of natural and primitive origin.

The uniformity seen with colouring is also a feature of their general build. The height range for Exmoor Ponies is naturally between 11.0 hands and 13.2 hands although the majority are 12.0 hands; the Exmoor Pony Society has height maxima of 12.2 for mares and 12.3 for males

Plate 19 *The facial markings of an Exmoor pony are most distinctive*

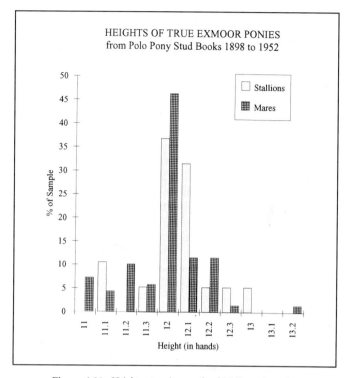

Figure 4.01 *Height range in sample of 88 Exmoor ponies*

but as Figure 4.01 illustrates, the tail end of the height distribution exceeds these. The graph is based upon a sample of 88 Exmoor Ponies registered (with heights recorded at four years old) in the Polo Pony Stud Book between 1898 and 1952 (and specified as pure-bred). With such definite rules within the Society, owners are somewhat reluctant to admit they have ponies which exceed the set maxima, but the 1976 census of registered Exmoor Ponies included a few technically "over-height" ponies and confirmed the range as being 11.0 to 13.2 hands.

Ponies below 12 hands are more readily accepted by the breeders of Exmoors but generally it has been assumed that ponies above 12.3 might well have some non-Exmoor blood. Certainly the majority of the ponies are around 12 hands but we must not dismiss the few larger ponies too hastily, for as these results suggest, they may be legitimate Exmoors. Such a distribution of size is the normal pattern for any natural population, with the majority falling within a small range and small numbers at both extremes.

Size is very much a matter of the length of the leg bones; these survive better than many other parts of the skeleton and have therefore been well-represented in finds of horse bones from prehistoric sites. Thus we can compare ancient pony anatomy with that of today's

Plate 20 *Comparison of metatarsals (shannon bones) L-R A) Arab B) Roman cross-bred F)Shetland-type G) Iron-Age Celtic H)Mantel collection 102, 000 B.P. I) Alaskan fossil pony J) modern Exmoor mare*

Plate 21 *Comparison of metatarsals (shannon bones L-R A) Larger Mendip fossil pony B) smaller Mendip fossil pony C) modern Exmoor pony mare D) smaller type of fossil pony from Dordogne, 32, 000B.P.*

Plate 22 *Comparison of metacarpals (cannon bones) L-R from A) Roman site B) Exmoor pony mare 1947 C) Brigantes site (Roman era) D) Mantell collection circa 102,000 B.P. E) Alaskan pleistocene river gravels F) larger type from Mendips*

Plate 23 *Comparison of modern Exmoor pony (top) and Alaskan fossil pony metacarpals (cannon bones)*

Plate 24 *Comparison of humerus bones (upper fore-leg) between modern Exmoor pony (right) and Alaskan fossil pony*

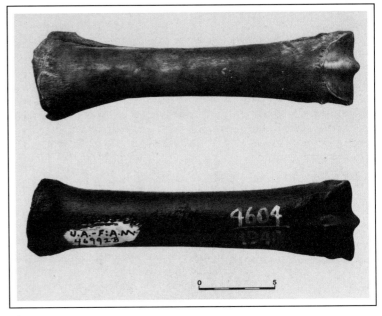

Plate 23

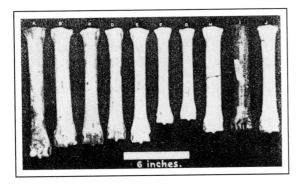

Plate 20

Plate 21

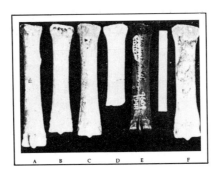

Plate 22

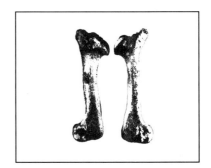

Plate 24

animals and if we look at the Exmoor Pony leg bones alongside those of British Hill Pony, again there are remarkable parallels as the photographs of bone collections reproduced from the "Speed Papers" show. The results of such comparative anatomical studies strongly indicate that the British Hill Pony skeletal characteristics survive in the Exmoor Pony.

This match is striking enough but the comparison holds true even further back for if Exmoor leg bones are set beside bones dug out of the Alaskan river gravels, they are indistinguishable. James Speed M.R.C.V.S. working at the Royal Dick Veterinary College in the 1950s discovered this remarkable likeness when Mary Etherington brought Exmoor Pony bones to Edinburgh for him to study. We will hear more of them later.

So we have striking skeletal uniformity in the leg formation and hence the size, between today's Exmoor and the ponies of very distant yesterdays both in Britain and far beyond. The size of these ancient animals was the product of evolution matching the ponies to what their environment could support. The fact that the Exmoor Pony is still so anatomically similar strongly supports the idea that Nature alone has shaped its evolution, for the effects of artificial cross-breeding usually stamp themselves clearly in equine bone structure.

Exmoor Ponies are very stocky with deep chests and large girths. Their build makes them enormously strong despite their relatively small size. F. J. Snell, writing his "Book of Exmoor" in 1903 records that there was a local Exmoor saying:

A long horse, with a short back; or a tall horse with short legs [30]

meaning that the body of an Exmoor is thick and robust. There is of course a range of "stockiness" just as there is with height. A famous horseman's saying is "No foot, no horse" and the feet of Exmoor Ponies are extremely strong and compact; they are blue-black in colour.

Whilst Man is well able to capitalise on the strength of Exmoor Ponies, as Chapter 10 will explore, all the features which these animals display reflect the work of Nature in adapting the ponies for survival rather than Man's handiwork. We will consider these adaptive characteristics in detail when we look at surviving, later in the book. For now it is worth re-examining the Exmoor to gain an overall impression of how its appearance reflects its needs.

Firstly, the colouring and markings; as we deduced when looking at the British Hill Pony idea, the markings around the eye and on the muzzle seen with many grazing animals probably evolved as a means of camouflage. The fact that these markings remain fixed characteristics of the Exmoor Pony strongly suggests that Man has not interfered with their breeding as they retain this primitive natural adaptation. The eye marking is often referred to in the Exmoor as a "toad-eye" but it is the structure of the eye rather than its colouring that gives rise to this term. The flesh immediately around the eye forms a raised rim above and below it which prevents water flowing into the eye by channelling it around the outside of the rim.

Plate 25 *Clayford Bracken Sweetie (8/33) showing the "toad eye", the raised rim of protective flesh highlighted by its mealy colouring*

Plate 26 *The hairs at the root of the tail are short and form a snow/rain chute, channelling water off the body*

As we will see in assessing survival abilities later, so many of the Exmoor's features are adapted to coping with the cold and perhaps more important, the wet conditions. The coat structure and the arrangement of long body hair are naturally designed to protect the animal. The coat is superbly efficient in expelling water and the openings to the body are kept small and well-insulated; this is why the Exmoor has small ears and a low-set tail which hangs close to the body. Exmoor Ponies have two phases of coat growth which provide them with a suitable coat to withstand the winter and a thinner summer coat. The long head, deep chest, tail

structure, beard, strong legs and small feet each have a function in terms of surviving the elements or escaping predators.

The teeth of an Exmoor Pony are particularly adapted to a coarse diet. The incisors (the front, biting teeth) emerge from the gums along a curved path so that they meet vertically. This formation means that the ponies bite food off cleanly with an efficient cutting action which does not tear and thus damage their food plants. Exmoors seem to retain this dental feature right into old age unlike many horses where the incisors angle forwards as the animal becomes elderly. Retaining an

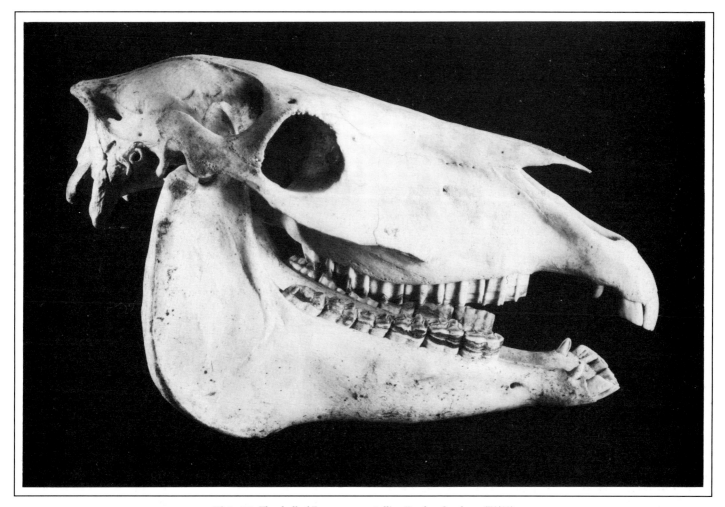

Plate 27 *The skull of Exmoor pony stallion Bracken Sundown (78/41)*

efficient bite is crucial to a pony surviving unaided and probably explains why the Exmoor has a long life-span. Exmoors often reach their mid-thirties and the record seems to be held by a pony that died in 1990 aged 42.

The molar teeth are very large and well-designed for their function. They are set into the jaw so that if you project the axis of each molar upwards, they meet at a single point; this design creates a strong chewing pressure which is required to deal with the tough, moorland plants. Just as the leg bone structure matches that of the British Hill Pony and its ancestors, this arrangement of the teeth seen in the Exmoor is the same

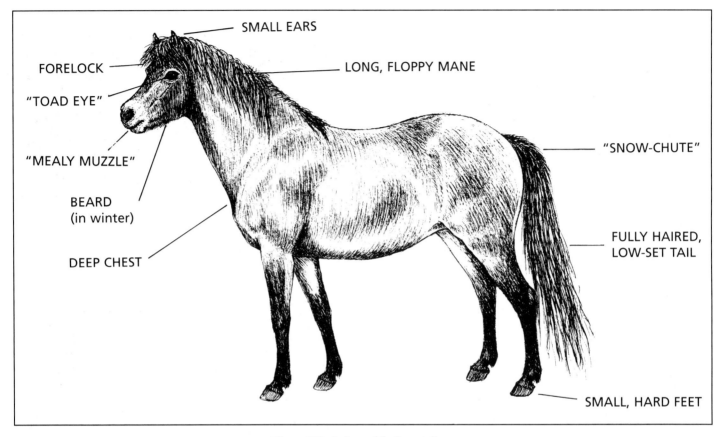

SMALL EARS

FORELOCK

LONG, FLOPPY MANE

"TOAD EYE"

"MEALY MUZZLE"

BEARD
(in winter)

DEEP CHEST

"SNOW-CHUTE"

FULLY HAIRED,
LOW-SET TAIL

SMALL, HARD FEET

Figure 4.02 *Features of the Exmoor Pony*

as described for one of the four basic types of ancestral equid which Hermann Ebhardt identified in his studies.

A standard description of the features of an Exmoor Pony such as illustrated in Figure 4.02 gives just the basics of identification. Once we delve further into the characteristics, we find that each has its special role to play in aiding the pony to survive, whether it be in obtaining food, avoiding being eaten itself or in tolerating and thriving amidst harsh weather. There is absolutely nothing which even hints at the hand of Man selecting artificially. The Exmoor Ponies therefore seem

to display a natural identity like fully wild animals; there is good cause then to consider them a race of ponies, not a breed which, by definition, is the end result of an artificial breeding programme.

The uniformity of Exmoors is a testament to a natural genetic make-up. Their foals are all born the image of their parents as with wild animals. This indicates that they have very little genetic variation between individuals as well as outwardly constant appearance. Exmoor Ponies seem to have recessive genes as the wild-type appearance usually gives way to the more

Plate 28 *Exmoor foals have their mealy markings from birth (Clayford Bracken Sweetie 8/33 and her 1991 colt)*

Plate 29 *Adult Exmoors with 6 month old foals during the gathering on Withypool Common, showing the uniformity of appearance common to all Exmoors*

dominant genes of other horses and ponies when they are crossed. Horses and ponies with cross-bred ancestry not only show variation between individuals but their variable genes make the appearance of their offspring a genetic lottery.

So this simple fact of every Exmoor being essentially the same as every other Exmoor is highly significant. We can justifiably view the Exmoor as something unique and not simply another breed.

Amidst all this emphasis on uniformity, we must not forget that even within a wild population of essentially identical animals, there is a degree of individual variation. Were it not so, research zoologists would never be able to distinguish sometimes hundreds of animals as individuals as with some of the famous projects on lions or chimpanzees. Exmoor Ponies as we would expect have subtle differences and given enough time to sit and study the herds, recognition of individuals becomes possible. Shading of coat, build, sometimes even personality and behaviour allow characters to become familiar. Whether the full range of natural variation in the British Hill Pony type has survived within the Exmoor Pony is an intriguing question that warrants some exploration.

The White Dimension

An Exmoor Pony should have no white markings, yet in researching the history of the ponies an unexpected question arises – was there once a grey/white strain within the natural race? Here we are thinking of a totally natural occurrence where a grey/white individual appears not as a result of introduced blood but as a genetic rarity.

As we will see in the next two chapters, the original wild population of ponies on Exmoor lived on what became designated as a Royal Forest, where once they probably numbered a thousand or more. When this homeland was sold, the numbers which had declined somewhat over the centuries were drastically reduced and the ponies were saved within small free-living herds elsewhere on Exmoor. The most famous of these herds was that belonging to the Acland family and there are records that within that herd there were occasional "greys". However, the Aclands sometimes put Exmoor mares to non-Exmoor stallions in-ground; from experience they knew the progeny would not survive living free and sold such crossed animals into domesticity. These Acland greys are described by different observers as dapple-grey or even very dark grey, so it seems likely these were indeed cross-bred animals. So we probably should not infer that these references to grey have anything to do with the natural breeding of the free-living pure-bred ponies.

In registering ponies in the early editions of the Polo Pony Stud Book, the Aclands were careful to distinguish where ponies were pure-bred Exmoors; this distinction was evidently recognised by them as important. There are a few fascinating registrations, for instance, the dam of one registered pony is given as grey and then the registration has the note:

dam, grand-dam and great-grand-dam pure Exmoor.

Are we to conclude then that grey was a legitimate if rare variety? Evelyn March-Phillips wrote about the Acland herd in 1896 and having explained that no ponies of mixed descent were retained in the free-living herd, says:

The colour is also imperative: the most usual is a brown-mouse colour, or brown inclining to bay, more rarely black or grey.[31]

The most stimulating hint of a natural grey/white individual comes from an early photograph published in *Farm Livestock of Great Britain* by Robert Wallace in 1907 (it is not known if the picture appeared in the first edition in 1885). The picture, reproduced here is entitled

Plate 30 *"Exmoor ponies brought down from the mountains" (reproduction of plate from* Farm Livestock of Great Britain *1907)*

"Exmoor Ponies brought down from the mountain" and there, within one of the Exmoor herds, is a grey/white individual. Yet this looks to be in all respects other than coat colour very like its fellow brown and mealy ponies. It is the same height, with the same build and, interestingly, has dark colouring on the legs and a recognisably light muzzle colour.

The obvious temptation is to dismiss this as a crossbreed but should we be so hasty in view of Evelyn March-Phillips' observations? Is this confirmation that occasionally a grey/white genetic variant occurred as the one or two Acland registrations suggest? The simple answer is we just do not know and probably never will; there is insufficient material on which to base a judgement but it remains an enticing side-track from the main story. It is an attractive hypothesis that such an unusual pony appeared from time to time given the traditional reverence for white animals and legends of their use in pagan worship. Would that not have arisen from the surprise and wonder when into a herd of dark coloured animals was occasionally born a foal which grew up to be such a dazzling exception?

Enough of such possibilities. We leave this grey/white Exmoor as just that, a possibility. If such individuals did ever exist naturally, we seem to have lost them from today's Exmoor population. Whether selected out deliberately or the genes lost when the population has at times been alarmingly reduced in numbers who can say? For now, let us return to the normal British Hill Pony brown and mealy wild-type and explore if there is any further evidence supporting or refuting the idea that it survives in the Exmoor Pony.

Bones and Blood

In examining the Exmoor Pony so far, we have found an animal which shows features which are both natural adaptations and also highly primitive characteristics which suggest a close relationship to the first British Ponies. The bone comparisons seem to provide striking evidence to support the concept that the Exmoor and British Hill Pony are one and the same animal yet the theories expounded by James Speed and Mary

Etherington are not well known and certainly not universally accepted. It is interesting to explore why this should be so and we must start by setting the scene regarding the Edinburgh research.

As we saw previously, James Speed was researching the development of ponies in Britain and by means of comparing bone structures was beginning to put together the picture of the original type of pony (which we have called here the British Hill Pony). He had identified the close match with its ancestors in Alaska by comparing British bones with those excavated from Alaskan river gravels by Otto Geist. Mary Etherington, a breeder of Exmoor Ponies and an Exmoor resident brought Exmoor Pony bones to Edinburgh and when they compared them to the British and Alaskan material, they found the amazing consistency.

For these Edinburgh researchers the match spanning so many thousands of years was an amazing discovery but the zoological establishment in Britain apparently failed to register any reaction. Perhaps being a veterinary anatomist and publishing in veterinary journals explains why the Speed work was overlooked by zoologists. It may also have been that there were even fewer people interested in pony history then than the few who work in that field today. Whatever the case,

Plate 31 *Mary Etherington with one of her Exmoor ponies, prior to moving to Scotland*

the Speed work did not deserve to be condemned to obscurity. Hermann Ebhardt co-operated with the Speeds in their work and between them they undertook the measurement and x-ray of thousands of bones. Dusty boxes simply labelled horse bones, long forgotten in museum store rooms, were at last opened and investigated as the Speeds toured Britain seeking ever more material for their research.

As they progressed with their study, James Speed and Mary, now Mrs. Speed, became more and more convinced that the Exmoor Pony represented a primitive survivor of the ancestral British pony and was not Man's handiwork. They had carried out so much investigative work but the papers they published only conveyed a small sample of their results, mainly in the form of photographic comparisons. They expounded their theories at length but included little of the hard data they had accumulated. The scientific world has to demand that scientists publish their results so that others can check and re-examine them before theories gain credibility. So today we have the limited amount of data which has already been described, matching the leg bones, but the majority of information amassed by the Speeds has been lost. Towards the end of her life Mary Speed destroyed all their original research documents, apparently weighed down by disappointment that their work had not made a significant impact.

Even though the Speed papers were republished in 1977 under the title *The Exmoor Pony – its origins and characteristics* the work remained little known for again it was not published within the zoological community but through the Rare Breeds Survival Trust. So today if the scientists are to confidently establish a relationship between the Exmoor and its ancient ancestors it will take more than just the few Speed articles; essentially, their work will have to be repeated. The museum store-rooms will have to be revisited and a standard set of measurements taken from the bones of various ages.

So, the bone comparisons we have so far from the Speed work are remarkable and strongly suggest the theory that the Exmoor represents a surviving population of British Hill Pony but it is not sufficient to present this as irrefutable fact. We also need to look at the question in as many different ways as possible and bones are not the only material which may hold the key to horse evolution. Blood and tissue are proving just as rich a source of information to the scientist although the techniques have mainly emerged due to economic factors.

The Thoroughbred Racehorse is a modern masterpiece of human horse-breeding skills and such animals can command huge prices. Where large amounts of money are paid for a single animal, it is vital to have reliable means of identification and confirmation of pedigree. To this end, various techniques have been developed which can assist in determining relationships and even, in the case of genetic fingerprinting, uniquely identify an individual. Before genetic fingerprinting, the technique of blood-typing was developed. This involved identifying the proteins in a blood-sample. Research scientists found this to be a useful method of studying relationships because the closer animals were related, the more alike their pattern of proteins were. In Britain this work was undertaken at the Animal Health Trust in Newmarket by Mr Mike Scott M.R.C.V.S.

Mike Scott was interested to test the blood of various horse and pony breeds to compare the results and as part of this study samples from eleven Exmoor Ponies were analysed in 1976. The results are very interesting as Mike Scott's report conveys:

> It must be emphasised that the eleven animals tested were not a representative sample from the Exmoor breed. The parentage of these animals is made up of just five stallions and six mares so there is bound to be a bias in the results. However, this does not deter from the fact that there are evidently some very unusual blood types in the breed. It is particularly interesting that the overall impression is one of a "primitive" breed, in that the blood types are those associated with the opposite end of the scale from breeds such as Thoroughbreds and Arabs.[32]

Perhaps most interesting was the Exmoors' form of proteins forming the Prealbumin system:

This system has proved difficult to work with because we have encountered a type that we have not seen before.

How frustrating it is for us that the necessary study to obtain fully representative results has still not been carried out. Other Exmoor Ponies have been blood-typed but elsewhere; thirty-eight of the ponies belonging to the Royal Dick Veterinary College in Edinburgh were sampled and the blood sent to the University of California in Davis in 1980 but the results require interpretation within some form of comparative study and at the time of writing such an interpretation has not yet been obtained. However, there are hints that this line of investigation could be most thought-provoking. Dr Oliver Ryder who studies the Przewalski Horse at San Diego Zoo has also had blood-typing carried out at Davis and in a letter to me wrote:

Of particular interest to you may be the finding of a unique form of prealbumin in Przewalski, not found in domestic horses. It will be most interesting to compare the data from Exmoors and Przewalskis! [33]

We have then in blood-typing and in genetic fingerprinting (which is carried out using tissue samples such as skin or even just a hair follicle) other means of studying equine relationships and ancestry. The results so far with regards to the Exmoor Pony support the view that it is a primitive animal and unlike deliberately bred horses. However, just as with the bone studies, so much more work needs to be done. If we are to understand how our different types of horse and pony are related and the ancestral sequence, then large numbers of individuals of all breeds need to be included in comparative blood-typing/genetic fingerprinting studies. We need the researchers working in different countries to jointly interpret their combined results.

Genetic studies do seem to hold most prospect of determining once and for all the significance of the Exmoor Pony. We saw earlier how first impressions regarding Faroese Ponies were that they were not closely related to Icelandic or Scandinavian breeds and hopefully future investigations will compare them to the various British Ponies. This should reveal whether the theory that the British Hill Pony was taken to the Faroe Islands is confirmed or otherwise.

It would be so satisfying if the writing of a book like this could wait until these studies are completed so that the ideas about the Exmoor being the surviving British Hill Pony could be more confidently stated or indeed dismissed should it prove otherwise. However, such academic studies take so long and often raise new questions to be answered; the telling of the Exmoor story cannot await such developments but the obvious message is that it will be a continuing story.

Fanciful Ideas

Having committed ourselves to considering all theories, we must pause to evaluate some of the more imaginative ideas which have been expressed about Exmoor Ponies.

Some early writers suggested that Exmoors were brought to Britain by the Phoenicians when they visited Cornwall to trade for tin. No scientific evidence has been found to support such an origin and the idea is inconsistent with the evidence of equine development we have reviewed already. We can probably allow this theory a decent burial without being accused of a lack of objectivity!

Similarly, the subject of Spanish influence lingers in respect of many of the British types of pony. According to the proponents of the hypothesis, horses from the Spanish Armada swam ashore when the ships were wrecked and bred with the British Ponies. Whilst a few individuals might have done so, it seems most unlikely that they could have had a major influence over such a wide geographical range. To subscribe to the Spanish theory would mean accepting the idea that the decks of each ship were packed with horses, that all took to the sea close to shore, survived and then ousted all the native pony sires from their herds. The truth is more probably that most of the unfortunate animals were dumped into the sea at an early stage, when defeat became obvious, and that most of them drowned.

Finally we come to "Katerfelto". Whenever the

ancestry of the Exmoor Pony is written about, eventually the name of Katerfelto will be mentioned. How can the Exmoor be an unmixed race of ancient pony? After all, didn't Katerfelto live and breed with the free-living herds on Exmoor and didn't he have Arab blood?

Katerfelto was the title of a novel written by G.J. Whyte-Melville in 1876. The novelist portrayed the horse as a very beautiful grey with characteristics suggesting Arab influence. On the very last page are the words which led to the whole mythology which grew up around the Katerfelto name:

> *But what became of the good grey horse? Tradition . . . affirms that he was never re-taken after his bridle broke, but passed on rejoicing to life-long freedom in the moor . . . Doubtless he joined those herds of wild horses and ponies, which to this day roam through the remotest coombes and moorland wastes of West Somerset and North Devon, free and unrestrained as the very breeze that sweeps across the scanty herbage on which they feed. Here it is presumed that he fulfilled his destiny.*[34]

In 1960 the Exmoor Review included an excellent article "Katerfelto – The Wonder Horse" by "H.W.K.". This was a detailed examination of the facts behind the myth and concluded that a horse called Katerfelto had indeed existed. So Whyte-Melville did not invent Katerfelto but immortalised a local equine celebrity which he must have heard about on his visits to Exmoor.

We can trace something of the history of the real Katerfelto but what sort of animal was he? H.W.K's article refers to a piece written by "Nimrod" in 1824 which stated that Katerfelto was the offspring of a beautiful black Galloway. Katerfelto was apparently dark bay in colour and around 14 hands. Why then did Whyte-Melville change fact to fiction in his story? Well, a grey (white) horse is far more the right image for an equine hero and when the novel was written in the late 1800s, the Arab was near worshipped within the context of horse-breeding in England.

"Nimrod"'s writings make no mention of Katerfelto having run wild on the open parts of Exmoor so the idea of his liberation after adventurous exploits probably is purely romantic fiction. However, the stallion was owned by the Warden of the Royal Forest of Exmoor, Sir Thomas Acland, and he may have allowed Katerfelto to run with his free-living Exmoor Ponies out on the Forest around 1790. His son wrote in 1886 that around that time his father owned about 500 Exmoor Ponies and that Katerfelto, if he existed, was supposed to have infused some Arab (or Spanish) blood into the population.

So now we come to the crux of the whole matter. It does seem likely that a non-Exmoor stallion, Katerfelto (exact breeding uncertain), was introduced to the free-living Exmoor Pony population. We must examine what significance this had. The scene awaiting Katerfelto was some 19,000 moorland acres upon which lived possibly 50 Exmoor Pony stallions with perhaps ten mares each (assuming ten mares per stallion, a reasonable zoological maximum). Even if numbers were managed, we can envisage perhaps 25 stallions but I think the higher number more likely.

Into this arena comes Katerfelto. Like all intruders he would have had to challenge an existing herd stallion for leadership of a harem or gradually poached a young mare or two from their bands. No Exmoor stallion I have encountered would have stepped aside and offered him a group of mares in respect for his wondrous form. No, they would have fought to keep their mares. Inter-male rivalry must have been highly active, so Katerfelto would have had a very hard time of it.

Did he succeed at all? The resident Exmoor stallions were perfectly adapted to their harsh environment and poor diet. Katerfelto was not of moorland stock and would have found life hard subsisting on the meagre rations offered by the moor. With his small head and possible Arab ancestry, his teeth would have been totally unsuitable for coping with the moorland plants. This "foreigner" would also have been severely tested by the winter weather without the specialised coat, the legacy provided for all true Exmoors. For these reasons, I suspect that the experiment of introducing Katerfelto into the wild was a dismal failure. I would be surprised if he was kept at large for more than one or two years.

If he did succeed in covering some Exmoor mares, it is

unlikely that this would have exceeded 20 per year and was more probably far, far less. The myth which has evolved about Katerfelto portrays him as the ultimate super-stud, mating with every mare he encountered and totally dominating the genetic future of the Exmoor race. No stallion mates with a group of mares and then moves on to challenge for another band and then another. He would quickly die from sheer exhaustion. In reality, he would have secured a small group of mares and concentrated upon safeguarding them.

So he might have sired some foals whilst with the free-living population. They however would have been recognisably cross-bred. In "Nimrod"'s words:

He stamped his likeness so decidedly on his progeny that they never can be mistaken by those who knew him.

Such crossed offspring, given that they were by this wonderful stallion, coveted by so many, would have found a ready market and would surely have been sold by Sir Thomas. Also, there was a recognition that cross-bred ponies could not thrive through Exmoor's harshest winters and this was the ethos behind the Aclands maintaining the true race. So again, Katerfelto's children would have been culled out of the herd.

A zoological perspective therefore sheds new light on the Katerfelto legend. Though his existence was fact, his significance has surely been over-dramatised. Gone is this wonder-horse that galloped across Exmoor displacing all the Exmoor stallions and infusing the whole race with Arab blood. When you really think about it, the story is biologically ludicrous. Far from being overwhelmed, the Exmoor Ponies' genetic integrity was probably unaffected. Yet Katerfelto left an enduring inheritance, a chaos of mis-information and misunderstanding which even to this day occasionally resurfaces to challenge ideas of the Exmoor's importance.

Expert Opinions

Returning to more scientific considerations, it is essential in exploring the status of the Exmoor Pony that we are careful to separate fact and opinion. We have looked at this pony and identified natural adaptations; we have seen the bone comparisons carried out so far and we have reviewed the observations regarding the Exmoors' blood proteins. Such information forms the basis of fact upon which we can assess Exmoor Ponies at present. However, as long as we remember that opinions are not proven data, we should not overlook the various statements which have been made about these ponies both supporting and refuting the idea that they are our ancestral pony race.

Firstly, we return to bones and to Cranborne Chase in Dorset. General Pitt Rivers, who has been called the "Father of scientific archaeology" excavated various sites around Cranborne Chase between 1880 and 1900. His credentials as a meticulous scientist are well established. Professor Glyn Daniel wrote of him:

In fifteen years Pitt Rivers transformed archaeology from the pleasant hobby of barrow-digging to an arduous scientific pursuit. There is no doubt that the modern techniques of excavation now practised in north-west Europe began in his work on Cranborne Chase.[35]

In the reports of his excavations, Pitt Rivers listed the animal bones he found in great detail and in many cases he recorded measurements of them. He carried out this analysis in order to compare the bones found in the excavations with those of contemporary domestic animals. Interestingly, in Volume II, he stated:

The Exmoor Pony is probably the nearest approach that can be found at the present time to the horse of the Romanised Britons in this district.[36]

So here again, and some sixty years before the Speeds carried out their work, we have bone comparisons yielding the opinion that the Exmoor Pony strongly resembles ancient ponies. This time the link is made to the ponies of the ancient Britons and brings an historical. perspective to add to the prehistoric comparisons.

Even before Pitt Rivers' work, the Exmoor Pony had

received recognition; the Encyclopaedia of Rural Sports published in 1840 stated:

> Strictly speaking it is doubtful whether we have any horses which as well deserve the term of thoroughbred as our Exmoor Pony.[37]

(the Oxford English Dictionary definition of "thorough-bred" being "pure-bred").

Earlier we referred to the opinion of the Danish Society of Horse Breeders that the Faroese Ponies most closely resemble certain British Ponies. Trondur Leivsson wrote:

> Mr Rasmussen made a description of our ponies, about twenty individuals, and his conclusions were quite evident, that the Faroese Pony does not resemble the Icelandic or Scandinavian ponies in particular. Another of Mr Rasmussen's comments was, that in his opinion, the Faroese Pony resembles closer to the Exmoor and Dartmoor Ponies in Britain, rather than to the Nordic breeds. We know for sure that in modern times the only import of ponies to the Faroes has been of domestic breeds from Norway and Iceland.

So here we have an opinion which lends support to the idea that the British Hill Pony may also have descendants upon the Faroe Islands. However, the Faroese Pony population does not show uniform appearance. Whilst some individuals are brown with a suggestion of lighter muzzle and a shape apparently like an Exmoor Pony, others show the colour variation and anatomy more like Icelandic Horses. This suggests there has been some Scandinavian/Icelandic influence in the past. Hopefully, future comparisons of blood will give us a clearer understanding of how closely British and Faroese Ponies are related.

One very convincing comment suggesting the Exmoor as the original native pony may be found in the pages of Points of the Horse by Captain Hayes, where he quotes Lord Arthur Cecil. We have already referred to parts of what he said but the quote in full is highly significant:

> In 1890 I went to the New Forest and found that for many years few if any stallions of the old true breed had been kept. As far as I could ascertain, the old type when it appeared, was singularly like the Exmoor, in the wonderfully sharp outlook, clean head and bright eyes and also, singularly enough, the tanned muzzle and flanks. I tried the experiment of bringing a few Exmoors into the Forest, and everyone of the old Commoners were unanimous (not knowing them to be Exmoors) in saying "Ah that was the old kind of pony which lived in the Forest."

Here we have observations from the ultimate experts in native ponies, the Commoners who owned them, and the words of these New Forest men identify the Exmoor Pony as the "old true breed".

As stated in the opening chapter, we have to take account of all data, theories and opinions if we are to be objective. As far as I am aware, there have been no discoveries which have undermined the theory of a close relationship between the Exmoor Pony and the British Hill Pony. Indeed in reviewing what has been written about equine origins and the history of British horses, it has proved singularly difficult to find statements which argue against the Speed/Ebhardt theories by offering alternative explanations. Anthony Dent wrote in The Pure-Bred Exmoor Pony in 1970:

> Some friends of the Exmoor Pony are in the habit of claiming that it is 'directly descended from the original wild horse of Britain'. What does directly descended mean? Either one is descended from some ancestor or one is not. There was not, in any case, any such thing as the original wild horse of Britain. In Europe in prehistoric times there were at least three varieties of wild horse; but it is highly unlikely that the Exmoor Pony – any more than any other British breed of horse – is descended exclusively from any of them.[38]

Yet being unlikely is no indication that a theory has been undermined. However, though there seems to be no scientific literature which explores the Speed/Ebhardt work and by reasoned argument highlights flaws in the conclusions, their ideas are still to be firmly established. There has been some progress, in that where the 1977 *Handbook of British Mammals* states that there is "no evidence" to support the idea that any British pony is the direct descendant of native wild horses, the 1991 edition has changed this to "little" evidence.

It seems likely that the lack of acceptance by the zoological community stems mainly from the fact that the information has never been adequately presented. As this book will demonstrate, the question of the significance of the Exmoor cannot be assessed without looking at information from many disciplines. It would seem though that as scientists take the trouble to look more closely at what has been discovered so far, the ideas are beginning to gain more credence.

However, neither those who support the theory or those who disbelieve it can escape the fact that far more research is needed to resolve the matter. At present then the British Hill Pony-Exmoor story is still in its infancy and we need many scientists from different disciplines to undertake detailed studies of both fossil and living animals of all types in Britain. The material is available yet so far the interest has not surfaced or studies have not progressed far enough to reach firm conclusions.

It would seem that some German zoologists have decided that there is sufficient basis for regarding the Exmoor as a possible second prototype horse (in addition to Przewalski's Horse) and valuing it accordingly. Both Exmoors and Przewalski Horses are exhibited at Sababurg Zoo. Perhaps this provides us with an important message. We have to look after the Exmoor Pony carefully even if at a later date new studies provide a different interpretation of its status. There would be little achievement in proving them to be the British wild horse only then to find that we are too late to conserve Exmoors in their natural state.

For us in our present search for understanding the natural history of the Exmoor Pony, we are left to make up our own minds as to what seems most probable. Perhaps we can assist this process by considering the implications of accepting the theory that the British Hill Pony survives in the Exmoor. If this is so, then it means that instead of altering the original pony population by introducing alien blood, as we have charted around the rest of Britain, on Exmoor alone Man conserved the native type. We have seen that the naturally adapted characteristics of the Exmoor Pony show no evidence of human selection, which implies that this pony population has not been through the processes of domestication and is genetically a wild-type. However, as opponents of the theory argue, this seems so unlikely. Throughout Britain, in some places which would appear just as remote as Exmoor, if not more so, Man was breeding the free-living ponies according to his design and obliterating the British Hill Pony

What was so special about the Exmoor locality? Could the people have taken such a different approach? Can it really be the case that the British Hill Pony escaped domesticity and submergence into a contrived product just on one small upland area and one which had no physical barriers to isolate it?

To answer this we must now travel to Exmoor and study its people as much as its ponies. We need to explore their history and find out what role the ponies played in the economy of the area. We have to discover whether historical records confirm or contradict the idea that on Exmoor, the British Hill Pony truly found an enduring sanctuary.

CHAPTER 5

THE PONIES OF THE
ROYAL FOREST OF EXMOOR

Early in the nineteenth century Thomas Carlyle wrote:

The history of the world is but the biography of great men.[39]

but the more we become involved in looking at history, the more we find that the experiences of ordinary people are just as important. In our journey through the recorded history of the Exmoor Ponies we will, it's true, meet monarchs and famous men but those who lived unexceptional lives and those whose names we do not know are just as important to our story.

The First Historical Records

We start in the summer of 1086, on a track leading down to the Manor of Brendon which lies on the northern edge of Exmoor. A group of six riders are making their way towards the hamlet and there is much activity ahead of them as their approach has been seen. The party is headed by a Commissioner in the service of William the Conqueror; we will call him Robert for like all the Domesday recorders, he failed to leave trace of his own identity. Robert and his scribe are accompanied by a priest and three guards. The priest has come with them to translate, for they cannot speak English. Robert

has been comforted by the presence of guards as they have passed through wild and lawless country inhabited by wolves and outlaws. Ahead of them is an uncertain welcome too for they are here to determine the level of taxation which will be levied on the manor and its tenants.

We don't know if Robert or someone like him actually visited the Exmoor manors or whether their owners were summoned to some centralised assessment. Wherever it took place, it must have been a difficult exercise as suggested by Anthony Dent and Daphne Machin-Goodall in *The Foals of Epona:*

The commissioners and their clerks met, in every township, the principal landlord or his bailiff, the parish priest and a deputation of the oldest tenants. Between them they stated the bounds of the township, the acreage of its ploughland, the rent it had been worth in Edward the Confessor's time and what rent the lord expected to get for it in 1086. Also what stock was running on the common. The commissioners and their clerks had no English. Neither, very often, had the landlord or his reeve, who spoke to the commissioners in French. The parish priest translated the evidence of the old tenants into Latin, in which language the clerks wrote down a complete economic picture of the township.[40]

However, if the Domesday recording was as popular as the Poll Tax introduction, it seems likely that the Norman Commissioners might well have had to seek out their information on site, particularly relating to manors distant from any town or city. So we will return to Brendon and our civil servants.

The Lord of Brendon Manor was a man called Radulf de Felgheres, a Norman who had been awarded Brandona, as it was called in those days, for his services to the King. The entry for it in the Domesday Book gives us a fascinating glimpse of this settlement:

This can be ploughed by eight ploughs. Of it Radulf has in demesne half a hide and two ploughs, and the villeins have half a hide and six ploughs. There Radulf has seven villeins and six bordars and five serfs, and one pack-horse and a hundred and four unbroken horses, and twenty-five head of cattle, and eight swine, and a hundred sheep and thirty goats, and thirty acres of wood, and two leagues of pasture, and it is worth by the year a hundred shillings, and it was worth thirty shillings when he received it.[41]

We cannot get side-tracked into interpreting all the details of life at Brandona in 1086 for our quarry is simply equine. Hope Bourne quoted the Brendon extract in her book *A Little History of Exmoor* and from it assembles a vivid picture of the manor and its agricultural life. Our interest lies in this, the first written reference to ponies on Exmoor.

It is worth digressing at this point to think a little about the words "horse" and "pony" because the modern-day differentiation between them is irrelevant throughout most of history and adds confusion to our story. MacDermot explained in his *History of the Forest of Exmoor* that the word pony was not used on Exmoor until probably the early 1800s. What we now call ponies were referred to as Exmoor Horses. He also tells that in the seventeenth century they were called "horse-beasts" or sometimes "widge-beasts". So we may

refer to Exmoor Horses or Exmoor Ponies and mean the same animal, the equid native to the area.

So what can we make of Radulf's one hundred and four unbroken horses? In *Foals of Epona* these are referred to as "104 unbroken mares" and the authors suggest this implies a total stock of about 400 animals. If, as Hope Bourne interprets, the manor had somewhere around 300 acres of land, such a large number of horses must have free-ranged over common grazings or up on the wild moorland above Brendon. The fact that they are specifically entered as "unbroken" suggests that they lived much as the ponies live today and that breaking individuals for riding animals might well have been an activity carried on at the manor. What is so frustrating is that the Domesday recorders were interested only in numbers for taxation assessment purposes; they were not interested in recording information for posterity and so included no details of what the animals looked like. We can say that in all probability these *equae indomitae* listed for Brendon were the free-living native ponies which had inhabited the wilds of Exmoor since Celtic if not prehistoric times, but probability is not proof!

Brendon Manor was not the only place where Robert's scribe itemised non-domestic horses although it was the highest count. The wording used at the manors of Cutcombe, Luccombe, Horner, Quarm and Lynton is different though, referring to *equi silvatici* with 39, 7, 5, 2 and 72 horses listed at these manors. There is agreement, between authors who have explored this, that although the word *silvatici* is derived from *silva* which relates to woodlands, this is not the meaning here (just as the "Forest" of Exmoor has nothing to do with trees but means a hunting ground). Thus we are not being told about woodland or forest horses. Instead, it seems that the words *silvatici* or *silvestres* were used to mean wild.

So, we know that these manors on the fringes of Exmoor had ownership of wild horses, sometimes in large numbers. Yet what of Exmoor itself? There were no roads or trading routes of any importance across the high parts of Exmoor and it must have been a wild and inhospitable place. Even centuries later when a man we

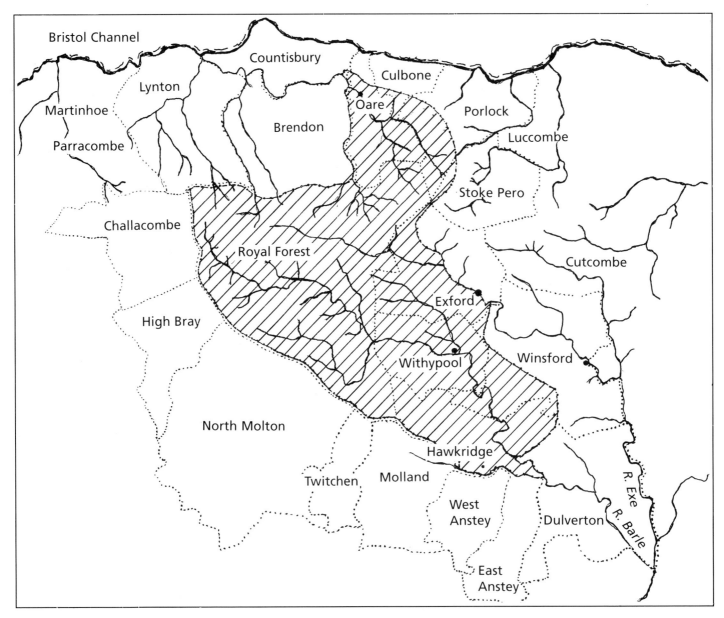

Figure 5.01 *Map of Exmoor Forest and surrounding manors/parishes (Domesday to Thirteenth Century)*

have heard of, Daniel Defoe, travelled around England and Wales, Exmoor was untamed and he described it in 1722 as:

a filthy, barren ground. It gives indeed, but a melancholy view, being a vast tract of barren and desolate lands.[42]

For the Norman commissioner and his party, venturing out onto the moors would have been a daunting prospect and perhaps they decided better of it and relied on information supplied by people who had experience of this wasteland. The Domesday Book makes very little mention of moorland places but we can read about three foresters who had land at Withypool. They were called Dodo, Almar and Godric and must have hated the Normans, for William the Conqueror gave their land to a Norman, Robert de Osburville. All we know is that they had half a hide of land (a hide is thought to have been around 120 acres) at "Widepolla". Figure 5.01 shows the extent of Exmoor Forest and the manors which surrounded it at that time.

There is an entry regarding Molland:

The king has a manor called Mollanda which Harold held on the day on which King Edward was alive and dead . . . . To the manor of Mollanda belongs the third penny of the hundreds of Normoltona and Badentona and Brantona, and the third animal of the pasture of the moors.[43]

MacDermot believed that "the moors" relates to the whole of the Exmoor hunting ground on which animals were grazed and rent was paid for pasture. Amongst these few comments about the main part of Exmoor, there is nothing about horses specifically. We know that sizeable numbers were owned by lords of nearby manors and perhaps grazed out on the Royal Forest, but we have no way of knowing whether there were others on the moor which belonged to the Crown. These would not have been recorded as the king would hardly wish to tax himself.

So facts are few from the eleventh century despite the Domesday record. There were horses on Exmoor which were described as unbroken or wild but we know nothing of their appearance or how they were managed. Yet how miraculous this Domesday exercise was; for all its deficiencies in our modern eyes, it provides even students of equine history with some information. Without it, our first records of the horses of Exmoor would be from less than five hundred years ago. So we have every reason to be grateful to the fiscal policy of William the Conqueror and to his civil servants who made this remarkable survey.

Very few of the Saxons who William had conquered twenty years earlier had any reason to be grateful to their imposed monarch. The Saxon lords had been turned off their manors which had been given as rewards for loyal service to the invading Normans. In addition, their new ruler proved to be almost eccentrically obsessed with hunting and this brought about the imposition of a very restricted way of life in the southern counties.

Historians have recorded that William the Conqueror *"loved the great deer as their father"*; he certainly loved to hunt them and this seems to have been the foundation of some of the most repressive policies ever felt by country people. It is probable that Saxon lords had already designated places such as the moors of Exmoor, Dartmoor and Bodmin Moor as hunting grounds over which they held rights. William took over these areas for his own hunting reserves but was not satisfied with these alone, perhaps because there were probably more deer in the true forests than out on the moorlands. Thus he also "afforested" most of Devon and Cornwall as well as his *Novae Forestae*, the New Forest; this term "afforestation" meant simply the designation of an area as Royal Forest, which meant a hunting ground.

Afforestation was accompanied by the introduction of incredibly harsh laws designed to protect the king's deer; William held the life of a deer to be much more important than the human rights of his subjects. Much has been written about the Forest Laws but it is the management of Exmoor Forest which interests us. It was all very well setting aside vast tracts of land as game reserves and imposing cruel laws but this required considerable administration and government. The head official, appointed by the king, was the Warden of Exmoor Forest. The first warden was Robert de Osburville who had taken over Withypool, Hawkridge and Exton manors. He paid a small rent to the Crown but then received all the income from renting out the moorland as grazing for the cattle, sheep and horses belonging to adjoining land-owners. His duties revolved around protecting the deer and ensuring they were always available to be hunted by the king. He was assisted by a Deputy Forester, Verderers to enforce the laws and Agisters to count the stock, a system which has survived to this day in the New Forest.

We will come back to the workings of the Forest later for most of what is known comes from the 1500s, 1600s and 1700s. MacDermot concluded though that it was little changed from when the area was first designated a royal chase. As we search through the pages of the history books, we find nothing relevant to our story other than changes of Warden until King John's reign. The repressive nature of Forest laws weighed heavy and eventually John was paid to dis-afforest Devon and Cornwall apart from his moorland hunting grounds, which of course included Exmoor. Later on, he was forced to do the same for parts of Somerset. Yet on Exmoor nothing changed, a theme which emerges time and again throughout its history.

Where are our moorland ponies through all this? They must have continued as ever to graze the open Exmoor country, their owners paying dues for these grazing rights but sadly no-one thought to write anything about the animals themselves. They were a source of income, not interest.

After John died there was much discontent registered about the extent of the area designated as Royal Forest and subject to its laws. Eventually Henry III established the boundaries by means of a "perambulation" but pressure to reduce the area continued. Further perambu-lations took place and eventually by the dawn of the fourteenth century Exmoor Forest had contracted to just the parish of Exmoor plus the parish of Oare; the latter was freed from Forest designation at some time later. The area which now remained as Exmoor Forest, less than twenty thousand acres, was of course the wildest part. The land which none had tamed remained the home of deer and ponies all year and was used for livestock grazing in its kinder months. If records were kept of its usage and income during these early centuries, none have survived.

Our written evidence of the Exmoor Horses prior to the sixteen hundreds remains just the Domesday entries. However, historians seem agreed that the arrangements documented in the seventeenth century for the running of the Forest were a continuation of the system which had been practised for the previous six hundred years. If only just one of those Wardens of Exmoor had written about his life we might have had some insight into these truly dark ages; yet writing for posterity would not emerge for many hundreds of years and we cannot even be sure these men were literate. Account books must have been kept but have never been found, so we are left without a real history of the people or their animals until much later.

Once we enter the seventeenth century there is a relative wealth of information but before we start to read again of the horses of Exmoor, we must visit yet another king of England who might have brought our story to an end prematurely.

Henry VIII and his Horse Laws

Henry the Eighth is certainly renowned for disposing of unwanted wives but his efforts to rid Britain of most of its pony stock are perhaps less well known. He passed an Act which restricted the export of horses and obliged land-owners to breed horses and increase the national equine resource. The Act also contained legis-lation regarding the size of stallions which showed a great prejudice against those of small stature:

Forasmuch as the breed of good and strong horses is a great help and defence to the realm and a great comoditie to the inhabitants thereof, which is now much decayed by reason that little stoned horses and Nags be suffered to pasture in forests etc. and to cover mares feeding there. Therefore for the encrease of stronger horses hereafter be it enacted that no commoner or commoners within any forest, chase, moore, marish, heth, common or wast grounde at any time after the 31st March 1543 shall have or put forth to pasture in any such ground etc. any stoned horse or horses being above the age of two yeare and not being of the altitude and height of 15 handfulls.

A number of counties were exempt from this part of the Act, including Dorset, Devon and Cornwall but Exmoor was, in theory, not safe from Henry's dictates. In another section of the Act there was an instruction to carry out gatherings on all the commons, chases, marshes and moors once a year and to destroy animals of small size. Fortunately here there was a loophole for no actual size was stated:

If there shall be found any mare filly fole or gelding that then shall be thought not to be able or like to be able to beare foles of reasonable stature, or not able or like to grow to be profitable labours, by the discretion of the drivers aforesaid then the same drivers shal cause the same unprofitable beastes every one of them to be killed.

We must be so thankful for this wording for, of course, once discretion comes into play and particularly when others have to determine "reasonable stature", such a law loses its bite. Those people carrying out the annual gatherings would have known well enough what size of animal their local heath or moor could support. Even where the more specific parts of the law were supposed to be enforced, we can imagine the reaction of the local people if they inhabited remote areas and had the independence of spirit which survives today. It would probably have been much the same as the attitude to possible E.E.C. regulations; if we don't agree with them we will carry on as we have always done and who will bother to come here to tell us differently?

There is a full description of these Tudor horse laws in *The Foals of Epona* and its authors explore just what motivated Henry VIII to enact such "heightist" laws. They suggest that the military use of horses at the time necessitated breeding large horses capable of carrying armoured soldiers but that perhaps the fact that his personal bulk made all but the strongest horses of little use to him had the greater influence.

So the small horses of Britain, those we now call

ponies, had a lucky escape. Their habitation of the wilder parts of the kingdom and being owned by men who had little time for laws which were to their disadvantage was the saving of the ponies. How significant the words we use can be, for our legal system continues to revolve around the debating of the meaning of "reasonable" and give a countryman powers of discretion and he will do as he thinks fit.

Exmoor then seems to have been unaffected by these events but earlier in the century Henry VII had brought one significant change to the area in the last year of his reign. He leased Exmoor Forest to its then warden Sir Edmund Carew in 1508; the emphasis moved from providing the Crown with deer to the grazing of stock on the moorland although some deer still had to be conserved.

There were many changes of ownership and warden during the 1500s and innumerable legal disputes regarding both deer and stock as well as the land itself. One such case is of interest to us from the year 1598 in the Court of Chancery – Thomas Webber, Deputy Forester and James Darche of Luxborough versus John Baker of Withypool and John Thomas of Bishop's Nympton. The point of contention seems to have been who exactly should receive the rent for animals grazed on Exmoor. F.J. Snell in *A Book of Exmoor* explains:

The point was raised, to whom – whether to Sir John Poyntz, Knight or to Peter Edgcombe, Esquire – the revenues should be paid by the country people who had or should put their "rother-beasts (horned cattle), horse beasts, sheep, swine etc" to depasture in the Forest of Exmoor.[44]

This was just one of the many legal wrangles between Poyntz and Edgcombe which dominated this period of Exmoor's history but it is one which specifically tells of our "horse-beasts". There is also reference amidst their quarrel to the local courts on Exmoor and this brings us again to the subject of how Exmoor Forest was administered and how the grazing of animals was managed. At last there is well documented evidence as we enter the sixteen hundreds having reached this point with just the merest glimpses of the ponies' earlier history.

The Free Suitors of Exmoor

It is five-thirty on a summer's morning in the early 1600s and we are at Wincombe Head near Withypool. There is a group of men, each standing beside his pony, quietly talking as other riders approach from the direction of Withypool and Hawkridge. Gradually, 52 men assemble having reported to the Deputy Forester who is in charge of the proceedings. These men are the Free Suitors of Exmoor and their duty today is to help with the round-up the horses on Exmoor Forest.

These are men of whom we know little as individuals; their lives were unremarkable and yet they figure as importantly in our history of the ponies as the kings we have also encountered. Let us choose just one of these mounted hill-farmers and we will call him John Hooper, a name which he will hand on to his descendants and which will be found on the list of Free Suitors in 1797. If we could meet with John and ask him about his life, he might tell it thus:

My farm is only small but with it comes the responsibility of being a Free Suitor. I hold the farm on condition that I work for the Warden of Exmoor Forest but in return I have some privileges. My duties are mainly to help drive the Forest to bring in the stock; we do this up to nine times a year. We go out once, nine days before midsummer for the annual drift or "prey" as we calls it for sheep. Then we go out two or three times rounding up cattle but not on set days. It's the same for the horse-beasts, no fixed dates but we drive for them more often, perhaps five times a year sometimes, three in summer and two in winter.

When we gather the horse-beasts or widge-beasts as we sometimes call them, we're usually back at the pound by mid-day; that's at Langacre Farm of course, where the Court is held you know. The owners have to come and claim their animals and pay their dues but often some aren't claimed. These animals stay in the field next to the Pound and if they haven't been claimed after a year and a day, they are forfeited to the Warden as estrays.

I'm one of 52 Free Suitors and we all come from either Withypool or Hawkridge parishes. We have to do other things apart from helping out with managing the stock on

Plate 32 *The Withypool pound site, beyond Landacre Bridge*

the Forest. We attend the Swainmote Courts where we deal with things like fining people whose animals have trespassed out on the Forest; one is held near the Pound at Langacre and the other in Hawkridge churchyard. We also help out with walking the Forest boundaries every seven years and of course we may be summoned to sit at an inquest if a corpse is found within the boundaries. We don't have to serve on any juries outside the Forest though.

We don't get paid for this work for the Warden but we do get rights on the Forest in return. Like all the Free Suitors, I can graze 140 sheep out on the moor during the day and there is talk that this may be increased to allow night grazing soon. I can also graze five horses or mares and their colts up to a year old, plus as many cattle as my farm will support in winter and some pigs. I can cut peat for fuel and heather and bracken for bedding in winter and can take some fish. Another good thing is that we don't have to pay any tolls for selling stock at the markets or fairs.

My father farmed before me and drove the Forest for the warden just as I do and his father did the same. My son will start riding the drifts soon once he's passed his eighteenth birthday and as long as one of us attends then we fulfil our suit. It's been this way for as long as anyone can remember.

Of course we are putting words into our contrived farmer's mouth; he would probably have spoken very differently in style of language and certainly with heavy Exmoor dialect but nonetheless would have provided us with this information. The facts presented by our John Hooper come from documents surviving from the sixteenth, seventeenth and eighteenth centuries; records of the Swainmote Courts 1541–59, depositions of witnesses in 1634–35 and again in 1678, the Parliamentary Surveys of 1651–52, the Forester's own record books 1718–1764 and the Forest of Exmoor Court papers from 1797. We owe so much to historians like Edward MacDermot and Roger Burton for their painstaking research and recording of such documents. Both provide a far more detailed picture than we can include here, as we must concentrate upon the ponies.

This system of the Free Suitors and their role in managing the animals on the Royal Forest probably has its origin much farther back in time. If we recall the wonderfully named trio at Widepolla in Saxon times, Dodo, Almar and Godric, they were described as Foresters and their work must have been similar to that recorded for the Free Suitors in terms of livestock control. Just picture the situation in Saxon times, when various manorial lords owned free-ranging stock which grazed up on the moors. Each animal must have had to be marked in some way to indicate ownership and the stock must have been gathered in at some time to remove the crop of young animals. We can picture our three Saxons and their fellow forest workers riding out across Exmoor for a drift just as in later centuries. The whole principle of the "wardenship" begun in the 1200s was the deriving of income from renting out the grazing and must have required similar management. In 1617, part of the evidence for a legal dispute tells us of Exmoor:

> It is a large ground, many thousand acres in extent and thirty miles round at least, time out of mind used for the pasture of great numbers of sheep, cattle and horse-beasts.

So the system of the Free Suitors described so well in later centuries was probably little changed from that which had operated on Exmoor for a very long time. Although it ended when Exmoor Forest was finally sold in the nineteenth century, the practices for managing free-ranging stock survive in the annual gatherings and brandings of the Exmoor Ponies which we will encounter in a later chapter.

The Suitors at Large

The Free Suitors were not the only people who grazed animals on the Forest for the land-owners and tenants of parishes (once manors) which surrounded the Forest had rights of common for which they paid fees. It was these Suitors at Large which provided the income for the Warden of Exmoor by grazing their animals on the Forest. The exact conditions of the Suitors at Large rights are not so well documented but MacDermot includes a deposition from one Thomas Smythe of North Molton in 1634 who said:

> The 52 Suitors and the tenants of the Lord of the Manor of North Molton may depasture their sheep, cattle and horses in their own right in the day time.[45]

Thomas Smythe also stated that they might depasture such sheep, cattle and horses in the Forest as they could run on their own tenements in the winter, but that the sheep and cattle were taken off at night. The Suitors at Large were not obliged to serve the Warden but did attend the Court.

Today we are bombarded with paper documents which convey all manner of useful and unwanted information but things were very different in those times. If fees had to be paid for grazing Exmoor, those fees had to be made known to the Suitors at Large. Thus the Forester had to send men to the nearby towns in early spring to proclaim the rates for pasturage that year. This probably meant the assigned man actually standing in the town square and calling out the rates for the practice came to be known as "crying the moor". It usually took place in South Molton, North Molton, Dunster, Barnstaple, Porlock and Combe Martin.

MacDermot lists the prices charged during the sixteenth and seventeenth centuries; for horse-beasts the cost was 4d. (four old pennies) a year up to 1628 but by 1652 had risen to two shillings. In 1654 it was up to five shillings but that must have proved unworkable for it reduced to four shillings the next year and remained at that price until the sale of Exmoor Forest in 1818.

The Exmoor Courts

The Swainmote Courts dealt with all the problems which arose with the system and there seem to have been plenty, usually concerned with non payment of fees and trespass of animals on the Forest and adjoining Commons. The title Swainmote apparently means "a meeting of free men" and Free Suitors and Suitors at Large had to attend; if they did not, they were fined. The information we have seen so far suggests that this arrangement was superbly efficient and the Warden of Exmoor had everything well under control. Perhaps for the most part the system did work well but there were certainly those who sought to exploit or avoid the rules.

In documents relating to a dispute between Slowley and Pearce in 1622 one witness suggested that the drifts were not always restricted to within the Forest boundaries:

> He hath often knowen that the cattle and horsebeasts of divers commoners of the commons adjoyninge unto the said Forest have bin sittinge quietly uppon the said commons late in the eveninge after sunnsett a myle from the said Forest and in the next morninge, very tymelie, the said cattle have bene taken in the praye or drifte of the said Forest and so driven to Wythepoole and there ympounded.

Only the Warden gained from such acquisitions and so presumably the Deputy Forester had so instructed the men riding the drift that day.

Another example of less scrupulous activity is given by Laurence Meynell in his book *Exmoor*:

> The forest pound at Withypool, which for centuries was the only one and which even when superseded by James Boevey's new-fangled affair up at Simonsbath still continued to function for a long time, was almost inevitably the occasion or scene of more than one dispute. As for

instance in 1658 when a Mr Harton from Porlock came, claimed and took away an impounded colt which was not in fact his at all, afterwards agreeing with the real owner (no doubt for a good consideration!) that they should both keep silent in the matter. A post-fact conspiracy which was blown sky-high when Mr Courtenay of Molland, who himself privately locked up Harton's real colt for straying on his land, announced the fact.[46]

MacDermot provides Mr. Harton's version of the incident:

> His version of the story of the wrongly claimed colt is that having missed for thirty-three weeks one of his colts, which must have strayed out of the Forest "into some remote place", after one of the drifts a neighbour told him it was at Withypool pound. He accordingly went there and found a mare colt like his own of the same colour and age, and with the same ear mark. Believing it to be his own, he claimed and took it away. Three days afterwards, one Vallacott of North Molton came and claimed it from him, and told him his colt was in the keeping of Mr. Courtenay of Molland. They both travelled to Molland and put the two colts together. Mr. Courtenay and others said it was very hard to distinguish them.

So perhaps this was more a case of confusion rather than an anything underhand. What is interesting for us is the reference to ear-marks as a means of determining ownership. Presumably this was in addition to the brand-marks which had to be applied to the animals of Suitors at Large, for the brands only signified the parish where the owner resided. The system of ear-marking continued into recent times to make identification easier where ponies of more than one owner lived together. Although the Exmoor Pony Society brand marks fully identify the ponies belonging each owner, they are difficult to read when the ponies have their winter coats at the autumn gathering.

Much of what we know from these early times comes to us in the form of records of legal disagreements of which there seem to have been an unending sequence throughout the history of Exmoor; one Exmoor farmer of today explained it simply, that in winter their hobby was hunting and in summer, litigation!

We now have a good picture of what life was like for the ordinary farming men like John Hooper and for the Deputy Forester and his Agisters over a period of several hundred years, between say 1500 and 1800. Now we must look at some of the other events relating to Exmoor during the period.

The 1600s

We start the 1600s with Exmoor Forest belonging to Charles I, though of course leased to the Warden, Sir Hugh Pollard by then. Once the Parliamentarians under Oliver Cromwell had disposed of the king, they turned their attention to dismantling the monarchical system. There was disapproval of the principal of the Crown owning land.

In 1651 Exmoor was once more visited by surveyors. Unlike our Domesday civil servant, we do know the name of this Cromwellian assessor; he was a Jeremie Baines and his task was to perambulate and define the boundaries of the Forest and to furnish a description of the property. This early "estate agent" was obviously not particularly impressed by what he found. He assessed the potential annual income of the 18,927 acres of the Forest at £473 and wrote:

> That the said Chase is mountainous and cold ground, much beclouded with thick fogges and mists, and is useful for depasturing cattle, horses, sheep and is very sound sheep pasture. But a very great part thereof is overgrown with heath and yielding but a poor kind of turf of little value here.

Despite this description, a buyer for Exmoor Forest was found and in 1652 it became the property of Mr. James Boevey. He chose Simonsbath as the centre of his moorland estate and there he built the first house on the Forest plus a new pound as we have heard before. It was here at Simonsbath Farm that later accounts tell of surveys of colts (thought to mean sales) and of castrating of colts; apparently an allowance of beer was

made to the men involved with this hard work. James Boevey was certainly not a man blessed with diplomacy for his actions during his ownership must have alienated most of the people in the surrounding parishes.

When the people of the nearby towns went to hear the Warden's men "crying the moor" in 1654 they were in for a shock; Boevey had more than doubled the pasturing fees. Where horses had previously been charged at two shillings a year, the fee became five shillings and there were similar increases for the sheep and cattle. The local people retaliated in several ways; some put their stock on the Forest and then refused to pay while others simply kept their animals elsewhere. So rather than increasing his income Boevey received less. Needless to say changes were made, the rates reduced and the farmers returned to using the Forest.

James Boevey seems to have spent most of his time in the Courts trying to prove that the adjoining commons were part of Exmoor Forest. The battle lasted over five years and went against him. In the course of it he had taken at least seventeen legal actions against his neighbours.

The Parliamentary period was short-lived and Charles II was restored to the monarchy. As part of this, all the previously held Crown lands were returned to him and Boevey had to surrender ownership after just eight years. However, he remained as Warden of Exmoor until 1696 having had the foresight to purchase a life interest in the lease.

Through all this exploration of the seventeenth century we have focused on the people and events but in truth have found little regarding our Exmoor Ponies, other than the fact that horse-beasts were an important part of the agricultural system and were allowed to graze the moorland all year unlike the sheep and cattle. This very fact of all-year habitation of the moor suggests that when farmers first settled the surrounding lands and established free-ranging herds of cattle and flocks of sheep, the horse-beasts were already there with proven ability to withstand the winters. This is however an interpretation not proof. Also, if we look at all the disputes relating to infringements of the rules of pasturage, there is little regarding the horses amidst the frequent lawsuits.

How many horse-beasts lived out on the Forest? We know that the Free Suitors could graze five horses or five mares and colts. Anthony Dent and Daphne Machin-Goodall interpreted this in *Foals of Epona* as follows:

> *This is not to be taken as five head, either mares or colts. The mare-and-colt is one unit; how many followers there were to a mare would depend on the time of year and the state of the market. In the early autumn we might reckon one foal to a mare, and either one yearling or one two-year-old unsold owing to lack of markets. Say an average of two "followers" per mare. Between them the suitors could run two hundred and sixty brood mares, with say five hundred and twenty young stock. A reasonable proportion of stallions is one to twenty mares; thirteen stallions (there were probably rather more), making a grand total of about eight hundred head, a figure that compares fairly closely with the numbers on the moor today.*

That was written in 1962 when the total of Exmoor Ponies and cross-bred ponies on Exmoor was far higher than today. This is possibly an over-estimate of the number of horses grazed on the moor by the Free Suitors but the evidence is ambiguous. In depositions from witnesses in a lawsuit in 1610, a John Beare of Withipoole stated:

> *. . . and they have also used to have for every suit five horses, mares and colts of their own, whereof no colt under the age of one year was accounted to be of the number, and that if they had any more going in the Forest they did ever pay the Forester for the same as others did.*

Yet in 1635, evidence for a bill brought by George Cottingham said of John Pierce of Withipoole:

> *3 suits belong to him and in right of each he is entitled to depasture five mares and five foals, or five other colts instead of the said mares and foals.*

Again in 1678 and 1692, the right of each free suit is defined as five mares and their foals until one year old.

If the right did allow just one follower per mare, it would mean the total number of Free Suitors' horses were five hundred and twenty, assuming all exercised their rights and this is doubtful. In the 1651 Survey of Exmore Chase by Jeremie Baines, we are told:

> *Memorandum that scarce any of the said Suiters which live in Hawkridg doe make any use of the said Chace, having large Commons of theire owne neare to theire tenements.*

So, if we assume only the Withypool Suitors ran horses to their full allowance, their population can be estimated at around 370. Yet this would not have been the total on Exmoor Forest for there were also the horse-beasts pastured there by Suitors at Large. We do not know if the Warden, James Boevey, owned ponies. It seems therefore that there was probably a minimum of around 500 horses at this time in contrast to the sheep which numbered about forty thousand.

Finally, we come to the statement in MacDermot's history, where he says that the horses driven five times a year were *"of course Exmoor Ponies"*. Sadly that is an opinion not a statement of provable fact. Yet when all the evidence from later history is assembled with the genetic and biological information we have about Exmoor Ponies, this is the most reasonable conclusion. However, we don't have a single description or drawing from those times to make it certain. This absence of certainty applies throughout this history until we come to the first photographs taken in the 1800s.

The 1700s

Margaret Boevey held the lease of Exmoor Forest for a short time but in 1704 one Robert Siderfin became Warden and it seems that only a small number of ponies were included in the transfer. Roger Burton records in *The Heritage of Exmoor* 1989:

> *Fourteen years later there was still only a small herd, with just two colts sold and six cut, and it is strange to find that the £4.6.0. realised by the sale was not included in*

the income of the Forest as was the usual custom. This happened again in 1719, when 13 ponies were sold for £23.2.6.[47]

Robert Siderfin died in 1720 and the Wardenship was taken over by two men in partnership, Robert Darch and James Hill. The Forester's Account Books suggest that they ran a small pony herd as seven ponies were sold for the large sum then of £17.0s.6d. The income from selling the same number the next year was just £9.10s.0d. showing how variable the horse market could be. Their customers for the moorland grazing were pasturing a total of 166 horses on the Forest in 1722 and there were of course still those belonging to the Free Suitors.

Darch and Hill were obviously more interested in their ponies than previous Wardens who had perhaps merely accumulated a few unclaimed animals. Their gradual build up of a herd, as recorded in the Forester's Books has been revealed by Roger Burton's careful scrutiny of these old records following on from 1721:

The numbers of ponies sold annually in the next ten years rose only slightly; the emphasis being placed on building up the herd, and though 38 colts were cut in 1731, only 10 were sold for £16.4.6. This policy continued; the numbers sold each year falling far short of the numbers born, and by 1736, when 34 ponies were sold for £39.0.0, the herd had grown considerably.

The death of Robert Darch in 1737, followed by his wife in 1740, changed nothing, even though this half moiety was now split between their two children, but in 1741, we find the price paid for ponies had dropped and only £23.8.6 was realised from the sale of 31 ponies. Three years later, in 1744, prices were at the other end of the scale, when most of the 19 ponies sold made £2–3 apiece, with a top price of £3.15.0.

The fact that 28 of the geldings in 1731 were not sold must reflect a lack of customers for they could in no way assist in building up the herd. These details show us how unstable the market for the ponies was with such wildly varying prices. From all these records and those of later dates we can compile a listing of the value of

YEAR	NUMBER SOLD	TOTAL PAID (£.s.d.)	PRICE PER PONY (£.s.d.)	DECIMAL EQUIVALENT (£)
1704	2	4.6.0	2.3.0	2.15
1719	13	23.2.6	1.15.6	1.78
1720	7	17.0.6	2.8.6	2.43
1721	7	9.10.0	1.7.0	1.35
1731	10	16.4.6	1.12.6	1.63
1736	34	39.0.0	1.3.0	1.15
1738	50	55.5.0	1.2.0	1.11
1741	31	23.8.6	0.15.0	.75
1744	19			2.5
1747	61	98.19.6	1.12.6	1.63
1748	105	117.0.0	1.2.0	1.11
1749	284	294.17.0	1.0.6	1.0.3
1773	36	73.9.6	2.8.0	2.04
1777	36	80.0.0	2.4.6	2.23
1780	47	88.3.6	1.17.6	1.88
1783	35	64.7.0	1.17.0	1.85
1785	20	60.16.0	3.1.0	3.05
1805	27	120.5.0	4.10.0	4.5
1807	28	144.4.0	5.3.0	5.15
1809	28	201.18.0	7.4.0	7.2
1805–1808	83	466.7.0	5.12.4	5.62

Figure 5.02 *Prices paid for Exmoor ponies 1704–1809*

Exmoor Ponies over many years as shown in Figure 5.02. We must keep in mind too that the animals were still not referred to as ponies. That word was only used in Scotland and did not reach Exmoor until Scottish shepherds arrived in the next century. Darch and Hill would have talked of their horses. We also have to be careful about the word "colt" in historical records; obviously where it is used in talking about cutting (that is castrating) it does refer to males as is understood today. Yet in the 1700s it still meant a horse of either sex but under four years of age.

The Forest Accounts of 1736 give us a wealth of information about the income derived from horses; there were the fees paid for grazing horses on the Forest which amounted to £7.12s.0d. There were 97 colts at two shillings belonging to commoners (presumably Suitors at Large) and five others grazed at four shillings each. As well as listing these, MacDermot also identifies one of the five as having come from Milverton and one from Old Cleeve. MacDermot continues:

Then follows a list of "Colts sold in the year 1736." Thirty-four were sold realising £39.9s.0d. . . . The highest price given for a single colt was £1.13s.6d. . . . the lowest figure was 16s.

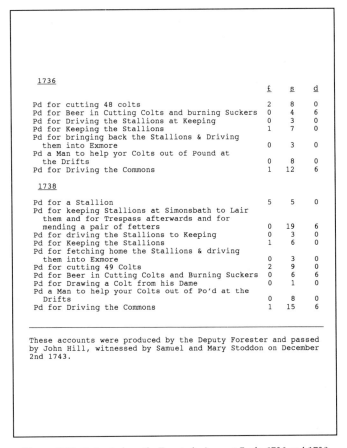

```
1736
                                                £   s   d

Pd for cutting 48 colts                         2   8   0
Pd for Beer in Cutting Colts and burning Suckers 0  4   6
Pd for Driving the Stallions at Keeping         0   3   0
Pd for Keeping the Stallions                    1   7   0
Pd for bringing back the Stallions & Driving
   them into Exmore                             0   3   0
Pd a Man to help yor Colts out of Pound at
   the Drifts                                   0   8   0
Pd for Driving the Commons                      1  12   6

1738

Pd for a Stallion                               5   5   0
Pd for keeping Stallions at Simonsbath to Lair
   them and for Trespass afterwards and for
   mending a pair of fetters                    0  19   6
Pd for driving the Stallions to Keeping         0   3   0
Pd for Keeping the Stallions                    1   6   0
Pd for fetching home the Stallions & driving
   them into Exmore                             0   3   0
Pd for cutting 49 Colts                         2   9   0
Pd for Beer in Cutting Colts and Burning Suckers 0  6   6
Pd for Drawing a Colt from his Dame             0   1   0
Pd a Man to help your Colts out of Po'd at the
   Drifts                                       0   8   0
Pd for Driving the Commons                      1  15   6
```

These accounts were produced by the Deputy Forester and passed by John Hill, witnessed by Samuel and Mary Stoddon on December 2nd 1743.

Figure 5.03 *Extracts from the Forester's Account Books 1736 and 1738 (from MacDermot)*

Figure 5.04 *Change in size of the free-living population on Exmoor*

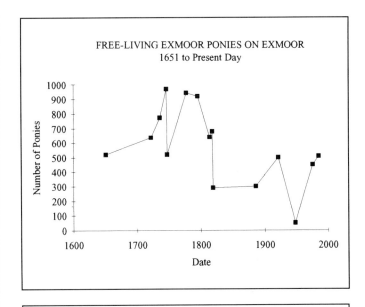

FREE-LIVING EXMOOR PONIES ON EXMOOR
1651 to Present Day

YEAR	WARDEN'S	NUMBER OF PONIES		TOTAL
		FREE SUITORS	SUITORS AT LARGE	
1086	?		800 E	800 E
1651	?	370 E	150 E	520 E
1722	100 E	370 E	166 R	636 E
1736	300 E	370 E	102 R	772 E
1746	450 R	370 E	150 E	970 E
1747	0 E	370 E	150 E	520 E
1777	422 R	370 E	150 E	942 E
1795	400 R	370 E	150 E	920 E
1814	480 R	40 R	120 E	640 R
1818	500 R	60 E	120 E	680 E
1819	20 R	150 E	120 E	290 E
1886				300 E
1921				500 E
1948				50 E
1976				99 C
1985				
1990				138 C

E =estimate   R=record   C=census

The details of payments made by the Warden for services relating to the management of the horses gives us a good picture of what went on. The extract from 1736 reproduced in Figure 5.03 tells us that 48 colts were gelded and that "suckers" (the old name for unweaned foals that is still used on Exmoor today) were branded. We also see a reference to "driving the stallions at keeping" and "bringing back the stallions and driving them into Exmore" which suggests a system was operated whereby the stallions were taken off the Forest, perhaps for the winter, much as is still the practice in many parts of the New Forest. The records for 1738 tell a similar story.

The involvement of the Wardens in horse-breeding continued, with William Draycott taking over from James Hill but later, presumably to capitalise before the lease expired, the Darch family and Draycott sold off their horse stock. Sixty-one were sold in 1747, 105 in 1748 and finally 284 in 1749. Thus some 450 horses were sold in these three years. It shows that the herd belonging to the Wardens had grown considerably during the previous fifty years. Taking these figures with the 100–150 which other people grazed for a fee plus the estimates of the Free Suitors' horses, the population was probably around a 1000 prior to this dispersal. At a stroke, the number, of Exmoor Horses was almost halved as Figure 5.04 illustrates.

Roger Burton suggests that this fluctuation in the horse numbers was probably a regular feature of changes of wardenship:

This has raised a point that has apparently escaped the notice of historians in the past, and it is highly probable that this was not the only occasion in the history of the Forest that on the termination of a lease – or when the Forest changed hands – the entire horse or pony herd belonging to the outgoing Warden was sold, leaving the incoming Warden to build up a new herd. It is, of course, possible that in many cases the new Warden took over the whole or part of the herd at valuation, but as we have just seen this was not necessarily so.

In 1767, after two Earls of Orford had held the lease,

it passed to Sir Thomas Dyke Acland I, the first of this family to hold the Wardenship. During the years between the dispersal sale and Acland's arrival there are no records of ponies being sold or colts cut as sources of Forest income. Presumably then this first Sir Thomas decided that he wished to own a pony herd himself and began the task at once. In 1768, 16 colts were cut and branded and apart from the following year, the numbers gradually rose each year. In 1772 the herd had increased to the point where a sale could be held and presumably the "crying a survey of the colts" was once again heard in the towns around Exmoor. By 1777 the records show there were 329 "old colts" and ninety-three foals belonging to the Warden:

Stock on the Forest in 1777

	Horses	Mares
Old Colts	164	165
Foals	47	46

The numbers are somewhat puzzling, being so even between the sexes. We would not expect to see so many adult males in such a situation of managed grazing, so we must view this record with some care. Perhaps a high number of adult males were gelded but it is difficult to see what purpose they would have served. We also find the use of the word "foal" as opposed to sucker or colt and also a reference to the sale of "Exmore Naggs". One other interesting point is that the only references to stallions are within the Deputy Forester's books and were payments for moving the stallions on and off the Forest, not income. Does this imply that only the Forester ran entire stallions on the Forest? Records of the stock grazed there by others include mares, colts, foals and geldings but not stallions. If this is the case, it means that the Deputy Forester actually controlled the breeding.

Again throughout these many records of horses on Exmoor we find just numbers and nothing about what sort of animals they were. However, we do have some important pieces of evidence that there was a recognised native Exmoor Horse, later to be called Exmoor Pony, and that local people clearly distinguished between this race and other horses. John Thorne farmed at North Radworthy near North Molton and we will quote from his diary elsewhere in this book. He took over the farm in 1790 when he was twenty-nine, on the death of his father. An inventory of the assets of the farm was made in that year and includes the following:

4 Pack Horses	£35	
6 Colts	£24	
2 Colts Exmore	£5	[48]

So John Thorne recognised clearly a specific Exmoor type. We can speculate that as this inventory was carried out on the death of John's father, the breeding of Exmoor Horses had been carried on during the older man's lifetime and perhaps before that.

About the same time, the Reverend John Collinson must have been touring the county of Somerset. He described each parish and its history in his book *The History and Antiquities of the County of Somerset* published in 1791. His entry for the parish of Exford provides another record of a particular Exmoor horse:

> *Among these is Exford situated . . . . in a fertile vale, surrounded by bleak and dreary moors. The environs for many miles were formerly a forest called Exmoor, now a wild waste, intersected by deep winding vallies and romantick hollows. As the only produce of this wild tract is pasturage, it is principally stocked with sheep and a small breed of horses and cattle from the adjoining parishes.[49]*

Finally, as the new century was fast approaching, John Billingsley wrote his *General View of the Agriculture of the County of Somerset in 1795*. Here too we find mention of the breed of Exmoor Horses:

> *Near the centre of this large tract of land is an estate called Simonsbath . . . . Here the forester has an annual sale for the small horses that are bred on the surrounding hills. The small horses (in the whole upwards of four hundred) are not taken into better keeping, nor to more sheltered*

> *grounds, during the severest winter. When the snow covers the forest to the depth of many feet, these hardy animals are seen in droves, traversing the little vallies and sheltered parts, gathering their scanty fare from the banks of rivulets and warm springs; but the sheep are almost all driven off for the winter.[50]*

How helpful it would have been if only Billingsley had employed an artist to accompany him and illustrate the book with pictures of the animals. We are however beginning to benefit in this last decade of the 1700s from the emergence of interest in describing and recording detail and in publishing books. Here we have confirmation of the existence and numbers of the Exmoor Horses and a vivid outline of their free-living way of life.

It is worth pausing before we enter the 1800s to review what we have discovered so far. Here in the late 1700s we are still seeing a way of life little different to that of the eleventh century. Throughout these many hundreds of years the people living around the edges of Exmoor Forest have grazed their horses out on its moors. From the Domesday records to those of Billingsley, these horses are identified as free-living. For much, if not all of the time, they have been managed by the officers of the Forest aided by the Free Suitors, or their equivalent, who in return have also run horses on the Forest. Finally, we know that some of the Wardens themselves have boosted the population with animals of their own.

Overall, our story so far has been one of considerable continuity with very little changing over a period in which dramatic changes occurred in less remote areas. It is sometimes hard to imagine just how isolated Exmoor was even at the end of the 1700s. The Reverend Collinson paints a picture of Withypool in 1971 which tells us of an inaccessible place amidst the moorland:

> *Its situation is full of the wildest scenery: the hills are very lofty; some of them cultivated, and others heath or waste land, covered with fern and wild thyme, with many whortleberry plants and curious mosses. A track winds*

beautifully along the slope of these heights, overlooking the recesses of the dell, which is divided into fine pastures. Here no carts nor wagons are ever used, the roads being impassable for wheel carriages, and scarcely pervious for horses.

Withypool was actually quite a centre of activities, as one of the Swainmote Courts was held there, so we can but imagine just how isolated the other hamlets and farms around the Forest must have been. The Forest itself had just one dwelling, the house at Simonsbath, until the 1800s.

We begin to realise that the rigours of hill farming and the very remoteness of Exmoor bred not only well-adapted horses but also a society of people who were very insular. They were steeped in the traditions of the moor and had little contact with the outside world. We will return to this again for this insularity persisted well into our present century. A local farmer recounted how even in the 1950s there were people on some of the hill farms who only left them once a year to visit the annual fair at Bampton.

The relevance of all this to the history of the Exmoor Ponies is that we have no reason to believe that the patterns of life, including the keeping of the local horse type as herds which wandered the Forest surviving on their own merits, changed until relatively recent times. However, we now move into the 1800s, a period in which changes did affect Exmoor and its horses and threatened to disrupt this enduring heritage.

The 1800s

We start this new century with the third Sir Thomas Acland (or rather his Deputy Forester as he was a minor) continuing to build up his pony herd and with something of a puzzle in the Forest records. The accounts for 1805, 1807 and 1808 show that 83 colts and nags were sold and here at last, the person who wrote these accounts troubled to list the colours of the ponies. There were 34 black, 17 bay, 9 dun, 20 grey, 2 chestnut and 1 piebald. How are we to interpret this? There are several explanations which can be offered.

The first point to consider is whether the Forester recorded colours because this was the first point at which a variety of colours was a feature of the Warden's pony stock. Alternatively, we might suggest that it was someone new writing the accounts but in fact William Lock was the Deputy Forester from 1782 to 1819. So why record colours then and not before? We do not know the answer to this and we do not know when variety of coat colour was first seen on the Forest.

We should now jump ahead to when Sir Thomas Acland III ceased to be Warden in 1818. He sold off most of his stock but he kept a herd of pure-bred Exmoor Ponies which he relocated to Winsford Hill. We will look at this more closely later. For now, the fact that he could confidently establish a pure-bred herd implies that there must have been control of stallions by the Deputy Forester on behalf of the Warden and that the stallions would have been what we now call Exmoor Ponies. We

Plate 33 *Sir Thomas Dyke Acland III (1787–1871)*

saw earlier in the Forest books how there were payments for moving the stallions onto winter keeping for a period of years and no mention of stallions in the listing of stock grazed by others. Colonel F.H. Reeks (agent for the Acland family 1929–1939) wrote about the history of the Acland herd in 1960:

> The 7th Baronet, who took the name of Dyke when marrying into that family, bought the remainder of Lord Orford's lease of the Royal Forest of Exmoor in 1767, and from that time he and his successors the 8th, 9th and 10th Baronets held leases from the Crown until 1814. They also held the office of Forester and as such were the only ones allowed to run stallions on the Forest.[51]

So we have confirmation that the Warden controlled the breeding of ponies as only his stallions could be part of the population on Exmoor Forest. If his stallions were not all true Exmoors, how then could a pure strain have survived to be relocated by Sir Thomas?

If the Acland stallions were all true Exmoors, the system on the Forest would have been much as on Withypool Common today. Mares and geldings of any breeding may be grazed there but only Exmoor Pony stallions. Thus, out on the Forest, there could have been mares and geldings of non-Exmoor or Exmoor-cross breeding as well as true Exmoor mares which could breed pure with the Exmoor stallions.

Despite the logic of it, there is no written record that all the Acland stallions out on the Forest were Exmoor Ponies. However, if some had been of other breeding, how then would our Exmoor race have survived? The characteristics of the Exmoor, particularly the facial markings, height and the low-set tail are so easy to lose, often in just one generation. If cross-breeding did occur at this time or earlier, the wild-type should have disappeared as it did in so many other locations and this should have been the end of the British Hill Pony. This did not happen and so the idea that the stallions were restricted to the Exmoor type seems the most convincing.

It is just possible that the Exmoor race might have survived even if other stallions had access to them in theory. If we suppose that there were Exmoor Pony stallions and there were other stallions too, what would have been the interaction between them and how would the social structure of the population have developed? We know from many anecdotes of Exmoor Pony owners that these ponies are racially prejudiced when given the choice. They will mix with their own kind in preference to other horses and ponies where they can. Even in exclusively Exmoor communities, mares can be very selective as to which stallion they will mate with. So if stallions of other breeding did have contact with them, perhaps the natural instincts of the Exmoor race kept them apart. We might also hypothesise that as the Exmoor race thrives much better than cross-bred animals on the natural diet, they would be fitter and thus more likely to succeed as herd stallions.

It seems most likely though that only Exmoor Pony stallions were run on the Forest by the Wardens. We will return to the subject of purity or cross-breeding later in the context of deliberate crossing versus pure-breeding. For now, we need to realise that once again there may be several interpretations of the little evidence that exists; in the end we must each decide which seems the most logical.

Whatever the circumstances of the horse population of Exmoor in terms of management, we are left with the varied colours recorded in the accounts. Here too, there is probably room for different interpretations. Bay and dun are recognised shadings of the brown coat colour still seen in Exmoor Ponies today. Chestnut and piebald are definitely totally alien and these three animals were not Exmoor Ponies but what of the greys and blacks? In the last chapter, we explored the idea of a natural grey variant within the British Hill Pony genetic make-up. If this is true, then we cannot dismiss these 20 greys recorded in the accounts as non-Exmoors for certain. Again we just do not know. The 34 black ponies have usually been assumed to be cross-breeds but there is an alternative explanation for these too. When recording coat colour today, the shades used are bay, brown and dun and this is judged at about six months old; but there is a small number of adult Exmoors which have very,

very dark brown coats. In recording such animals when sold, did William Lock decide that calling them black was very much easier than writing very, very dark brown 34 times?

Perhaps not; perhaps those who interpret these records as meaning that only 26 of these ponies were true Exmoors are right. As Roger Burton suggests, Sir Thomas may have been culling his herd to rid it of these non-Exmoor animals. Whichever is true, through artificial stallion management or through natural equine social order, the Exmoor Pony race persisted and did not disappear into a melting pot of pony genes.

In 1808, the young Sir Thomas Dyke Acland III came of age and took over the running of the Forest with just six years of the lease remaining. His efforts at obtaining a further lease were unsuccessful, prompting him to offer to buy Exmoor Forest from the Crown. The administrators for the Crown were already having thoughts as to Exmoor's potential for growing trees and they decided that this should be its future, rather than sell it to Sir Thomas or anyone else. A last perambulation and survey of the Forest was carried out in 1814-15 and the area was divided up by an act of parliament that year. Sir Thomas Acland received an allocation of 3,201 acres near to his estate of Holnicote. Each Free Suitor was awarded 31 acres while some 4,700 acres went to the Suitors at Large as a group. This left the Crown with 10,262 acres near Simonsbath for their tree planting scheme.

This final survey provides us with the one full census of ponies on Exmoor Forest prior to 1976! As shown in Figure 5.04, all the population totals at other points in history involve some degree of estimating. Even this census is not crystal clear; it shows that there was a total of 640 ponies with 480 belonging to the Warden, 40 to the Free Suitors and 120 to the Suitors at Large. This may be a low figure because the wording for those other than Sir Thomas Acland's refers to "mares and foals" and it is not clear whether the figures are for mare and foal units or really mares plus foals. So it is possible that the total might have been 800.

This plan to plant oak trees on the Forest was still being examined in 1818 but was also abandoned in that year. Roger Burton says that it is thought that Sir Thomas Acland persuaded them that the project would not work. If it was him, he achieved his desired result, for the Crown put its Exmoor land up for sale. Sir Thomas no doubt constructed his bid on the basis of the potential income from the grazing. He had the records and experience as Warden to allow him to calculate a sensible price and his bid was 5,000. However, the Crown received other bids; Lord Fortescue offered 30,000 but even at this price he too was unsuccessful. Ultimately it was an ironmaster, Mr John Knight, from Worcestershire who purchased Exmoor Forest for the staggering sum of 50,000.

John Knight also bought many of the allotments of land which had been given as compensation to the Free Suitors and Suitors at Large. There was little point in these individuals each enclosing their 31 or 14 acres respectively and Knight's offer to buy them back must have been welcomed. Sir Thomas Acland also sold his 3,201 acres to John Knight, who ended up with about 16,000 acres in total.

Sir Thomas Acland III must have been bitterly disappointed at this outcome. For him as Warden, the Free Suitors and the Suitors at Large, it was the end of a way of life that went back hundreds of years. They must have wondered what would become of the ancient traditions of pasturage and Forest law. 1818 was then a watershed in Exmoor's history and in the history of its ponies too.

From this point onwards we must follow three almost separate stories as we see the ponies dispersed on the sale of Exmoor Forest. We know already that Sir Thomas Acland III retained ponies and took them to his land near Ashway Farm to continue his breeding of the Exmoor Pony. John Knight provides the second path to follow for he acquired Exmoor Ponies from the Aclands and embarked on an attempt to "improve" them. Finally, and all too often overshadowed by the Acland story, there is the history of the ponies bred by the hill farmers in the parishes around Exmoor.

CHAPTER 6

THE DISPERSAL, CONSERVATION, AND DECLINE OF EXMOOR PONIES

The Acland Herd of Exmoor Ponies

There is little recorded about the sale of the ponies in 1818 but Sir Thomas Acland III's son, another Thomas (see Figure 6.01), wrote in 1886:

All that I know of Exmoor Ponies is that my father, when lessee of Exmoor prior, I think, to 1815, when he was in Vienna, used to have about five hundred ponies running wild . . . . There was a great sale when we were in Vienna and it must have spread the breed about.[52]

We do know that his father had no wish to abandon his breeding of Exmoor Ponies, despite having lost Exmoor itself and sold his allocation of 3,000 acres to John Knight. In a wonderful article for the *Pall Mall Magazine* of October 1896, Evelyn March-Phillips wrote extensively of the history and then status of the Acland herd:

At this time Sir Thomas was outbid for the Crown lands by the father of the present Sir Frederic Knight, and there followed a great sale of his ponies, which must have spread the breed far and wide. Four stallions and some mares were sent to Ashway, a little farm on Winsford Hill; and from this stock springs the present pure herd, which are therefore no longer to be found on the forest proper, but which range over the great moorlands which lie adjacent.[53]

Seven years after this article, R. J. Snell published his *Book of Exmoor* and tells us that there were 20 ponies in all taken to Old Ashway where there was a fine stretch of moorland. These were to be the nucleus of a new herd. Yet before both these writers, Sir Thomas's son had written an essay "On the Farming of Somerset" for the *Journal of the Royal Agricultural Society of England* in 1850 and in it he said:

It must not be forgotten that Somerset possesses one of the purest breeds of the native English horse, the Exmoor Pony; the breed is carefully kept up by Sir Thomas Acland on Winsford Hill.[54]

After losing Exmoor Forest, the Acland family continued to spend part of the year on Exmoor, staying at their property at Holnicote. Sir Thomas still employed a manager or "pony-herd" to look after the ponies and his name was John Rawle; he had been pony-herd for the previous Sir Thomas Acland II too, probably since 1785. He lived at Old Ashway farm. In his *History of*

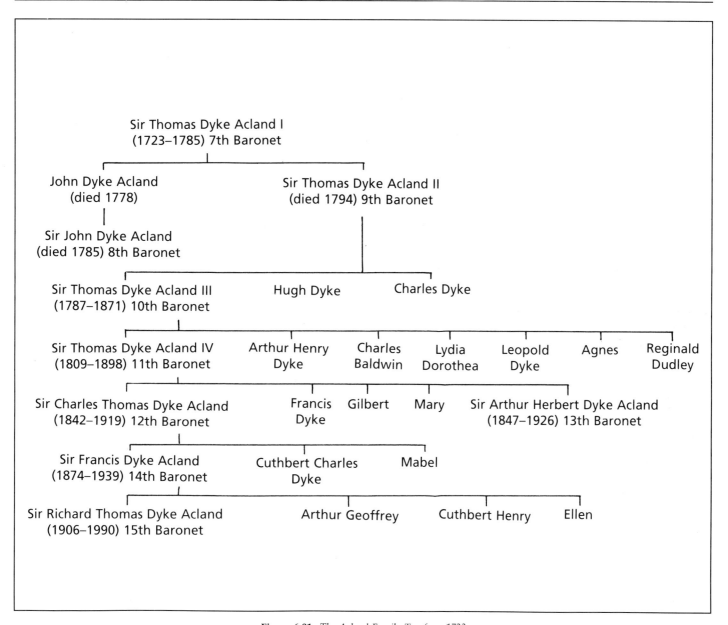

Figure 6.01 *The Acland Family Tree from 1723*

Selworthy written in 1897, F. Hancock gave a description of Rawle:

> He was a man of great strength, and could go into a herd of ponies and bring out unassisted in his arms any one of the little whinnying creatures, a feat which required skill, as well as strength, for the ponies fight very fiercely with their tiny forefeet. Rawle entertained for the head of the Acland family of the day the sentiment of a feudal retainer for his chief. It is said that when he accompanied Sir Thomas on any expedition, and his master entered a house for refreshment, Rawle stood at the door like a sentry, watchful and immovable, however long the delay, until "his honour" reappeared. Sir Thomas's wish was law to him.[55]

We have evidence of his dedication in a delightful story which John Rawle himself left for us in his diary and to which Evelyn March-Phillips added some details, probably related to her by his son. In 1835, he was asked by the Baronet if he would accompany two ponies to Carlsruhe in Austria, as a present for the Duke of Baden. Although it is unlikely that Rawle had travelled very far before and he was not a young man, he undertook the task which proved to be quite eventful. He had with him a pass covering the export of the two ponies but during the trip, one of the ponies foaled. He hid the foal under the straw and concealed it from the Customs officials. Eventually, he delivered the now three ponies to the Duke's establishment on 26 August. Sir Thomas's mother was staying with the Duke and the next morning asked for Rawle only to find he was already on his way home as Sir Thomas would need him for shooting black-cock on 1 September.

Sir Thomas Acland III was committed to breeding the Exmoor Ponies without introducing non-Exmoor blood, in contrast to John Knight and some of the Exmoor farmers who were cross-breeding extensively. We will come to these crossings later. Acland had apparently experimented earlier and concluded that the original strain, which was conserved throughout, was best left unaltered. Evelyn March-Phillips recorded:

> Experiments have been tried from time to time of introducing fresh blood, but the inevitable conclusion has been that, though the progeny may be improved in the first generation, the second is in every instance inferior to either of the grandparents. Since this was established, all foreign strain has been carefully weeded out and none of mixed descent are now left in the herd.

Perhaps here we have reference to culling out non-Exmoor animals at the sales in 1805–08 when different colours were mentioned. Certainly Sir Thomas Acland was renowned after 1818 for breeding the pure Exmoor Pony strain. Sir Walter Gilbey in *Ponies Past and Present* wrote in 1900:

> When Sir Thomas sold his Exmoor property to Mr Knight he removed his original uncrossed stock to Winsford near Dulverton; these ponies alone preserve the full characteristics of the old strain; they run from 11.2 hands to 12.2 hands, are dark brown with black points, and have the mealy tan muzzle.[56]

Richard Rawle, who took over as pony-herd from his father said that the herd was kept "not for profit but for example". The Acland ponies were identified by a distinctive anchor shaped brand-mark, which had been used since about 1797. It became recognised by many as the symbol of a true Exmoor Pony. While the principle of pure-breeding was adhered to, Sir Thomas did not give up the idea of improving his ponies and decided to experiment by giving Nature a helping hand. Around 1876, a new system of management was introduced whereby, after the annual gathering, a number of the best mares and foals with most potential were driven down to the Acland estate at Killerton in Devon. This was aimed at giving the youngstock better grazing and a kinder climate in the belief that this would improve them in adulthood. The mares stayed just a few months but the foals were kept at Killerton for a year or more. F.H. Reeks, who managed both Killerton and Holnicote in the 1930s, described the system:

> In the old days as soon as the mare suckers were weaned, sometime in November, they were driven by road to Killerton, where they were put out in what is known as the Back of the Park. The best of the colt foals went with them,

where they thrived on the better grazing. They stayed at Killerton until the following June twelve months, when they were brought back to Winsford Hill.[57]

This practice continued for many years. Sir Charles Acland said in 1903:

> *For the last thirty years we have been in the habit of taking about twenty of the best mares, with their foals, down to the better climate and grass at Killerton, where the young ones spend a year or so. And the result has been twofold. First of all, "emollit mores, nec sinit esse feros" (which means "it softens the character if it is not allowed to be wild"); and secondly, the chests are widened, and as a direct result, the shoulder rendered more sloping and the humerus more upright and the action improved. But the quarters are entirely another matter, and I am afraid many of the tails come out as low down in 1900 as they did in 1870. Experience has taught us that the original strain of blood is as good as any cross we can devise, and that no cross will combine good qualities through two generations with any degree of certainty.*[58]

From what we now know of breeding Exmoors in domestic conditions and raising them on richer habitats than Exmoor, it seems likely that the improvement the Aclands obtained was more from the annual careful selection than from a response to an easier first winter. Whilst the individual ponies wintered at Killerton may well have grown better than their counterparts up on the moor, it is most unlikely that this would have become an inheritable trait within just thirty years.

The numbers of Acland ponies grew quickly from the 20 retained in 1818. When writing in 1886, Sir Thomas Acland IV referred to the family having had 80–100 ponies since the time of the great sale. Gathering the ponies in from Winsford Hill and Ashway Side was an annual event. With no fees to be collected, there was no need to bring in the ponies more than once a year, as had been the practice on the Forest. This annual round-up was described by Evelyn March-Phillips in 1896 and is worth quoting at some length:

> *About once a year the herd is driven together and inclosed, to be counted, branded, and a certain number selected for sale or breeding purposes. It was my good luck to be present one day last autumn when the proprietor of the Holnicote ponies was thus taking stock. It is only at these times that any one can judge of their numbers and condition – any one , that is, except the pony-herd, the son and worthy successor of old John Rawle; he knows each one, as a shepherd knows his flock; can answer for the age of each, and has its parentage and its pedigree at his fingers' ends. For a day or two before the muster he had been out on the hills, riding round with his son and his dogs, driving down the stock. The ponies tend to run in droves, especially when scared, and this makes them easier to manage; but even those who know their haunts may ride for an hour without finding one.*
>
> *At last all are gathered within the low stone walls of the yards at Ashway, where stands the herd's cottage, below Mounsey Hill and above where the Barle flows under the great Druidical boulders of Tarr Steps, the witches' bridge.*

Plate 34 *Acland ponies at Old Ashway Farm (reproduced from* Pall Mall Magazine *1896)*

Plate 35 *Acland ponies at Old Ashway Farm (reproduced from* Pall Mall Magazine *1896)*

Behind the little pastures the purple folds of moorland stretch away to the sky, with Dunkery Beacon's dark ridge towering over all. The grass and bracken are turning orange, and here and there in the hollows the low, wind-swept beeches gleam gold and russet in October sunshine. In a small yard, against an old barn or barton, are penned up the fathers of the flock – spirited little fellows, with high crests and sweeping tails, plunging, fighting, rising to bite one another's manes. Hard by, a whole bevy of ponies frisk and scamper round a larger yard, while in a third the little mares move placidly, their foals stepping demurely at their heels, with pretty baby dignity.

The foals look very tiny, and their legs are not so long and lanky in proportion to their height as those of foals usually are. Their small bodies are covered with a thick, fur-like coat, and their short rough manes stand crisply erect; while the bright, mischievous eyes of the full-grown ponies gleam through shaggy locks, tumbling in all directions. The judging goes on – some twenty are marked to be sold "to Bampton Fair". Mothers and infants are told off to the rich meadows of Killerton. Here and there a faulty animal is drafted. A strong well-shaped black has failed to acquire the indispensable mealy nose; and notwithstanding undeniable merits, the fact goes forth that he is to run no more with the herd. All above two years are branded with the anchor on the near flank – for nearly a hundred years the badge of the Holnicote herd.

There are suggestions in later correspondence that the Acland ponies not only ran on Winsford Hill and Ashway Side but also on South Hill and Bradley Moor. This might explain how the total was around one hundred, certainly more than Winsford Hill alone could have supported. Richard Rawle's successor, Tom Parkman, considered three stallions and 30 mares to be, the maximum that could be run on Winsford Hill. We also see in this extract another reference to selecting against anything thought not to properly marked. This is a fascinating account of the management of the Acland ponies in 1896 and when we come to look at management today in a later chapter, the continuity and lack of any real change will be evident. We also learn from this article that Sir Thomas's herd included six stallions, named Prince of Wales, Duke, South Hill II, Colonel (described as a beautiful little four year old) and two young ones.

The ponies to be sold were walked to Bampton for the Fair held in early November and their auctioneer was a Mr Daniel Evans who we will meet again shortly when looking at other Exmoor Pony breeders of the times.

The Acland ponies at the end of the 1800s probably had little contact with people other than at the annual gathering. Sylvia Calmady-Hamlyn, who was the secretary of the Dartmoor Pony Society for many years, wrote in a letter dated 1955:

I used to know the Acland ponies well and once old Sir Thomas Acland offered me any two I liked running on the hill if I could get near them – I couldn't.[59]

In 1898, Sir Thomas Acland IV died and his son Charles inherited the title. Richard Rawle was still the pony-herd. Mr D. J. Tapp of Dulverton, writing in 1946 recalled:

The Acland herd was known and talked about all over the land. There were approximately 80 ponies on Winsford Hill in the summer. The suckers were sent down to Killerton Park in the autumn. Those that were drafted in Sir Charles' time were sent to Bampton Fair. That was a great day for a lot of us. I used to be one of the helpers. Sir Charles used a pure-bred Exmoor Pony for shooting black game. When the dog, a Pointer, marked, he would get off and a boy who had walked with him, or the keeper, would take the pony. Sir Charles spent half his time with the ponies at Holnicote. He used to have all sorts of games with them.[60]

So, at this time and perhaps since 1818, some ponies were kept at the Holnicote property as well as those on Winsford Hill. Sir Charles Acland's niece, Maimie Acland, wrote of her uncle in a letter written in 1960:

Uncle Charlie, though he did like horses and went to see the ponies on Ashway Side and took me with him, was not a bit of good about the history or really, bless him about horses! Parkman often wished to differ violently![61]

Tom Parkman thus took over as pony-herd sometime between 1898 and 1919 for it was in this latter year that Sir Charles Acland died. The title passed to his brother Arthur. It seems that the pony herd was reduced in size at this time and that Acland ponies were purchased by at least two other local breeders of true Exmoor Ponies, William Westcott of Zeal and William Crockford of West Hawkwell.

Sir Arthur Acland held the baronetcy for just a few years and died in 1926. His son Francis succeeded him. Sir Francis was to be the last Acland to own the herd of Exmoor Ponies. Tom Parkman retired early in the thirties and he was not replaced, perhaps hinting that Sir Francis did not have such an ardent interest in the ponies as his predecessors. In fact his ancestors must have turned in their graves when he committed the cardinal sin of sending eight of the Acland Exmoor mares to run with Lord Fortescue's non-Exmoor stallion.

Tom Parkman's daughter, Gladys Bawden, recalled this event in correspondence in 1962; apparently the mares were returned to the herd in foal and possibly some of the resulting fillies were retained, certainly no colts. Later culling of animals with this Fortescue blood is thought to have ended the influence of this ill-conceived project.

Prior to Tom Parkman's retirement though, far more prudent management had been practised as he had acquired stallions from Mr Crockford's herd. Although all originated from the same Acland foundation stock at 1818, the herds had gone their separate ways and this introduction of less closely related blood was a wise move on Tom Parkman's part.

The Acland family had kept a private stud book but this was lost in a fire at Holnicote during the Second World War, an incalculable loss. However, it had been possible to register ponies in the Polo Pony Stud Book since 1898 and there are a number of records of Acland Exmoor Ponies. Interestingly, as ponies of any breeding

Plate 36 *Sir Charles Acland's Stallion "Dunckery" Reserve Champion at Islington Show 1916 (reproduced from* Polo Pony Stud Book)

could be entered in the Exmoor section if they were bred on Exmoor, the entries for Acland ponies often specifically stated that both sire and dam were pure-bred Exmoor Ponies. This was undoubtedly to distinguish them from the animals registered by Lord Fortescue. We have one early photograph, from these Polo Pony Stud Books, of an Acland bred stallion called Dunckery, which won at the 1916 London Show. In 1921, the Exmoor Pony Society was formed and Sir Francis Acland was elected its first vice-president. It was Lord Fortescue who became the first President. We will look at the early days of the Society later in this chapter.

The history of the Acland family's ownership of Exmoor Ponies was approaching its end. Around 1927 Old Ashway farm with its moorland known as Varle Hill and Ashway Side was sold to Mr Frank Green. His great-nephew, Colonel Simon Lycett-Green wrote about these events in the herd Stud Book in 1952 and his writings were reproduced in the 1990 *Exmoor Pony Society Newsletter*:

> On this hillside existed a herd of wild Exmoor Ponies, the original Acland herd. They are the oldest herd remaining and for years have been distinctively marked with their Anchor brand. Under the terms of the purchase, the herd of ponies became the joint property of Sir Francis Acland and Mr Frank Green but they remained as wild as stags or foxes. They were only touched when they were rounded up once annually for branding which was no mean feat, carried out with the aid of the local farmers and witnessed by the Secretary of the Exmoor Pony Society. Otherwise they had free warren of the previously held Acland estate and they fed off the hill.[62]

Sir Francis Acland died in 1939 and his son Richard inherited his half share when he assumed the title. Prior to this we have heard of the ponies grazing Winsford Hill as well as Ashway Side; Sir Francis had sold Winsford Hill in 1926 but apparently rights for grazing the hill had been retained.

Frank Green was obviously the more interested partner; the Acland bond with the ponies had been weakening in the time of Sir Richard's father. Thus at some point Frank Green bought out Sir Richard Acland and became sole owner of the herd. The Acland family had conserved the true Exmoor Pony for over one hundred and seventy years. Thus the story of the Exmoor Pony and that of the Aclands is intertwined and those of us who admire the ponies today owe so much to this family.

Simon Lycett-Green wrote that Frank Green was highly committed to the ponies:

> he always maintained that they were part of the estate and could not be separated from it. He regarded himself as keeper of the herd rather than owner.

This was surely an attitude that would have found favour with the earlier Sir Thomas Aclands. Gladys Bawden wrote in 1962 in a letter that Frank Green occasionally requested her father, Tom Parkman, the retired pony-herd, to go with him to Ashway Side and look at the ponies. He also forged a close association with the Westcott family, who by now had a wealth of experience of breeding Exmoors, and benefited from their advice and from exchanging stallions with them.

F.H. Reeks, who was Steward to Sir Richard Acland, wrote about the round-up and inspection of the Anchor herd in 1937 during the Acland-Green partnership, in an article for the 1970 *Exmoor Review*:

> The first time I saw the ponies was at a round-up in the early autumn of 1937. The farmers had ridden the Hill the day before, and some 30 to 40 ponies were collected in the yards at Old Ashway. So far as I can recollect, the Society's inspectors then were the late Maurice Westcott and Harry Williams. Tom Parkman had been in charge of the Acland herd since he took over from Richard Rawle. I knew very little about Exmoors in those days and Tom Parkman's life had been spent with them. I relied on his judgement.
>
> I have many vivid memories of the Old Ashway round-ups. The yards were full of completely wild and unbroken ponies . . . .we all had to be "pretty dapper on our veet". When a sucker or older pony was chosen to be taken out for inspection, one young man would slip on a halter and the

Plate 37 *Gathering Exmoor ponies on Winsford Hill in 1938*

Plate 38 *Bringing the Acland ponies back to Old Ashway Farm in 1938*

other would seize the pony's tail at the extreme tip in order to keep well clear of the flying heels. Both would then pull or push as the case might be until the pony was clear of the milling herd and produced before the inspectors.

Stallions and mares were dealt with in the same way, but rather more respect was paid in the case of stallions, who were quite capable of standing on their hind legs, boxing with their fore legs, and using their teeth at the same time if the opportunity presented itself. On one occasion when we were half way through the job, the lower gate of the main yard was found to be partly open. One stallion made a rush for it and got through. The rest of the herd followed before we could lift a finger; some got through the gate and others jumped it or the rails at the side, and within a few seconds the whole lot were streaming on to the road and back to the Hill.

Our history of the Acland herd has now reached the outbreak of the second world war and the time of near disaster. Simon Lycett-Green wrote of the events which nearly wiped out the herd:

During this time the herd numbered approximately forty. They were always ruled by one stallion and the laws of nature. Younger stallions were driven off although at breeding times some seemed allowed to have a few mares in attendance. Old age and accident were the controlling factors in numbers and so they lived looking after themselves as far as possible.

The dark days of the 1939–45 war brought dark days, too, for the Acland herd. They remained living on the hill and at the time of meat rationing and shortage, some criminal butchers visited Exmoor and trapped the majority of the herd in one of the narrow lanes and stole them away. They must have employed some local aid but the criminals were never caught. Frank Green spent several hundreds of pounds in trying to trace the ponies and it was ascertained that they were taken as far as Cumberland.

Only about a dozen survived the tragedy and they were taken into the fields far from the moorland roads and there they remained for the rest of the war. In fact Frank Green would not let them onto the hill again and they remained in his enclosures. There is no doubt that Frank Green, with his

own years creeping into the nineties, became more zealous in his care of the ponies. He would not trust anyone to touch them and about 1948 he stopped the Exmoor Pony Society from visiting and branding the ponies. By this time they had begun to increase once more to approximately twenty. The old stallion became too old and had to be destroyed, his place being taken by a younger pony of the herd.

We will return again to the effects of this disaster when we look at the genetics of the Exmoor Ponies in a later chapter. It must have been a devastating blow to Frank Green and no wonder that he became so protective of what remained of the herd. The theft of the ponies was no doubt motivated by the fact that people were hungry and there was considerable profit to be made by the unscrupulous. Those responsible probably had no idea of the importance of these particular ponies but would such knowledge have influenced them anyway? We must be thankful that on that night 12 of the group escaped this fate to continue the line.

About 1950, Simon Lycett-Green bought Old Ashway farm from his great uncle and the ponies were returned to Winsford Hill. He and his daughter, now Mrs. Rose Wallace, reorganised the herd and culled out a number of ponies at this time. Colonel Lycett-Green recalled in his article:

So the Simon Green family took possession of the herd with a view to guarding and protecting the ponies' rights and interests. However, they too had to recognise that the keeping of ponies in the days of more intensive agriculture is no easy matter. If allowed to graze on the hill they break into the best crops of some neighbours and so they have to be kept in the enclosed land. This has meant a limit has had to be imposed on their numbers. The question of size of the herd was not too difficult for when they were taken over it was discovered that a number had small white marks or other blemishes not truly indicative of a pure-bred Exmoor; so they were reduced to twelve mares and a stallion. These were the remains of the Acland herd but it is hoped that they may remain on their rightful ground for many years and that they will continue to breed and raise stock worthy of their ancestors. Simon Green has passed his guardianship of the ponies to his daughter Rose in the hopes that she will continue to love Exmoor and its ponies and that if ever circumstances should make it necessary for her to part with the property she will do all she can to preserve the life of the Acland herd.

So once again the work of rebuilding the herd had to begin. Where, in the early 1800s, Sir Thomas Acland III's ponies numbered around 500, in the 1940s the population was almost lost. Fortunately though, ponies from the Acland herd had been sold to other breeders in 1818 and 1919 and from the 1920s demand for Acland ponies grew, both on Exmoor and elsewhere. Thus others of this ancient lineage survived and contributed to other Exmoor Pony herds. Yet it is sobering to look at the chart of population size in Figure 6.02 and realise that the world-wide total of Exmoor Ponies has only recently regained and over-taken the 500 level.

The history of the Acland herd goes on. Mrs. Rose Wallace is still the owner of the herd which lives free on Winsford Hill. Now we must return to the year 1818 and to the sale of the bulk of the Acland ponies, to follow the fortunes of the Exmoor Ponies which became the foundation for other herds.

The Knight Ponies

When John Knight became the owner of Exmoor Forest, he acquired some of the Acland Exmoor Ponies. Sir Walter Gilbey says in *Ponies Past and Present* that:

It is stated that only about a dozen mares were left in their old quarters.

Roger Burton though, in his *Heritage of Exmoor*, believed there to have been about 30 left behind by Sir Thomas for John Knight. Perhaps this was a private sale agreed before the large dispersal sale. It is hard to believe it would have been a gift, given that Sir Thomas could have had few kind thoughts for the man who had so totally out-bid him for the Forest.

We have been reminded throughout of how Exmoor

Plate 39 *The Acland/Anchor herd on Winsford Hill*

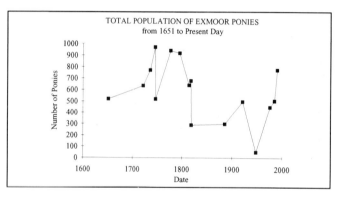

YEAR	Warden's	Free Suitors	Suitors at Large	Total
1086	?		800E	800E
1651	?	370E	150E	520E
1722	100E	370E	166R	636E
1736	300E	370E	102R	772E
1746	450R	370E	150E	970E
1747	0E	370E	150E	520E
1777	422R	370E	150E	942E
1795	400R	370E	150E	920E
1814	480R	40R	120E	640R
1818	500R	60E	120E	680R
1819	20R	150E	120E	290E
1886				300E
1921				500E
1948				50E
1976				450C
1985				507C
1990				777C

E=estimate   R=record   C=census

Figure 6.02 *Change in size of the total Exmoor pony population*

Forest was an isolated wilderness and it is worth re-emphasising that this was as true in 1818 as in any of the centuries before. The farmhouse at Simonsbath was still the only dwelling on the Forest and there was no road system, just ancient tracks. The Forest was not fenced and only separated from the adjoining commons by boundary stones. It was a wild land fit only for the grazing of animals.

However, John Knight saw it quite differently. He had tamed and improved heathland before and he saw great potential in Exmoor, which presumably explains the huge price he was willing to pay for it. His ambition was to turn this barren landscape into a thriving agricultural community. He began by enclosing his property within a wall which ran for nearly 30 miles and he established the first true roads. He continued the renting out of the grazing to some extent but his main interest was in re-claiming the moor for more productive agriculture.

It would be all too easy to spend time looking at this ambitious project in detail, for it is a fascinating story of a man's self-belief and determination to challenge Nature. Yet we are concerned with the ponies. Suffice it to say that, in the end, Exmoor largely defeated John Knight and an enormous amount of his money was spent without much to show for it. C.S. Orwin's *The Reclamation of Exmoor Forest* written in 1929 is the definitive account of the Knight era and tells the story of this battle so well.

John Knight was then a man who believed in change and progress. He tackled the business of breeding ponies with his universal approach that what Nature had created, he could improve upon. It is impossible to say whether this stemmed from arrogance or from a mission to aid the advancement of his country. So, when he acquired his small foundation herd of Exmoor Ponies, a project was immediately begun to try to breed a larger animal.

To achieve this he crossed some of his Exmoor mares with Dongola Barb stallions and Thoroughbred stallions. He found a ready market for the progeny locally as hunters. However, there was a price to be paid for this "improvement" of the ponies for the cross-bred stock could not themselves rear foals if over-wintered out on the moorland. Back in 1657, a yeoman of North Molton called Nicholas Slader had almost predicted the outcome of these experiments when in testimony he said:

> *The land and soyle of Exmore is a very cold, course and barren soyle, and doth produce a course, mossy and sower grass only serviceable to keep beastes alive, and not to grow and improve them.*[63]

Frederic Knight took over from his father in 1842. We can imagine how disappointed John Knight was by the time he left Exmoor. After spending twenty four years and quite literally a fortune (Roger Burton estimated it at 100,000, equivalent to about 30 million today) his great dream had not been realised. Frederic Knight carried on the work but instead of trying to farm the whole estate as his father had done, embarked on a programme of building and developing farms which he then rented out. This was a far more practical approach.

Frederic, later to be knighted, also continued pony breeding but the lessons had been learned and the use of large horse sires had been abandoned. In 1850, there was a sale of Knight equine stock but the pony stud was retained and by then numbered somewhere between 100 to 400 (sources disagree on this point). It is also impossible to say how many of these had been bred true and how many were cross-bred to some degree; certainly cross-bred ponies were sold at Simonsbath over the next few years. Was this a culling out process to leave just the stock which had not been experimented upon? It seems probable that few had escaped some degree of crossing as other pony types had been brought in.

So, from his nucleus of thirty Acland ponies in 1818, John Knight and then his son had built the numbers back to the levels of their predecessor but the true Exmoor Pony was probably a rarity out on the Forest some fifty years later. Frederic Knight also faced the reality by the 1860s that pony breeding was not producing the maximum income from the land and that sheep would generate better profits. By the time he died in 1897, just 60 Knight ponies remained. Instead of keeping ponies on until three or four, the practice of selling the crop as suckers had been in use for some time. Roger Burton suggests that some of the reduction in numbers may also have been from natural causes as in the winter of 1896-97 many of the Brendon ponies died "as a direct result of the severe drought in the previous summer".

These remnants of the Knight pony herd were bought by Viscount Ebrington who later became Lord Fortescue. By 1910 there were just 16 ponies, three in 1928 and by 1930 they were gone.

Roger Burton summed up the impact of the Knights upon Exmoor:

Exmoor today is still very much as Sir Frederic Knight left it, and it is, I believe, a blessing that he did not have the means to do all he intended, for in failing to complete his mighty task he has left Exmoor with a delicate balance of farms and wild moorlands that in many ways complement and supplement each other.[64]

The ponies though suffered the full force of the Knights' desire for change; they were easy to alter, unlike the Exmoor terrain that resisted so hard. Just think how different the Exmoor Pony story might have been if John and Frederic Knight had worked as hard to conserve the true ponies as they did to redesign them. Fortunately, as we know already, the Acland family were guardians of the native animals but they were not the only ones. In the parishes bordering the Forest were many families who, like Sir Thomas Acland III, were to become pioneers in the field of conservation. So once again we return to 1818 to trace the story of some of the other pure-bred Exmoor Ponies which left the Royal Forest.

The Exmoor Breeders

The history of the Acland and Knight ponies has been fairly easy to chart, for being men of wealth and position, they or their employees could devote time to keeping estate records. Also they attracted attention because of their social standing and some of their contemporaries wrote about them. Few visitors to Exmoor in the late 1800s who wrote of the area failed to mention the Aclands and the Knights. However, it was quite a different story for the hill farmers who battled the Exmoor environment in the parishes around the Forest to earn their hard living. Their time was and still is needed for the farming itself, not writing about it and they attracted little attention. Fortunately though, there are snippets of information and also the knowledge which has been passed down through several of the families to the present day. So we can construct something of this part of the Exmoor Pony story which is just as important as the Acland history.

The first Exmoor character we meet is Daniel Evans, who was quite a late-comer in the story. We will look at him first because of his close association with the Aclands. He was born in 1825 in Devon and at some time prior to 1861 moved with his wife to Winsford, where he became the publican of the Royal Oak. He was obviously quite a businessman because he was also a general merchant, a farmer and an auctioneer. He farmed 48 acres and employed two labourers. Daniel Evans acted for many years as auctioneer of the Acland ponies which were sold annually at Bampton Fair. F.J. Snell described him in *A Book of Exmoor* as "A kind and genial host"; he goes on to tell us of Daniel Evans the auctioneer:

In writing of Bampton Fair it would be unpardonable not to say something about Mr. Daniel Evans and his mart. Until the resuscitation of the lime and stone industry obliged him to move on, Mr. Evans annually located himself in the yard opposite the Tiverton Hotel, amidst picturesque surroundings, but rather cramped. His rostrum is now erected in Orchard No. 2, where he likewise has a sale-ring, and his mealy-mouthed ponies – all pure Exmoors – are secured in pens. It is not too much to say that for many people his familiar figure has become a symbol of the fair; but besides being a symbol, "Sir Thomas' poor auctioneer" – Mr Evans does not look poor – is one of the most entertaining of men, with a fund of good stories, wherewith he contrives to relieve the monotony of business. He once told an interested audience of the gentlemanly habits of a stallion called "South Hill". In the paddocks round

Ashway, where this pony ran with the mares, he was frequently seen to rise on his hind-legs, open the gate with his fore-paws, and keep it open while the ladies of his seraglio passed through to the moor.[65]

This sounds as if Daniel Evans could rather embroider and exaggerate stories for his audience. Snell obtained this tale from Evelyn March-Phillips' article and in this she says that the pony-herd and other witnesses vouched for the truth of this story. It does sound as if they might have been pulling her leg.

Daniel Evans not only auctioned Exmoor Ponies but bred them himself as well; he was allowed to run his mares with the Acland ponies on Winsford Hill. Possibly the oldest photographs surviving of Exmoor Ponies are those which were used in Captain Hayes' *Points of the Horse* published in 1904, which date from 1897. One shows a stallion "Royal Oak" being held by Tom Callaway who was helper to the pony-herd Tom Parkman. This stallion was a prize winner at Islington Hall in 1897; he was bred by Daniel Evans out of one of his mares by an Acland stallion. Royal Oak had been

Plate 40 *Mr Edward Mucklow Junior's mare, Gladys (reproduced from Points of the Horse 1904)*

sold to a Mr Edward Mucklow Junior, from the north of England, who also owned the mare, Gladys, in the second photograph which is reproduced here. We know little of Edward Mucklow except that he wrote to Captain Hayes:

They are the foundation of the best Polo ponies, mated with a Thoroughbred horse, not too big. Ponies bred this way are extraordinary jumpers and lovely hacks.[66]

Daniel Evans owned an unknown number of Exmoor mares which he must have purchased privately from the Aclands or perhaps taken as his commission as auctioneer.

Seven years before Daniel Evans was born, the end of the Royal Forest resulted in the 1818 dispersal sale and some of the local farmers, including redundant Free Suitors from Withypool and Hawkridge, purchased Acland Exmoor Ponies either to add to their existing stock or to start herds. We have to remember that the Free Suitors had, for whatever reason, reduced the number of ponies they collectively ran on the Forest to just 60 by 1818. It is also important to note that the bordering parishes had their own tracts of common land on which these farmers held grazing rights.

One family has already been mentioned, the Westcotts of Zeal, who were later to help and advise Frank Green. D.J. Tapp of Dulverton, who was himself an Exmoor Pony breeder, wrote in 1946:

Mr. Westcott of Zeal always had an excellent herd. He started with Acland stock. That was old William Holcombe Westcott. He was a masterpiece. A heavy-walking sort of man.

Presumably, farming at Zeal in Hawkridge parish, he had been a Free Suitor and purchased Acland ponies at the dispersal sale. He was obviously as committed to the breeding of the true Exmoor as the ex-Warden, for the Westcott family were to become enormously respected for their knowledge of Exmoor Pony breeding. William's son Richard was one of the members of the first ever committee when the Exmoor Pony Society was formed in 1921 as was A.G. Westcott who farmed at Porlock.

Plate 41 *The late Sidney Westcott, leading the ponies to Old Ashway Farm after the Winsford Hill gathering*

In 1931, the family moved to Draydon farm near Old Ashway. Here William's grandson Charles Maurice Westcott and his sons, Sidney, Bob and Charlie, continued the tradition of breeding Exmoors.

The Exmoor Pony Society allocated herd numbers to breeders and Sidney Westcott registered his ponies in herd No. 10 as well as herd No. 1 (which his father founded). His brothers Bob and Charlie owned No. 28 and No. 7 herds respectively. Sidney was very active in the Society, like his father, and is perhaps best remembered riding at the head of the Anchor herd as they were brought down from the Hill after the gathering each year. He managed the breeding policy of the Anchor herd for many years. Sidney Westcott died in 1978. His brother Bob and his sisters now live at Tippacott,

Brendon and register within herd No. 10, while Charlie and his wife Linda farm at Clitsom, Roadwater. Both families continue to breed, inspect and judge Exmoors.

The Westcott No. 1 herd, founded on Acland stock originally, also came to influence the breeding of the Anchor ponies over a hundred years later, for one of their stallions, Crackshot II, ran with the Anchor herd between 1955 and 1960. The first Crackshot and Caractacus were also No. 1 herd stallions and both of these were bought by Miss Etherington (later to be Mrs. Speed) and taken to Scotland to form Herd No. 2, now owned by the Royal Dick Veterinary College of Edinburgh. So the Westcott family have played a significant part in the history of the Exmoor Ponies since 1818.

Alongside William Westcott at the 1818 dispersal

sale was a Withypool farmer, Nicholas Milton, who was tenant of Lower Landacre and a Free Suitor. He also bought Exmoor Ponies then, or perhaps earlier, and established his herd on Withypool Common. His great-great-grandson is Fred Milton who farms Weatherslade, Withypool and who still breeds Exmoor Ponies on the common. In 1968, Fred Milton wrote an article for the *Exmoor Review* in which he chronicled the family history, including the pony herd:

Nicholas Milton, my great-great-grandfather, was 36 when he became tenant of Landacre in 1807, so was just in the prime of life for hard work. He was interested in Exmoor Ponies and kept a number on the Common. His sons also learned to look after them, especially young Nicholas II, who spent much of his time riding his pony, shepherding and looking after the stock of ponies.

I met a dealer from Reading some years after he had retired from business, and he told me he had bought scores of Exmoor Ponies from my grandfather and the family. The "pure-breds", he said, "with the well-known mealy muzzle, were outstanding and surpassed all others in stamina."

My father, Charles John Milton, was born at Dadhayes, left school at the age of 13 and came to live at Weatherslade on his birthday. He took a very keen interest in Exmoor Ponies, and in 1890 played the responsible part of collecting, marking and selling for his father, uncles and brothers. During the 1880's the sales for Exmoors were good, but early in the 1890's the prices at Bampton dropped considerably, although those at Bridgewater kept up. The following year arrangements were made to rail the ponies from Dulverton to Bridgewater, but the overhead cost of transport and forage very nearly cancelled out the extra money made. The next year they drove the ponies on foot to Bridgewater, a two-day journey, lodging a night at Crowcombe about half-way. This also did not prove successful, the ponies being tired and sore-footed. So it was decided to revert to Bampton. Nevertheless, contact had been made with dealers from the north, who promised to come to Bampton in future. So the sales improved again and stayed steady for several years. The colts of two to three years in age were in demand and sold for pit ponies. The

fillies also went for cross-breeding for riding ponies and light carthorses.

I was born at Weatherslade and have lived there all my life. At an early age I learned to ride a pony. Father also bought summer grazing for cattle in other parishes, often 8–10 miles away, so I spent eight hours in the saddle on many occasions. In 1930 prices fell badly. Sheep and lambs fetched only a few shillings, two-year-old Devon cattle 10–12 and Exmoor Ponies 2–3. In the depression that followed, it was very difficult to make a living at farming. But we survived it all.[67]

Fred Milton has a keen sense of family tradition and the breeding of No. 23 herd out on Withypool Common continues to be as important to him today as it was when he became owner of the herd in 1946. The Miltons were exhibitors at the first ever Exmoor Pony Society show held at South Molton in 1921 as were the Westcott family. He too has been on the Exmoor Pony Society committee many times and is again, as this book is written. He is still a Society Inspector and Judge. His great-nephews, Robin and Rex Milton, help him with the practical management of the herd.

Plate 42 *Mr Fred Milton judging the Exmoor Pony Society stallion parade*

Just a few miles from Withypool is the village of Twitchen and on a nearby enclosure called Lydon's Moor, are some six Exmoor mares of No. 44 herd which has belonged to the Thorne family for many generations. In 1945, W.G. Thorne wrote about his father's involvement with Exmoor Ponies:

My father lived at Brightworthy (adjoining Withypool Common), sixty-five years ago. He kept from 15 to 20 breeding mares and a stallion. He used sometimes to take as many as 50 ponies to Bampton Fair, by road all the way. He was a speculating kind of a man. I daresay he would have bought in some to sell again. I've heard him say he attended Bampton Fair every single fair – without a break – for 50 years. His ponies were always pure-bred. He used to ride out on the hill and come home at night and say to us: "I've seen a beautiful sucker to-day. I must see if I can't buy that." [68]

W.G. Thorne's son, the late Leo Thorne, wrote in the 1974 *Exmoor Pony Society Newsletter* that his grandfather started the herd at Brightworthy in 1865:

He stayed there until 1880, when he moved to Higher House, Twitchen, my present home. He retired in 1903, when my father took over the farm together with my grandfather's best ponies. One of the best ponies that my father bred that I can remember quite well was a stallion called Jan Ridd. In 1913 the late Lord Poltimore, of Court Hall, started a herd of Exmoors and he persuaded my father to sell him Jan Ridd. Lord Poltimore died in 1917 when he looked like building up a fine herd and they were all sold; one can only say the pity of it all. My small herd of ponies have descended down from my father's and my grandfather's ponies. [69]

So far, it has been impossible to determine absolutely whether the Thorne family are descended from John Thorne who we met in 1790 at North Radworthy. Given the locations it seems very likely and thus the family's herd of Exmoors may go back much farther than Brightworthy in 1865. Whether there was an unbroken link in the breeding of the ponies we do not know.

Miss M.G. Etherington gathered together several reminiscences of the local breeders in her booklet *The Little Horses of Exmoor* published in 1947. This included a piece by William Crockford of West Hawkwell Farm, Luckwell Bridge:

My father always had pure-bred Exmoor ponies and so have I. They run on an allotment called Codsend Moors all the year round. That moor adjoins Dunkery and it is very cold and rough there in winter. Ponies eat up a lot of the rough grass which makes it come up sweeter in the spring and summer next year for the sheep and bullocks. On good land Exmoor Ponies may get fatter but they do not gain any height. I do not think they can gain height without crossing. I like a pony with short ears, broad forehead and nostrils and a nice mealy nose. I have seen the ponies grazing peacefully with the deer and I think the ponies, like the deer, have always been natives of Exmoor.

If they are to be used as children's ponies they should be handled young. When we take them to shows they are brought straight off the moors and are not got up for the show in any way whatsoever. I had a mare called Ladybird that I bought when the late Sir Thomas Acland had his sale at Ashwick. She was the winner of many prizes and all the ponies I have are her descendants. She was branded number 2 in my herd which is Herd No. 12 in the Exmoor Pony Society's Stud book. I joined the Society when it was formed.

When I was a lad I remember buying some suckers from the late Mr. Dick Westcott of Zeal. They cost 4 pounds each. I also bought a young mare sucker from a neighbour and often wished I had kept a stallion from her. I have sent ponies to Scotland at different times: some to Dalbeattie, some to Peebleshire. Exmoor ponies are good because they have great strength to carry weight on the moors, are very sure-footed and of very hardy constitution. [70]

During the late 1940s, Bill Western bought West Hawkwell Farm and became owner of No. 12 herd, taking over from William Crockford's daughter. The ponies still inhabit Codsend Moor today and Bill Western is still serving on the Exmoor Pony Society committee. His grandson Michael is training to be an inspector and so the tradition continues.

Plate 43 *William Crockford with his prize-winning Exmoors at Exford Show*

Plate 44 *Tom Pring (far left) showing his ponies*

We have followed the generations of Exmoor families, the Westcotts, the Miltons, the Thornes, and the Westerns, some since Exmoor ceased to be a Royal Forest, and have seen the Exmoor Ponies as part of their lives throughout. There are several other local families

who were once part of conserving the pure-bred Exmoors and we have just a few records of these. Tom Pring wrote in 1946:

> *I've been a breeder of the Exmoor Pony practically all my life. I am a member of a family who rented under the late Sir Thomas Acland near Old Ashway, where he kept his famous herd of pure-bred ponies, and they were a grand lot. He was the only landowner who set out to preserve the native breed and well he did it. When I came home from school, a neighbouring boy and I used to go out on the hill on our Exmoors and I used to ride round helping my father with the shepherding when I was five. In those days – back in the '80s – nearly every pony on the hill would be a mealy-nosed Exmoor.*[71]

David Tapp, who we have quoted before, said that his father farmed Knaplock, close to Winsford Hill, around 1860 and that "he was mazed about Exmoor Ponies". He tells us that he used to ride an Exmoor to school and his father said it was the safest way to go as an Exmoor will never falter.

In the mid to late eighteen hundreds, while these farming families were breeding true Exmoor Ponies, there were others who just as enthusiastically decided that cross-breeding was the best policy. The ponies running on the commons near Brendon, Oare and Porlock to the north of Exmoor Forest soon became mongrelised. What led to this dichotomy in approach, with one faction totally dedicated to pure-breeding and the other to crossing? Perhaps Sir Thomas Acland IV provides the clue to this in the essay on farming he wrote in 1850, for he described the Exmoor hill-farmer as well as the agriculture:

> *He is many miles from a market town, with the sea on the north and the forest on the west; he has therefore comparatively few opportunities for intercourse with others, and is chiefly dependent for his ideas on the traditions of former generations, his own observation, and the improvements which may be brought into the district by owners of property or new tenants.*

The isolation of Exmoor was indeed considerable.

Wheeled carts were not used in the locality until around 1830, presumably reflecting the absence of any substantial tracks; people and possessions were transported by pony or pack-horse and these were used to draw sledges across the fields. MacDermot tells us that even the Government ordnance map of 1809 is:

> hopelessly inaccurate in its delineation of the Exmoor country, and leads one to think that there was good ground for the local tradition that the surveyors never went over the moor at all.

The arrival of John Knight on Exmoor certainly introduced new ideas to the area and some farmers followed the Knight example and turned to using non-Exmoor stallions, abandoning the traditional way in favour of this "modern" approach. So why did some families resist this "progressive" influence?

It is surely no coincidence that the pure-bred herds of Exmoor Ponies survived mainly in the parishes of Withypool, Hawkridge and their neighbours, with those families who had close association with the ex-Warden, Sir Thomas Acland III. He advocated breeding the ponies in the traditional way. The redundant Free Suitors would probably also have resented the arrival of John Knight and the loss of their ancient privileges, making them more entrenched in their view that they wanted nothing to do with this in-comer or his ideas. Their loyalty to the Aclands and the old ways would have been reinforced.

Those who had been Suitors at Large or new arrivals to Exmoor had no such tradition or prejudice against the Knights; they had paid in the past for pasturage and all that changed was the person charging the fees. So perhaps there was far more potential for introducing new ideas in the parishes to the north of the Forest. We must be eternally thankful for the conservatism of the few families who along with the Aclands ensured the Exmoor Pony survived these revolutionary times. They deserve our admiration for then, as now, the Exmoor Pony breeders did not succumb to the economic temptation of crossing. The placing of tradition over financial reward is well illustrated by the story recalled by one Exmoor breeder of the two Williams cousins having their photograph taken to celebrate their accomplishment of getting ponies to Bampton Fair between the wars, where they received on sale less than the minimum commission of half a crown.

We know from other areas of the country how easy it was to totally eradicate the British Hill Pony, simply by the wholesale conversion to cross-breeding. The ponies escaped this fate on Exmoor due to its almost island-like status. Amidst the rapidly modernising industrial world of Britain as a whole, it remained a backwater where its people clung to their established customs. Unlike other remote parts of Britain, Exmoor experienced the impact of just a single influential outsider, who failed to convince all as to the merits of progress. Perhaps most important of all, Sir Thomas Acland III appreciated that the true native pony was the "fittest" for Exmoor and worth preserving. He and those he influenced came to be conservationists long before the "green" era.

The Birth of the Exmoor Pony Society

Although the Knights' experiments with crossing ultimately taught them that the moorland would not sustain the less hardy progeny, the principle was not abandoned completely. The Barbs and Thoroughbreds departed but they had also purchased non-Exmoor pony stallions. It is not clear whether their later pony stud bred pure Exmoor or used these other pony sires. Out on the northern commons, the farmers certainly continued experimenting with crosses and succeeded to a certain extent; their crossed ponies, still with much Exmoor blood, could rear foals and just about survive if not thrive, except in very bad winters. So cross-breeding and pure-breeding both continued on the geographically separate commons.

In 1912, the president of the Board of Agriculture and Fisheries formed a committee to advise him regarding the "improvement" of Mountain and Moorland Ponies. Their report makes fascinating reading; they concluded that attempts to introduce non-native blood were not productive given the reduction in hardiness. However, they recommended the interchange of stallions of the Mountain and Moorland breeds as a means to improving the pony stock generally:

> *thus introducing the qualities and improvement desired from those herds which have already shown their ability to stand the hardships inseparable from the life of a Mountain and Moorland pony. This life being the most valuable agent in making ponies a useful factor in national horse-breeding.*[72]

The idea of invigorating domestic pony stock with the hardy genes from native ponies was sound enough. However, the references to interchanging stallions were ambiguous, for they could be interpreted as exchanging stallions within a breed to avoid inbreeding or as exchanging stallions between the breeds. In fact the Chairman of the committee, Lord Arthur Cecil, certainly implemented the latter system in his dealings with New Forest Ponies, introducing Exmoor stallions among others to the New Forest as we have seen earlier in this book. Mr A.C. Mardon, who wrote recommendations regarding Exmoor in the report, stated that if there was difficulty finding Exmoor stallions to put on some of the commons "in this case Fell Ponies would be gladly accepted". There is no record of this being put into practise. Interchange was then most probably seen as a mixing of any of the native breeds. From our perspective this report was not very helpful to the Exmoor Pony for it created even more encouragement to cross-breed.

At this time, the aim of so many pony breeders around the country was to produce a suitable mount for the Polo field and for hunting; undoubtedly breeding programmes which blended native pony with a certain amount of "foreign" blood were proving highly successful. The whole ethos of "improving" the native free-living pony stock was in part a recognition of their importance but at the same time failed to emphasise, if not appreciate, the need to conserve the raw materials separately. The Board of Agriculture report identified all the Mountain and Moorland ponies as having a common ancestor but failed to realise that this "British Pony" was still in its unaltered state in the few pure-bred Exmoor herds.

It is not surprising that the Exmoor Ponies were not recognised at that stage as special. In terms of registering ponies in the early Polo Pony Stud Books, the majority were cross-bred and only a few of the Acland pure-breds were included. So Exmoor must have been viewed from afar as no different from say Dartmoor or the New Forest. It is interesting though that Lord Arthur Cecil did visit Exmoor, presumably later, and was taken to see the Acland herd on Winsford Hill. He obviously recognised their value then for he wished to buy the entire herd! The offer was refused but as we know he certainly purchased some Exmoor stallions.

The 1912 report was valuable though for all its shortcomings for it recommended that District Associations be set up to look after the interests of each breed and to administer grants and premiums awarded by the Board to encourage breeding. There appears to be no record of any formal association being formed on Exmoor at that time as a result of the recommendation, but the idea eventually took root. The formation of Breed Societies began over the next few years but it was not until 1921 that the Exmoor community took action.

Come now to the Red Lion Hotel in Dulverton on a Friday evening in March 1921. Every seat in the room set aside for this special meeting is taken and there is a hum of chatter as the assembled company await the start of the proceedings. Lord Fortescue is seated at the top table and opens the meeting which has been convened by Mr David Tapp. Lord Fortescue begins by explaining that the Board of Agriculture is trying to encourage the breeding of native ponies, as numbers of horses are low following the war. He reads a letter from Lord Poltimore, saying that the difficulties facing the Exmoor Pony breeder today are the scarcity of pure-bred stallions and the continued pressure to breed larger ponies to command higher prices.

Lord Fortescue reads the first proposal to the meeting:

> *That it is expedient to form an Exmoor Pony Society and to compile a register of Exmoor Ponies on the lines of the Exmoor flock book; and a register of the brands in use by the members of the society.*[73]

Mr Tapp seconds the motion and says that the Exmoor Pony will be the best anyone can buy because they have the biggest heart and lungs of any horse in the world. There is much applause at this and no doubting the shared enthusiasm for the ponies. Some discussion about brand marks ensues and this is finally deleted from the proposal to be thrashed out at a later date.

We move on to the second proposal:

That up to the 31 December 1923, ponies shall be admitted to the register if recommended by not less than two inspectors and approved by the committee, but that after that date no ponies shall be admitted to the register unless they are the offspring of ponies registered in the society's stud book.

This is carried almost unanimously and then the meeting moves on to electing officials for the new Society. Lord Fortescue is elected as President and Mr. Reginald Le Bas becomes its first Secretary. A provisional committee is formed and Lord Poltimore, R.S. Westcott of Hawkridge, Tom Parkman of Ashway, W. Pring of Champson, D.J. Tapp of Highercombe, Mr. Perkins of Lynton, A.G. Westcott of Porlock, G. Molland of Simonsbath and F.G. Heal of Exford are elected as its members. Their task is defined as being to consider the appointment of inspectors to pass ponies for registration in various groups of parishes and to present their recommendations within three months.

These speeches from the inaugural meeting were reported in the local press in detail under the headline "The Pure-bred Exmoor Pony – Society for its maintenance formed at Dulverton." The report described the above events and went on to explain how the meeting debated the defining of a true Exmoor Pony:

In order that a decision could be come to on the question of size and general qualification of ponies for entry in the stud book, draft proposals were laid before the meeting to the effect that the inspectors should be guided by the following rules:

No pony to be above 13.2 hands or, if under four years old, likely to exceed that height.

No pony to be eligible unless the sire and dam were both genuine hill ponies and free from any cart-horse or hackney cross.

In cases where nothing is known of the breeding, ponies may be admitted if obviously of moorland type and free from above disqualifications.

The question of size was not settled without considerable discussion. Mr R.S. Westcott spoke strongly in favour of the limit being 12.2 and many were in agreement with him, while others held that 12.3 or 13 hands should be the limit. Ultimately the Chairman took the feeling of the meeting with the following results – 12.2 as the maximum for mares and 12.3 as that for stallions. The other rules were passed and in the matter of colour it was agreed that bays, browns, blacks and greys should be admissible but not chestnuts.

We have seen in an earlier chapter that the actual height range seems to be between 11 hands and 13.2 hands at the extremes but with the great majority of both stallions and mares being 12 hands. This reporting of the definition of rules certainly conveys the idea that the height maxima agreed were very much a compromise, rather than a firm belief that stallions should be allowed to be bigger than mares. We have also explored the idea that grey might be a rare but natural variant and questioned as to whether black really meant black. Given that the Society was being formed specifically to preserve the pure-bred ponies, it is hard to imagine that they would allow a definition that permitted inclusion of cross-bred ponies.

A few months later, a second meeting was held, this time at the Carnarvon Arms and the draft rules were presented to the members. The objects of the Society were defined:

To improve and encourage the breeding of Exmoor Ponies of the moorland type, to form a stud book for the breed, to institute annual shows of breeding stock and produce, to examine and approve all pony stallions to be used in the district for breeding of Exmoor Ponies and to award premiums for the same; to arrange for the exchange of stallions for use within the district and for importing suitable stallions from outside the district, and to pass all ponies intended for registration in the Exmoor section of the National Pony Society's stud-book or for exhibition at the society's shows.

The rules were confirmed as presented at the first meeting with the definition of an Exmoor being:

Height – mares not exceeding four years and upwards 12.2; sires not exceeding the same age, 12.3. Colour – black, bay, brown, dun, with a mealy nose, and grey but not chestnut.

Dr Collyns, the author of a classic book on the Red Deer, suggested there should be a more detailed description including such points as strong, compact cannon bone and clean heels; these points were added plus the stipulation that no white markings of any kind were permissible in a true Exmoor Pony. Agreement was also reached upon brand-marks and it was decided that all registered ponies would be branded with a society brand, a four-pointed star, with the owner's herd number and the number of the pony in the herd. Thus, the system was established, which continues today, whereby an Exmoor Pony's pedigree can always be obtained by checking its branded numbers against the stud-book.

So the Exmoor Pony Society had been born and christened. Lord Fortescue and Sir Francis Acland were confirmed as President and Vice-President respectively and David Tapp, who seems to have been the drive behind the whole enterprise, was elected as the first Chairman. By the time they met again for the first annual general meeting in March 1922, much progress had been made. Mr Le Bas reported that 111 mares, 18 mare suckers, 11 stallions of one year and upwards and 8 horse suckers, a total of 148 ponies, had been registered and branded. The Society had grown to 25 life members and 46 annual members. By the following March, a further 82 ponies had been registered.

The original intent had been to close the stud book at the end of 1923 but we learn from the proceedings of the 1925 AGM that this rule was deleted for the inspectors felt they would be excluding some legitimate Exmoor Ponies which had not yet been inspected. These early years saw the establishment of classes for Exmoor Ponies at South Molton show and at Exford Show locally but breeders also began to take their prize animals further afield. However, their experiences were quite sobering at first when they found their ponies, taken from the moor, competing against ponies of native breeds which had been bred on studs and specially prepared for the shows. Four Exmoors competed at Islington in 1924 and the Secretary reported that "we were handsomely beaten". Again credit goes to the Exmoor breeders for they resisted the temptation to adopt the fashions of the show-ring; they set the rule that Exmoor Ponies should always be shown in "natural condition".

By 1927, around 350 Exmoor Ponies were registered with the Exmoor Pony Society (EPS) and a selection of the best were entered in the Exmoor section of the National Pony Society Stud Book. The EPS report for that year stated that there had been a steady improvement in the quality of the ponies presented for branding over the six years. However, these were hard times for breeders:

The Society in common with horse breeding generally is suffering from the depression in industry and agriculture and modern conditions generally. The coal strike and a falling market for ponies adversely affected the sales in 1926 and this reacted on the Society, causing some breeders to drop out.[74]

Whilst a few fell by the wayside, the core of Exmoor breeders carried on, their enthusiasm and commitment undiminished. The records of the Society, listing the members of the Committee during the twenties and thirties, repeat the key names again and again – Parkman, Westcott, Crockford, Tapp, Thorne, Pring, Williams. The Society was however beginning to expand, for in the thirties the market for Exmoors began to improve and as suckers were sold away from the moor, so the spread of Exmoor Pony enthusiasts widened.

The Exmoor Pony Society today is the product of that extending of horizons, for while some of the Exmoor families remain a focal point within the Society, there are small breeding herds spread from Scotland to Cornwall. At the founding of the Society, the numbers of Exmoor Ponies on the moor and on farms were estimated at about 500 in total. The population size was to fall drastically and only surpass that level again in the late 1980s.

The Second World War

The 1940s were catastrophic for some of the free-living Exmoor Ponies. We have already charted the decimation of the Acland/Anchor herd when most were stolen and presumably butchered. Elsewhere on the moor, ponies were facing different threats. American tank and gunnery crews stationed on Exmoor and practising on Brendon Common apparently tired of inanimate targets and trained their guns on the moorland animals,

Plate 45 *In the 1930s and '40s, Exmoor ponies began to find new homes away from Exmoor*

Plate 46 *The riding school in Kingsley Green, Surrey 1936/37, showing the popularity of the Exmoor at that time, with three out of seven pupils riding Exmoor Ponies.*

Plate 47 *Prime Minister (stallion bred by Sir Francis Acland and owned by Mary Etherington) served with the "Exmoor Mounties"*

including ponies. It is not certain how many true Exmoors were amongst the animals lost but locally this is remembered as yet another reason why numbers fell so dramatically.

Another wartime problem was the absence of many of the young men who normally undertook the active management of the herds. We cannot be sure whether the Society functioned at all because either no records were kept at this time or they have been lost. Generally, and understandably in wartime, the ponies were not uppermost in people's minds and the pony breeding declined. The gates across Exmoor's roads fell into disrepair and some of the commons ceased to be safe havens for the true Exmoor; some farmers withdrew their remaining ponies back onto farms.

Yet a few Exmoor Ponies also served the war effort. The 1st Somerset (Minehead) Battalion of the Home Guard had to patrol almost the whole of Exmoor and the Brendon Hills. They formed mounted patrols and are believed to be the only Home Guard unit which were issued with cavalry equipment. By August 1940, the "Exmoor Mounties", largely those associated with the

Devon and Somerset Staghounds, numbered around 50. Their mounts were various, including some bicycles amongst the horses and ponies; a few rode Exmoor Ponies. To begin with the Mounties armed themselves with shot-guns but eventually obtained rifles. Jack Hurley in *Exmoor in Wartime* wrote:

> *Among places from which the Mounties kept watch were Brightworthy Barrows and the corner of Alscombe Common, on the Withypool-Sandyway road. Patrols did duty in fours each night, and were accustomed to long rides to the guard points.*[75]

We can perhaps picture the scene, as they rode across the moor in the darkness; how slowly the hours must have passed as they kept vigil. We can be proud that a few were accompanied by Exmoor Ponies.

Towards the end of the war, it emerged that the numbers of true Exmoor Ponies had declined disastrously; an optimistic estimate would be that about 50 remained on Exmoor and no herd of any size had been established elsewhere at that time. So the Exmoor Pony was very nearly wiped out. Once again, one individual with great vision, a worthy successor to Sir Thomas Acland III, played a major role in ensuring its survival. In the village of Withypool lived Miss Mary Etherington, daughter of the rector and a keen breeder of Exmoor Ponies. When the appalling position of the moorland herds became evident, she cajoled and encouraged the local farmers to put every effort into breeding the ponies and rebuilding the herds. She helped campaign successfully for the introduction of cattle grids to restore the integrity of the commons and allow the farmers to restock them with both sheep and ponies. Fortunately, Mary Etherington has left us with her own words describing these times in *The Little Horses of Exmoor*:

> *The idea of telling the story of the Little Horses of Exmoor came when the war ended and it was found that a mere handful of this ancient breed remained. In 1946 there were only six pure-bred filly foals born on Exmoor. This caused widespread concern. The wild ponies on the moor have a warm corner in the hearts of many people in*

Plate 48 *Mary Etherington riding Foxglove (48/28) on Exmoor in the 1940s*

different parts of the country. Numbers of questions were asked. "Why have the ponies gone? Where have they gone? Can they be brought back?". All this led to still further questioning about the habits and ancestry of the breed. People wanted to know "What is an Exmoor Pony? Where did it come from? What is its origin?

Miss M.G. Best, who has made a life-time study of the native pony breeds from the naturalist's point of view, has tracked the little horses in their wanderings from prehistoric times down to the present-day and has shown us what a rich inheritance we have in this rather desolate corner of moorland. The four breeders, W. Crockford, T. Pring, D.J. Tapp and the late W.G. Thorne have written from their own experience and knowledge. They are well-known in the West Country. They have carried on the main tradition of the Acland herd and kept the breed pure. This they did in spite of great difficulties and very little encouragement.

The true Exmoor Pony is a fixed type. It has survived from the prehistoric past in spite of many threats of extinction. The threat today is probably greater than it has ever been. There are two main reasons for this: the demand for horse-meat and the destruction of the common gates. The long queues outside the horse-meat shops in London answer the questions "Where are the ponies going? Can they be brought back?" but the gates are really the main cause of the trouble. If motor drivers had not been allowed to ruin Exmoor as a stock-rearing district, many young mares and stallions would have been left on the hill and the fact that those which were sold became meat would not have mattered, the breeding stock would have been maintained.

Motor drivers will not open and shut gates which were put up to prevent stock straying off the commons. The result has been that thousands of acres of valuable grazing have been lost and the country has been robbed of food which was so badly needed. The Exmoor Horn Sheep and the Exmoor Pony which have grazed the hill together with the deer, from the earliest times, are both in danger of becoming extinct.[76]

The decline in pony breeding had therefore started with the arrival of the motor car and the wartime events added to the problem. Mary Etherington was tireless in her drive to save the ponies. She sought the help of the Natural History Museum in London for she believed that if the ponies' ancient ancestry were appreciated then more effort would be made to conserve them. She met an unreceptive audience there and her friends, the Westcott family, recall that the zoological establishment viewed her as simply a nuisance and were unwilling to investigate. The Zoological Society of London did however take the matter seriously and in 1946 exhibited an Exmoor stallion (Caractacus 1/9) and mare (Foxglove 48/28), in Regents Park zoo for four months, to draw the attention of the public to the plight of the breed and the importance of conserving these ponies as foundation stock.

The attitude of the Natural History Museum management is hard to understand given that they once recognised the Exmoor and the Shetland Ponies as desirable

Plate 49 *The Speeds' research herd on the Pentland Hills in Scotland*

for their collection of indigenous mammals; certainly no studies had been undertaken subsequently to devalue the ponies' status. Perhaps it was the obscurity of the few families which conserved the true Exmoors amidst the more publicised cross-breeding activities which accounts for the disinterest. However, they did suggest to Miss Etherington that she should contact the Royal Scottish Museum.

Mary Etherington set off for Scotland having successfully acted as a catalyst on Exmoor, where breeders were sorting out their stock and re-establishing herds on the commons. She took with her some Exmoor Pony bones and her Exmoor Ponies. James Speed wrote of her arrival in an article for the *Exmoor Pony Society Newsletter* in 1981:

> *Then, in the early fifties Mary Etherington arrived in Edinburgh. She had been working whole-heartedly to*

help save the remnants of the Exmoor Pony herds and was finally advised by the British Museum to come to Edinburgh to see if she could get some backing for her claims about the scientific importance of Exmoor Ponies. The Royal Scottish Museum & the Museum of Antiquities had already had dealings with me about Celtic ponies and their harness so that when Miss Etherington arrived with a collection of Exmoor Pony bones, they at once brought her to me. That collection of bones, the skull and metacarpals in particular, spanned the centuries, for here was the ancestor of, or the direct descendant of, our prehistoric native pony.[77]

Mary Etherington and James Speed married and worked together comparing prehistoric and historic pony bones from all over the country with bones of native ponies. They established a research herd which they used to test out the Exmoors' powers of survival, running them on the Pentland Hills near Edinburgh.

They published a number of scientific papers presenting their ideas but the zoological establishment was unimpressed. Their failure to win the Exmoor Ponies the recognition they felt the ponies deserved was a life-long source of disappointment to Mary and James Speed.

From our perspective though, the Speeds should have felt more than satisfied with their contribution to the Exmoor story. Had Mary not persuaded the Exmoor farmers to revive their efforts at conserving the true Exmoor Pony, then would the population have recovered? If she had not pursued her academic interest and met James Speed, would either of them have ever reached the conclusions they jointly presented, so stimulating further research in future years?

This is perhaps a suitable point at which to bring this history to an end. The early '50s were a happier time for the ponies. Their numbers were starting to increase again and their homelands were once again returned to them. New free-living herds were established with the Speeds in Scotland and with the Dean family in Cumbria. The Exmoor Pony Society found renewed vigour and a growing band of enthusiasts. So we will close at 1953. Why then? Well that year a budding zoologist was born, destined to become addicted to Exmoor Ponies and write their story, and she is not ready yet to be classed as history!

The Historical Perspective

Acceptance of the Exmoor Pony as the surviving British Hill Pony is obstructed by the difficulty in believing that a population could have survived all this time in an area of the British mainland. Zoologists are now well accustomed to finding that Nature may take an unusual course with island populations but how, they ask, could such a remarkable survival story have occurred on Exmoor? Many find it impossible to believe.

To appreciate the Exmoor Pony story though, requires a wide approach for zoology, archaeology, palaeontology and social history are all key elements; studying just one, leaves much of the overall picture unseen. It is a jigsaw which has many pieces.

The close similarity between the Exmoor Pony and what we know and deduce about the British Hill Pony could be explained in several ways. We know from zoological studies that wild type characteristics will sometimes re-emerge in populations which suffer intensive natural selection in very harsh environments. This is happening with the feral horses on Shackleford Island off the east coast of North America. Alternatively, the wild form can sometimes be recreated from artificially crossed populations by continual selection by the breeder of the ancestral features when they re-occur; this has been the method of "breeding back" a replica of the European Tarpan, another possible prototype pony. Finally, a primitive animal may continue to the present-day virtually unchanged if left subject to the laws of Nature rather than Man, as with Przewalski's Horses before they were driven to extinction in the wild.

The history of the Exmoor Pony helps us to assess which, if any, of these explanations applies. The ponies inhabit a wild and harsh place in which the ancestral adaptive features remain advantageous. However, there is nothing to suggest that conditions have been extreme enough to have reselected those characteristics from a domestically altered population such as on Shackleford. In fact, we know that occasionally, in the hardest winters, the ponies were given a little hay, cushioning them from the full force of natural selection. It seems reasonable therefore to reject this as the likely explanation for the surviving wild-type.

Our history of the ponies certainly suggests that in this century, the Exmoor breeders have specifically selected good representatives of the original pony type. This may possibly even have emphasised some of the ancestral characteristics, producing more clearly marked heads than before and perhaps favouring a smaller overall size of head. We know that certain herds were deliberately conserved and protected from cross-breeding from 1818 onwards. Thus at no point in the history do we see true "breeding-back" from crossed animals to restore the full array of Exmoor characteristics. Certainly, once the loss of hardiness was understood, those who were crossing ensured a high proportion of Exmoor blood but none could conceal the effects of the alien introductions.

Plate 50 *Teagle Mistaken Identity, Mr & Mrs Cambell's Thoroughbred—Exmoor Cross (14.3hh at 2 years old)*

The experiences of those who have experimented with crossing tell us clearly that the wild-type genetic blueprint is always altered to a recognisable extent, even in the first generation. The mealy muzzle rarely comes through undiluted, the cannon bone of the leg changes and the low-set position of the tail usually alters. So it is most unlikely that today's Exmoor Ponies are the result of breeding back programmes.

We come then to the last option, that our Exmoor Ponies are the British Hill Pony. We looked at evidence which tends to support this from anatomical and physiological studies earlier. Yet to make sense, for this to be possible, requires that the British Hill Pony experienced unique conditions on Exmoor alone, throughout the whole of its original range. We can identify three main factors which led to the emergence of pony breeds elsewhere in Britain. Firstly, the impact of horses imported by the Romans or their auxiliaries; secondly, contact with new ideas and animals along major trading routes or from local centres of trade; finally, the introduction of foreign stallions by influential landowners.

Our historical journey through the centuries of Exmoor's history have shown that this small upland area did indeed have a unique passage through time. Its

isolation made it almost an island. Although Exeter became a Roman city, contact between Exmoor and the Romans was minimal. There were no routes of importance across Exmoor, no large commercial centre or port nearby and no dwellings upon it throughout much of its history. Then, when change threatened this long continuity through the ideas of the Knight family, some of the Exmoor people held true to their traditions. This conservationist approach to their way of life and their animals was totally insular within a country that was forging ahead with progress. The British Hill Pony had a last refuge, protected by the commitment of the people to their own heritage. The ponies survived not in spite of human interference but because it was uniquely constructive on Exmoor.

Exmoor Ponies cannot be exactly the same as the ancestral form for Nature will have changed them over thousands of years in subtle ways to fit their modern homes. Man has influenced them genetically, through selecting what he views as the best of the original true Exmoor. We have to acknowledge that the population was not kept entirely free of outside blood; that is why today the ponies are so rigorously inspected and anything with white marks rejected. Yet this has to be kept in perspective: the Exmoor is in a similar position to the zoo populations of Przewalski's Horses.

When Przewalski Horses were brought out of Mongolia to found the captive groups, some had an infusion of domestic Mongolian pony blood. Zoos have systematically selected against this and purged their stock of its influence, as far as possible. The essence of their wild characteristics is unscathed and no-one would dream of allowing them to decline on the grounds that they were impure. In just the same way, the Exmoor breeders have culled any ponies which even hint at the influence of the few non-Exmoor animals which possibly contributed to the herds and the ponies represent their ancient race without dishonour. They can be viewed as a genetic wild-type just as much as the Przewalski's Horses, or the Scottish wild-cat or the Red Deer, which like Exmoors have had their purity "nibbled at the edges" by the products of Man's animal breeding.

There will still be many who cannot accept this interpretation of the Exmoors' history and biology for, after all, it remains a theory. We have had to use logic and deduction as well as the evidence presented and this will not satisfy the academic, nor should it. We should welcome any serious study of the Exmoor Pony even if its result is to show us a less romantic explanation of why it is so like the British Hill Pony. Countless bones lie in the stores of museums awaiting study; the blood of horses and ponies may hold the clues to ancestral relationships. Hopefully, this book may stimulate other academics to take up the challenge. As Elaine Morgan wrote in *The Descent of Woman:*

an establishment, however august, cannot put paid to an idea by spluttering at it. Nor can it be snowed under by politely declining to discuss it. It can only be killed by people who have considered it, have found reasons for rejecting it, and are prepared to state them.[78]

In the absence of a more convincing explanation, I believe we have on Exmoor a zoological treasure, the last remnant of the original British Hill Pony.

Let us continue our travels now, returning to the present, and go to Exmoor to explore the Natural History of the remarkable Exmoor Pony.

CHAPTER 7

HOMES, HERDS AND HABITATS

Spanning the border between Devon and Somerset lies Exmoor, an expanse of high moorland patterned with deep, wooded combes and enclosed farmlands. Its northern boundary is a dramatic coastline of high cliffs falling away into the Bristol Channel and it extends some 20 miles southwards and 35 miles from east to west. Exmoor, the last refuge of our once widespread British Hill Pony, became a National Park in 1954 and some 265 square miles lie within the designated area. About thirty percent of this is moorland, heath or rough land. Rising from sea level to over 1,700 feet at Dunkery Beacon, Exmoor blends many elements of rural landscape and wilderness into a unique character.

To adequately portray Exmoor would require a book in itself. Perhaps even then it would fall short of conveying the indefinable magnetism of the place for those who love nature in its untamed state. S.H. Burton in his book first published in 1952 introduced Exmoor in this way:

Not in the whole of Britain is there more varied beauty in so small a space as can be found inside the boundaries of Exmoor National Park. It is so short a distance from North to South, from East to West; yet the contrast between, say,

the wooded valleys near Cloutsham and the brooding moor at Rowbarrows is so complete that they might be hundreds of miles apart instead of barely a mile. Perhaps this endless variety is the secret of Exmoor's fascination.[79]

Our visit to Exmoor and its ponies takes us only to the high moorland and we will tour the homes of the free-living pony herds shown in Figure 7.01. We will see where they live, how their herds are formed and function and the importance of their habitat. Yet for anyone to truly understand the natural history of the Exmoor Pony they must come to know Exmoor itself in all its variety. They must come to know the small hill farms which border the open moorland and appreciate the struggle to gain a living from Exmoor's inhospitable land. They must see Exmoor in high summer, with its walkers and tourists, showing its gentle face, then return again in winter to stand out on the moor in driving rain with all the beauty hidden in an Exmoor mist.

Exmoor is undoubtedly a remarkable place, quite unlike nearby and better known Dartmoor. Exmoor is known best perhaps for its population of wild Red Deer and for the classic love story of Lorna Doone set amidst its wild grandeur. We have seen how throughout history

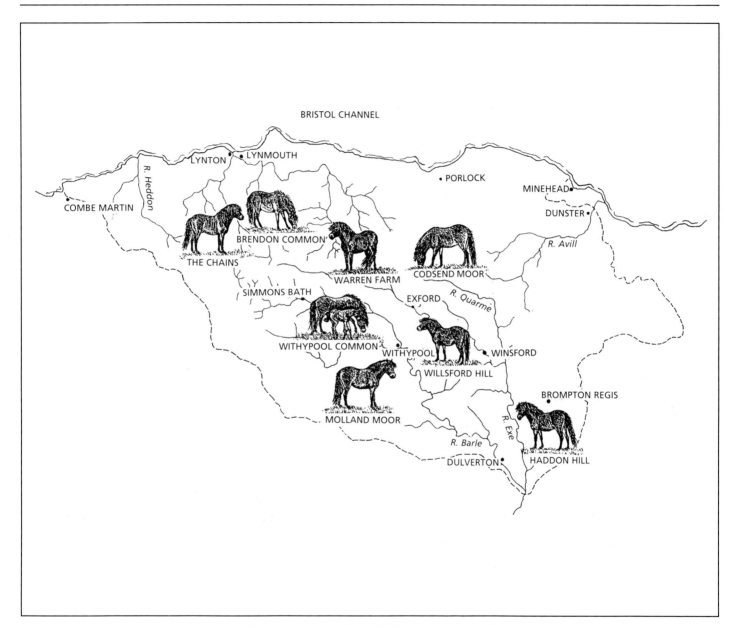

Figure 7.01 *Locations of the free-living Exmoor pony herds on Exmoor*

it has been an island of continuity amidst a sea of development and change. While changes have come to Exmoor, it retains that special character which is summed up by the National Park's own description *"Exmoor – where time runs slowly"*. Approaching Exmoor from Taunton, the National Park begins at the foot of the Brendon Hills and as you climb up the long hill it is as if you have passed through some unseen gateway and leave the pace and pressures of life behind.

Driving on through Wheddon Cross and Exford our first visit is to Winsford Hill and perhaps the best known of the Exmoor Pony herds, the Acland or Anchor Herd. Our tour will then take us to nearby Withypool Common, Molland Moor, a small enclosure on Codsend Moor and on to Warren Farm, Brendon Common, the Chains and Haddon Hill. For anyone wishing to visit the herds of true Exmoor Ponies running free, it is important to know exactly where to look, for they are to be found only in these few locations. People may visit Exmoor and think they have seen Exmoor Ponies but may have only encountered mongrel ponies which graze some of the other Commons in small numbers. These are ponies on Exmoor, not Exmoor Ponies.

Today's tour, in the summer of 1991, will allow us to meet the resident Exmoor Pony stallions with their herds. However, by the time these pages are read, some stallions will have been moved to other locations and there will be new characters to encounter on a visit to the moor.

The Homes of Exmoor Ponies

Winsford Hill

Between the valleys of the rivers Barle and Exe is a high ridge of heather moorland owned by the National Trust. This is Winsford Hill, an area of 1,760 acres rising to 1,395 feet above sea level. The B3223 Dulverton to Simonsbath road runs along the highest parts with the land to either side falling away into the river valleys.

Winsford Hill is very popular with visitors to Exmoor, offering spectacular views and lying just above Exmoor's most famous attraction, the clapper bridge, Tarr Steps. There is also an intriguing antiquity close to the lane

down to Winsford village, the Caractacus Stone, so called due to its inscription which translates as "Kinsman of Caractacus".

Most of the vegetation close to the roads is dominated by heather, while the slopes of Winsford Hill tend to be mixed communities of grasses covered extensively by bracken. There are only a few small and stunted trees, mainly hawthorn and rowan, and only small amounts of gorse present. Generally, Winsford Hill as a habitat offers very little rich vegetation and parts of it are quite impoverished. However, the lie of the land is such that there are many sheltered spots which animals may seek out to avoid the elements. There are also many places which cannot be seen from the roads which provide seclusion and privacy when animals wish to avoid the many visitors to Winsford Hill (or to elude me during field work!). In fact, many visitors to Winsford Hill remain unaware of its pony population as it is frequently possible to drive along all its roads and not to see a single pony.

Our historical review of the Exmoor Pony told the story of the famous Acland pony herd. As outlined, the Acland herd passed into the ownership of the Green family and today is owned by Mrs. Rose Wallace of Mounsey, Dulverton. The herd runs on Winsford Hill, leased from the National Trust, and is often referred to

Plate 51 *Loganberry A/201 (centre) and mares on Winsford Hill*

Plate 52 *Cracker A/9 (far right) with his herd on Winsford Hill*

as the Anchor Herd. This naming relates to the use of an anchor symbol as a brand mark rather than a herd number (as used by all other Exmoor herds). The ponies are managed by Mr Derek Sparkes from Old Ashway Farm, which nestles close by in the Barle valley.

The Acland herd of Exmoor Ponies live on Winsford Hill geographically isolated from all other ponies. There is no access to any other part of the moor where Exmoor Ponies live and there is no mongrel population sharing the area with them. Although in terms of ownership it is a single herd, numbering usually around forty adult ponies with a few youngstock, the natural arrangement is for the ponies to live in smaller herds each focusing upon a stallion. Usually there are two stallions present although on infrequent occasions there have been three. During this tour the two resident stallions are Loganberry A/201 and Cracker A/9.

Exploring Winsford Hill then we may encounter two main groups of ponies each with a stallion. We will undoubtedly also find a few small groups of mares, perhaps in twos or threes, a little separated from the nearby larger group. Searching for the ponies, we will also meet the sheep and cattle which are grazed there.

If we are very fortunate, and have chosen an early morning for our walk, we may be rewarded with a sight of the magnificent Red Deer, which favour some of the quieter parts of the area.

It may be that driving across Winsford Hill you may find the ponies without much effort, but there are always greater rewards for donning the boots and walking the moor, particularly at dawn or dusk. You may come upon the ponies on a summer evening at one of their favoured water-holes where the mares wade into the pool to drink and foals race and chase amidst the rushes. You might trek up onto the Hill amidst a February snow-storm and look out across the frozen heather at stillness, only to hear suddenly from behind a stand of gorse a snorting and whinnying. You may find the ponies scraping the snow off their food, their thick coats protecting them from the elements.

This then is the home of the Acland ponies, Winsford Hill. It is a home of great beauty but a demanding habitat for any animal. From its high point at Wambarrows we can look westwards across the Barle valley to the village of Withypool and its Common, our next destination and another of these few precious homes of the Exmoor Pony.

Withypool Common

Withypool Common lies to the west of the quiet village of Withypool and is an undulating area of heather and grass moorland. It rises between 850 and 1,398 feet above sea level. The river Barle winds across the narrowest part of the Common and on through the village. There are stunning views upstream towards the ancient hill fort of Cow Castle. Three roads cross Withypool Common and together with the river divide it naturally into three main areas, Withypool Hill, Brightworthy Barrows and Bradymoor.

Withypool Hill is a place of interest for archaeologists as it boasts the best example of a stone circle on Exmoor, although the unwary walker is more likely to trip over the stones than be astounded by them. The area is mainly covered by heather. The highest point of the Common is Brightworthy Barrows, separated from Withypool Hill by the South Molton road. It rises steeply out of Knightoncombe and is the remotest part of the Common. It is mostly an area of mixed heather and grass moorland with gorse and bracken but there is also an area of purple moor grass near Green Barrow. On the northern side it falls again steeply into Dillacombe and across to the lane leading to Landacre Bridge which crosses the river. Beyond the lane there are grassy slopes which drop steeply down to the river.

Beyond the the Barle lies Bradymoor which rises from the river to the Common's northern boundary and this is again mixed heather and grass moorland with gorse and bracken. There are a few hawthorn and rowan trees, but far less than on Winsford Hill.

Many visitors are attracted to the area by Landacre Bridge where the river is usually shallow and children can delight in searching for small fish. The bridge itself is the oldest packhorse bridge on Exmoor and behind it lies the farm of Lanacre. Withypool Common was originally administered by the Lord of the Manor, the owner of Lanacre Farm. This system survived until 1922 when the payment of dues was ended. The Common today is managed by the Withypool Commoners' Association which came into being in 1949 after a period in which local farmers had worked for the welfare of the Common and had persuaded the County Council to replace gates across the roads with cattle grids.

Commoners' rights are attached to twenty-three farms and properties which are close to or border Withypool Common. Thus their owners or tenants can graze animals upon the Common according to these rights and within the rules of the Commoners' Association. Until fairly recently, the regulations were that sheep could graze the area from April to December but must then over-winter on their home farms. Cattle could live out all year but must be fed in winter off the Common. Only the ponies were permitted to live independently and continuously throughout the year. The rules now also permit the grazing of cattle and sheep on the Common during the winter. We will consider the effects of this change of management later in the book. The numbers of grazing animals are limited under the Commoners' rights, relating to the acreage of the farms. It is not a place favoured by the Red Deer.

The 1,923 acres of Withypool Common have long been home to free-living Exmoor Ponies, perhaps even before 1818. Today a population of around 40 adult ponies live there. Number 23 herd is owned and managed by Mr Fred Milton of Weatherslade Farm and Number H8 herd by Mrs Creenagh Mitchell of Knighton. The herd of mongrel mares which used to share the Common has gone now but one or two mongrel mares may occasionally run with the Exmoors.

Part of the Commoners' agreed system is that only true Exmoor stallions may be put on the Common, hence ensuring that no crossing damages the breeding of the ponies. As on Winsford Hill it is usual to find two stallions on the Common. The ponies focus into two main herds, although this can be easily disrupted as we will see later. In 1991, the resident stallions, are Mrs Mitchell's Dazzling Boy 85/32 and Mr Milton's Prince Harry II 23/202 and they run with around 25 mares and a few geldings. 1990 saw the end of an era; the stallion Golden Gorse died aged twenty seven, having spent his whole life on Withypool Common. Prince Harry II, his son, carries on the line.

We will become more familiar with the ponies of

Plate 53 *Ponies from No. 23 herd on Withypool Common*

Plate 55 *Prince Harry II (23/202) crossing the River Barle on Withypool Common*

Plate 54 *Creenagh and Bob Mitchell with Heather Moonshine 78/46 at Knighton*

Plate 56 *Dazzling Boy 85/32 (right) with visiting mare Acacia A/299*

Withypool Common as we explore their natural history further because these Exmoors were the subject of three years' intensive research back in the '70s. This will be referred to as "the Withypool study". The Withypool ponies were selected because unlike Winsford Hill, there are very few places on Withypool Common where the ponies can conceal themselves. Also, the Common offers a much more varied array of habitat types to study.

Yet visits to Withypool Common can be so much more than just field trips to study the ponies. There are many wonderful experiences that can make this part of Exmoor draw you back again and again. The sight of the first foals of summer revelling in the sun, while buzzards mew overhead. Later, as the moon rises, those foals racing in sheer joy, silhouetted against the sky. The beauty of Landacre bridge, a kingfisher perched on the thorn tree beside it, the hour too early for visitors. And once a dawn, when a stag wandered quietly through the pony herd, intent on its path towards Cow Castle and unaware of its watcher.

As with all the homes of the free-living Exmoor Ponies, Withypool Common is a fully enclosed area and its ponies are isolated from all other pony populations, unless there is human interference. Just occasionally a careless walker will leave a gate open which gives access to a pathway to Molland Moor and there have been a few instances of a stallion visiting its neighbours briefly. However, these neighbours are also Exmoor Ponies and Molland Moor is next on our itinerary.

Molland Moor

Despite its local name, Molland Common, this is not really common land as with Withypool, but is part of the Molland estate, and as such is private land in a single ownership. It lies along the southern boundary of the National park and extends just over 2,000 acres. Several lanes cross the area but carry far less traffic than on Winsford Hill or Withypool Common as fewer visitors seem to visit Molland. For those who do, the views across to Dartmoor in the distance are breathtaking.

Molland Moor is made up of extensive flat regions separated by small valleys following the streams which cross it. In the northern part of the Moor is an area known locally as "Soggy Moor" which is very wet and boggy. According to local memory, a tank sank beneath the mire here during exercises in the Second World War. Molland Moor was also reputedly inhabited by a Puma back in the '70s, long before sightings of the "Beast of Exmoor" began to be reported.

Like Winsford Hill, the vegetation of Molland Moor is predominantly rather poor heather-dominated communities, without the areas of grass moor found on Withypool Common. Again, a few hawthorn and rowan trees struggle to exist on this exposed ridge but there is a small wooden combe on the southern flank.

It is a quiet part of Exmoor and as such often favoured by the deer in search of their peaceful existence. Cattle and sheep are grazed on the Moor and it is home to our third population of Exmoor Ponies. These are herd number 99 and belong to the Dart family of Great Champson, Molland. A single stallion, Prince Arthur 23/142 who was bred on Withypool Common, ran with a herd of about seventeen mares until recently. Often the ponies formed several small groups. Sadly, in May 1991, Prince Arthur was killed in a road accident. Whilst the mares are indeed Exmoor Ponies, unfortunately only about seven of them have been officially registered. With so few herds living free and so few habitats available, these ponies of Molland Moor are of great importance. Every encouragement must be given to ensuring the continuation of the herd.

From this large expanse of heather and bog, we now journey to a quite different location, where Exmoor Ponies live in great isolation. We travel back through Withypool and Exford, out onto the Cloutsham road to Codsend Moor. Shortly after leaving Molland Moor though, we come to the Sandyway pub which looks out across a large enclosure of moorland, known as Lydons Moor. A group of six Exmoor mares live within this enclosure, belonging to Mrs Mary Werner of Twitchen. These mares form herd number 44, but run without a herd stallion, so are not truly a herd in its natural sense.

Plate 57 *Herd No. 99 near Litton Water on Molland Moor*

Plate 58 *Prince Arthur (23/142) and young mare on Molland Moor*

Codsend Moor

On the south-west flank of Dunkery Beacon, above the River Quarme, lies Codsend Moor. This small area, of about 1 square mile, slopes down from 1,500 to 1,000 feet above sea level. It is divided up into a series of rectangular enclosures of around a hundred acres each which afford views of Winsford Hill across the Exe valley.

The enclosures, whilst small, are relatively rich habitats for grazers in moorland terms, as grass predominates without bracken cover. Cattle, sheep and Exmoor Ponies share the second Codsend enclosure which covers 111 acres. Two streams rise in the enclosure, creating boggy ground, especially in the central parts.

To visit Codsend Moor, the car must be left behind and the path to Dunkery Beacon followed. The enclosures then lie to the right of the footpath but with their thick beech boundary hedges, many walkers must pass the ponies without realising they are there. The land is private and no footpaths actually cross it, so Codsend is a very remote and undisturbed home for Exmoors, a fact reflected in the shyer behaviour of this herd. Those wishing to visit the Codsend ponies should make arrangements with their owners.

These Exmoor Ponies form No. 12 herd and belong to the Western family of West Hawkwell Farm, Luckwell Bridge. The herd is a small one, as its home is so restricted, and a single stallion, Hawkwell Caligula 12/136, runs with just twelve mares. For a short period the ponies were released onto the open moor running from Dunkery Beacon to Porlock Common, there being no cross-bred stallion on the area. However, the experiment was curtailed because the Exmoor Ponies were drawn to the coastal vegetation and made their home dangerously close to the main Minehead to Lynmouth coast road. These rare ponies could not be placed at such risk. Hopefully, once a new cattle grid prevents access to the main road, these ponies may again be liberated onto the larger area of Dunkery.

As with all the free-living groups of Exmoors, the Codsend ponies live out on the moor all year round. Because their enclosure is so unnaturally small they cannot always live an entirely independent life. The vegetation is restricted in quantity and variety. So, in extreme conditions, a small amount of hay may be used to supplement their natural diet. However, the resources of Dunkery Beacon are potentially available to them as the ponies are well able to break out of this enclosure if they choose to.

Codsend Moor is thus an isolated home for Exmoor Ponies. It is an eerie place with its own legend of a girl who perished in its bog. Yet it can be a stunningly beautiful place, free from people, the breeze carrying the calls of lapwing and curlew, while hares race across its lower slopes. The ponies seem to share the resentment of intrusion which all Codsend's wild inhabitants display.

The Forest of Exmoor

In our tour of Exmoor Pony herds so far, we have visited enclosures of varying sizes which lie on the fringes of the Forest of Exmoor. Now we must set out to find the Exmoor Ponies which live on the Forest itself.

In 1980 the National Park Authority, responding to concerns about the future of the Exmoor Ponies, made a real commitment to their conservation by establishing two herds to be owned and managed by the authority themselves. It was a momentous step forward in the conservation drive because for the first time some Exmoor Ponies came under the protection of a body responsible to the public. It was also a high profile statement of how important the conservation of the true Exmoor Pony was deemed.

With great historical significance, one herd was located back on the Forest of Exmoor. The ponies were returned to a home they had probably held for thousands of years, having lost it to the economic drive for ever more sheep during the late eighteen hundreds. To see this herd it is necessary to make arrangements with

Right: Plate 59 *No. 12 herd on Codsend Moor*

Inset: Plate 60 *Mr Bill Western and Mrs Gill Langdon with Hawkwell Lady Margaret (12/82)*

the National Park for this entails a visit to Warren Farm as the herd grazes out on the inaccessible moorland beyond.

Warren Farm lies off the Exford to Simonsbath road up a long track which winds up the side of a cleave and crosses the River Exe. S.H. Burton was greatly impressed by Warren and described it thus:

Surrounded by this magnificence, Warren Farm is splendid in its loneliness. Few homesteads in England can rival Warren in the romantic appeal of its setting. Faced by the steep walls of the valley, backed by one of the loneliest and loveliest stretches of the moor, the farm is Wordsworthian in its austere grandeur; "alone amid the heart of many thousand mists".

The farmhouse was built around 1842 and is a fine example of the buildings constructed by Frederic Knight. Today Warren is the home farm for the Exmoor Ponies which form herd number H52.

The ponies live free out on the vast expanse of open moorland which lies north of the farm. They can wander over some 2,000 acres of this, restricted by the deer fences which cross the Forest. The moorland here is bleak and uncompromising, a place of little natural shelter. The soil is sparse and peaty and mainly heather covered but there are also many wet areas with moor rush and deer sedge growing in tussocks out of the bogs. There are no real footpaths across the moor here and walkers have to follow the animal pathways. In consequence few people visit this remote place and the ponies therefore have little contact with visitors.

A herd of 13 mares lives with one stallion, currently Knightoncombe Lackey H8/61, a son of Dazzling Boy who runs on Withypool Common. There are no other ponies on this part of the moorland but they share their home with cattle, sheep and deer. This isolated part of Exmoor is well liked by the Red Deer as it receives so little disturbance. It was on a walk from Warren Farm, out across the bogs and heather, that the then Head Warden Cdr Jim Collins and I watched a herd of 19 stags quietly resting and feeding, a sighting never bettered in either's experience.

Plate 61 *Knightoncombe Lackey (H8/61) with his herd beyond Warren Farm*

The ponies on the Forest beyond Warren are living in perhaps the most natural surroundings of any of the Exmoor herds today. Although just fourteen, where once many hundred roamed according to historical record, their habitation of the Forest once again is undoubtedly of great importance. The Exmoor Ponies have reclaimed a home that was rightfully theirs.

Brendon Common

Back down the Warren Farm track to the Simonsbath road and our route now takes us through Simonsbath itself. As we pass the church on our right, images arise of the many pony sales held here before the church was built and how an Exmoor Pony was once roasted here for a feast! On up the hill and we take the B3223 Lynton road out across Brendon Common.

Crossing the Common in the 1970s and early '80s, the pony herds seen then were of crossbred animals, as was the case for much of the last hundred years. However, on Brendon Common as elsewhere on Exmoor, the numbers of mongrel ponies seem to have fallen significantly over the last ten years, with no consequent increase in the numbers of Exmoor Ponies. This presumably reflects the poor economics of breeding ponies. There are still some cross-bred ponies on Brendon Common and of more interest to us, a group of eight Exmoor mares.

These Exmoor mares form herd number H67 and belong to Mr Len South of Farley Water Farm, Brendon. They cannot lead a totally free existence because they have to be brought onto their home farm to foal and then mate with an Exmoor stallion. With a cross-bred stallion running on the Common, this form of management is the only way to ensure that the mares are not covered by a non-Exmoor. Their home farm is however little different to the moor itself with vegetation of deer sedge, heather, bracken, a few thorn trees and areas of bog.

When out on Brendon Common, the mares can roam over some 2,138 acres of rolling heather moorland similar in nature to the land beyond Warren Farm but with the intrusion of the road and various footpaths. Several streams rise on the Common, flowing down into the famous Doone Valley and boggy areas lie at their sources. As elsewhere, the ponies share this home with sheep, cattle and Red Deer.

The Chains

Standing upon Brendon Common and looking westwards across Cheriton Ridge we can see higher land beyond, known as the Chains. This is an inhospitable place, forming the watershed for Exmoor. The rivers Barle, Exe and West Lynn have their sources on this remote part of the moor. The steep slopes are around 1,500 feet above sea level and are covered by blanket bog, the water table being very close to the surface. It is a very exposed and desolate region with no roads and just a single footpath skirting its eastern edge.

Until recently this was home to a breeding herd of Exmoor Ponies belonging to Mr G. Ford of Manor Farm, Cheriton. One stallion and about 25 mares, mostly of Withypool Common origin, formed herd number H23, running within an enclosure of 1,160 acres

extending over the high part of the Chains. Sadly, the Exmoor stallion has been replaced with a non-Exmoor animal and although the true Exmoor mares remain, their progeny is now cross-bred.

This is a loss to the breeding population which can be ill-afforded, not only because of the small numbers of free-living Exmoors in total but also because this herd was living such a natural life in its isolation. They shared their environment with a few cattle, sheep and deer but were rarely contacted by people. The Chains presented an important refuge where the laws of nature were pre-eminent. Trekking up onto this boggy wilderness and viewing the ponies, we can only hope that the next stallion to be used will once again be a true Exmoor.

Haddon Hill

The home of the second Exmoor National Park herd is quite a contrast to the isolation of the Forest, although no less harsh in its own way. To visit this herd we must travel down off the moor to Dulverton and up onto a high ridge above the Exe valley. Haddon Hill is a small area of heather moorland situated above Wimbleball Reservoir just within the boundary of the National Park. The reservoir was created in 1980 and attracts many visitors. Haddon Hill, with its views across the lake also became popular with walkers.

One stallion, Snoopy A/253, and six mares originally

Plate 62 *Herd H42's 1991 stallion, Snoopy (A/253)*

from the Acland herd live on the 400 acres of open heath and their home is high and bleak. The vegetation is mostly heather dominated and rather poor but there are also areas of grasses and gorse. Whilst most of the hill is very exposed, there are a few small stands of trees which afford a little natural shelter. The herd number is H42 and, as with the Warren herd, it is managed by the National Park Authority.

Whilst the Warren ponies are rarely in the company of humans, visitors are a regular factor in the lives of the Haddon ponies with walking and riding popular on the hill. The ponies share the area with sheep and deer but cattle are not grazed here. If visited on a summer day with the water glistening below, Haddon Hill seems an idyllic home for any animal. Return in winter when the temperature is near freezing and rain drives relentlessly across the hill and the true challenge to its inhabitants becomes obvious. As with all of the Exmoor Ponies' homes we have visited, only the toughest of animals can survive in such places.

The Free-Living Community

Our tour of Exmoor and the homes of its free-living Exmoor Ponies is at an end although we will return to Withypool Common to learn more of their way of life. We have visited all those places where these ponies live in natural surroundings, wandering over enclosures of open moorland ranging from just a hundred acres to several thousand. Some have been easy to find, by simply driving across popular parts of the moor, while others live out their lives without disturbance and must be sought on foot.

There are some free-living Exmoor Ponies in other parts of the country and one herd abroad. To see these requires a grand tour from Cornwall to Scotland and across the Channel to Denmark. Our itinerary begins with a visit to a herd which has only recently been established on a small outpost of moorland in Cornwall.

Visitors to Helman Tor, an archaeological site administered by English Heritage, overlooking Lostwithiel, now encounter a living reminder of the ancient past. The boggy moorland and granite outcrops are home to the

Plate 63 *A newly established free-living Exmoor herd on Helman Tor, near Lostwithiel*

stallion Tawbitts Mr Toff H17/3, six mares and a young colt who will take over as stallion in 1992. The herd has been established by Mr and Mrs Girdler of Higher Trevilmick Farm which lies on the flank of the Tor. The ponies have access to some of the rougher land on the farm and that, with the Tor, gives them some fifty acres for their home. The Tor itself has a mixed vegetation of grass, heather and bracken with plenty of gorse. The lie of the land and the granite rocks provide a home with plenty of shelter to be found.

The largest free-living herd away from Exmoor is in Cumbria and we travel north to a windswept fell near Brampton. Tarn House is a 6,000 acre expanse of rough moorland at about 1,000 feet above sea level and comparable to the environment on Exmoor. The vegetation is predominantly bent grasses with bracken and some gorse but there is heather, moss and cotton grass too. The lower parts of the area have some birch and holly trees which provide shelter. This wild and beautiful fell is home to herd number 14, owned by Mr Peter Dean of Kirkhouse, Brampton. The herd was formed in 1958 and ponies were bought from many different sources on Exmoor to ensure that the full span of bloodlines was

Plate 64 *Herd No. 14 at Tarn House, Cumbria*

represented. Eight female lines have been conserved within herd 14. Today, the stallion Crasus 14/75 runs with 14 breeding mares at Tarn House. They range over the full 6,000 acres except when the sheep which share the fell are lambing and the ponies are then restricted temporarily to a 150 acre enclosure. The youngstock are kept separately from the breeding herd and ten graze an enclosure of 112 acres at Talkin Fell nearby.

Like all the free-living groups away from Exmoor, herd 14 is important because its ponies, like those on Exmoor, are subject to the full effects of Nature in terms of survival. They act as reservoirs of animals from which the herds could be rebuilt if, perish the thought, any catastrophe befell the populations on Exmoor. Herd 14 would be particularly valuable due to the number of lines represented in it. We will return to this theme in the final chapter.

Before leaving Cumbria, we should visit the small village of Dockray-in-Matterdale near Penrith in the Lake District. We set out from the village across an empty landscape and on an isolated fell find the Exmoor Ponies of herd No.37 belonging to Miss Veronica Watkins. No stallion runs with the two mares and five geldings in this 100 acre enclosure, yet they are an important small group

because their owner has observed their free-living habits over many years. We will hear more of them later when we look at how Exmoor Ponies survive. For now, we look northwards from Cumbria and head for Scotland to find our last British free-living herd.

Seventy miles west of Inverness, the west coast of Scotland is a chaos of sea lochs, peninsulas and islands. Between Loch Broom and Little Loch Broom the land rises from sea level up to the heights of Ben Ghobhlach at 2,053 feet. Scoraig is a small community of a dozen or so households, situated towards the tip of the peninsula some 5 miles from the nearest road. This is a truly remote place, accessible only by walking those 5 miles along a narrow cliff path or by boat across Little Loch Broom. Four thousand acres of common grazing land is now home to a herd of Exmoor Ponies owned by Mrs. Debbie Davy at Achmore and the herd number is 21. A visit to this herd is a real expedition but those who have made the long trek return with tales of stunning scenery and ponies living in natural splendour. Currently, Mr P. Dean's stallion Octavius 14/57 is on loan to Scoraig and he lives there with ten mares and two filly foals. Another herd 14 stallion, Domitian 14/82 will join Octavius on Scoraig in the near future.

Plate 65 *Exmoors at Scoraig, North-West Scotland*

The herd ranges over the hillside moving between the sea-shore and the mountain-side up to 2,000 feet. A deer fence runs down to the beach and splits the grazings into two enclosures. The hillside has a thin peat soil which is eroded in many places so that rocky areas alternate with peat bogs. It is a harsh place for humans and ponies alike for over 60 inches of rain falls a year and it is always windy. The wind creates a chill factor which wipes out the advantages of the closeness of the Gulf Stream. It is a cold, wet place in winter. The Exmoor Ponies share this home with cattle, sheep, Red Deer and feral goats. The available menu is principally heather, sedges, rushes, moss and bog grasses. There is virtually no gorse or trees and just a few stands of bracken. Down by the sea there are a few grassy lawns which are heavily grazed by all the animals. In winter

the cattle are removed onto the crofts but the sheep and ponies stay out all year.

The existence of a free-living herd at Scoraig is important in a historical context, for the British Hill Pony has returned to a former home in Scotland. The wildness of Scoraig means that its Exmoors are another important breeding group where Nature will continue to shape the ponies.

In order to visit our last free-living herd we must leave Britain and travel to Denmark. In 1963, a group of Exmoor Ponies were exported to the 400 acre island of Taero, south of Sealand, to establish a breeding herd. The ponies on Taero survive without any assistance on open grazing which constitutes about a third of the island. The vegetation is mixed grassland and there is one small wooded area which provides the only shelter.

Plate 66 *Exmoor herd on the Island of Taero, Denmark*

The ponies make use of this during the hot summers on the island but tend to stay out in the open during the cold winters. There is free access to the sea-shore as on Scoraig. About half a mile from Taero is Lilleo (Little Island) which is a narrow spit extending a further half mile. The ponies frequently wade out to Lilleo at low tide when the water is about three feet deep. They graze there during the day but are careful to return before the evening when high tide increases the depth of water to 6 feet.

Although some progeny have been sold out of the herd, there are no records of any new blood being introduced. Until recently, there were 17 ponies in the herd but this has been reduced to a smaller group of one stallion and four mares with foals. Whilst the foundation stock sent to Taero twenty eight years ago were registered Exmoor Ponies, none of their offspring were ever inspected or registered. The last registered mare died in 1990. Thus, the ponies remaining are un-registered and so their numbers are not included in the statistics that follow. We will be revisiting Taero though when we look at territories and diet.

Returning to Britain it is pleasing to finish this tour by planning some further visits in the future. New free-

living groups of mares and geldings have recently been established by the National Trust in Dorset and Devon and English Nature in Cornwall. Their primary purpose is to graze nature reserves but hopefully, they might one day become breeding herds. This would be a welcome boost to the population of Exmoors which remain under free- living conditions.

Population Size

Figure 7.02 shows the results of each census carried out since 1976 and the growth in numbers across all categories is very encouraging. Some 777 ponies (free-living plus domesticated) were located in the 1990/91 census. However, this is still a very small population size and the Exmoor rightly remains classified as a very rare animal. To put this in perspective, there are

	DATE OF CENSUS			
	1976 (counted)	1976 (+ estimates)	1985/86	1990/91
TOTAL POPULATION	450	536	507	777
Stallions	30	33	47	42
Breeding Mares	167	350	290	274
Non-breeding Mares	130			150
Geldings	113	140	170	166
Colts 2 and under	10	13	included above	71
Fillies 2 and under	included above	included above		74
DETAILS OF SUB-POPULATIONS				
Ponies abroad	31	58	30	40
Domesticated sub-population	348		365	580
Free-living sub-population	102		142	197
On Exmoor	88		115	138
Elsewhere	14		27	59
Stallions	8		9	11
Mares	94		133	121
Others (youngstock not included in stallions & mares plus geldings)	0		0	65

Figure 7.02 *Comparative census results*

about 950 Przewalski Horses, a recognised "endangered species", in zoos and reserves world-wide.

It may seem from our tour that free-living Exmoor Ponies are plentiful but this is not so. The herds we have visited totalled in April 1991 just 197 animals – 11 stallions and 121 mares, the rest youngstock and a few geldings. This is a tiny population and consequently very vulnerable. The fact that we have some 580 Exmoor Ponies also living in domesticated circumstances does not really provide adequate back-up to the free-living group. Where Exmoors are domesticated and several generations are bred away from moorland life, we cannot be sure that they will retain the ability to live naturally. We will examine this and its implications further later on.

So in assessing the state of the Exmoor race, we really have to look at the two sub-populations separately. On that basis, despite increasing by a marvellous 93% since 1976, the 197 free-living ponies remain exceptionally rare within a race which is in total rare by any standards.

Home Ranges

With our tour of the free-living herds now complete, we return to Withypool Common to find out more about how the ponies live and behave. Between 1974 and 1978 the ponies on Withypool Common were the subject of detailed scientific research, giving us an insight into how they use and relate to their moorland home.

Anyone visiting one location regularly begins to appreciate that there is some pattern to where the ponies may be found. There are places in which they are seen frequently and places which are used rarely or not at all. Unless they are on a particularly small area, such as Codsend, the ponies range over some but not all of the land available to them. With many animals there is a difference between the total environment available to them and the total area they actually use. The area they use regularly is their "home range".

A home range is the part of the environment an animal or herd of animals uses for its day to day life and is completely familiar with. It contains all the resources the herd needs for food, water, shelter and rearing the young. So, the range must be large enough to supply all the ponies' needs but is not limitless. This is because under truly natural conditions the farther animals wander, the more likely they are to encounter dangers. The smaller the range is, the better the ponies will know it. Thus when disturbed or frightened, they will know exactly the safe routes to follow and the places of refuge.

So a home range is a delicate balance between the need to wander in search of food, water and shelter and the need to restrict the herd to familiar ground. Such a relationship with the environment has obviously evolved in the totally natural state when wild ponies were subject to predation. The pattern of behaviour is fixed within their genes and persists because it still helps them to survive even today. Whilst not hunted, the ponies are subject to considerable disturbance and these home range responses enable them to minimise the stressful effects.

There is no set size for a home range because it depends upon the availability of food and water and the lie of the land. Ponies with access to rich grassland might require a smaller range than those on poorer heather moorland. However, the location of water-holes or rivers and the proximity of sheltered places can also determine whether the range will be large or small. In addition, the presence of other pony herds will have an influence because they will each be competing for the best home range.

Exmoor Pony Home Ranges

In 1974 when observations of the ponies began, there were two stallions on Withypool Common, Golden Gorse (23/69) aged eleven and Royal Duke (23/06) aged four. At that time, Royal Duke had just four mares regularly living with him in a group. This small herd was frequently to be found just a short distance from the main herd with Golden Gorse. By April 1975 Royal Duke had become more successful and his herd was comprised of ten mares. The increase came from mares which had left Golden Gorse's herd. By this time separate home ranges had begun to emerge. Generally, Golden Gorse's herd lived mainly north of the River

Plate 67 *A home range must include suitable places for rearing the young—mare and foal on Winsford Hill*

Plate 68 *A home range provides the necessary resources of food and water*

Plate 69 *Golden Gorse 23/69 (left)*

Plate 70 *Royal Duke 23/06*

Barle on Bradymoor, while Royal Duke and his mares occupied a home range between the river and Brightworthy Barrows.

However, the situation had not yet stabilised and when the ponies were released after the October gathering, one large herd formed, including both stallions, adopting the former range of Golden Gorse's herd. Eight mares resumed the home range south of the river, previously occupied by Royal Duke. This arrangement lasted until February 1976 when Royal Duke and three more mares rejoined the group south of the river.

After this the relationship between the two home ranges varied. Sometimes the ranges were totally separate, not overlapping at all, so that the two herds kept apart. At other times, the ranges overlapped considerably, although the herds rarely encountered each other, occupying any one area at different times. Even in months when overlapping ranges were recorded, the most favoured parts of those ranges, known as core areas, were still Bradymoor for Golden Gorse and his mares and between the river and Brightworthy Barrows for Royal Duke's herd.

Some light was shed upon why the home ranges were sometimes totally discrete by looking at which months

were involved. It emerged that during 1975 the herds kept to completely separate ranges during April, May and June (the main period of foaling and mating). This occurred again in 1976, continuing into July. This cannot be the whole explanation though, because after September, the ranges only overlapped for two further months and a more stable arrangement of non-overlapping home ranges developed.

Overall, the question of discrete or overlapping ranges seemed to relate to the relationship between the two stallions, obviously at its most sensitive during the breeding season. As time went on, Royal Duke matured, building his herd to equal that of Golden Gorse, who of course lost mares to him. The two stallions seemed to tolerate each other less and less. The result of this seems to have been that eventually, as if by gentlemens' agreements, they favoured a home range upon which the other did not encroach. Whilst they had kept mainly to their own areas north and south of the river, even when the total ranges did overlap, the river finally became recognised as a boundary between them.

This home range system does not mean that the herds never moved into each other's area, for home ranges refer to routine, day to day existence. There were occasions when something happened to frighten one

Plate 71 *Mare crossing the River Barle on Withypool Common*

or other of the herds and under those circumstances the normal arrangement was disrupted. One such occasion was when the local fox hunt crossed Withypool Common, the noise of the hounds alarming Royal Duke's herd. The ponies moved north of the river to a position close to Golden Gorse, perhaps for safety in numbers. On another occasion a group of riders galloped noisily towards the ponies and Royal Duke and his mares again sought the safety of Bradymoor. On neither occasion was there any response from Golden Gorse.

So a system of separate home ranges developed gradually between these two herds as the younger stallion matured. At the same time there were two herds sharing Winsford Hill. Their stallions were Mounsey Hill (10/44) and Hannibal (A/162). These stallions were aged five and six, and so were very close in their stage of maturity. Again, the home ranges seemed to be separate, with no overlapping recorded, although they were studied far less than those on Withypool Common.

Are Exmoor Ponies Territorial?

It might be tempting given such division of the available environment into separate ranges to talk of territories but this is not really appropriate. A territorial system is one in which the exclusivity of the home range is actively and positively maintained by behaviour involving aggression and display. Some equine species are truly territorial. Grevy's Zebra and the African Wild Ass both establish and defend territories by aggression, with stallions fighting at range boundaries. They also advertise the boundaries of their territories by marking them with large dung piles.

No signs of such behaviour between Golden Gorse and Royal Duke or between Mounsey Hill and Hannibal were seen or reported when out on the moor. Golden Gorse and Royal Duke did fight briefly on one occasion but this was after the gathering when on their home farm in a situation of enforced, unnatural proximity. Only one confrontation between them was witnessed on the Common, involving snorting, squealing and nipping each others' necks but they separated quickly and calmly went their own way. This was nowhere near the boundary between their ranges and nothing like fights witnessed occasionally between New Forest stallions. With these ponies, like Exmoors, serious confrontations seem reserved for situations where an unfamiliar stallion intrudes.

Relationships between neighbouring stallions which are well established rely more on low key snorting and squealing. On Withypool Common, one skirmish did occur between an intruding stallion and a young colt in 1990, involving both animals rearing up on hind legs but the youngster quickly withdrew. Immature Exmoor colts kept in close proximity to each other have been seen to play-fight as if practising the skills they might one day need.

Plate 72 *Pinkworthy Centaurium H9/5 (left) and Pinkworthy Corylus H9/6 play-fighting*

The boundaries between the Withypool Common ranges and those on Winsford Hill were walked regularly and there were no signs of large dung piles. However, in Cumbria and Scotland under free-ranging conditions, large accumulations of dung have been seen but unrelated to stallion interactions. So it does not seem as if Exmoor Ponies display territorial behaviour despite their tendency to develop separate home ranges. Yet could this be in some way related to their environment and the fact that there is little competition for females or food?

Studies of horses in various wild situations have suggested that territorial behaviour may evolve in response to conditions where herds have to compete for food or water, or where stallions have to compete strongly for enough mares. A great deal of light was shed on this when Dr Dan Rubenstein studied the feral horses living on the inhospitable Shackleford Island off the east coast of North America. The island, just 20 miles long and about half a mile wide, is a barren place where about 100 horses live free from human interference. It is thought they are descended from horses which swam ashore from shipwrecks.

Here the scientific study identified two different systems of home ranges operating. In the least impoverished part of Shackleford, the horses showed no territorial behaviour in maintaining their home ranges. However, the horses on the other two-thirds of the island did aggressively defend territories. These lived in an environment made up of three habitat types. There were areas of saltmarsh, grassy areas which occasionally had pools of brackish water and finally the beach habitat with dunes. The study concluded that in order to survive, the horses needed access to each of these three areas and thus it was crucial to ensure that a herd had a home range in which they were all available. This required each herd stallion to defend the boundaries of its range vigorously.

One instance of highly aggressive behaviour between Exmoor stallions is known. Until recently, the population on the island of Taero, in Denmark, numbered 17 including seven adult males. According to the caretaker of the island, there has been a considerable amount of fighting between them each spring. Three unsuccessful stallions were eventually forced off the island. Two swam about 2 miles to the nearby island of Bogo and one covered a similar distance, swimming to the mainland. When Helen Poulsen, an Exmoor Pony Society member, visited Taero in June 1991, she found that the ponies were in two groups:

> One of the two small herds into which the ponies are split consisted of seven ponies – one old stallion, one mare and foal, three colts and a filly. These were on Taero. The main group had waded out to graze on Lilleo and there was a younger stallion, three mares and foals and two yearling colts. The younger stallion had replaced the older male as the dominant herd stallion this spring.
>
> We decided to herd the ponies back onto Taero so that everyone could take a closer look. While the herd stood some way off-shore, the stallion approached us very warily, seemingly most concerned about the vehicle. Only when he had come onto Taero did the rest follow. Once back in close proximity to the other group, the older stallion was confronted by the dominant stallion and retreated out onto a spit. Also, there was a three year-old stallion which was on its own, having been "cast out" by the other ponies. He approached the herd but was quickly chased off by the dominant stallion.
>
> This lone male has obviously seen some vicious fighting and most of the males are scarred. The caretaker said that ponies had been forced through a double-strand barbed wire and electric fence during fights.[80]

Helen filmed the ponies during her visit and the behaviour between the stallions is fascinating to watch. Here we have Exmoors that have had to establish a hierarchy amongst the males through extensive fighting. This has led to the decision to sell off all the surplus males. What a contrast to the peaceful arrangements seen on Exmoor. On Tæro though, breeding females are a scarce resource and competition for the right to breed has produced this highly aggressive behaviour. The film records the dominant stallion dunging several times around his herd and driving other males away.

However, without a detailed study we cannot assess whether any true territories have been established.

We have learnt from comparing the Taero and Exmoor situations that inter-stallion behaviour and probably home range/territory establishment is variable. Where a resource is limited, as with females on the island, then stallions will develop their rivalry to its full extent. Most Exmoor Ponies live today in places, which though fairly harsh environments, do have food and water available throughout the Commons or enclosures. They live in populations where there are far more mares per stallion than would occur in the wild. Thus there are no severe pressures upon the gentlemens' agreements which seem to exist.

However, as the ponies have never been watched continuously, we do not know whether some confrontation or fight is involved in defining the boundaries between exclusive ranges at the outset. There were no such reports from local sources. The demands of defending a territory are great. Where space and resources are not constraints, and where there is a low density of males with numerous females, perhaps the territorial instincts become replaced by avoidance of contact. Stallion interaction declines to simply repelling any challenging approach by another male. No animal will waste energy defending a territory if it is not crucial to survival or to the chances of it reproducing.

On some occasions the Withypool herds were approached by unfamiliar geldings and the stallions reacted aggressively, kicking, biting and chasing the intruder away but not out of their home range. A mature stallion does appear to tolerate juvenile males within close proximity, as Golden Gorse tolerated Royal Duke at first. Both these stallions accepted the presence of two yearling colts in 1978. It may be important that such young males have been born into the herds rather than introduced. In 1976, Dazzling Boy was released as a two-year old onto Withypool Common but was unsuccessful in establishing himself. He was driven off the Common onto an adjoining enclosure and had obviously been on the receiving end of some aggressive behaviour. We do not know though whether this was the result of one of the resident stallions objecting to his presence or whether he was disciplined by mares, who can administer some fairly rough justice to inexperienced colts.

Changes Following Royal Duke's Departure

The home range system described for Withypool Common was one which evolved as the relative maturity of the two stallions equalised. It developed into this fairly stable division of the Common into separate ranges for normal existence but with a mutual tolerance of overlap if disturbance occurred. Unfortunately, when Royal Duke was removed from the Common in 1980, the study had come to an end and so the emergence of the new herd stallion was not charted in such detail. He was a son of Royal Duke, called Aga (23/138), and was only a yearling when Royal Duke's reign ended. Only two foals were registered as by Aga during his seven years on the Common, and those were in 1986 which suggests that perhaps like Royal Duke he had to establish his herd gradually. Royal Duke achieved a stable group of ten to twelve mares when he was five. Sadly Aga was killed in a collision with a car in 1986.

With no resident stallion in the second herd, the home range and stallion behaviour undoubtedly changed. More mares lived with Golden Gorse and he extended his range once again to overlap the second herd's considerably. During 1988 and 1989 a mature Exmoor stallion escaped onto Withypool Common and for a short time the two herd system returned, although we don't know if he poached mares back from Golden Gorse.

Dazzling Boy had been released again when older, during the later part of Royal Duke's time on the Common and did successfully establish a small herd. However, he was not continuously present as he and his mares were often taken back onto their home farm during the breeding season. When free, his herd favoured the area between Withypool Hill and the road down to Landacre Bridge and this home range seems to have overlapped with Royal Duke's. Perhaps this arrangement was acceptable as there was a respite from it when the stallions were most aware of each other during the early Summer. Even when Dazzling Boy was absent, his group of mares continued as a separate group, occupying the same home range and were not absorbed into Royal Duke's herd.

In 1990, Golden Gorse died and this had a profound effect on the herds. A two-year old son of this marvellous old stallion was tolerated by him and living on the Common but Prince Harry II (23/202) had failed as yet to establish his own herd. Without Golden Gorse, the main herd system broke down and it was almost impossible to predict where the mares would be. Dazzling Boy and his mares were temporarily living on a neighbouring enclosure, so no mature stallion was present. The mares divided up into smaller groups ranging from Bradymoor to Withypool Hill. It is reported that the mares had become unsettled for a month or two before Golden Gorse's actual death, perhaps indicating his failing strength and suggesting he may have died of natural causes.

An eleven year-old stallion, Prince Arthur (23/142), was brought to the Common from neighbouring Molland Moor in an attempt to restore the herd structure and breeding activity but soon disappeared. He had returned to his former home, proving that the ponies can find ways through the boundaries of the enclosure if the urge is strong enough. Prince Harry II was seen mostly in the company of his mother and did not attempt to assume the role of herd stallion. Interestingly, an older gelding living in the herd began to behave much as a herd stallion would do and provided some focus for the confused mares.

Thus, the mares of Withypool Common will have to reform their social structure around the young Prince Harry II as he matures and it will be interesting to see how this process develops. If only we had continuous study of these ponies we might clarify just how the patterns of ranges evolve. From this study of the herds on Withypool Common we have seen that home ranges are an expression of many environmental and behavioural factors. They must be big enough to serve all the herd's needs but no bigger. Home ranges of all female groups will readily overlap, but the inter-relationship between stallions creates pressures to minimise contact. With sufficient resources available to all and enough mares to permit natural sized groups for both stallions, the Common is shared peaceably and there is no need to waste effort defending a whole range; driving off intruders is enough.

During the period when Golden Gorse and Royal Duke were both running with herds of about fourteen mares each, there was also a herd of mongrel mares living on the Common. These were taken onto their home farm to mate with a stallion as no cross-bred entire males are allowed on the area. The mares tended to stay close to their farm as they had to be fed during the winter. Their range encompassed the south flank of Withypool Hill, overlapping just slightly with Royal Duke's. The Exmoor stallion seemed to have little interest in these mares, confirming the racial prejudice often seen with Exmoors which tend to favour their own kind given a choice, even in domestic circumstances. However, just once within the four year study, the mongrel herd and Royal Duke's herd were seen together. A combined herd formed and stayed together just three hours. The mongrel mares then returned south with no attempt by Royal Duke to keep them. Perhaps the mongrel herd had been frightened and this was similar to Royal Duke's herd seeking refuge on Bradymoor.

The Size of Home Ranges

The studies of the herds on Withypool Common, Winsford Hill, Molland Common and Codsend Moor showed that the size of a home range is related to the richness of the food available and its distribution, and to competition for food from other ponies and from sheep, cattle and deer. It may be that availability of and competition for water and shelter might similarly influence range size. Also, the social organisation of the herds and the stallion inter-relationships are factors affecting the extent of a home range.

The diagrams in Figures 7.03 to 7.06 show the position and sizes of all the herds' ranges studied back in the '70s and it is clear that they varied considerably from place

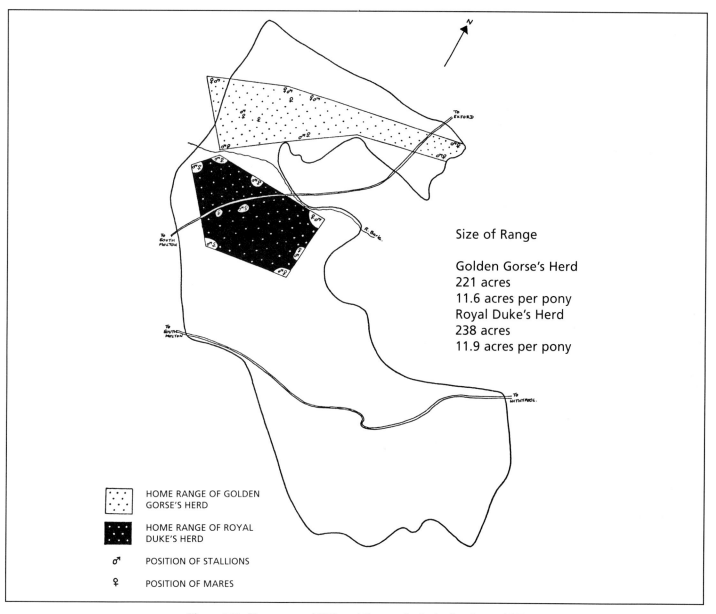

Size of Range

Golden Gorse's Herd
221 acres
11.6 acres per pony
Royal Duke's Herd
238 acres
11.9 acres per pony

HOME RANGE OF GOLDEN
GORSE'S HERD

HOME RANGE OF ROYAL
DUKE'S HERD

♂ POSITION OF STALLIONS

♀ POSITION OF MARES

Figure 7.03 *Home ranges of Withypool Common herds, April to August 1977*

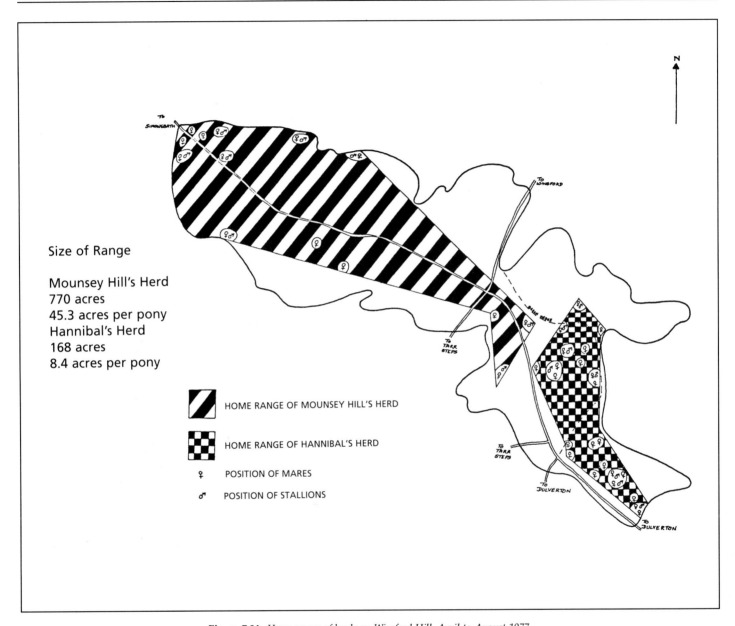

Size of Range

Mounsey Hill's Herd
770 acres
45.3 acres per pony
Hannibal's Herd
168 acres
8.4 acres per pony

⧄ HOME RANGE OF MOUNSEY HILL'S HERD

▦ HOME RANGE OF HANNIBAL'S HERD

♀ POSITION OF MARES

♂ POSITION OF STALLIONS

Figure 7.04 *Home ranges of herds on Winsford Hill, April to August 1977*

to place. However, as the number of ponies in the herds also varied it is easier to look at the ranges in terms of size per pony. If that is calculated we are still left with differences which need explaining.

It seems that the smaller ranges of Withypool Common and Codsend Moor reflect the better quality of food available to those herds compared to Winsford Hill and Molland Moor. If the vegetation of each area is looked at in terms of being rich, intermediate or poor, Codsend is entirely rich grazing and Withypool Common has 30% rich, 60% intermediate and 10% poor. Both Winsford Hill and Molland Moor have only tiny amounts of rich vegetation and 30% and 45% poor vegetation respectively.

Yet the richness and availability of their food is not the full explanation of the varying range sizes because we still have the wide difference between the two herds on Winsford Hill with no obvious difference between the vegetation in each range. Perhaps some factor of water distribution or shelter might account for this and obviously more studies are needed to fully comprehend just why one range should be much bigger than another.

All of the herds on Exmoor that were studied lived within enclosures of less than 2,500 acres. Are the boundaries of their homes limiting factors in themselves? The only situation where ponies have been observed on a much bigger area to date has been on the Cumbrian Fells, where the single group had a home range of about 6,000 acres. However, without a detailed study of the vegetation and geography of the area we cannot be sure that this suggests bigger ranges if the ponies have more freedom. As ever, far more research is needed.

So there are no hard and fast rules about how much land an Exmoor Pony herd needs or will use. Their home ranges are as big as they need to be and as small as they can be.

Home ranges are therefore that part of the animals' environment over which they roam and which represents home. They are made up of places with which they are completely familiar and in which they will live given a lack of disturbance. Walk out over Withypool Common or any of the other homes of the ponies and you will find clear trails used regularly by them, just as we use clearly defined roads and paths. Watch the herds regularly and favourite places are soon identifiable; places for times of sunshine and others for when it rains or snows, and places of seclusion when visitors invade their home. So a home range may be the whole area which the herd utilises but Exmoor Ponies show various preferences for certain parts of their environment. If we are to understand the patterns of their habitat use, we must find out about these preferences and what motivates the ponies to favour some places above others.

Favourite Places

We now stay on Withypool Common for a while to investigate which parts of the ponies' home ranges are used most. Figure 7.07 shows the places preferred during the period April 1975 to March 1977. Those north of the river are the preferred or "core" areas shown by Golden Gorse's herd and those south of the river are the core areas for Royal Duke's herd. Core areas are thus those parts of a home range which are used most frequently.

These areas were identified, as were the home ranges themselves, by recording the locations of all the ponies at regular intervals over thousands of hours. The most frequently used places were mapped out and those areas then studied carefully to identify what attracted the ponies to them. With both herds there is a similar story.

Firstly, unsurprisingly, the core areas were in places where there were high proportions of the ponies' favourite food plants. There was also a definite relationship to the location of water. The most intensively used places were areas close to streams or liable to occasional water cover. This was true throughout the period but the preference was even greater during the drought conditions in the summer of 1976. The ponies probably find the grass growing near streams to be of better quality and also drink from the streams. This explains why the herds did not make regular visits to the river to drink.

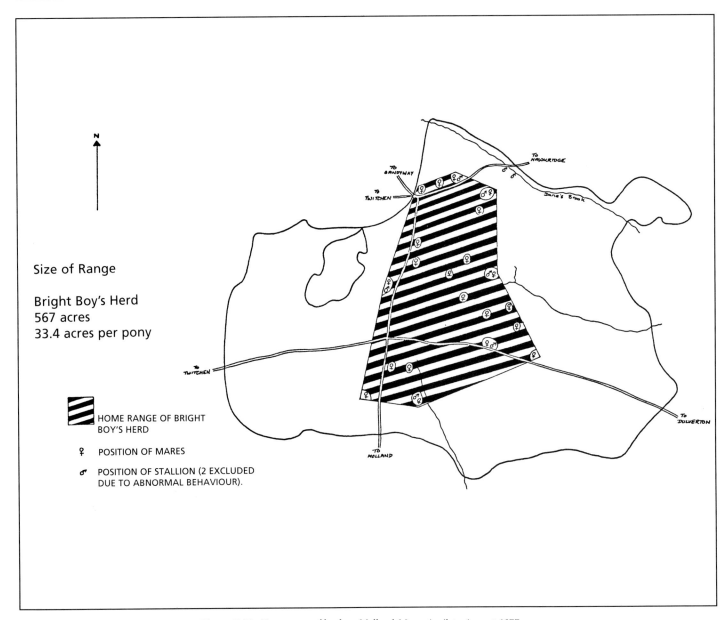

Size of Range

Bright Boy's Herd
567 acres
33.4 acres per pony

HOME RANGE OF BRIGHT BOY'S HERD

♀ POSITION OF MARES

♂ POSITION OF STALLION (2 EXCLUDED DUE TO ABNORMAL BEHAVIOUR).

Figure 7.05 *Home range of herd on Molland Moor, April to August 1977*

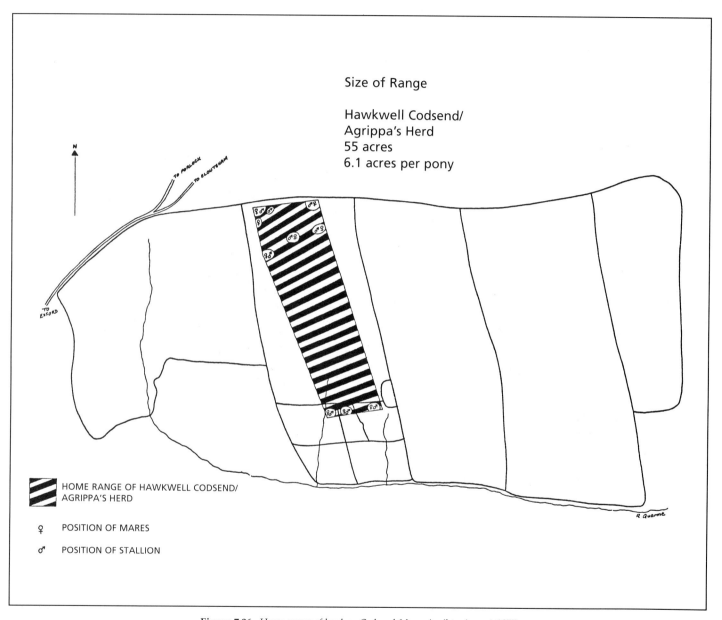

Size of Range

Hawkwell Codsend/
Agrippa's Herd
55 acres
6.1 acres per pony

HOME RANGE OF HAWKWELL CODSEND/
AGRIPPA'S HERD

♀   POSITION OF MARES

♂   POSITION OF STALLION

Figure 7.06 *Home range of herd on Codsend Moor, April to August 1977*

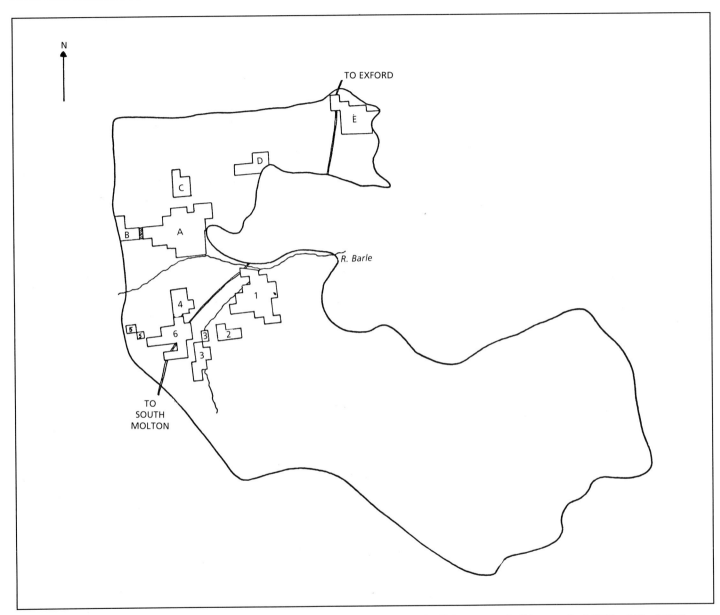

Figure 7.07 *Core areas in Golden Gorse's herd's home range (A–E) and in Royal Duke's herd's home range (1–6) between April 1975 and March 1977*

Both herds had some favoured places which offered them good shelter either from nearby hedges or from the lie of the land. Area C on the diagram is a sheltered hollow at the top of one of the streams draining Bradymoor and areas E and 5 are well protected by the boundary hedges. Areas 2 and 3 lie in Dillacombe sheltered by the land rising either side of the stream.

The places used most by the ponies seem to have been uninfluenced by the presence of roads or footpaths. There was no attraction to or avoidance of these features. The selection of the core areas was a response by the ponies to the natural factors in their habitat.

The free-living herd at Scoraig in Scotland have a far more varied choice of habitats available to them and their owner Mrs Davy has observed that their patterns of use relate to natural factors:

> The ponies have definite circuits as they move around the hill – I think these are seasonal and dictated by the weather. In summer they will go fairly high on the shoulders of Ben Ghobhlach and can be difficult to find. In good weather they'll also graze around the lighthouse on Cailleach Head which is on high cliffs and very exposed but in bad weather they are rarely there. Most of the time they move along the north shore or near Camas an Lochain, a fresh water lochan several acres in extent in a basin towards the west of the peninsula. In very poor weather they are often there as it is sheltered or in the sheltered valleys which run back from the north shore. In very snowy weather they're often found on Carn Dearg, a rocky area jutting out into Loch Broom, bisected by small steep valleys, probably because there is often less or even no snow there when the rest of the peninsula is white.[81]

Moving Around the Range

Whether we ride horses or not, most of us are familiar with the four paces of movement which horses or ponies can adopt, the walk, the trot, the canter and the gallop. These are natural movements for a pony, not something taught to create a riding animal. Each pace is used at some point in the daily lives of free-living ponies.

With all animals, life is a constant balance between expending energy and obtaining food to supply energy. Therefore the effort devoted to any activity is usually the minimum so that energy is not wasted. So it is with the Exmoor Ponies and the majority of all movement throughout their home range is at a walking pace. There are however two distinguishable types of walking.

As the ponies graze, they slowly move forwards by means of small paces which are essentially undirected. Different individuals in the herd move in various directions so that the herd gradually spreads itself over its chosen grazing area. This is behaviour we might call "wandering". The other form of walking is "travelling". This is where all the members of the herd move from one area to another. It is purposeful and directional, with all individuals walking along the same route. Most of the movement of the ponies is wandering and this can be seen throughout most of the ponies' day but travelling was recorded in just 20% of the hours studied on Withypool Common. In most cases, the wandering of the herd involves moving no more than 100 yards or so while travelling by its very nature takes the herds 400 yards on average.

The purposeful walking to move the herd from one area to another occurred mostly at dawn, then around noon and again at dusk. Although no night studies were possible within the Withypool Common study, the ponies were known to have travelled again during most nights, by where they were found the next morning.

The ponies trot on various occasions, sometimes as part of normal movement and sometimes as part of their response to being disturbed. Once a herd has begun travelling, the last few individuals may delay leaving and then will trot to catch up the herd. Their approach at a trot will often stimulate the others in front of them to trot for a short distance. Also, the foals will often have to trot in order to match their mother's walking pace.

If the ponies are approached by people, a regular minor disturbance, they usually walk away maintaining a certain distance between themselves and the people. If several people approach and are insufficiently calm and quiet, the ponies often trot away over a larger distance and do not usually resume their original position.

Free-living Exmoor Ponies only canter or gallop infrequently, with the exception of young foals which do both regularly as part of play. Stallions will canter and gallop when chasing away intruding geldings or in pursuit of a mare before mating. Mostly though, these faster paces are reserved for "fleeing" (the response to major disturbances). Apart from when the ponies are gathered off their moorland enclosures once a year, as part of the management of the herds, fleeing happens relatively rarely and usually involves disturbance of the herds by riders.

On Withypool Common, during the three years of observations, there were three occasions when fleeing was seen and these involved the riders following the fox hunt or rather noisy approaches by riders. In each case the distances the ponies covered were not that much greater than normal travelling distances but the ponies either cantered or galloped. These occasions of escaping from some threat each involved the herd crossing the river. Perhaps placing themselves beyond such a natural boundary removed the need to run further from the disturbance. This type of reaction has been recorded for

Plate 73 *Mare and foal fleeing*

Mountain Zebra in Africa which are far more tolerant of observation by people if there is a stream between them and the observer. Similarly, the Exmoor Ponies were rarely alarmed by events taking place on the other side of the river.

Returning to the more normal activity of travelling from one part of their range to another, Exmoor Ponies follow well-defined pathways and regularly take the same routes. The paths are clearly worn away on areas of heather and gorse but are less defined on the grassland as the ponies will tend to wander and graze over the grassy areas. The use of familiar routes is important to animals which seek to avoid threats by fleeing. If threatened by predators in the wild, escaping along a well-known pathway is more likely to be successful than rushing through unknown terrain. The flight can be more rapid and the animal knows what to expect and where it may find refuge. Although predators and hunters ceased to be a threat to Exmoor Ponies several centuries ago, this instinct still allows them to minimise the stress of when they are disturbed. As we shall see in a later chapter when we look at the annual gathering of ponies, those on Withypool Common at least always follow the same route as they seek to escape the pursuit of the riders.

Well worn pathways can also be important to the ponies in coping with hazardous terrain. On Codsend Moor there are patches of deep bog down the centre of the enclosure and riders following a hunt have been seen to cross the area without following the pony paths and sink up to their horses' bellies. The pony paths navigate a safe way through the mire. Walking on Withypool Common, along Dillacombe stream, the going is very boggy but the pony path provides a firm crossing. The Exmoors also have a natural awareness of the dangers of boggy ground and an inherent ability to navigate safe passage across unsafe terrain. In her article on Exmoor Ponies written in 1896, Evelyn March-Phillips wrote:

The instinct of these ponies for bogs is almost infallible. A rider tells me he has ridden one across a wide, shaking bog, where men and horses were sinking on either hand; *the pony, left to his own devices, patting with short steps lightly, quickly and fearlessly over the treacherous ground, hitting upon the soundest tussocks with a security only possible to the native horse of the forest. Up-country horses may have found their last bed in the 'Devil's Stables', as some significantly name the worst part of the vast bog called the Chains; but it is strange indeed if a pure-bred Exmoor has been led to stall there.*[82]

Such routes across open moorland are used by both the ponies and the sheep; they are also followed by sensible walkers and sometimes develop into quite well-worn tracks because of the human usage. Whether the paths are made by the ponies and followed by the sheep or vice versa no-one can say. Perhaps it is most likely that each makes its own but they have the sense to follow each others' routes when they find them, much as we people do now.

We have seen then that the Exmoor herds utilise their home ranges in ways which relate to the distribution of food, water, shelter, other animals and other ponies. They have a firm geographic awareness and move within their ranges accordingly. They react quite calmly to minor disturbance by people through maintaining a distance from them but not running away. They will respond to major disturbance, particularly by riders, by fleeing. This tolerance of minor disturbance has evolved within recent times as the herds were once much more sensitive. As recently as the nineteen-sixties they would run away from people, according to those who visited the herds in those days.

Gradually over the last thirty years, as tourist numbers have grown, people have become an inescapable part of many Exmoor Pony homes. The ponies have adapted to this by modifying their behaviour. If they had not, they would be fleeing so often in summer, their feeding routines would be constantly interrupted and there would be harmful effects on young foals. So the ponies have learnt to put up with us and this recognition of a set distance at which they remain calm is important for anyone visiting the herds.

The Exmoors are not tame though. This tolerance of

closer approach is their natural strategy for coping with what they cannot avoid in a way which conserves their energy. Visitors to the herds need to remember this and cannot expect to ever approach close enough to touch the ponies. These animals have no interest in visitors' food and do not behave as some ponies in the New Forest and on Dartmoor do. Exmoors do not approach people. The Exmoor Ponies on areas which are visited regularly by tourists will allow people to approach so far but no further. So, if visiting them for the first time, it is best to walk up to them very quietly and calmly and not to try to get too close. Once you trespass into their area of discomfort, they respond and will move away. As mentioned before, ponies in isolated locations where few people are seen retain more nervous behaviour and a more careful approach is needed.

Keeping Away from People

Whilst the ponies on Withypool Common, Winsford Hill and Molland Moor have become more approachable as described, they have also adapted their own behaviour to avoid people. On Withypool Common the study of core areas in the ponies' ranges did not show any avoidance of places used by tourists but when the timing of the herds' occupation of sites was studied it revealed a strategy of avoidance.

Studies of the New Forest Ponies and the ponies on the Gower Peninsula in Wales, carried out before my study of Exmoor Ponies, had shown that in both places the ponies had a set daily routine. When the Exmoor Ponies were studied on Withypool Common, it was important to find out whether they too showed a predictable pattern of which part of their range they could be found in at particular times of the day. Thus the positions of the herds at dawn, 0900 hours, noon, 1500 hours and dark were extracted from all the observations between April 1975 and March 1977 and analysed, correcting for changes in British Summertime to natural "Pony Time".

Golden Gorse's herd showed avoidance of disturbance by people and traffic. The area of their home range crossed by the road to Exford was mostly used by the ponies at dawn and then 0900 hours. The presence of droppings on the road also revealed that the ponies used the road areas during the night. There were much fewer recordings of the herd being near the road later in the day. The areas of their range well away from the road showed far more occupation at noon and 1500 hours. Figure 7.08 shows the time of day with the maximum number of records of the herd being present for each part of the range. By favouring Area A early in the morning, the herd was minimising its contact with vehicles and people. From mid-morning onwards the amount of traffic increases, particularly in summer, when tourists also park and picnic along the edges of the road up on Bradymoor. By the time the people arrived the ponies had moved into the interior of their range and were thus far less likely to be disturbed. This is not to say they were never found near the road later on but the pattern of avoidance predominated.

Royal Duke's herd lived on an area of the Common which had much greater access and thus disturbance, with a longer stretch of road and a well used track to Fernyball. Also areas adjacent to the track and close to Lanacre Bridge are favourite places for visitors to the Common to park their cars and picnic. They also spread along the river. Figure 7.09 shows the times each section was favoured by Royal Duke's herd. We can see a similar pattern with the areas suffering disturbance later in the day used mostly by the ponies at dawn and 0900 hours. Again the interior parts of the range saw most use from noon onwards. These patterns were most pronounced during the summer tending to confirm that the ponies were deliberately organising their movement around their ranges to minimise their contact with the human race and vehicles.

While both herds seemed to show the same strategy of timing in relation to people, this was much more pronounced with Royal Duke's herd. This was probably because there were far more areas where disturbance was experienced within this herd's home range. Golden Gorse's herd had only a small part of their range which was regularly invaded by people. Royal Duke's herd showed a predictable pattern on many days, occupying

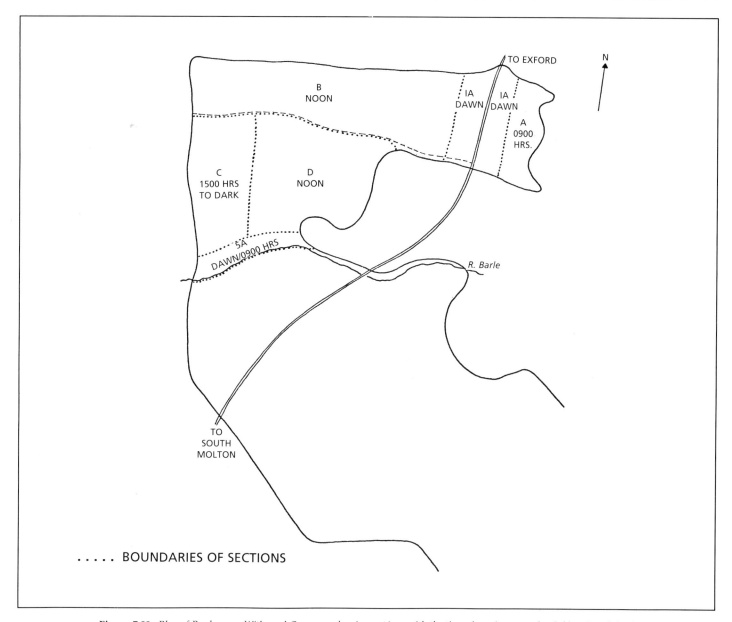

N

TO EXFORD

B
NOON

IA
DAWN

IA
DAWN

A
0900
HRS.

C
1500 HRS
TO DARK

D
NOON

5A
DAWN/0900 HRS

R. Barle

TO
SOUTH
MOLTON

. . . . . BOUNDARIES OF SECTIONS

Figure 7.08 *Plan of Bradymoor, Withypool Common, showing sections with the time of maximum use by Golden Gorse's herd*

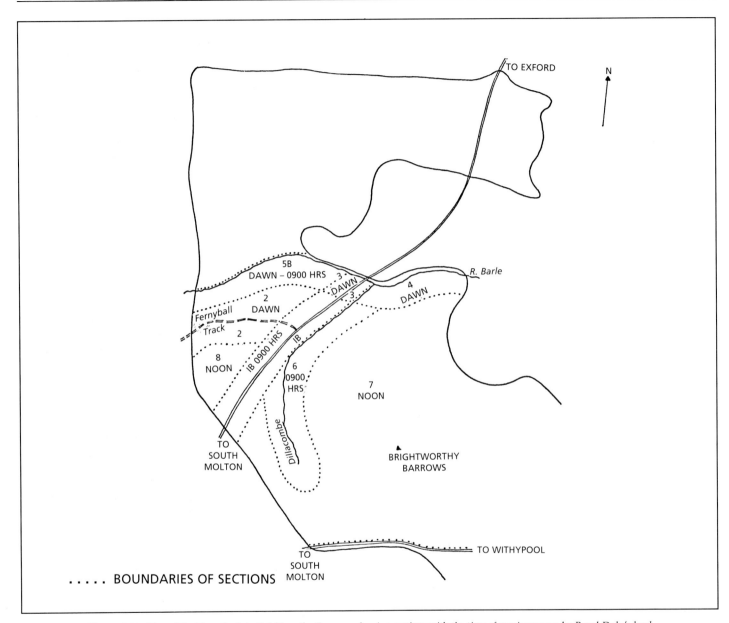

Figure 7.09 *Plan of the River Barle to Brightworthy Barrows, showing sections with the time of maximum use by Royal Duke's herd*

the area around Fernyball track at dawn and through until 0900 hours. By noon they had usually moved into Dillacombe or up onto Brightworthy Barrows far from disturbance and they stayed there throughout the afternoon. As the light faded they were equally likely to stay up on the Barrows or to move back down by the road. The pattern was not so pronounced during the winter.

With Golden Gorse's herd there was no such set routine discovered. Although when they used the area near the road it was most likely to be early in the morning, they did not seem to seek it out as a regular pattern. Similarly, within the interior of their range there seemed no pattern to when they would be in one particular place. This must surely have been because they experienced a great deal less disturbance throughout most of the home on Bradymoor. Perhaps this also explains why the senior and dominant stallion had laid claim to a home range north of the river rather than south.

The behaviour of the Withypool herds in avoiding those places favoured by visitors during the "tourist hours" is probably true for Winsford Hill, the other well-used area. Although no detailed recording was done on Winsford Hill, the information collected did seem to suggest a similar way of dealing with the summer's intrusions. The Winsford Hill ponies were certainly within sight of the road far less often during the summer months. Most visits to the herds were around mid-day and usually they were to be found in locations distant or concealed from people.

Exmoor Ponies today mainly live in places which they must share with human visitors. Exmoor has been "discovered", though the numbers of visitors is still small if we compare it to somewhere like the Lake District. People are a regular and inescapable fact of life for the Exmoor Ponies living on the accessible parts of the moor. Just as the ponies are adapted to living independently in their natural habitats, they have also adapted to the intrusion by people. They have developed an awareness of when they may use particular areas in privacy and when they must leave them and move away onto those parts of their range which visitors rarely disturb. It is a sensitive response to this noisy and disruptive two legged animal which they have to tolerate.

This is an important aspect of their free-living existence, for the Exmoor Ponies have adapted to Man's disturbance and shaped their natural use of their home range to minimise contact. The shyness and nervous behaviour once so important in avoiding predators is no longer appropriate in dealing with the day to day non-threatening approaches by people. So it has been modified through the generations, as Nature continually selects the best ways for an animal to relate to its environment.

A Natural Way of Life

Golden Gorse and Royal Duke, our "leading males" in this in-depth look at the Exmoor Ponies' way of life are sadly both now dead. Their legacy exists not only in their descendants out on Withypool Common but in the pages of a scientific thesis and in this book. They and their mares, several of whom still graze the Common, have shared their life with us and allowed us to know a little about what life is like for a free-living Exmoor Pony.

We have to remember though that these have been only glimpses into their world and much more research is needed. We know how the Withypool Common herds at that time organised their lives and related to their habitat. We cannot be sure this holds true for all situations, although many of the observations of Winsford Hill tend to confirm the patterns seen. We need to have ponies on many thousands of acres with great variety of habitat types and a project of continuous observation before we can define the "rules" of Exmoor Pony ecology.

What we have seen so far is that these ponies live a life in harmony with Nature, subject to its laws where Man does not interfere. They have great knowledge and understanding of their homes. They use this to maximise their ability to thrive in harsh surroundings and to minimise anything which interrupts the important business of surviving.

CHAPTER 8

SURVIVING

The terriblest winter this year ever since that one in 1776, that is thirty-eight years ago. Began the 6th day of January, snow and three or four snows else, then a day's rain and froze to the ground, bushes, trees, hedges, broke them all down with the weight, which was two and three inches thick in some places of ice. Then before it broke away it snowed two nights and most two days with a tempest of wind that blowed the snow in the biggest drifts ever known. The ice lay on the ground for more than a week.[83]

So wrote farmer John Thorne of North Radworthy in the winter of 1814, giving a vivid picture of the harshness an Exmoor winter can bring. Throughout historical records there are accounts of the hardship people and animals suffered in such extreme winters. One farmer in 1607 wrote about the hard frost and snow which lasted about five weeks, while another in 1676 said:

The frost is recorded so great that the oldest man living did never know the like for everything was so hard that meat could only be roasted; because they could get no water for to boyle the pot.[84]

R.D. Blackmore wrote of this winter in his novel *Lorna Doone*, having listened to stories of it handed down through his family. In his chapter "The Great Winter" he described it thus:

That night such a frost ensued as we had never dreamed of, neither read in ancient books, or histories of Frobisher. The kettle by the fire froze, and the crock upon the hearth-cheeks; many men were killed and cattle rigid in their head-ropes.[85]

Should we think that such winters were only known long ago, the events of 1962/63 remind us that our climate can spring these nasty surprises upon us at any time. In the *Exmoor Review* of 1963, C.H. Archer noted that the average temperature over December, January and February was 32 degrees fahrenheit (zero celsius), which would have been normal for southern Sweden. The cold weather persisted for 71 days until 3 March. Snow fell over a period of 57 days and stayed on the ground much longer. These conditions were similar to the winter of 1946/47.

When we visit Exmoor, bathed in summer sunshine with its expanses of purple heather high above the waters of the Bristol Channel, glistening below, it is hard to envisage these onslaughts that winter can bring. The eloquence of these descriptions makes us realise what a challenging environment it can be for human and animal residents. The harsh elements and the depredations of winter involve Exmoor's animals in a battle which they must annually win if they are to reach

Plate 74 *No. 12 herd on Codsend Moor*

maturity and breed, so fulfilling their biological purpose. Whilst thankfully not every winter is like the extreme cases cited here, each one brings conditions which only the hardy can survive. The combination of persistent wind, cold and rain can be even more difficult to cope with than snowfalls.

Harsh weather and scarce food make winter the main threat to the survival of the Exmoor Ponies now that there are no natural predators. The wolf was hunted to extinction centuries ago. The struggle to survive also involves the ponies in competing for the limited resources with various animals which share their habitats. A further factor in surviving is coping with the parasitic creatures which seek to exploit the ponies themselves. So there are many aspects of a natural existence which can mean either life or death to an individual animal. These are the pressures which ruthlessly ensure that the strong survive and contribute to the next generation, while the weak perish. It is the ability of the Exmoor Ponies to win these natural

struggles that places them close to the wild extreme of our wild to domestic spectrum. Hope Bourne summed them up in her book *Living on Exmoor* saying:

> *Wild creatures they surely seem, despite their nominal ownership by the farmers of the hills, living their lives on the open moor, in summer, in winter, in storm and sunshine and snow, handled by man only once a year and dependent only on their own hardiness and courage for survival.*[86]

She also makes us realise that the survival capabilities of the Exmoor are exceptional when compared to ponies whose characteristics have been altered by man:

> *It is noteworthy that any sort of cross-breeding has the effect of reducing the natural hardiness of the Exmoor. Only ponies of the old stock can survive such a winter of snow as that of 1947 unfed and unhelped on the open moor. In that great winter most of the Exmoor Ponies of Withypool Hill came through to the spring unharmed, while the cross-bred ponies suffered terribly and many died.*

So just what is it that enables the Exmoors to survive and indeed thrive in these difficult surroundings? To discover this, we must look closely at how they deal with the elements, find their food, and relate to other animals.

Adaptations to the Climate

To appreciate just how well adapted to coping with winter weather Exmoor Ponies are, you must visit the moorland on a cold, wet, winter day. Equipped with thick jumpers, waterproofs and wellington boots, hike out across the moor, find the ponies and you will see survival at work. The driving rain and wind, so icy cold, will chill you to the bone and soon have you retreating to the log fire of a local hostelry, there to marvel at the resilience of these animals.

The Exmoor Ponies withstand these appalling conditions by means of numerous adaptations of their bodies and their behaviour. Whilst people take cover from the hostile elements, they endure them. They stand, rear into the wind, tail tight against the body, heads down and continually eat. They may be in the lee of gorse bushes if the wind is severe but often remain out in the open taking whatever shelter they can from hollows and hedges. Whilst you shiver in inadequate man-made coverings, the ponies graze on in no distress.

The key to their ability to thrive in harsh climates lies in their coat structure and the arrangement of hair on their bodies. Visit a tame Exmoor Pony in the rain and it will look very wet, yet if you put your fingers beneath the surface of the coat, the skin is dry and warm. This is because the Exmoor Pony grows a special winter coat each year. In late August or early September this double-layered coat begins to grow. The undercoat is made up of short, fine hairs which can be thought of as "thermal underwear", which insulates the pony's body from cold. Over this undercoat the hairs grow longer and coarser and are greasy, giving the pony efficient water-proofing.

In Cumbria, Veronica Watkins has observed the phases of coat over many years. She explained to me:

> *If a pony goes away in the summer for a week or two, it needs to be back in September to get its winter coat fully grown by the end of November. In fact mine start growing their coats in August. The ponies put all their energy into building up this woolly under-coat and long hairs over it to shed the rain. I think it is the thick build-up of grease that takes a lot of protein to produce. They are never too lively during this time.*[87]

This outer "raincoat" is wonderfully adapted to its task of expelling water from the animal. The hairs grow in a pattern which diverts water away from the vulnerable parts, where the animal might get chilled, and off the body. Figure 8.01 shows this drainage pattern of an Exmoor Pony. James Speed explained it in this way:

> *A closer look and we find that the hair has aggregated into little triangular areas, the apices forming converging points for the water, and all these apices are pointing in the direction of the flumina or "hair-streams". The hair-streams may end at a fringe such as the beard, the fringe down the mid-line under the neck, the back of the thigh – which is joined by the lateral hairs of the tail when the tail is pressed*

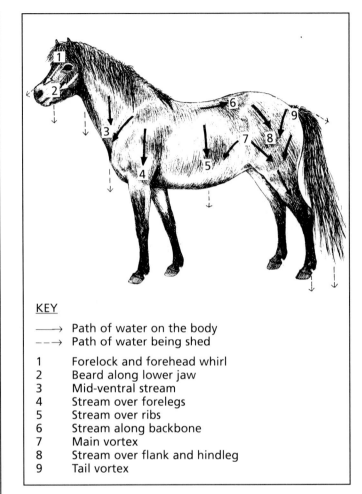

KEY

⟶   Path of water on the body
- - ⟶   Path of water being shed

1   Forelock and forehead whirl
2   Beard along lower jaw
3   Mid-ventral stream
4   Stream over forelegs
5   Stream over ribs
6   Stream along backbone
7   Main vortex
8   Stream over flank and hindleg
9   Tail vortex

Figure 8.01 *The Exmoor pony's water dispersal system*

> *close – and the back of the cannon and fetlock tuft, or they may be turned aside by a "whorl" or vortex so that they are kept clear of the eyes, the flank in front of the thigh, the breast and so on. It is quite certain that these vortices are placed in exactly the best positions to divert the run of the rain-water from sensitive or comparatively unprotected areas.*[88]

Plate 75 *Snow-thatched ponies on Winsford Hill*

The efficiency of the thermal insulation of the coat can best be seen in snow. As the snow falls, it actually collects on top of the ponies, a phenomenon known as "snow-thatching". The snow does not melt as insufficient body heat escapes through the thick coat. Thus the pony's body is not soaked by melt-water and the snow can be shaken off the coat periodically.

In April or May, depending upon weather conditions, the ponies begin to moult out this winter coat and the summer coat develops. This lacks the thermal under-layer which is no longer needed, but still shows the drainage arrangements which are always essential in our climate. Whilst the winter coat is thick, shaggy and greasy, the summer coat is sleek and shiny, giving

Plate 76 *The summer coat is single-layered and sleek*

the ponies a very different appearance. Foals born in summer are born with a summer coat, but if a foal is born late in the year, it arrives with a winter coat structure matching its mother's physiological state. This happens very rarely, as the ponies have a distinct breeding season, and is yet another strategy for increasing chances of survival. The record for an untimely foaling seems to rest with a Withypool mare who gave birth on Christmas Eve; the foal was naturally called Noel.

Persistent rain is far more usual than long periods of snow, although these too are a factor in the local climate as we have seen from the extracts quoted. Rain is perhaps even a greater threat coupled with cold for it can readily lead to exposure. It is hard to envisage the sheer misery of the intense cold and the seemingly endless rain. Hope Bourne escapes neither living so close to Nature and her words bring home to us what Exmoor inhabitants must endure:

Plate 77 *Dazzling Boy (85/32) part-way through moulting his winter coat. After a rainy night, the water dispersal patterns in the coat are evident*

January – cold grey days and bitter winds, and black frosts that set hard in the earth. Now winter has set its teeth in the land, and for the week past an ominous leaden sky has pressed down on field and moor, and all life has shrunk into itself under the stiffening cold. The bitter north-east wind pierces like a knife blade, shrivelling all vegetation, licking the moisture out of everything and giving the ground a dry, brushed look, seeking out all the chinks in the armour of one's clothing, and biting at one's nose, ears and fingers. A blue-grey fog of coldness lies over the hills, cheerless and drawing dawn and dusk together without any noonday brightness.

February – Under the leaden rain-filled sky the moor lies desolate; wind-lashed, streaked and curdled still with snow, rolling in heaving undulations like the billows of a tideless sea, reaching up to dark skylines swallowed in grey cloud. Soaking bent and sodden rush, black dripping heather,

bracken soaked to dark mahogany and the icy white of snow a livid dappling in every hag and hollow. There is no life, no sound but the beating rain, no voice but that of the wind. It is loneliness and desolation, the western land as was in the beginning, storm swept and primeval.

So coping with the icy-cold rain is crucial to survival. This water dispersal function is the clue to understanding the purpose of the long hair of the forelock, mane, beard and tail. All of these serve to channel rain off the body or away from especially delicate areas.

The long, floppy mane directs the water down over the shoulders and off the side of the animal. The forelock channels rain down the mid-line of the head between the eyes and the beard, absent in the summer, collects and sheds it. Exmoors are sometimes criticised within the equestrian world for having low-set tails. Yet

Plate 78 *The mane, forelock and beard are all adapted for shedding water*

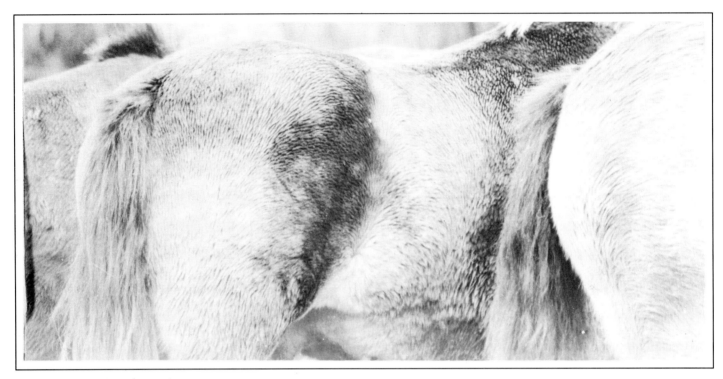

Plate 79 *Short hairs at the base of the tail form a snow and rain chute*

this is the best natural solution for protecting the rear body openings and the long hair drains the water from the rump down to the ground. At its root the tail has a fan of shorter hairs, known as a "snow-chute" but in truth more a rain-chute for again the function is to move water outwards away from the sensitive openings.

There are further anatomical features which are also protective for the ponies. Any description of an Exmoor Pony will refer to it having "toad eyes". This is often thought to mean just the oatmeal coloured ring around each eye but it refers more the surrounding rim of raised flesh. This makes the eyes very prominent, hence the comparison to a toad. The flesh bulges in this way because the eye socket is shallow. The bulk of the eye pushes the encircling fat outwards, so raising the skin.

Plate 80 *The raised flesh around the eye protects it from water and the short ears are well defended from the elements*

The shallowness of the socket allows considerable mobility of the eye and hence a wide angle of vision. Such an extensive field of view is an obvious advantage to an animal which has predators. The rim of flesh also prevents water from running into the eye, so the feature is doubly useful.

To survive wet and cold conditions, it is important for all body openings to be protected. Hence an Exmoor Pony's ears are small and lined with short hairs to protect the skin and to minimise heat loss. Even the length of the pony's head, again often criticised by those committed to breeding "pretty" horses and ponies, has been explained as being an adaptation to the winter climate. It provides a long distance of membrane between the nostrils and the lungs, to warm the air breathed in.

So Exmoor Ponies have a whole arsenal of natural weapons with which to battle the elements. With such characteristics they are able to carry on their lives, not only surviving the winters but thriving. It is this difference between thriving and surviving which distinguishes them from cross-bred ponies. James Speed wrote to me about the importance of the adaptive characteristics and how they were diluted in other breeds of ponies:

Do remember that our mountain and moorland ponies are for the most part mixtures but still with much of the original Adam (Exmoor) in them, so that Exmoor Pony features such as the toad eye can reappear. In other words, all Exmoors have the toad eye, but other hill ponies may or may not have it. It is constant in Exmoors but not in others. The same holds for the coat. You will see the original coat pattern of flumina and vortices in a pure Exmoor Pony and if any other pony has it, it is fortunate to have retained this Exmoor characteristic in spite of mixed ancestry. I have never seen the perfect pattern in other ponies although I expect it could happen.[89]

We have already seen that in particularly harsh winters many cross-bred ponies may perish whilst most Exmoors survive but most winters do not present such an ultimate test. On Exmoor and on other moorland habitats, cross-bred ponies somehow manage to live through most years but it is perhaps an unperceived form of cruelty. Such mongrel ponies, which are rarely blessed with an adequate winter coat or the protective features seen as an invariable rule for the Exmoor, are forced to live often cold and wet. They have no way of avoiding such distress. They indeed survive most of the time but do not thrive. A visit to such cross-bred herds in foul weather will leave an impression of some individuals in utter misery, a great contrast to the Exmoors who carry on seemingly contemptuous of bad weather.

The importance of the specialised winter coat and body hair cannot be over-emphasised for it makes the difference between life and death in really extreme conditions. For every Exmoor foal born, its coat structure will determine its chances of survival if it is to remain in a moorland herd. If it has a faulty coat formation then it is likely to succumb to really testing weather. James and Mary Speed studied the coats of native ponies in great detail, revealing the special characteristics of the Exmoors. They kept a research herd of Exmoors on the Pentland Hills in Scotland and watched to see how they fared in bad winters. They found that the pattern of whirls and vortices in the layout of the coat was crucial and that any animals with imperfect structure experienced difficulties in extreme conditions.

James Speed believed that the central forehead whirl was a good indicator of the efficiency of the coat as a whole. He said that if this whirl was single, neat and tidy and situated correctly on the mid-line down the head, then the coat was properly formed. If the whirl was ill-defined, multiple or wrongly sited then such an animal was likely to be less well-protected overall. Such a pony was still a legitimate Exmoor Pony but when natural selection sought out weakness through the pressures of winter, this would be a significant factor.

If we leave the fireside of that local inn and once again brave the elements to find some Exmoors, we can look at them with great respect, understanding that they owe their hardiness to an inherited survival kit. The mane, tail and beard are no longer just attractive features; now we see them as perfectly designed for water dispersal. The lie of the coat is no longer taken for granted but appreciated for its intricacy and efficiency. Judgements as to size or position of features, so important in domestic horse-breeding, become irrelevant; all is shaped by Nature to fit the animals for their natural life.

The free-living ponies also have an instinct for finding what natural shelter there is within their home ranges. Sometimes they seem to be out on an exposed hillside but when that place is visited in bad weather, it actually offers protection from nearby banks or hedges or perhaps even just a slight hollowing in the land. Often in driving rain or snow, the ponies will move into an area of sizeable gorse bushes and the thickness of the vegetation protects them to some degree. Some Exmoor residents believe that the ponies may even sense the approach of snow as they seem to seek out a part of their range which is safe from drifting snow before a blizzard hits.

Yet this is not an infallible sense. There is a story of disaster which has been passed down through the Milton family of Weatherslade. Hope Bourne relates it thus:

Again one turns into the blankness of the snow. Where are the ponies now, I wonder? Somewhere down in some south-facing, north-sheltered combe, tails to the wind. It is seldom they come to any harm. The little horses will survive where sheep and cattle perish, delving in the snow with their forefeet in search of food, and mouthing the whiteness for a drink. The moor farmers say that the proof of a pony's breeding is whether it can survive, without any feeding or aid from man, a hard winter on the hill. The true Exmoor succumbs rarely to the hardships of Nature, though half-bred stock may suffer much under severe conditions.

Yet once a herd of good ponies did die in the snow, on Withypool Hill. I have heard it told that in a great blizzard of the 1880s a group of ponies took shelter in the corner of the moor where the big hedges of Brightworthy and Knighton come together, and that there the drifting snow built a great wall around them, so that they were shut in, and there they perished.

Plate 81 *Ponies on Winsford Hill using the bank and beech trees for shelter*

Plate 82 *Hollows in banks provide a welcome respite from the wind*

Fortunately, the ponies' innate instinct for safe places rarely lets them down as it did in this unusual tragedy which has long been remembered locally. Hope Bourne observed an Exmoor herd in the winter of 1978 moving, when the snow started, to an area of clefts in the hillside which seemed to offer shelter. As conditions worsened the ponies left this apparent refuge and after a few hours, there was a drift of about thirty feet deep covering where they had been. It may well be that in a totally free situation their instinct is to move to a more generous habitat during the worst of the winter weather. James Speed told of a herd of Exmoors which disappeared from some high moorland in Scotland during a terrible period of snow. He thought they had died but when the snow cleared, they were not on the hills. The herd had moved down off the high ground and were living on the seashore.

The hardiness of Exmoor Ponies is comparable to that of truly wild animals and is based upon a combination of anatomical features and behavioural responses. Just how remarkable their survival capabilities are is reflected in the judgement of the farmer who told James Speed that in the worst of winters, the sheep die first, then the cattle, then the deer but last of all the Exmoor Ponies. This is a legacy from their wild ancestors which shows no signs of man's interference.

The Moorland Menu

Finding enough food and water is the preoccupation of all living creatures, for if they fail to satisfy their energy needs each day, they decline and ultimately die. This is true whether an animal is provided with food or has to forage unaided. Ponies kept domestically rely on their owners to provide all their requirements; this dependence is the essence of domestication. Free-living ponies have to rely on what the natural environment can provide and their own abilities to make the most of the natural provisions.

Exmoor Ponies inhabit areas which, with the exception of Codsend Moor, offer a wide variety of vegetation types and food plants. They have an extensive menu to choose from. As we have seen earlier, water is readily available throughout the enclosures, either in rivers, streams or water-holes. If we visit a free-living herd in order to see what they eat, we are faced with a problem. When a pony feeds, with its mouth at ground-level, it is almost impossible to be sure which plant it is eating, if it is feeding on an area of mixed vegetation. So studies of diet cannot rely on observation alone.

This unfortunate fact of zoological research life introduces the researcher to the delights of analysing dung. If you cannot be sure what is going in at one end, you can at least make certain by studying what comes out at the other end. During the Withypool study, this was the method used to establish just what the Exmoor Ponies in Golden Gorse's herd ate. Firstly, microscope slides of the cells of all the main plants on the Common were prepared and photographed, to provide an identification

Figure 8.02 *The main plants on Withypool Common's moorland menu*

samples were collected and treated so that the plant fragments could be extracted and mounted on slides. These were then compared to the reference photographs and the original plant identified. Peering through a microscope at hundreds of such slides is an unforgettable experience. Eventually, the images of tiny plant cells seem to become fixed to the eyeballs and are still there even when you close your eyes. Instead of counting sheep at night, you continue to count the number of bumps on the cell walls to discover which grass species is which. Yet it is all worthwhile for a picture emerges not only of which plants are eaten but also in what proportions.

The principal food plants available to the animals grazing Withypool Common are shown in Figure 8.02. Five main grass species are distributed on this part of the moor; Red Fescue, Sheep's Fescue, Common Bent, Purple Moor Grass and small amounts of Reed Grass. There are three types of heather with Ling, Bell Heather and Cross-Leaved Heath although Ling predominates. Most of the gorse is Common Gorse but there is also some Western Dwarf Gorse present. Bracken and the Soft Rush are common. Although Bilberry is quite widespread south of the river, it is not so abundant on Bradymoor. Obviously, the flora of the Common contains many more species than those listed, but only in small amounts. Those illustrated constituted the "main courses" on the menu.

As Figure 8.03 illustrates, for the year as a whole, just over half the food eaten consisted of the softer, palatable grasses, the Fescues and the Common Bent, which is unsurprising. Heather formed 10% of the diet with only slightly smaller proportions of rushes and gorse. Purple Moor Grass formed only five percent and Bracken only just registered. Bilberry was found in just a few samples, insufficient to record in percentage terms. Perhaps this is because it is not widespread on Golden Gorse's herd's range. Fifteen percent of the fragments could not be identified but were a mixture of many different types. The importance of having a varied diet such as this lies in maintaining the availability of food and coping with seasonal shortages. Taking a selection of plants cushions

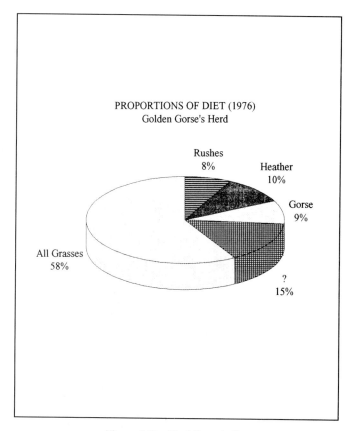

Figure 8.03 *The full year's diet*

the vegetation from intensive use of any one species and hence avoids over-grazing. Also, if one food item ceases to be available periodically, the ponies can compensate by increasing their use of other plants.

Another aspect of diet which the study revealed related to the animals' preferences. If the proportion of a food in the diet matches the proportion of it in the mixed vegetation available, we can view this as showing no particular attraction to that plant. However, if there is a greater percentage eaten than is represented on the ground, this reflects preferential selection by the ponies. This type of analysis showed that the Exmoors studied showed positive preferences for the Fescue and Bent species of grasses and for rushes and gorse. The amounts eaten were probably limited by how much the ponies could find. Heather was selected in smaller proportions than it was available and we can conclude that it has far less appeal. One plant which seemed to be particularly enjoyed by the ponies was Montbretia, a member of the Iris family, which grows in very small amounts by the river. They would wade through the water specifically to eat the leaves and beautiful orange flowers in summer. It was a rare delicacy and the supply was quickly exhausted.

It is easy to understand why the ponies favour the softer grass species; these combine good energy supply with pleasant taste as does the Soft Rush. The preference for gorse is harder to appreciate, given its prickly form, but it is a rich energy source. Its selection is highly seasonal and the preference for it is very high in winter and low in summer. Heather is not a particularly good source of energy and is of course very woody and perhaps unpleasant in texture. Similarly, Purple Moor Grass is a much harsher in texture and not very palatable. Only negligible amounts of bracken were seen in the diet and this reflects the fact that when immature,

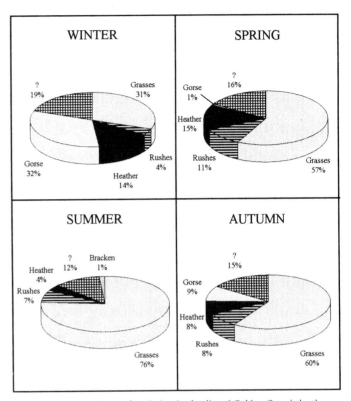

Figure 8.04 *Seasonal variation in the diet of Golden Gorse's herd*

the bracken fronds are highly poisonous. The ponies only sampled the tips of fully grown fronds occasionally.

These choices and partialities become clearer if we look at the way the diet varied over the year. Figure 8.04 shows the proportions of foods eaten during each season. Summer is the time when the ponies really exercise free choice because the plants are at their peaks of availability. Their preference for grasses shows clearly with over three-quarters of all their food intake being made up of the soft grass species. Small amounts of heather and soft rush are also eaten. Bracken only registers in the summer when the fronds have reached full height.

As autumn arrives, the grasses stop growing and so

Plate 83 *Exmoor ponies have tough mouths and strong teeth to cope with coarse food such as gorse*

the amount available to the ponies diminishes and a smaller proportion of their food needs can be met by grass. They compensate by increasing the amounts of rushes and heather eaten and also by resorting to the energy rich gorse, although still in relatively small amounts. The winter diet shows the autumn trends have continued with the Exmoors only able to find just over a quarter of their diet as grass. Rushes have also reduced, heather increased but the most striking change is that gorse has become the predominant item chosen from the impoverished menu.

As spring comes, assuming it is not delayed and the grass resumes its growth and becomes more palatable, the quantity of grasses again reaches the autumn level and gorse is just a minor element. Heather and rushes continue to be important secondary choices.

We have to remember that this is not the definitive version of an Exmoor Pony's diet because the information comes from just one herd and from one year. The year studied was rather unusual as it was 1976 when there was an extensive hot, dry period in summer which reduced the amount of grass available later in the year. So it may be that the dependence upon so much gorse in winter was exaggerated to some extent. In 1989 and 1990, Dr Elaine Gill included Exmoor Ponies in her comparative study of free-living ponies on Dartmoor, Exmoor and the New Forest, looking at diets and condition. She found a similar picture of the Exmoor diet and also identified mosses as a major ingredient. Interestingly, although the summers of 1989 and 1990 were also very dry, Dr Gill found much lower usage of gorse and heather in the winters which followed. They were however very mild winters by comparison with 1976/77. It may be though that the quality of gorse and heather on Withypool Common has further deteriorated.

The Exmoors' use of gorse as a winter food source is very important and a key to how they can thrive and maintain good condition, as it is rich in nutrients. The ponies show no reluctance when eating gorse and although have been seen trampling the shoots to crush the spines before eating, they will also simply bite off the gorse and eat it without apparent discomfort. The inside of their mouths must be very tough. It seems likely that this depends upon the state of the gorse. If it is relatively young the ponies can cope with the spines but where the spines are hard as well as sharp, they choose to soften them by trampling. Studies in the New Forest have concluded that the animals which maintain condition are the ones which will eat significant amounts of gorse. The ponies there which lose condition to varying degrees seem to lack either the instinct or the willingness to tackle this prickly food. Gorse offers ponies a double resource as it provides a combination of food with shelter and in deep snow can be the only plants readily available.

In conditions of snow-cover, heather can be reached if the snow is not too deep, by pawing the snow away from the vegetation. There are also other ways in which Exmoors have been known to cope with winter shortages. James Speed observed that in severe conditions when heather and gorse could not supply enough food, the Exmoors dug up bracken rhizomes to eat. This has to be a final resort, emergency rations, for the digging requires using precious energy. The rhizomes are a rich supply of starch but in most conditions the cost of reaching them would outweigh the benefit. This behaviour has not been recorded on Exmoor itself. Dead beech leaves and thin twigs are consumed to supplement the winter diet and the ponies will also take small quantities of green beech leaves in spring. In situations where Exmoors have had access to woodland, they have been seen to take elm and pine shoots too.

We saw earlier how a group of Exmoors in Scotland escaped the worst of winter by taking a holiday by the sea. These ponies supplemented their rations by eating seaweed and this has been seen elsewhere. The ponies living on the isolated peninsula of Scoraig in Scotland have free access to the shoreline and regularly eat seaweed, particularly in spring and autumn. Unlike the Exmoor Ponies, the cattle and sheep on Scoraig have to be given regular doses of mineral supplements, specifically copper and cobalt; perhaps the ponies obtain these trace elements from the seaweed. The menu of the ponies on the island of Taero also includes seaweed.

Plate 84 *Exmoor ponies on the Danish island of Taero eating seaweed*

We have just a few hints that Exmoors may have physiological strategies which account for their maintaining good condition when other ponies are recognisably in difficulties. James Speed escorted a visitor from the German Ministry of Agriculture on a visit to see Exmoor Ponies back in the 1950s. Surprisingly, this gentleman took a great interest in the ponies' droppings. He explained that having watched the ponies for a considerable time, he observed that the nearby birds took no interest in the dung. This he felt showed that the ponies digested their food most efficiently, leaving little of energy value to be passed out the body. He saw this as a contrast to most horses and ponies which produced dung still containing useful amounts of food for birds. This anecdote does suggest that the Exmoor has a far more efficient digestive system than many ponies. Thus, as well as the capability to adapt their diet to seasonal variations, perhaps the ability to extract the maximum food value out of the plants is another key to their hardiness. Such a study of energy intake and loss is a research project awaiting an enthusiastic student.

Another physiological aspect which might shed light on the different survival capacities of various horses and ponies is the rate at which the animal's metabolism works. Very little information is available as yet and certainly nothing on Exmoor Ponies but the studies so far are interesting. The metabolic rate of Thoroughbreds has been found to be far higher than that of Welsh Cobs. It is tempting to think that the bodies of free-living ponies would function at an even slower pace, again due to a poorer diet and as an adaptation to using energy efficiently. Having observed her ponies over many years, Veronica Watkins believes that there is also a change in level of activity during the winter:

> I think they semi-hibernate in the shortest days, under their thick coats, so only need a little food to keep their energy up, if they can keep dry and out of the wind.

Yet how are we to find out? To measure metabolic rate, the animals must be tested in a relaxed state and no free-living pony is relaxed when confined enough to attach electrodes! Japanese scientists have done some work by attaching electrodes and a radio transmitter and re-releasing the animals. Maybe this is a further project in need of a researcher. Certainly we do know that the Exmoors manage their "energy budget" very well and reduce their levels of activity in winter. They devote most of their time to feeding and far less time is spent resting or socialising. The fact that reproductive activity is suspended in winter as we will see later is also related to conserving precious energy and concentrating on just surviving.

There are also body characteristics which are adaptations to subsisting on impoverished diets and surviving winters. Sometimes Exmoors are criticised for being broad in the back and having a large girth but there are good reasons for this. The large body cavity provides room for a high capacity digestive system which is needed if large quantities of rough material are to be consumed to generate internal central heating. The teeth of Exmoor Ponies are particularly important in dealing with some of the items on their menu. As outlined in Chapter 4, the cheek teeth (the grinding molars) are large and well designed for chewing the tougher plants. They are set into the jaw at angles which maximise the chewing pressure that can be exerted. The front biting teeth, the incisors, emerge from the gums along a curved path so that the upper and lower incisors meet cleanly and vertically. This means that the food plants can be bitten off cleanly rather than torn and damaged.

There have been some rather extravagant claims that the Exmoor Pony possesses an extra molar tooth compared to all other horses and ponies and this is just not true. The process of "chinese whispers" seems to have been at work for the research on which this assertion was based does not say this. Hermann Ebhardt did say that the Exmoor had an extra branch of the main blood vessel supplying the jaw. He suggested this represented the beginnings of the development of an extra tooth to provide improved mastication of food. He reported that he had only seen this arrangement in Exmoor Ponies. However, X-rays of a few other breeds have also shown this development to some extent and its significance is not certain. It might simply be the additional blood supply required by a large jaw-bone.

The large jaw is important to the Exmoor in that it is an essential bed for the sizeable teeth which are themselves so well adapted to natural feeding. If Exmoor Ponies are cross-bred it is essential to keep this in mind when selecting the other parent.

Exmoor Ponies are renowned for obtaining a good living off their poor moorland vegetation. In early spring, perhaps the most testing time when the deprivations of winter have been endured for many months, they still appear in good condition without much loss of body substance. Visit the New Forest or Dartmoor and whilst some individuals will have coped, others exhibit varying degrees of leanness. There is no easy explanation of this. So many factors are involved; the vegetation, the diet, the physiology, the reproductive state, the parasitic burden and probably factors of inheritance too. So further studies of Exmoor Ponies will not be mere academic exercises but may help in defining what is required in animals if we are to expect them to survive the free existence unaided. Greater awareness in this respect would hopefully lead to less occasions where unsuitable cross-bred ponies are forced to endure a miserable existence.

Free-living Exmoor Ponies can find all their own food without help from us, if they are given a sufficiently large moorland home where the vegetation is well-managed and not damaged through over-grazing by domestic stock. We have to beware of thinking that their survival abilities are unlimited. They cannot be expected to prosper on tiny areas or on exhausted ground or if they are kept in numbers which the land cannot support. The perils of over-population can be seen with the Red Deer in Scotland where sizeable culls are sometimes needed; if these are not carried out then many of the deer may starve. The Exmoor Ponies' self-reliance is an important dimension of their wildness in natural conditions. Without our help they will survive as a population although if conditions become very hard, the weak might succumb. Whilst this is an inevitable part of natural selection, it is not in the best interests of the hill farmer, for whom the ponies are a source of income, minor though it is. Thus, when food is hard to obtain in long periods of snow, some owners of herds may put hay out for the ponies but this is by no means a regular event nor is it done for all groups.

Plate 85 *Herd No. H8 ponies on Withypool Common are sometimes given a little hay in snowy conditions*

The first record of providing some emergency supplies for the ponies comes from long ago. John Thorne, who's diary we have read from before, wrote further of that terrible winter in 1814 saying "forced to give hay to the Exmore colts and other colts". This was obviously a most unusual occurrence. Around the turn of the century, a little hay was put out for the Acland ponies in the hardest winters but rarely eaten to any extent. The significance of giving this aid in times of exceptional hardship must not be exaggerated. Perhaps in freak conditions it might make a crucial difference but where it is not provided, the majority of Exmoor Ponies still survive, as is recorded for 1947 on Withypool Common and from the Chains in more recent times. However, it might protect the weak from the rigorous laws of Nature.

Perhaps in this context we should think hard as to whether interfering is in the ponies' best interests. It might save an individual, but ultimately such intervention may weaken the population as a whole. We will consider this further in the final chapter.

Sometimes it may be that taking hay to the ponies can be counter-productive in immediate terms not just in its impact on cushioning weak individuals. If hay is taken by helicopter it is generally dropped up on the high, exposed ground and might well lure animals from safer, sheltered places. We know too that such charitable actions are not always appreciated as might be expected. In the winter of 1962/63 ponies on Dartmoor were not coping well and food was being dropped by helicopter. This was televised and perhaps explains why one Minehead resident, who could in no way have seen the Exmoor Ponies, pressed the local authorities for similar action. Despite assurances from the owners that their Exmoors were in no difficulty, hay was dropped on Bradymoor, only to be ignored by the ponies. Another owner relates how in his early days of owning Exmoors there was an extensive period of snow cover and he was concerned about his herd. He battled through the snow for several miles with some hay only to find that the ponies merely sniffed it and walked away. So sometimes when we perceive them to be under pressure, the ponies may not be in real difficulty.

Any truly successful animal is probably an opportunist and the Exmoors are no exception. The hill farmers have to feed their cattle each day in winter out on the moors and the provision of hay or silage is sometimes exploited by the ponies. However, the farmers involved will often chase the ponies away. If they take the food meant for the cattle it erodes the meagre profits of the hill farmer by increasing his costs. Such poaching of the cattle food is an occasional bonus, not a vital part of surviving for the ponies.

There are many reports that Exmoor Ponies, even in domestic circumstances on farms, show a preference for natural food rather than hay. If they are kept in fields where there are natural hedgerows they will obtain as much as they can from this source before resorting to prepared fodder. Where owners can keep their Exmoors on rough grazing, winter feeding of hay is reduced. It is all a matter of what is available in their habitat, captive though it may be. If they are unfortunate enough to be kept in small wire-fenced fields, then of course they cannot be expected to sustain themselves and will need feeding appropriately. Out on Exmoor, the ponies do not approach humans seeking food as ponies on Dartmoor and the New Forest are known to do. So the message is clear, Exmoor Ponies ask only to be provided with a suitable natural habitat and then they would rather have nothing to do with the agricultural equivalents of "fast food".

Competition

Living off the moorland vegetation is challenge enough for any animal but there is a further dimension which makes the task even harder. This is competition, where the use of a resource such as food by one individual reduces the amount available to another. Where food is plentiful and the density of those requiring it is low, the relationships between animals may not be noticeably competitive. Where food is limited, the effect of competitors makes the struggle for survival that much more difficult. Those competitors will be the other individuals of the same race plus other species which use the same resources.

Plate 86 *Exmoor ponies and red deer grazing together in Draydon Fields, near Dulverton*

The homes of the free-living Exmoor Ponies are enclosures of varying sizes and availability of food plants. The ponies do not have their habitats to themselves but share them with several other types of animals which have similar diets. Some are wild creatures and others are the hill farmers' stock. As we found when visiting the herds, Red Deer inhabit Winsford Hill, Molland Moor and Brendon Common but are not continually resident on the other areas. Rabbits are present in some places but their numbers are so low that they are not a significant competitor at present. Hares were seen slightly more often during the studies of the herds but also have little impact upon the competitive scene. Sheep are grazed on all the areas where there are Exmoor Ponies and cattle are present on most. Various types of cattle and sheep are used but they have to be the hardy breeds. The local strains are the Exmoor Horn Sheep and the Devon Red Cattle but many other varieties are favoured as well. On Brendon Common there are also the cross-bred ponies.

There have been no detailed studies of the diets of sheep, cattle or deer on Exmoor which we can compare to what we know of the Exmoor Ponies' feeding. However, research from other parts of upland Britain shows that there are a number of plants common to both sheep and ponies' diets in a variety of situations. They are then direct competitors to some degree but their preferences show different seasonal patterns. There seems to be less of an overlap between ponies and cattle so they may not compete with each other as strongly. Red Deer have been intensively studied in Scotland and have a much more varied diet as they utilise many different habitats. On Exmoor they can exploit the woodlands, the open moor and the enclosed fields of the hill farms, for their jumping abilities make them contemptuous of most artificial barriers. So there is some similarity in food selection but no great competitive pressure on the ponies from the deer.

Where many different types of wild grazing animals cohabit, the pressures of competition usually force each species to specialise in some way. This results in the different animals using different parts of the same food plant or using it at different stages in its growth cycle. Specialising in this way can result in a species being able to exploit an opportunity which others cannot and we call this adapting to fit a "niche". It is such specialising that enables so many different kinds of antelopes to live on the grasslands of Africa because it has minimised competition between them. This adapting to different niches is part of the very process of evolution itself and occurs on the way to separate species developing. It is though a wholly natural process. On Exmoor, the mixed communities of grazing animals have not arisen naturally. While the deer and Exmoor Ponies have probably shared the moorland for thousands of years, the sheep were an artificial introduction. It is likely that wild cattle once roamed Exmoor perhaps up to the Iron Age. How closely the primitive Devon Red breed is related to them is uncertain and other breeds have also been introduced into the moorland communities.

The blend of natural and introduced animals means that regulating the competitive interaction between the species cannot be left to natural development of specialisations. This is a process which requires thousands of years. While it is undoubtedly at work on the moorland, its timescales are too long for the hill farmer who must exploit the capacity of the moor to the full. Thus an important part of the science of hill farming is the calculation of stocking rates, for it sets the level of competition the animals will experience. Graze too many animals then some will lose condition and the returns will diminish; graze too few and the productivity of the moorland is under-utilised.

The community of animals on Withypool Common is regulated by the Commoners' Association. They use the stocking rates drawn up by the Commoners in 1818. This allows each farmer with rights an allocation in terms of "sheep equivalents" related to the acreage of the home farm. The allowance is one pony or cow per 10 acres and 1.25 sheep per acre. One pony or cow is deemed as equal to five sheep and the allocation for one type of animal can be taken up by another using this formula.

The original rules required, in winter, the removal of the sheep and whilst the cattle could remain, they had to be fed. The system was clearly based upon the understanding of competition between the species acquired through experience. By changing their rules to allow grazing of all stock throughout the year, the Commoners' Association have now abandoned the traditional practice of resting the moorland. It is surely no coincidence that the vegetation has noticeably deteriorated in recent years. Also, the intensity of competition must have been considerably raised which must be to the detriment of all the stock including the ponies. The long-term negative effects of the current system may prove to far outweigh the short-term gains.

We can see that the Commoners of Withypool who drew up the original management system recognised that they had created a community which needed regulating to maintain a natural balance. Where such controls are absent or less carefully determined, the degree of competition between the grazing animals may be much greater and the pressures on the environment lead to more damage. Sadly, there are areas on Exmoor which have not been carefully managed over a long period of time. The effects of this can be seen on the terrain and in the condition of the animals. This might be food for thought for the Withypool Commoners' Association.

So competition is part of every-day life for free-living animals but do the Exmoor Ponies show any awareness of this? Within their own populations, the ponies compete with each other as they all require the same food. The establishment of home ranges is a response to such competition, ensuring that a herd has sufficient resources available to it. It is a dividing up of the environment which is part of instinctive behaviour not a conscious understanding of competing with each other. If food is in short supply then competition can become more obvious in that the hierarchy of position within the herd comes into play and the more dominant individuals will take priority. Giving way to a senior pony was not seen when the ponies were feeding on natural vegetation but when a group obtained access to cattle fodder in small quantities their rivalry emerged.

There seems to be no awareness in the ponies that the sheep, cattle and deer are competitors. The ranges of all these four species overlap and although Exmoors are rarely seen mixed in with cattle, associating with sheep is not uncommon. However, most of the time they keep apart. Deer and ponies will mix but this is not often seen. The important point is that they do not drive any of these other animals away. Their competitive instincts are preoccupied with other ponies of their own race and of different breeding. There is however one way in which the competition between the ponies and the sheep is reduced, which does show some specialisation similar to our African example. Whilst some plants are sought by both species, the ponies and sheep favour different vegetation types in which to find them. During the Withypool project, sheep preferred the totally open swards of grass whilst the Exmoor Ponies more often selected the areas lightly covered by bracken when there was a choice available. Studies on Dartmoor have also suggested that sheep, ponies and cattle have different preferences for vegetation types. So Nature is assisting the establishment of balance in these moorland communities.

The one animal which competes with the moorland grazers but which is in no way controlled is of course the human visitor. This conjures up the vision of people lying on the moor eating grass, which is of course ridiculous although we do pick the Bilberries which are delicious to man and animals alike. The main way in which we compete with the ponies and the agricultural stock is through inconsiderate use of the moorland. Several of the homes of the Exmoor Ponies are visited by many people in summer, usually in cars. Cars are thoughtlessly driven onto the moorland vegetation, sometimes considerable distances off roads and sadly often causing damage to the vegetation. Every patch that is ruined is a lost meal for the animals and if the public appreciated this perhaps more care would be taken. Education will undoubtedly prove to be crucial in the conservation of Exmoor and its animals.

We have concentrated here on looking at competition for food but of course any necessity of life may be competed for. On Exmoor water is freely available but in other circumstances, where it is a scarce resource, rivalry for it may be intense. This is particularly relevant to the situation of the Przewalski Horse when it still lived wild in Mongolia. Water-holes are few and far between and needed by both the wild animals and the people with their domesticated flocks and herds. The struggle between the Przewalski Horses and the nomadic people involved competing for access to the water. Where people were using a water-hole, it became inaccessible to the wild horses and it is thought this was one of the factors which lead to the extinction of Przewalski Horses in the wild. Shelter too can make the difference between life and death so with some animals this is also the object of rivalry.

Any animals living independently have enormous problems to overcome if they are to survive. They must endure climatic extremes and must forage successfully for food and water. This is challenge enough but the struggle is intensified through being only one of many who seek the same resources. Competition with one's own species and with other animals adds that extra dimension of difficulty to the business of surviving.

The Enemy Within

Even when an animal succeeds in obtaining enough food and water and avoiding ill-effects from exposure to hostile weather, the battle is not necessarily won. A further challenge comes from within, from parasites living inside an animal. The Exmoor Ponies are no exception and their capacity to thrive and maintain good body condition also relies on natural ability to cope with worm infestation.

Regular worming is essential when keeping horses or ponies in domestic circumstances, as is careful management of fields to minimise re-infestation. This involves clearing dung from the fields and stables to remove as many worm larvae as possible. There are also various systems of rotating animals between fields; sheep will not be contaminated by equine worms and vice versa, so they can usefully clean each other's pasture. Where such management is not carried out, the grass soon becomes "horse-sick" and the parasites reach damaging levels. A whole array of drugs have been developed to destroy different species of equine parasites. The main types of worms involved are Red Worm, Lung Worm, Round White Worm and Seat Worm. The larvae of Bot Fly also live in the digestive tract. Red Worms usually present the most serious problem and can cause severe loss of condition and ultimately death if not treated. With all worms, animals under three years of age are most susceptible to the harmful effects.

These internal parasites are not simply a part of domestic environments although their presence is concentrated in small enclosures. They are an inherent part of the moorland communities too and present a threat to the free-living ponies, who are continually involved in the parasites' natural life-cycles. As most of the Exmoor Ponies exhibit no obvious symptoms of infestation, we need to explore just how they manage to cope. We also have to identify what leads to some individuals experiencing problems.

The worm burdens of Exmoor Ponies have been studied and, yes, again this involves the researcher collecting and analysing dung. This seems to be an inescapable part of being a zoologist! It does however have its good side for the researcher must stay close to the ponies; usually they are observed from a considerable distance to avoid influencing their behaviour. So a few hours can be spent in companionship with the herd, coming to know them as individuals, noting their differing personalities. There was one occasion early in the study, when Royal Duke's herd were just becoming familiarised with their human follower and the stallion decided to investigate me more closely. He approached and sniffed me from top to bottom very carefully and then moved away, apparently satisfied that intentions were honourable. A marvellous, literally breath-taking moment never to be forgotten. However, back to the dung.

By counting the worm eggs in the dung, we can determine the degree to which the host animal is infested with the adult worms. It is a rough and ready process, complicated by seasonal variations due to the worms' life-cycles but it gives a reasonable picture of what is going on. The samples from adult Exmoor Ponies showed that they carry worm levels which in domestic circumstances would be treated. Yet they do not show the loss of condition which would be expected at these levels. This implies that they have a much higher tolerance of internal parasites when living in a natural environment. It must be at least partly environmentally related because Exmoors seem to be as vulnerable in domestic conditions as any horse or pony.

Certainly the habit of wandering over their range, grazing different areas as time progresses, minimises their contact with their own dung. Also they share the habitat with other grazers which has some cleansing effect. Yet we can see that the parasites still invade and manage to establish populations inside the ponies at significant levels, so it is not solely a matter of avoidance. The answer would appear to be that the Exmoors' greater tolerance depends upon them obtaining natural worming agents in their diet. We do not know exactly what plants provide this treatment. It is yet another study which is required. However, we have some clues that pine shoots may be one such agent. In Scotland it was observed that after eating pine shoots, the dung of

Exmoor Ponies was full of adult Red Worms which had been expelled from the gut. The ponies on Exmoor do not have access to pine, so there must be other food plants which perform this service.

It may also be a case of whether high worm counts lead to poor condition or whether a pony in poor condition becomes more susceptible and the worms multiply and cause more damage. Thus factors of diet and reproductive state may be influences on the ability to tolerate the worms. The state of the vegetation does seem to be important. Most of the Exmoor herds were examined and worm counts were higher (and the condition of the ponies not as good) where the vegetation was poorer, either in terms of the availability of favoured foods or due to deterioration in the vegetation generally. We have to be careful in assuming this is the whole story though because it might be that different herds have varying access to plants which contain anti-worm substances.

If we are to ensure that the homes of free-living Exmoor Ponies are adequate, it is important that we do find out more of this relationship between quality of habitat, body condition and parasites. The Exmoor Ponies have been included in such a study by Dr Gill (albeit in less detail than the main subject, the New Forest Ponies) and this should provide some answers in the future.

Where environmental deterioration is significant, we humans must look to restoring the natural balances necessary to allow the Exmoor Ponies to thrive. Sometimes though, where the majority of ponies exhibit no symptoms of parasitic damage, an individual may be in trouble. This inevitably means that the individual in question is weak by comparison to its fellows and that left to Nature would probably perish or fail to breed. As we have seen this callous rooting out of weakness maintains the hardiness of the population as a whole. Thus, such an individual should not be assisted to continue as a free-living pony and should be removed from the herd, treated and moved into domestic surroundings. The owners of one or two herds have begun in recent years to give their ponies worming

treatment when they are gathered onto the far[...]
the autumn for a day or two. This probably ass[...]
ponies as they go into the winter months but s[...]
the process of natural selection which is the [...]
of the Exmoors' hardiness. Whilst such w[...]
undeniably well-intentioned, in the long-t[...]
obstruct the conservation of the Exmoor[...]
animals in difficulty, the traditional practi[...]
effect of Nature and deals humanely wit[...]
We will return to this theme in the fina[...]

The crucial time for each pony seem[...]
years, perhaps often explaining th[...]
which have no identifiable cause[...]
become infected by internal paras[...]
obtain the necessary bacteria fo[...]
the foals instinctively eat som[...]
ingest the larvae of the wor[...]
feeding well and without of[...]
of the worms is controlled[...]
is less robust, they may r[...]
damage which cannot b[...]
ward sign of the effects [...]ally
bloated belly and po[...]n with
foals, which should perha[...]ers some
degree of weakness. In adults, [...]n and out
of the gut, visiting arteries, live[...]ing of the
body cavity depending on type of wo[...] They feed
from the host's blood and can damage the liver. The
outward effect when damage occurs is usually loss of
body substance rather than bloating. Seat Worms are not
as damaging but are a source of great irritation for the
ponies as they cause itching at the base of the tail. Foals
and adults alike are glad of the few wooden posts and
road signs in the enclosures as these make wonderful
scratching sites.

Sometimes though Nature itself can place even greater
burdens upon the ponies. The winters of 1988/89 and
1989/90 were unusually mild and we might think this
would be welcome respite for the ponies. Yet, in the
spring of 1990, the Exmoors looked generally poorer
than after the severest of winters. Why should that be? It
seems likely that worms might be involved. Normally,

Plate 87 *Road signs make effective rubbing posts to ease the irritation caused by seat worms*

the life-cycles are such that the numbers of eggs shed in
the dung diminishes significantly in winter. It may be
that the absence of cold conditions affected the ponies'
internal metabolism and allowed the parasites to continue producing eggs at high levels for longer. Thus
the normally reduced contamination of the grass in
winter failed to occur. Also, the milder conditions would
perhaps have allowed the eggs to remain active longer
on the ground, where normally there would be a
reducing potential for re-infestation. So, the ponies may
not have had their usual season of some respite from
re-infection by worms. The unnaturally mild weather
probably also affected the nutritional value of the
vegetation. This is pure speculation but when one of the
older Exmoor farmers was questioned about the poorer
condition of the ponies, he believed it was because there
had been no real winter.

So internal parasites are really another competitor, for
they compete for nutrients within the body fluids. There
are also various external parasites which place demands
upon an animal too. All these uninvited guests represent a tremendous challenge to any animal and Exmoor

Ponies seem able to meet this in most natural circumstances. The way they do this is far from clear but the importance of conserving the natural balance of their habitat cannot be over-emphasised; their survival will depend upon it.

Predators

Another harsh fact of life is that where you have populations of grazing animals, there are usually various types of carnivores which prey upon them. Predators usually take the sick, old or weak young animals, which are the easiest to catch. Whilst this is of course a matter of torment and death for the individual taken, it is again Nature weeding out all but the strongest for the long-term survival of the species. So avoiding predators is another dimension of surviving.

Britain is most unusual in that its free-living ponies no longer face the threat of natural predators. Its island situation allowed the human population to eradicate the carnivores which threatened their domestic animals many centuries ago. On mainland Europe such total destruction was never possible though numbers and distribution were greatly reduced.

If we go back to prehistoric times, the wild ponies had many types of predators including lions, hyenas, leopards, sabre-tooth tigers, bears, wolves and human hunters. The threat from these animals cultivated wariness and a preference for open country where the ponies had unrestricted views all around. The woods and forests were dangerous places for they offered the predators concealment. By grazing out on open terrain, predation could be restricted to the taking of isolated or weak animals, while the stronger members of the herds survived through co-operative behaviour. The formation of a herd is itself a survival mechanism for animals which are too large to find refuge from predators; there is safety in numbers.

Just two of the ancient predators survived into historic times along with humans and these were the bear and the wolf. According to Anthony Dent, bears were certainly in Britain in Roman times as some were exported to Rome, presumably for a most unhappy fate

in the Coliseum. There is some evidence that they were still present in the eighth century in England but Dent believes that bears were wiped out earlier in Wales specifically because of their threat to horse-breeding. He also cites the situations in Slovakia, the Carpathian and the Bosnian mountains in Europe. In these places, herdsmen regard bears as a greater menace to horse herds than the wolf, although the bears do not seek out and follow the horses. Rather they are opportunistic and will take foals if they encounter them by chance. Given the history of free-living ponies in Britain, bears and ponies must have formed a predator-prey relationship for a very long period.

Wolves are more diligent predators where horses are concerned. In the European locations quoted, wolves will move down to the low ground when herds are moved to their winter grazing, so that they may continue to prey on them. Like the bear, wolves were a danger to Britain's ponies over thousands of years and Man did not finally exterminate them until relatively recently. The last British wolf is thought to have been shot in Scotland in 1743. The demise of the wolf had occurred earlier in northern England, around the 1500s and even earlier than that in the south. Anthony Dent records that King John kept a pack of wolf-hounds as well as stag-hounds on Exmoor but that the wolves were probably gone by 1200.

Prior to the wolf's extinction in Britain, farmers with stock must have employed herdsmen specifically to protect their animals from attack. They must also have lost a certain proportion of their stock to wolves particularly where they grazed on unrestricted areas. There were obviously financial benefits when the wolf disappeared, in terms of reduced wage costs as well as no losses of the animals themselves. This makes it easy to understand why inducements were offered to kill wolves and this was probably far more important than any perceived threat to people themselves.

So today's Exmoor Ponies and all the free-living pony communities throughout Britain live at peace, with the wolf long gone. Yet they retain many of the instincts they needed when the packs of sleek, grey predators shared their homes and fed on them. Watch a herd of Exmoors and you will find that there are always two or three ponies which remain alert, acting as sentinels while the others rest. While the ponies feed, they continually look up and about them, scanning the horizons, checking for signs of danger. Just occasionally they have been seen reacting to a large dog rushing towards them and their behaviour is similar to that still seen where free-living ponies are preyed upon by wolves.

Perhaps our best description of ponies' defensive reaction to wolves comes from Portugal, where the feral horses or "garranos" have been studied in the Peneda-Geres National Park. Here the wolves present a particular threat to isolated horses but their attack on a herd has also been witnessed in winter. It seems that a herd is well able to defend itself and that when the attacking intentions of the wolves are recognised, the horses form a circle with the foals in its centre, well-protected. The mares face inwards and as wolves approach and attack, they lash out with their hind hooves, delivering disabling kicks. The stallion remains outside this defensive wheel and attacks the wolves with feet and teeth, defending his mares and offspring.

Reports from Canada also tell how wary horses are even of individual wolves and will move away, with the stallion bringing up the rear. The Caribou however seem to have evolved a remarkable ability to tell whether they are threatened by wolves. When wolves are hunting, they raise their hackles and the Caribou detect this and will flee. When not hunting, the wolves' coats lie flat and the Caribou will graze on whilst a pack passes by. We don't know if wild ponies ever showed such behaviour. It was suggested that as part of the research at Withypool an experiment on reaction to wolves might be carried out. The proposal was that I should obtain and wear a wolf skin (having anointed it with wolf urine) from a zoo and then approach a herd! Suffice it to say that the idea was not put into action. Anthony Dent does relate that ponies within earshot of the wolves at Whipsnade Zoo did not react to their howling.

In the last chapter, we saw that Exmoor Ponies on

Plate 88 *Ponies form a defensive circle in response to attack by wolves*

the moor have become much less nervous of human presence in recent years. Man ceased to be a true predator a long time ago. Certainly in prehistoric times as discussed, the wild ponies were an important source of food for people but as farming replaced hunting this moderated. It did not however cease and Celtic people still ate horse-meat. Given the effort required to hunt free animals it is more likely that the Celts kept horses domestically to provide food but they may still have taken some from the free-living pony herds. As we have seen, when the Christian church became influential, the eating of horse-flesh was banned as part of the drive to stamp out pagan life-styles. Today, the legacy of that ban persists and the British generally have a cultural distaste for the idea of eating horses.

Whatever the predator threatening them, healthy animals which are not vulnerable due to age or youth must avoid being killed. Where predators and prey are in balance, the hunting does not threaten the population as a whole because the majority survive. Thus they have to be well adapted to eluding the attentions of the carnivores. Textbooks on horse anatomy describe in great detail the structure of the horse's legs and how they evolved into superbly efficient running machines. The strength of the hoof is crucial and the Exmoor Pony has hooves which are notably more robust than found in domesticated breeds. So they are well-adapted to both fleeing and fighting with their feet. As we have already seen, their colouring and marking are probably adaptations for camouflage.

Today the human owners of the Exmoor herds do still remove animals; they have to maintain the population size within the limits of what the land will support. If an elderly pony becomes weak or sick it is usually removed from the moor and the same is true of any foals in distress. This mirrors the effect of predation.

Free-living ponies have thus enjoyed lives free from attack for the last few centuries and have not faced the tooth and claw threats their ancestors confronted. This must inevitably have affected their behaviour but as we see, their defensive instincts lie just hidden, re-surfacing when danger presents itself. For a few Exmoor Ponies there may have been a far more recent reminder of the power of the carnivore. On Molland Moor, during the 1970s, there were rumours of a puma at large, supposedly having been released out on the moor. When Exmoor Pony owners were asked about causes of death amongst ponies, the owners of the Molland herd reported they had lost a few foals which had been badly mauled, presumably by a big dog or cat! We cannot know if this was "the puma" or indeed if the foals were killed or died naturally and then became carrion. This was long before any of the reports of the "beast" of Exmoor which, if it exists, is supposed to be feline. Whether such a big cat existed then or exists now on

Exmoor is not certain but if it does, there have been no more reports of ponies being preyed upon. It just reminds us that once there were dangerous creatures which made survival even more of a challenge.

Surrender

Death is a part of the life of a herd just as it is with all living creatures and there are both natural and unnatural causes. When free-living ponies become elderly, they become less fit to cope with the struggle to survive and begin to lose condition. The owners of the herds keep a careful watch for old ponies which begin to fail and usually remove them rather than leave them to their fate. They may be put down by the vet or sometimes moved to "retirement quarters" where food and shelter are provided. The effect on the free population is the same as if they had died. Exmoor Ponies can live a long life even out on the moors; Golden Gorse was twenty seven when he died and mares have been known to reach their mid-thirties.

Death also comes naturally to a proportion of the foals born each year, presumably those with weaknesses, never destined to survive. Unfortunately, post-mortems are rarely carried out, so there is little firm information about causes of death. The local hunt kennels usually receive the corpses and they have reported that sometimes foals are malnourished and riddled with worms. Often there is no obvious cause of death and the favoured suggestions are pneumonia and bracken poisoning (foals being born often when the uncurling, immature fronds are at their most poisonous). We do not really know for sure and it would aid our understanding enormously if fatalities were investigated scientifically.

Just occasionally a mare may not produce enough milk. During the Withypool study this occurred once for certain and the foal was removed to be hand-reared and sold away from the moor. Perhaps this is more common than we can detect and contributes to the weak condition which allows worm damage or pneumonia. There was one case of a mare actually rejecting her foal but this is most unusual with free-living ponies. Again the foal was removed and did not rejoin the herd. In all such cases intervention does not interfere with Nature as the effect is equivalent to the death which would have resulted. Over a three year period, foal mortality on Withypool Common proved to be due to natural causes in 83% of cases while the other 17% arose from accidents or unnatural hazards. 12% of all foals born in 1975 died within their first six months and in the next two years, this increased to 24% and 27%.

The main unnatural factor in the ponies' environments is the motor car and road accidents do account for some deaths of both adults and young. Fortunately this is not such a problem as in the New Forest but is regular enough to be of concern. The skull pictured in an earlier chapter came from the stallion Bracken Sundown killed by a car on Winsford Hill back in the sixties. Royal Duke's son Aga, who succeeded him on Withypool Common, met an untimely end through a collision with a vehicle, as did Prince Arthur and a mare on Winsford Hill in 1991. One of the foal deaths during the study was due to a car as were three mare fatalities. Also, watching the ponies over several years, many near-misses were seen. In the New Forest there are experiments being carried out to cut the speed of vehicles and so far this seems to be reducing the number of animal deaths. Hopefully, through education, those living on or visiting Exmoor can be made aware of the need for care but similar measures may prove desirable.

When gates across roads were first replaced with cattle grids there was one instance of an accident to an Exmoor Pony. The spaces between the bars of the grid were too large and a stallion broke its leg and had to be destroyed. The grid was rebuilt with the correct spacing. However, they may still present a hazard and ponies have occasionally been known to jump them.

People can also bring dangerous materials into the ponies' homes. On one area, where the boundary hedge separated the moor from a farm, the farmer had been careless. Plastic feed sacks had blown over onto the moorland and one foal was seen chewing at these. In this case it lost interest and the sacks were taken away but potentially plastic is a harmful material. The plastic rings on sets of cans taken on picnics present a real threat to smaller mammals and to birds but would also harm a pony if eaten. Cans and the ring-pulls from them could also prove damaging. The plastic sack episode was not the only problem the ponies faced near this particular farm for on another occasion a foal was seen tangled up in a length of wire. Fortunately it eventually managed to free itself. Another case of entanglement, this time in barbed wire, occurred once elsewhere. The colt was badly cut and it had to be rescued. Again, the theme of caring for the ponies' homes and keeping them free of unnatural elements surfaces.

There have also been fatalities due to factors in the natural environment which are most unusual. One exceptionally dry summer, several ponies were found dead on Winsford Hill and when examined were thought to have died of poisoning as their livers were very brittle. The theory was put forward that the very low water level in the streams had given them access to plants they did not usually encounter but we will never know if this was truly the cause. A story of unusual death has come down through Mr Fred Milton's family about the severe winter of 1881. We have already talked of a group of Exmoors which became trapped by drifts and perished. The stallion with that group was the only pony to break out of their snow prison but luck was not with him. He was found dead, pulled down by a huge, solid ball of snow weighing about two hundred-weight, which had accumulated on his very long tail. Perhaps twigs or similar had caught in his tail as he struggled out and allowed the snow to form around them for no comparable event has been recorded elsewhere. The Milton family though decided from that day on to partly cut their ponies' tails. This probably aids recognition of their animals far more than it actually affects survival in snow.

One potentially fatal accident befell a young foal and was photographed by John Keene prior to him rescuing the animal. A mare close to the river was behaving in a most agitated way and on investigation, her foal was found in the river with its leg stuck between rocks. On another occasion a mare was found stuck fast in a deep, narrow ditch. She had walked in at one end where the

Plate 89 *This foal's leg was trapped between rocks in the river*

cutting was very shallow and carried on until only her head was above ground, as the ditch had progressively deepened. She could not or would not turn around and if left might well have perished. In this case, the mare had been handled and allowed herself to be assisted to escape. It may be that her history was significant; she had not lived on the moor until she was four and perhaps had developed insufficient wariness. Developing awareness of hazards and learning how to survive is crucially important in the early years. This is why older ponies should always be included with young stock if a new free-living group is established.

Without such "aunties" the inexperienced youngsters may not fare well and this suggests strongly that surviving is a matter of learning as well as instinct.

The majority of free-living Exmoors have inherited a wonderful survival kit which allows them to live free successfully. They grow up in a herd community and acquire the herd wisdom of how to cope with testing conditions. They are the "fittest" referred to in this book's title. These Exmoors thrive and grow to maturity. Only then, when they breed can they achieve Nature's purpose, the passing on of successful genes to the next generation.

CHAPTER 9

BREEDING

In the summer of 1960, a very special filly foal was born into the free-living herd of Exmoor Ponies on Withypool Common. As all true Exmoor Ponies are virtually identical in markings, there was nothing at the time to make her distinctive but she was destined to be quite remarkable some twenty years later. In her first autumn, she was gathered in off the common along with all the other ponies and taken to Weatherslade Farm, where she passed the Exmoor Pony Society inspection and was registered. Mr Fred Milton, her owner, gave this filly the name "Red Bay" and judged her good enough to remain with the herd. So, while the other foals were sold, Red Bay returned with her mother to the moorland to become, in time, a breeding mare herself. What then was to be so special about this mare?

One morning in May 1980, high up on the northern part of the Common, known as Bradymoor, Red Bay gave birth to a colt foal. There was nothing unusual about that but a short while later she repeated the event and produced a second colt. Twins are very rare in native ponies and, even when occasionally born, it is not unusual for one or both to die, even in domestic conditions. Red Bay not only gave birth to twins but she reared both successfully, without any assistance, out on the open moor. Mr Milton remembers this happening

only once before, in the 1950s, and those twins were sold at Bampton Fair. Red Bay reared her colts well and both grew strongly. When their turn came for inspection in the autumn, both colts passed and were named Red King II and Red Boy II; both had been sired by the stallion Royal Duke.

Happily, we can follow the story of the twins further, for they stayed together and can be seen today, as geldings, at Tettenhall Horse Sanctuary, near Wolverhampton. Their owner Mr Billy Wilson tells us:

> *The twins are fully matured as good examples of Exmoor Ponies. They do stick closely together and live with a family of 16 pure Exmoor Ponies here at the Sanctuary. They were two years old when I bought them from Fred Milton and they were very difficult to handle at first. Each was broken to saddle; Red King went through a year of schooling to ride and became very quiet. With no-one available to do more with them, they remain turned out with the herd and surprisingly, Red King has gone back to being wild much more so than his brother.*[90]

So we are very fortunate in being able to see how Red Bay's twin sons developed and they are a living tribute to her outstanding quality as a free-living mare. Twins then are the exception and we must return to Exmoor to

Plate 90 *Red Bay 23/62 with twin colts on Withypool Common in 1980*

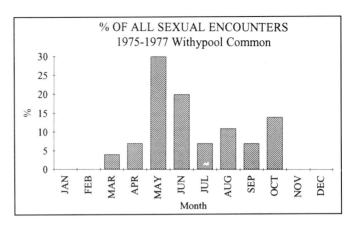

Figure 9.01 *The breeding season*

look at the normal breeding activities of the free-living herds.

The Breeding Cycle

Visiting the free-living Exmoor Ponies in winter, we would see a group of animals obsessed with just two things, obtaining enough food and finding natural shelter where they can. As we have seen, winter is all about individual survival so sex is an irrelevancy. From October to early March, the herd stallion shows no interest whatsoever in his mares, for there is a specific breeding season with free-living Exmoors and all sexual activity is suspended during the harsher months. This dormant period is known technically as anoestrus for the mares do not come on heat (are not in oestrus) and so fail to attract the stallion's attention.

Figure 9.01 shows this separation into a breeding and a non-breeding season; it is known as a monoestrus cycle and is seen with many types of horse living free, such as New Forest Ponies and Mustangs in America. It all depends upon the response of the ponies' hormonal systems to factors such as day-length, light intensity and diet. It is thought that there is hormonal sensitivity in the stallion as well as the mares. Thus when the days shorten, the sun shines less brightly and the nutritive

value of the food declines in the autumn, the ponies' sexual systems "close-down" for the winter. This is an important survival mechanism because energy must be conserved as we have seen in the last chapter and no unnecessary activity can be sustained. Of course many of the mares will already be growing a new foal and this is unaffected by the anoestrus period except that it benefits from the mare concentrating on feeding.

The exact timing of the beginning of each year's breeding season varies a little depending on the environmental conditions but is usually in March. Longer, brighter days and increased temperatures in spring stimulate the production of follicle stimulating hormone which triggers the onset of the oestrus cycle in the sexually mature mares. During the Withypool study in the '70s, behavioural observations were made over thousands of hours and few matings were seen in March, although the stallions were certainly interested and made unsuccessful approaches. In a study of Welsh ponies it was found that foals conceived in March were carried as much as a month longer than those conceived in June, thus timing the birth for more suitable conditions in the main foaling season. So it is advantageous if mares do not conceive early in the mating season. Of course this is not conscious family planning on the part

Plate 91 *Dazzling Boy (85/32) and Knightoncombe Muslin (H8/33) mating*

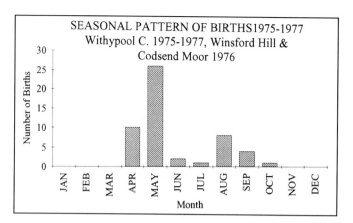

Figure 9.02 *The foaling season*

of the ponies; perhaps the effectiveness of the mare's oestrus builds up slowly at the start.

Mares who are not already carrying a foal come into oestrus about every twenty one days, until they conceive and then they cease to be sexually active throughout the pregnancy. The gestation period is approximately eleven months. About nine days after giving birth, there is a "foal-heat" when conception can occur again but generally this does not take place until the next oestrus, twenty one days later. Thus, for most mares, conception a month after foaling plus the pregnancy of eleven months, times the next foal for about the same time the following year.

The Foaling Season

Free-living Exmoor Ponies have a definite foaling season which, as with many animals, is a response to living in a highly seasonal environment. The chances of foals surviving are considerably greater if they are born during the summer, when weather and food supply are at their best. During the Withypool study, the births of foals were logged over a period of three years. Figure 9.02 illustrates that the foaling season spanned April to October but that the majority of foals, some 69%, were born in April and May, mostly in the latter. A similar seasonal pattern has been identified in the New Forest. The earliest foaling seen, during the study on Exmoor, was on April 18th on Codsend Moor while the latest was on October 22nd on Withypool Common.

Occasionally, a mare may fail to conform to the natural cycles and seasons; we have already heard of the foal born into No.23 herd on a Christmas Eve. So there may be births which occur outside the main season but overall the ponies are adapted to breeding mainly in early summer. This is certainly the best start for a foal, for it then has several months of kinder weather and good milk supply (as its mother is feeding well) before the onset of its first autumn and winter.

Zoological researchers are not kindly treated by the animals they study. After spending day after day watching a group of mares, the least they might do is to have the decency to foal while the observer watches. Yet this reward is almost always withheld. No foalings were seen during the Withypool study and similarly, the American researchers who observed Mustangs failed to see a birth. The stories of mares in domestic conditions seemingly hanging on until their owner's back is turned are many. It seems likely then that a mare has some control over the timing of her foaling and can delay to a certain extent until she is relaxed.

Fortunately, on an August day in 1989, when Frances O'Connell, an Exmoor Pony Society member and veterinary student, was visiting Exmoor, luck was with her and she witnessed a birth. Happily for us, she had her camera with her and captured a wonderful series of photographs of what followed. Frances takes up the story:

It was a warm, sunny afternoon as my two companions and I drove slowly across Exmoor on the look-out for Exmoor Ponies. We had driven all the way down from Edinburgh to attend the annual Exmoor Pony breed show but also planned to spend some time on the moors looking at the wild ponies about which we had heard so much.

As soon as we crossed into the common land I began to scan the horizon for any signs of pony life. The wild, open beauty of the place took my breath away and my eyes were constantly distracted by the vista of hills and valleys, bracken and moorland. There was also an indefinable "something more"; maybe it was the knowledge that I was gazing across part of Britain's heritage which had remained unchanged for generations that gave Exmoor its extra time-less quality. All we needed now was a herd of Exmoor Ponies to complete the scene.

We came across our first group of ponies quite accidentally as we stopped to admire one particularly breath-taking view. The ponies just materialised on the slopes below us and we watched them as they grazed steadily down the hill. Flushed with our first sighting of a herd we returned to the car and carried on.

We stopped again on the far side of Withypool Common just past Landacre Bridge, which is a favourite spot for picnickers. Sure enough, a couple of cars were parked on the river bank and some children were splashing about in the water. We scanned the hillside and spotted an unmistakable brown form in the distance, so we set off on foot, crossed the river and headed up the slope. As we got nearer we realised there were a lot more ponies than any of us had imagined as more and more heads popped out of the bracken. There must have been at least forty animals in the herd including all the mares and foals around us.

Suddenly we spotted the stallion. It was the grand old man – Golden Gorse himself who was already then twenty six and had probably sired more Exmoor Ponies than most people see in a lifetime. This was a real find for us. He looked us up and down and obviously decided we were harmless enough as he resumed the serious business of eating grass while keeping an eye on his charges scattered over the hillside. We didn't want to disturb the ponies, so we settled down in the bracken close to the main group. They didn't interfere with us so we didn't interfere with them. I could have stayed there for hours, watching the foals playing in the bracken and listening to the quiet munching of the grass. There was continually something interesting to watch.

My eyes rested on a mare who seemed rather restless. My first thought was that she was in season and was trying to attract the attention of the stallion as she paced back and forth, raising and lowering her tail. Suddenly as she turned towards us, the explanation became obvious – she was the most hugely pregnant pony I had ever seen and I gasped with excitement as I realised she was shortly to give birth.

Surprisingly, the mare took no notice of us sitting only 30 feet away or even of any of the other ponies close by and she made no attempt to distance herself from the group. Finally she seemed satisfied with the patch of ground she had chosen and settled down to the serious business of labour. The place she had selected was literally right in the middle of the herd which surprised me as I had always believed that mares took themselves off to some distant, secluded place to foal. Maybe we have always been wrong in our assumptions; so few foalings are ever observed in the wild that we really don't know for sure. It would certainly make sense that the safest place to foal would be surrounded by the herd.

She looked quite a mature mare and we guessed that she had been through it all many times although probably never with such an excited audience before. Even then, I still didn't really believe she was actually going to give birth right then and there in front of us but that is just what she did and all in about twenty minutes. The other ponies took very little notice, apart from one who stayed close by her side and intently watched her tail-end the whole time.

Interestingly, it wasn't a fellow mare or even the stallion but an adult gelding. We didn't know why he was running with the herd but, more intriguingly, we had no idea why he was the only one to stay by the mare. She took very little notice of him but it would be nice to think that she derived some comfort from his presence. Maybe he was her usual companion in the herd or perhaps they were related. We don't know and it may have been that he was just nearby at the time.

Throughout the early stages, the mare remained standing on the same spot. Her ears were back and she seemed to have an expression of inward concentration and she made no sound. Within minutes her efforts were rewarded as the glistening foetal membranes containing the amniotic fluid appeared. At this point she lay down so all we could see was her head through the bracken. The gelding moved closer until his nose was only inches away from her rump. She let out a low groan and strained again; he seemed to huff gently as if to encourage the mare. I clenched my fists willing everything to go smoothly as, if anything went wrong there would be no way to help. She was, after all, a wild pony and we had no right to interfere. Only the fittest can survive on Exmoor.

A couple of minutes later, she heaved herself to her feet and turned round and we caught our first glimpse of the foal as his nose and feet were just peeking out from under her tail. I heaved a sigh of relief as the foal was coming the right way round. So far, so good. Again she turned around and lay down, then stood up and went down once more as if she couldn't quite decide how to get comfortable. The contractions were coming more regularly now and we knew it wouldn't be much longer.

She lay down for what was to be the last time. Occasionally, her head came up when she appeared to be giving an extra hard push. Finally she was still. I wanted to leap up and rush over to where she was lying as the tension was almost unbearable but I knew better than to do so. Suddenly, what I can only describe as a glistening white cap appeared in amongst the bracken fronds behind the mare. This was our first proper sight of the seconds-old foal as he struggled to sit up, still covered by the membranes.

The mare lay still for a few moments and then heaved

Plate 92 *Bright Bay (23/80), aged 21, giving birth on Withypool Common in 1989*

Plate 93 *Bright Bay cleaning her new-born foal*

herself to her feet. She seemed to know instinctively that she had to break open the foetal sac as quickly as possible before the foal suffocated inside. Many mares actually stand up at the moment of foaling and so the membranes break open themselves as the foal drops to the ground but not this time. The mother bit open the sac and began to lick the foal's *head clean with vigorous movements of her tongue. She nickered softly to her new son and his head turned to her in response. It had all taken such a short time. Carefully and systematically, she dried him all over and began to eat up the remnants of the membranes. This is both a valuable source of nutrients to the mare as well as a protective measure to destroy traces of the birth which might attract predators.*

The gelding was still standing by and cautiously approached the foal but the mare was not going to allow anyone near her newborn foal and warned him away. Several other mares now also showed an interest in the new arrival but they too were warned off to a discreet distance and stood together with the gelding sniffing the air curiously. Within minutes, the foal made several determined efforts to rise to his feet although he still had a broad band of membrane tangled around his middle. What with that, his ungainly legs and the effects of gravity, he didn't quite make it and flopped back into the bracken.

I could have sat there all evening entranced but sadly we had to leave. I looked back for a final glimpse and saw that the foal's curly coat was just beginning to dry and his shiny wet ears which had been slicked down to his head were beginning to prick up. The mare looked up at us as we slowly backed away. I wonder what she was thinking. Although her brand-mark was not very clear, we thought it was 23/80, a twenty three year old mare called Bright Bay. She had given us an afternoon on Exmoor which I will never forget.

As we neared the road, a family of German tourists was just climbing out of their car. We exchanged greetings and they told me that they were on a ten-day holiday in Britain and were going to visit as many of the British parks and moorlands as they could manage. They did not seem very impressed with Exmoor and the father said to me: "New Forest Ponies were much more friendly and came right to the car and ate crisps and sweets from our hands. Whereas these ponies never seem to do anything so interesting". I just turned and looked back at the brown shapes on the distant hill and smiled secretly to myself . . . . if only they knew! [91]

The Exmoor Foal

Exmoor foals are born with the well-defined mealy muzzle and eye ring shown by the adult ponies but have a much paler coat colour. They are born pale brown or fawn and gradually darken as they mature, often passing through a rich, sandy-coloured phase. They show the natural fixed blueprint of markings from birth and, as in adulthood, the differences between foals are quite subtle. After about six months, when they have grown their first winter coat, they have the adult coloration. This gradual darkening with the development of the winter coat does not occur evenly over the whole body but frequently begins with the head, sometimes producing dark-faced foals at the intermediate stage.

At birth, the foal has a short, stiff mane, no forelock and a short curly tail, all much lighter in colour than those of the adults. This erect mane gradually grows in length and begins to fall over to the side and between the ears. Eventually it becomes the long floppy mane seen in the adults but even at the yearling stage, the mane can still be quite upright; it varies from individual to individual.

During the Withypool study, the heights of foals were estimated and most of the foals of up to one week old were close to 7.3 hands. Their rate of growth was fastest in the first two weeks of life and then gradually slowed; most foals grew to 75% of their adult height within their first year.

Although few are privileged enough to witness a birth, observing young foals at play is easier to experience. There is little to compare with sitting quietly on a summer's evening watching as the young foals become skittish and decide to test out their now firmer legs. They run in great circles around their mothers and their joy is obvious. Then they will run back to her and play, pushing into her side and ducking under her neck. The mares are so gentle with their offspring at this stage. The bouts of madness are soon over though for the young foals quickly tire and after a quick feed will lie down to rest again.

As the weeks pass, the foals become more adventurous. Their circles become larger and their speed

Plate 94 *The foal's first efforts at standing were unsuccessful and it rested beside Bright Bay*

Plate 95 *Young Exmoor foals have the mealy markings but a lighter brown coat colour (Knightoncombe Muslin H8/33 showing dappled summer coat, with 1991 foal)*

Plate 96 *By six months old, foals have grown their first winter coat and are much like the adults except for the short mane and tail (herd 23 on Bradymoor after the gathering)*

Plate 97 *As the foal grows older, the upright mane lengthens and begins to fall to one side*

increases with their growing confidence. Gradually they discover that other foals make better play-mates than mother. As they play, the foals in fact are testing out many skills they will need as adults. Their speed and sure-footedness will be important and when young colts rear up together, it is in practice for any masculine confrontations they may face. Their encounters with adult ponies also teach the foals their place with their mother and introduce them to the hierarchy within the herd.

Plate 98 *Play is an important rehearsal for adult life—Knightoncombe Goldcrest (H8/77) and Knightoncombe Double Dart (H8/78) play-fighting*

Reproductive Life

Studies in the New Forest have shown that most mares do not begin oestrus until their third summer when they are two years old, although a few did start their reproductive life at about fifteen months. We have no detailed information about free-living Exmoor fillies but during the Withypool study, no two year-olds produced a foal while 50% of three year olds gave birth. There were no matings seen between stallions and yearling fillies. So it would seem that the onset of oestrus is around the third summer on Exmoor too.

The age at which a mare ceases to breed varies considerably. It is dependent upon the mare's health and that in turn may depend upon the environment she lives in. Often the state of the teeth will determine how well a pony can feed and thrive. If all is well with her dentition and general body condition, a mare may continue to breed, though advanced in years. The record to date seems to be an Exmoor mare from Codsend Moor who successfully reared a foal at thirty five years old! This was exceptional and, generally, mares continue breeding into their mid to late twenties. For example, Figure 9.03 shows the number of foals registered to mares of different ages for Herd 23. If mares are seen to have difficulty in over-wintering, they are likely to be removed from the moorland life by their owners, so we cannot be sure what the normal limits are for free-living mares.

A breeding life of twenty years is therefore seen with some free-living Exmoor mares. We do not have much information about stallions because the moving of stallions, often away from the free-living herds, frequently comes before their natural decline in fertility. This is because exchanging stallions is a means of controlling in-breeding. However, in some cases, moorland stallions have lived out all or most of their reproductive life with the same herd. On Withypool Common, for example, Golden Gorse 23/69 was herd stallion with No. 23 herd for over twenty years; his sire, Forest 23/33 was herd stallion for thirteen years. On Codsend Moor, two stallions served for ten years each, Tommy 12/19 and his son, Aclander 12/34. These few examples are insufficient though to define the fertile life of a stallion out on the moor. Again, it will vary with the animal's condition and the quality of its habitat.

On Withypool Common during 1975–77, the foaling patterns of 18 mares which could be easily identified were studied and the results are shown in Figure 9.04. Over the three years, seven of the mares produced two foals, six gave birth once, four had a foal each year and just one was barren throughout. This was a small sample and research in the New Forest has confirmed that the majority of free-living mares will foal twice in succession and then have a year's break. So, with Exmoor mares having a potential breeding life of around twenty years, they could contribute about 13 foals to the population. There are of course some which produce more and a few which prove to be totally barren.

Unfortunately, we cannot get true breeding statistics from the Exmoor Pony Society stud book because it

Plate 99 *A herd No. 12 mare, aged 35, with her foal on Codsend Moor*

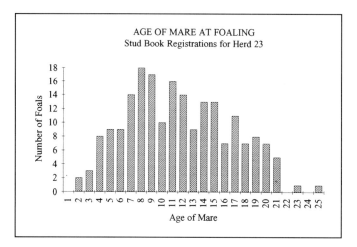

Figure 9.03 *The number of foals registered to mares of different ages*

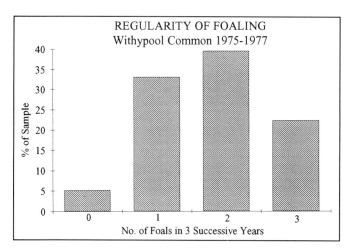

Figure 9.04 *The foaling frequency for a sample of 18 mares*

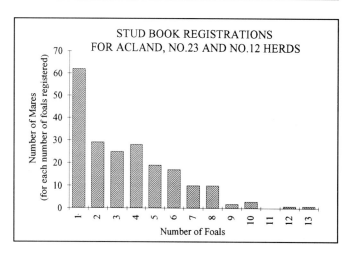

Figure 9.05 *Breeding performance of free-living mares*

records only those foals which pass inspection, which is not necessarily the total offspring for any mare. However, if looked upon as minimum figures, the information in the stud book provides interesting profiles of the breeding performance of moorland mares, as shown

in Figure 9.05 (based on analysis of registrations up to and including 1989). We can see that most mares had just a single foal registered but perhaps these mares were not long-serving members of the herd. For the rest, there is a fairly even spread from two to four foals per mare, declining numbers from five to eight foals per mare and only a few achieved nine or more registered offspring.

The free-living Exmoor Ponies are socially grouped in herds where a number of mares live with a herd stallion. The number of mares associated with a stallion will depend upon the maturity of the male and what other stallions are present on the same area, as we saw with the Withypool herds in Chapter 7. About 15 mares to a stallion would seem to be the maximum desirable for a stable situation. In unmanaged situations where stallion numbers are not restricted, as with Mustangs, herds are often composed of less than six mares with a stallion.

During the breeding season, mature stallions can be very possessive about their mares but where stable herd situations exist, they seem fairly relaxed. During the time Royal Duke was building his herd on Withypool Common, Golden Gorse displayed herding behaviour quite frequently. He could be seen driving mares which had strayed away from his herd back into the group, with his neck and head held low to the ground and stretched out before him. Most mares would comply without dissent. On one occasion though, a mare was seen to make a purposeful break for freedom. She failed to get away from Golden Gorse and the stallion proceeded to discipline her quite roughly, pushing her back into the group and even pushing the mare down on the ground. The next summer though, there was much less of this possessive behaviour.

We should not think that the herd stallion always reigns supreme and "calls the shots". Some mares have very clear ideas of how they wish to lead their life. During the Withypool study, one mare demonstrated a totally emancipated approach to breeding. She lived all year with the younger stallion, Royal Duke, but one day in May left the herd. Royal Duke did not try to stop her and she crossed the river and walked up the hill onto Bradymoor. There she stayed for two days, mating with Golden Gorse, and then she calmly walked back to her cuckolded partner, Royal Duke, and rejoined his herd.

Mares can also prove quite daunting for a young stallion and certainly the older mares teach a new herd stallion his manners. Inexperienced stallions have to suffer a probationary period in which they often receive quite hard kicks in the chest as their reward for amorous advances. Eventually they are taught their place and come to be fully accepted by the breeding mares. As mentioned earlier, stallions rarely if ever show interest in yearling fillies when they have plenty of mature mares available, in the free-living situation. Sometimes though, young mares can be pretty shameless. One young stallion was receiving considerable discouragement from the older mares in his group and when he was kicked away, a two year old mare would frequently present herself as consolation!

Mating takes place at any time of the day or night but one group of Exmoor Ponies in Germany appeared to prefer the darkness. Their owner wrote to ask if Exmoor Ponies were particularly shy as he never saw them mating but could hear their squeals after dark! Photo-graphing ponies mating can have its pitfalls too. Near to the end of the Withypool study, the photographic collection was still missing a picture of mating, when Royal Duke decided to oblige. Several photos were taken in quick succession accompanied by my exclamations of delight. Unfortunately, the ladies picnicking nearby were unaware of the circumstances and looked very strangely at this woman so enthusiastically photographing the passionate ponies!

The Productivity of the Herds

The herds of Exmoor Ponies out on the moor have been established by their owners in a way that maximises the productivity of each group. Harem groups of mares, each with a herd stallion, are the most efficient way to utilise restricted grazing rights, although, as we will consider later, it may not be the best way to genetically manage the populations. During the Withypool study, the productivity of the herds was investigated.

It is easy to calculate productivity, given that the identities and ages of the mares are known. The number of potential foals is calculated by taking the number of mares of three years and over. The number of actual births are counted and then expressed as a percentage of the potential births; this percentage is the population's productivity. It was measured for the herds on Withypool Common and Winsford Hill between 1975 and 1978. Figure 9.06 shows that over a four year period, the results were alike for both places. Productivity will obviously be affected by the level of fertility of the stallions but the similar pattern of results suggested that something environmental was at work.

The conclusion of the study was that the fall in productivity in 1977 was a result of the drought conditions in 1976 which had led to reductions in the quantity and quality of vegetation available to the ponies from autumn 1976 onwards. During that 1976/77 winter, five aborted foetuses were reported from a herd of mongrel mares which shared Withypool Common and were fed each day. Without such regular close contact with the Exmoor herds, we cannot know whether such natural abortions accounted for the fewer foals the following summer but

Plate 100 *With this year's foal successfully born, sire and dam share a tender moment.*

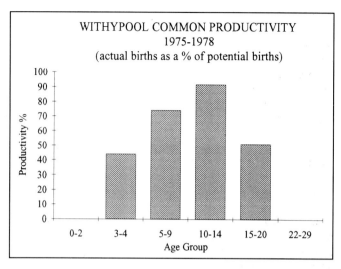

Figure 9.07 *Variation in productivity with age of mare*

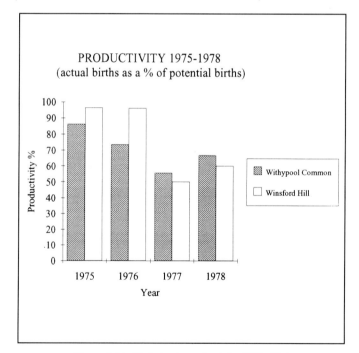

Figure 9.06 *Variation in productivity 1975–1978*

it would seem likely as the mares would probably have been pregnant before the difficult conditions arose.

Mares of different age groups also show differing productivity. Figure 9.07 illustrates this and shows that between 1975 and 1978 the highest productivity on Withypool Common (92%) was amongst mares between ten and fourteen years old. The results showed a build up in productivity to this peak, then a fall with older mares. Mares over twenty couldn't be included in the study as only one mare came into this category and this was an insufficient sample.

The success of breeding in the moorland herds therefore depends upon many factors, some under their owners' control and some naturally independent. The age structure of the herds, the numbers of stallions and the numbers of other stock which compete for food resources all affect breeding rates and can be managed. However, so much depends upon the health of the mares which in turn is affected by their natural habitat and weather conditions. Careful conservation of their moorland homes is thus important in maintaining a successful breeding population of Exmoor Ponies.

Natural versus Unnatural Influences

Whilst looking at reproduction, we have seen many natural responses on the part of the ponies, yet it is in this area of breeding that most of the artificial elements of their life are to be found. If we are to assess their place on the wild to domestic spectrum later, we must understand clearly the areas in which free-living Exmoors are different from wild animals.

The main reason for the domestic influences upon the herds is that they live now on small geographically isolated areas of moorland. Each sub-population exists as if on an island for there can be no movement of animals from one place to another unless deliberately arranged by the owners. The smallness of their homes, around two thousand acres at most, means that the numbers of ponies which can be grazed on any one area is small. Also, grazing rights are restricted because cattle and sheep are usually also grazed on the same areas. With a finite limit to the number of ponies which can be run on any area, the hill farmer must design his herd so that he makes the best use of the grazing rights. This inevitably means one or two stallions only with the maximum number of mares.

This management system also means that the offspring have to be taken away from the herd as numbers cannot build up; if youngstock are to remain then older ponies must make way for them. Also, old ponies are rarely part of the herd system because if they find over-wintering difficult or cease to breed regularly, their owners will remove them. So the free-living herds have unnatural age structures with very few young and old animals as permanent members of the herds.

The most significant effect of this is that young males are seldom left in a herd. If it occurs, there will be perhaps just one colt being brought on for a future herd stallion. This means that the herd stallions are always selected by humans not by natural selection. In unmanaged situations such as with the Mustangs, the sex ratio of the whole population is 1:1 and there are bachelor groups as well as harem herds. The young males compete vigorously with each other and only the strongest will be able to successfully challenge a herd stallion and assume the role himself. Thus the fittest males breed and contribute the best adapted genes to the future.

With the free-living Exmoor herds, the owners' selections can only be based upon judgement of external characteristics and some consideration of the closeness of relationship to the breeding mares, to control inbreeding. In essence, the colt that looks the best is likely to be selected and undergoes nothing comparable to the trials he would endure to become a herd stallion in the wild. The effect of this is that human preferences and judgements have to some extent weakened the impact of natural selection. This is true of course with the filly foals chosen to remain in the herds as well. Although all the chosen ponies must have adequate survival capabilities, this artificial selection cannot guarantee that the genetically fittest are the ones to breed. In 1859, Charles Darwin wrote of the inadequacy of human choices in his *Origin of the Species*:

> As man can produce a great result by selection, what may not natural selection effect? Man can act only on external and visible characters: Nature, if I may be allowed to personify the natural preservation or survival of the fittest, cares nothing for appearances, except in so far as they are useful to any being. She can act on every internal organ, on every shade of constitutional difference, on the whole machinery of life. Man selects only for his own good: Nature only for the being which she tends. The slightest differences may turn the nicely balanced scales in the struggle for life, and so be preserved. How fleeting are the wishes and efforts of man! how short his time! and consequently how poor will be his results, compared with those accumulated by Nature during whole geological periods! Can we wonder then that Nature's productions should be far "truer" in character than man's productions; that they should be infinitely better adapted to the most complex conditions of life, and should plainly bear the stamp of far higher workmanship? [92]

Darwin's words are relevant even for breeders of Exmoor Ponies because human selection has overshadowed natural selection in terms of breeding since 1818. We cannot know exactly how significant human choices are, for we have no way of testing which animals would have ben successful if there had been no interference. It would certainly prove an interesting experiment if we could allow a group to live unmanaged on a large, remote area and after several generations compare the most successful animals with those living in the Exmoor herds today.

The geographical isolation of the moorland herds has also produced some effects which would probably not have occurred if the groups had been in contact with one another and ponies were freely able to move around. Traditionally owners have been rightly proud of their ponies and have tended to line breed rather than freely mix the blood from different locations. This has inevitably led to the emergence of some identifiable strains within the population. Thus we can recognise an Anchor pony or a Withypool pony or a Codsend pony. In a totally free state, this would probably not be the case unless small groups became isolated by a natural barrier from the others.

The Gene Pool

When animals reproduce, they pass on all the information needed to form their offspring within the chromosomes contained in their eggs and sperm. Chromosomes are made up of genes which are like a blueprint for how each cell of the new animal should form and function. With the exception of identical twins, every living organism is unique as no two animals can have exactly the same set of genes . So if we think about the Exmoor Pony population, as with any population of animals, their total genes form what we may call the gene pool of their race.

Man has had an overwhelming effect on the Exmoor Pony gene pool. Every time he cross-bred without conserving the pure animal, the gene pool of the true race shrank. Each time the population was reduced, the variation within the gene pool became more limited. Thus by losing the British Hill Pony everywhere except Exmoor, the gene pool was decimated. Then by gradually reducing the numbers on Exmoor, the trend continued. Eventually, with the devastation to the population in the Second World War, the gene pool went

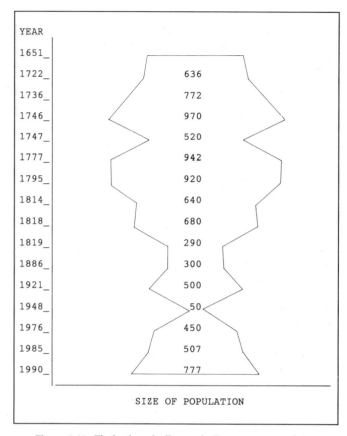

YEAR	
1651	
1722	636
1736	772
1746	970
1747	520
1777	942
1795	920
1814	640
1818	680
1819	290
1886	300
1921	500
1948	50
1976	450
1985	507
1990	777

SIZE OF POPULATION

Figure 9.08 *The bottle-neck effect on the Exmoor pony population*

through a bottle-neck, as Figure 9.08 shows. The genetic variation that existed when around 500 ponies were left was little enough; with numbers reduced to about 50, the gene pool was squeezed into a droplet.

This means that the ponies alive today can only represent the various combinations of genetic material which were present in the surviving fifty animals. Thus, we should not be surprised at how similar the genetic profiles of the individual ponies studied so far have proved to be. The blood-typing results we reviewed in Chapter 4 showed us animals with little variation between them and the funnelling of the gene pool has contributed to this. It also means that we cannot dismiss lightly the idea that there were other variants in the population in earlier times. Indeed the limited photographic history that exists suggests that the Exmoor Pony population is more uniform now than at the beginning of the century. This arises from both the narrowing of the gene pool in the 1940s and the effect of fashion and selection in the management of the breeding of the ponies.

Nature thrives on variation. The whole process of evolution depends upon the endless production of small changes allowing species to become better adapted to surviving. People, however, are only comfortable with clearly defined entities and this has had its impact upon the Exmoor Ponies. Breeders over the centuries have not produced their own version of an Exmoor Pony but rather have channelled its development down a narrow path. Today's Exmoors have their natural blueprint but it is one which Man has made more fixed than Nature might have. It seems probable that had a large population of British Hill Ponies survived in the wild, they would show a greater range of subtle variations than we see in our Exmoors today.

Perhaps this is easiest to understand if we think of an analogy. Suppose that the entire human population of Great Britain were wiped out except on Exmoor. The remaining people would all still be human beings but would not represent the full range of variation in human characteristics. Regional features, languages, dialects and customs as diverse as those from Scotland to Cornwall would not be present in the surviving population. Thus the Exmoor survivors could only contribute their characteristics to the new Britain. This would be a funnelling of the human gene pool.

Our Exmoor Ponies are truly then just a remnant of the British Hill Pony population. The genetic information as to what a British Hill Pony should be like has been passed down through the generations and Man's breeding management has reinforced the design that Nature formed thousands of years ago and continues to modify.

Bloodlines

One of the major problems that results from a constriction to the gene pool of a species is that very few bloodlines are present in the population after funnelling. As we have seen, the Exmoor Pony population on Exmoor was reduced to around 50 animals after the war, representing very few family lines. From the records of the Exmoor Pony Society stud book, it seems that we have either two or three stallion lines and the bloodlines within the mare population await detailed analysis. Preliminary work suggests that the mares go back to a foundation stock of just six stallions and seven mares.

Figure 9.09 shows the male lines represented in the stallion population up to April 1991. This is based upon the stud book issued before 1980 plus subsequent registrations. In the 1980 issue, the registration details for Crackshot I (1/10) had been amended to show Caractacus (1/9) as his sire, thus reducing the number of masculine lines in the stallions from three to two. The parentage of Crackshot I is the subject of continued dispute within the Society. If Crackshot I is really the son of Caractacus, then this would have meant Caractacus sired him when he was just one year old. This is not impossible given that No.1 herd was not free-living but remains unlikely. Both Caractacus and Crackshot I were sold to Mary Speed and taken to Scotland. According to James Speed, the two stallions were not father and son. Both stallions were registered in the Polo Pony Stud Book, Exmoor section, and Crackshot I's sire was given as an Acland stallion. As this entry is below that for Caractacus, it seems likely the latter would have been identified as the sire if he had been so. Probably then, they were not father and son. Yet they could easily have had the same Acland sire, so we may yet have just the two bloodlines.

There are of course many links between the stallions shown in the two/three bloodlines through their maternal relationships. This makes the study of the population very complex and the full contribution of the foundation animals will not be fully understood until the recently computerised stud book is analysed and inter-

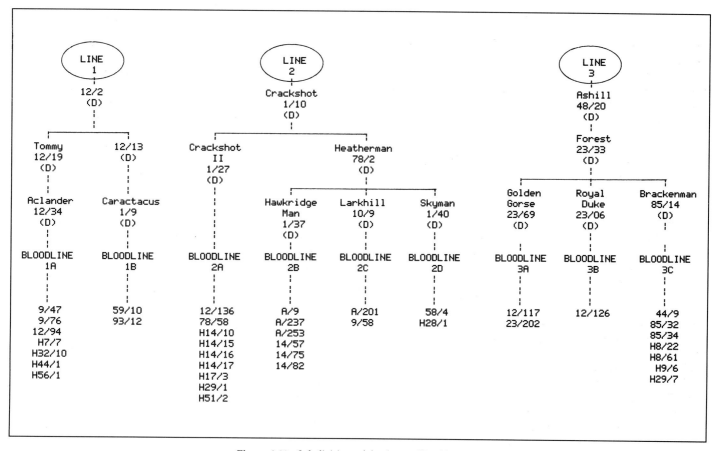

Figure 9.09 *Sub-divisions of the three stallion bloodlines*

preted by professional geneticists, particularly in the case of the mares.

Stallions being fewer in number are a more manageable subject. In 1984, the Rare Breeds Survival Trust analysed the stud book which they had on their computer. Their technical consultant Lawrence Alderson prepared a report on the contribution of the stallion lines in the colts registered in 1981 and 1983. He looked at the influence of three stallions on the breeding of the colts, Heatherman 78/2, Aclander 12/34 and Forest 23/33:

My report of April 1983 compared the relative contributions of Heatherman, Aclander and Forest to the breed born on the 1981 registrations of male animals. The results were as follows: Heatherman 13.83%, Aclander 9.47% and Forest 12.69%. Since that time, the influence of Heatherman would seem to have increased, and the 1983 registrations of male animals would indicate that this contribution is now more than 3.5 times higher than that of Aclander and almost 2.5 times higher than that of Forest.[93]

The message from this report was that one stallion line was becoming predominant. In terms of genetically managing the whole population this was undesirable as the amount of genetic variation was not being maximised. A more healthy population would be one where each line was equally represented in the new offspring. Lawrence Alderson calculated a contribution rating which showed the bias towards the Heatherman line and the results are shown in Figure 9.10. He found that of 33 colts born in 1981 (considering both male and female contributions), only three were not related to Heatherman and only one was free from both Heatherman and Aclander blood. Lawrence Alderson concluded:

> *The influence of Heatherman is spread throughout the breed, while the influence of Aclander, and especially of Forest, is concentrated strongly in limited portions of the breed.*
>
> *My principle recommendation is that the breed should be divided into breeding groups, based initially on sire lines, and that the best females should be used for line-breeding within each group, while the majority of females are mated according to a cyclic system of breeding. This policy is designed to maintain bloodlines and control inbreeding.*

It is hoped that this analysis will be updated and extended once more recent data has been input to the computer system.

Obviously, it is the contribution of the stallions in the population of foals which gives the true picture of bloodline representation. A balance of contributions to the new generations is the healthiest state. Some stallions may be used far more than others and we know that there are certain stallions which are hardly ever bred from. So simply looking at what stallions are available is not sufficient and we do need the 1984 report updated. However, bearing this limitation in mind, we can look at the representation of each bloodline subdivision in the population of licensed stallions in April 1991.

In terms of availability of stallions, we have in Britain nine of bloodline 1, nineteen of bloodline 2 and ten of

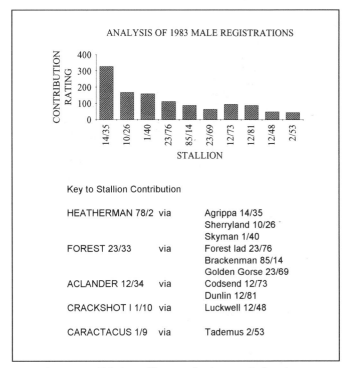

Figure 9.10 *Relative stallion contributions to colts born in 1983*

Plate 101 *Mounsey Hill (10/44)—from one branch of bloodline 2 which in terms of direct male inheritance has died out*

Plate 102 *Caractacus (1/9)*

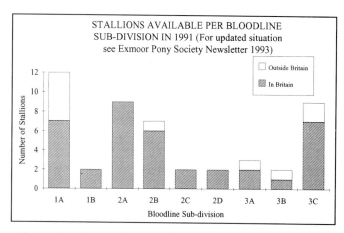

STALLIONS AVAILABLE PER BLOODLINE
SUB-DIVISION IN 1991 (For updated situation
see Exmoor Pony Society Newsletter 1993)

Figure 9.11 *Number of licensed stallions in the population in April 1991 representing each bloodline sub-division*

Plate 103 *Aclander (12/34)*

bloodline 3 (abroad, the figures are 5, 1, 4). However, if we consider the bloodline sub-divisions, the picture is alarmingly unbalanced. Figure 9.11 shows the relative representation of each bloodline sub-division in the population of licensed stallions in April 1991. In bloodline 1B, which goes back to Caractacus (1/9) there are just two fully licensed stallions but only one of these is bred from to any extent, Don Quixote (59/10).

Lines 2C, 2D and 3A each also have just two stallions but only one active to any degree, while Line 3B is now down to a single stallion since Prince Arthur was killed on Molland Moor. Undoubtedly, measures must be taken without delay if we are not to lose some of these bloodline sub-divisions and this will have to be a co-ordinated approach. Ensuring their availability is the most urgent problem but then there is a pressing need to encourage a more even usage of the full range of stallions in breeding new generations.

Several important lessons emerge from these studies of bloodlines in the stallion population. Firstly, if a stallion and/or his progeny are highly successful in the show ring, then those who breed and buy Exmoor Ponies for the purpose of showing will understandably tend to use that stallion more than others. In a breed with such small numbers, this means that other stallions do not contribute as much to the new generations. Variation is reduced and the breed as a whole begins to drift towards one particular type.

The second message that comes from this work is that if the genetic health of the population is to be maximised, then breeding has to be scientifically managed, along the lines suggested by Lawrence Alderson. Only through a Society-wide breeding policy can we ensure that we do not lose any of the scarce bloodlines. Each individual breeder will naturally wish to follow his or her own programme but in that way each may think that someone else is keeping a particular line going. For example, in 1977 a colt which was the only male representing one of the bloodline branches was almost lost as it was to be gelded. Happily it was reprieved and later licensed. This was most important as only one filly of that line was still living. However, this stallion has not been used to any extent for breeding and the situation remains far from satisfactory.

Some Exmoor Pony owners are undoubtedly uncomfortable with the idea that we should breed from ponies just because they are from rare branches of the bloodlines. Opinions have been expressed that such rarities are rare because they are not good Exmoors and their lines should be allowed to disappear. If such rare lines are not being used because the animals in question have disqualifying faults, then the argument is a fair one. However, if they are merely not the fashionable type or have had little opportunity to show what they can produce, we should be breeding from them. The population is so restricted that we cannot afford to lose any legitimate variation.

Gaye Sinclair M.R.C.V.S. has painstakingly identified mares belonging to poorly represented bloodlines and in a number of cases found that they are in non-breeding situations. Unless there is a just foundation for questioning their validity as Exmoor Ponies, the zoological view would be that these rare ponies should be relocated into breeding groups if possible, even if they are not the type which is nowadays favoured. The Exmoor Pony Society therefore faces a difficult task for it must find a way to meet the needs and aspirations of its members yet if it is to fulfil its objective of conserving the ponies long-term, it cannot allow the loss of any more genetic material. We will return to this challenge in the final chapter.

Inbreeding

One of the main reasons why it is so important to conserve all the surviving Exmoor Pony bloodlines is to minimise inbreeding. The whole population is very closely related, given that the number of animals was so small following the war. With such close relationships, high levels of inbreeding are always a potential problem. There is no cure for inbreeding but preventative measures can be taken by planning breeding carefully so that high inbreeding levels are avoided.

The degree of inbreeding in an animal is really the closeness of the relationship between the egg and the sperm which created it. The closer they are related, the higher the level of inbreeding in the offspring. It is generally accepted in the field of animal breeding that populations where animals are highly inbred are likely to produce problems. Breeding experiments have shown that the fertility, performance and the adaptability of groups of animals decline overall as inbreeding intensifies.

However, this general principle conceals the fact that inbreeding may produce some very good individuals even though it harms the total population overall. This is why quite often some of the most impressive animals may have pedigrees which are almost an advertisement for inbreeding. However, repeated many times, they will be in the minority and often real problems may emerge such as hip displacement or declining fertility. Scientists have found that moderate levels of inbreeding coupled with rigorous culling of poor offspring generally produces an improvement in a population. This probably explains the improvement in quality reported in the early years of the Exmoor Pony Society's activities. Yet when inbreeding exceeds a certain level, there is loss of vigour. The levels can be monitored by calculating from pedigrees a coefficient of inbreeding. It is rather a complicated process but the result is a percentage figure.

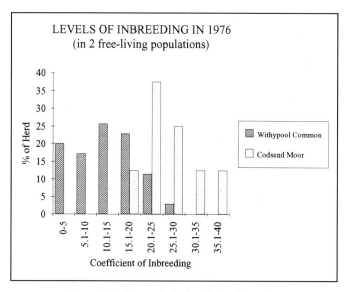

LEVELS OF INBREEDING IN 1976
(in 2 free-living populations)

Withypool Common
Codsend Moor

Figure 9.12 *Range of calculated inbreeding values*

Once values rise over 25% the negative effects begin to emerge and after about 40% in some cases lines can die out altogether. However, the animals used to determine these guidelines were not horses and certainly not Exmoor Ponies, so do these rules apply?

The inbreeding values were calculated for the ponies in two of the free-living herds in 1976, an onerous task as personal computers were not then available. Figure 9.12 shows that the levels of inbreeding were happily below the 40% watershed. They were significantly higher in the Codsend Moor herd than for Withypool Common because of the much smaller size of population on Codsend Moor and the presence of just one stallion. On Withypool Common, the presence of a second stallion Royal Duke improved the situation, because seven of Golden Gorse's daughters left their sire's herd and bred with Royal Duke.

Whatever led to these seven fillies leaving their sire's herd, it was obviously not a fully effective system for avoiding inbreeding as eight remained with Golden Gorse. Any offspring from those eight and their sire

would have been much more intensively inbred. However, on Codsend Moor, neither of Hawkwell Codsend's daughters produced foals by him suggesting perhaps that some degree of natural prevention may exist. Unfortunately, the information we have on this aspect of breeding is too limited to draw firm conclusions.

In a television documentary, one Exmoor resident expressed concern about inbreeding and the wish that "one day someone will find something to put it right". It can, of course, only be prevented and to do that requires careful management. Generally, the means of keeping inbreeding down to moderate levels has been the periodic changes of herd stallions. Introducing a new stallion which is not closely related to the young mares brings the level of inbreeding down at once. For example, the coefficients of inbreeding for Codsend Moor were below the supposed critical level of 40% but if Hawkwell Codsend had sired a foal out of his daughters, those foals would have been 80% inbred. This stallion was replaced by one from herd 14 and his offspring from those same young mares had inbreeding coefficients of just around 10%.

Exchange of stallions is therefore a way of managing inbreeding levels but has to be thought out carefully. Firstly, changing a stallion too frequently can be very disruptive in terms of the social life of the herd and may depress productivity. If an owner wishes to keep some of the resident stallion's daughters in the herd, that is the time to change to a stallion distant enough from their breeding. So if a stallion is selected carefully enough in the first place, he may remain until any of his daughters are retained and reach breeding age. In selecting a herd stallion, inbreeding can be kept to acceptable levels if the breeding of potential stallions and the mares is studied. Generally, if the stallion and the mares are not closely related then their progeny will have acceptable levels of inbreeding and should be fit.

The skill in managing herds is to assess that degree of relationship and to know when breeding is too close. Here the scientists can help with their calculations of inbreeding coefficients. The potential values for foals from each mare with a prospective herd stallion can be determined so showing if a stallion is a good or bad replacement when the time comes to change. This is particularly important if herd owners wish to breed true to a specific line. Inbreeding here will inevitably be higher than using a different bloodline, so it can be crucial to know which colt would produce the lowest level of inbreeding in the offspring. Selection of a prospective replacement stallion may often be according to its outward quality yet its inward genetic suitability is just as important to ensuring quality in his foals. With the computerisation of the Exmoor Pony Society stud book it should in time become a simple matter for herd owners to request an inbreeding potential analysis of the colts they are considering for herd stallions.

Given that all today's Exmoors are descended from so few animals because of the gene pool funnelling, the population is inevitably quite highly inbred. A number of the free-living herds have been run with sons taking over from their sires as herd stallions and breeding with sisters. Once we have fully analysed the stud book, we may find overall levels of inbreeding at times in the past or present which would alarm the geneticists. Yet we have little evidence that the population has suffered particular problems from this. The reason must surely lie in the fact that the breeders have so diligently culled any sub-standard or unfit animals. If prospective inbreeding is calculated and considered in the future management of herds, there might be fewer such animals to exclude from the breeding population.

The management of free-living herds is no easy task. Understandably, there is the family and herd tradition which makes it desirable to line breed rather than introduce blood from other herds. Yet each herd's pedigrees show that interchange has been required from time to time. As with most in life it is a matter of moderation and degree. Knowing just how much inbreeding is acceptable and when it has gone too far are the skills required to maintain a genetically and outwardly healthy herd. In the future, computerised study of the pedigrees will help herd owners to judge the inbreeding question more confidently.

The Balance of Breeding

Studying the way of life of free-living animals is a far from comfortable task in the winter months. While the Exmoor Ponies are marvellously adapted to the cold and wet conditions, people are not and Exmoor would test the resolution of the most dedicated observer. Yet each spring brings rewards which soon replace the miseries of winter, particularly the appearance of the new foals. Sir Alfred Munnings captured the joy of this time of the year with just a few lines in his poem *An Exmoor Lane*:

> *And in the spring the little foals are born;*
> *And there they lie, all basking in the heat*
> *Of some gorse-scented, blazing April morn*[94]

How well he conjured up the magic of warm spring mornings when the foals revel in the sunshine, replete and safe, protected by their watchful mothers.

In Nature's philosophy, successfully rearing a new generation is all that really matters; to perpetuate the species is the fundamental purpose. In so many ways, the Exmoor Ponies have natural breeding habits yet these are counterbalanced by the unnatural influences that come with human ownership.

We have seen that the ponies have a natural reproductive biology, with a clearly defined part of the year in which all mating and foaling takes place. This monoestrus system ensures that foals are born at the best time of the year. Also, the ponies live in groups where a herd stallion and a harem of mares form a natural breeding unit, although sometimes the number of mares with each stallion is higher than would probably exist in the wild. So there is much in their breeding which does conform to Nature's design for horses.

However, we have also come to realise that the ownership of the ponies and the management of the herds imposes unnatural influences upon their breeding. These mostly affect the population genetics and revolve around the fact that owners select the animals which are allowed to breed rather than Nature testing out which are the fittest. However, we must not forget that even though man may shape their genetic development in this way, Nature continues to exert its own effects

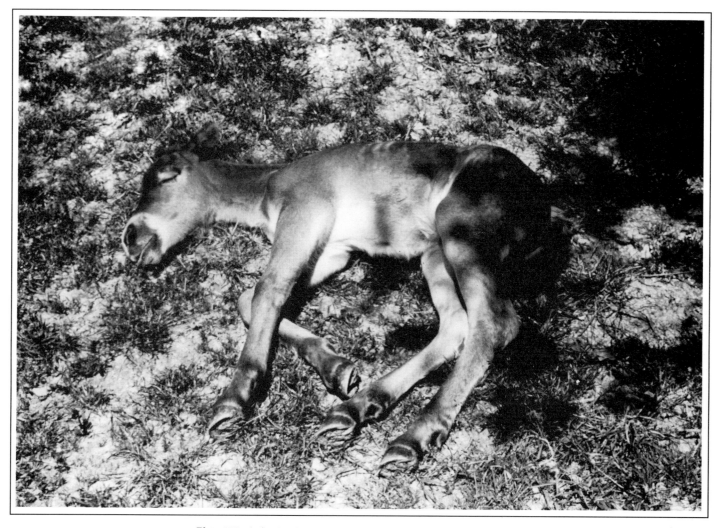

Plate 104 *A sleeping foal, once inspiration for Sir Alfred Munnings' poetry*

through continually testing each animal in terms of surviving to breeding age.

In breeding terms then, Exmoor Ponies show elements of both wild and domestic influences and we will have to take account of these when we finally assess their status. In today's world, conservation is often a case of careful management rather than simply leaving a species alone. If we are to conserve the natural blueprint of Exmoor Ponies, managing the genetic health of the population cannot be neglected.

CHAPTER 10

EXMOOR PONIES AND MAN

Since Man first fashioned a crude spear and became a predatory animal, the story of wild horses has been closely intertwined with that of the human race. Once it was realised that there could be more to the relationship than simply eating horse-flesh, the association between people and horses blossomed into a partnership which quite literally changed the course of human history. No book about the Exmoor Ponies would be complete if we ignored its role in the human-equine alliance and we must look at how Exmoors are used in domestic circumstances as well as how they exist in natural surroundings. However, Man is also a crucial factor in the story of the free-living herds. We have seen how important this has been historically and it continues to be so. Before leaving Exmoor then, we will take a closer look at how the free-living herds are managed.

The Moorland Year

For all but a few days each year, there is very little contact between the owners of the free-living herds and their ponies. Managing moorland herds has to be according to the principle of minimum intervention in their lives in order to allow Nature to remain the dominant force. Whilst owners check their ponies regularly to ensure all is well, close contact with them is restricted to just a short time each autumn, providing the ponies encounter no unusual problems.

Early summer is the time when the first foals are born into the herds and of course the mares receive no assistance in the process of giving birth. They spend the summer raising their offspring independent of their owners out on their moorland homes, which provide a kind environment at this time of year. Yet one aspect of their home, its finite extent and consequent limited grazing rights, means that this scene of adult ponies living alongside foals cannot continue indefinitely. Not all the new arrivals can remain in the herds, for the numbers would soon exceed what the moorland enclosures could support. Thus, their days of freedom are numbered. Also, to justify their existence as a marginal part of the hill farming system, Exmoor Ponies, like all free-living ponies, must provide their owners with an annual income from the sale of foals.

By October, the foals are well grown and can be weaned from their mothers. If left out on the moor, they will become increasingly independent but will continue to be suckled for a considerable time, often until the next foal is born if the mare is tolerant. This is a considerable burden on the mother through a winter when she has

Plate 105 *Most foals are only temporary members of the herd*

to obtain enough nourishment for herself, the newly-growing foal inside her, and for her foal at foot. Being able to cope with such demands is part of being fit to survive and the Exmoor Pony has these capabilities. However, in most years, perhaps only one or two will keep their foals to add to the herd if old ponies have died or are to be taken off the moor. For most foals, October represents a momentous change and the start of a very different life.

The Gathering

On Exmoor, bringing the free-living ponies off the moor to their home farms is called "the gathering" and this is a far more appropriate term than "round-up". Round-up conjures up images of the American wild west, of cowboys cracking whips, shouting, chasing the Mustangs at a frantic gallop, the horses wild eyed and terrified. Gathering ponies on Exmoor is today a much quieter, controlled affair which seems as familiar to the adult ponies as to the riders involved. Apparently, it was not always so calm but in recent decades it has been appreciated that the more restrained approach is actually more efficient and is certainly better for the ponies. Perhaps too, the fact that the ponies themselves

have generally become more accustomed to humans means that they are easier to gather.

The scene today at a gathering on Withypool Common begins with a handful of riders, occasionally one or two actually mounted on Exmoors themselves, setting off armed with the knowledge of where the ponies were the day before or a few hours earlier. The free-living ponies certainly seem to realise that these are riders with intent, not just casual passers-by, and when they detect the purposeful approach, the ponies set off at a canter rather than a furious gallop.

Plate 106 *The Withypool gathering*

As part of the Withypool Study, the route taken by the ponies during a number of gatherings was plotted and, as later observations confirm, the ponies have a well-defined response to the gatherers. Those grazing south of the River Barle follow tracks down to the far western boundary of the Common where they cross the river and head up onto Bradymoor. They move diagonally across the south facing slopes and head for the funnel of moorland which ends at the gate to Kitridge Lane. Undoubtedly, they are driven by the riders following behind them but there seems to be the memory of all those previous gatherings and remembrance of the route they have to follow.

Some years, the gatherers may miss one or two ponies; if the weather is misty, it is all too easy to over-look a few individuals. Generally, all are rounded-up without too much difficulty if the riders are skilful. The ponies are opportunists though and if given a realistic

Plate 107 *The Exmoor Pony Society secretary, David Mansell, helping to gather the Withypool ponies*

Plate 108 *The Withypool ponies are given time to rest at the end of the gathering*

gap in the line of riders, will attempt to evade capture. The pursuit is of course quite a test for the foals, particularly any which were late arrivals, and so the ponies are rested before they are driven off down the lane to Weatherslade Farm.

There are a number of records of the Withypool gathering; it has been filmed at least twice for television

programmes and I have written about it before. Whilst well photographed, the search for a written account of gathering the ponies on Winsford Hill proved fruitless; if none exists, this is surely an oversight which has to be remedied. Where Codsend Moor is concerned, we are more fortunate. Mr Ernest Painter, Anne Western's father, described gathering day for No. 12 herd in an article for the *Exmoor Review* in 1989, capturing so well the atmosphere involved:

A wet morning on Exmoor is wet! Half a dozen subdued riders and as many foot followers as could be press-ganged gathered at Hillhead Cross and, after a briefing, set off to gather up eight skittish young mares from Alderman's Barrow to join No.12 Herd. This went without incident until the mares were approaching Codsend Moor, where the track led between fairly high banks. Turning on her heels the leading filly took the bank in one slithering scramble, followed by the rest, and they were suddenly streaming across the Moor and disappearing into the mist. The riders, hampered by the banks, lost time in getting after them, and were further hampered by the boggy ground which the ponies had crossed without hesitation. By dint of some hard riding "the Cavalry" managed to outflank the ponies, and they were gradually shepherded back to Codsend, where No. 12 Herd had meanwhile been collected and held in a tight bunch in a corner near the gate.

The milling, excited mob of ponies was urged out of their moorland home onto the track along the flank of Dunkery, and they set off at a good pace, keeping well together. Thankfully the rain eased and the mist lifted and the sight of these wild creatures, huddling together with the primitive instinct of the herd, but moving purposefully, was heart-warming. They were led by the stallion "Tawbitts Mr Toff", the whites of his eyes flashing with excitement, the carriage of his head on his thick strong neck declaring his courage and defiance; the pack followed, the suckers – the unweaned foals – keeping up at the feet of their dams. They passed through Dunkery Hill Gate without hesitation onto the half a mile or so of road, before they were turned into the narrow traffic free lanes which make this part of Exmoor such good riding country.

Plate 109 *The Winsford Hill gathering*

Plate 110 *The Winsford Hill gathering*

Plate 111 *The Winsford Hill ponies are driven to Old Ashway Farm after being gathered*

Plate 112 *Confined at Old Ashway Farm, the adult ponies are very wary of human contact*

The final hurdle was at Luckwell Bridge, where the ponies were turned onto the busy B3224, the main east-west route across Exmoor. All traffic had to be stopped because

there was no stopping the herd on the move. Lorry drivers and motorists were all co-operative, and were rewarded with a rare and beautiful sight. The Herd were moving at full stretch, skidding round the Old Inn on the corner onto the road with clouds of steam rising from their wet backs, the suckers valiantly keeping up with their mothers in the scrum of hooves. A further quarter-of-a-mile up the hill they were turned into the Farm gateway, and safely corralled to await inspection and selection for the Herd Book in the case of the foals.

Next day the Herd were taken back to their Moorland home. Whether by instinct or intelligence, they know their way, and the return home is no problem.[95]

The aim of the herd owners is always to keep the herd in-ground for the minimum amount of time and so gatherings are usually planned for the day before the Exmoor Pony Society inspectors are due. The mares are usually kept in for the inspection day so that the inspectors may see them too if they wish and so that the breeding of each foal can be accurately determined. However, as soon as possible, the adult ponies are returned to the moorland. The release of the ponies is as interesting as their capture for as Ernest Painter so rightly says, there is a strong purpose displayed once freedom is regained. On Withypool Common, the ponies are released from two different locations (at one time from three) and usually resume their original groupings very quickly, returning to their favoured home ranges.

Inspection and Marking

We explored earlier how the Exmoor Pony Society was born at a time when cross-breeding or so-called improving was the fashion of the day. The objective of the Society then was to ensure the survival of the true Exmoor Pony and it remains so today. In order to do this, it was necessary firstly to identify those ponies left on Exmoor which had not been cross-bred and to mark them in a way which stated to all that they were true Exmoor Ponies.

Thus, a system of inspection was created, whereby two of the Society's appointed inspectors would assess each animal presented for registration in the newly-formed Society's Stud Book. At this stage the inspectors

had to examine both young and adult ponies and in this way the foundation stock for the Stud Book was approved. Later, in 1961, the Stud Book was officially closed which meant that after that date, ponies could only be inspected and accepted as foals – no adult Exmoors which had not been located by that date could be registered subsequently.

With many breeds, registration is automatic if a foal is from two registered parents but this is not the case with Exmoor Ponies. Although the progeny from two registered Exmoors must by all logic be an Exmoor Pony, the Society maintains its system of inspection and for very good reason. Breeders of Exmoors are the guardians of the British Hill Pony genetic heritage and safeguarding the purity of the stock is paramount. Although the extent to which alien blood influenced the Exmoor race in the past is known to be minimal, there is a continued mission to purge the ponies of any such factor. This means that a foal does not have a place in the Stud Book by right but on the basis of it being free from any non-Exmoor attributes. Also, with relatively high levels of in-breeding in some cases, it is important not to accept any animals which show physical deformities.

Inspection day is therefore quite literally a day of judgement. Each foal is thoroughly examined to ensure it is true to type and shows no undesirable features.

Plate 113 *The foals are separated to await inspection at Old Ashway Farm*

Plate 114 *Inspection day line-up at Old Ashway Farm in the early 1970s (L–R Robert Govier, Claud Govier, Robert Westcott, Derek Sparkes, Sidney Westcott, Lillo Lumb, Ken Govier, Percy Needs. Front Row—Colonel Reeks and Mrs Rose Wallace*

The main disqualifiers for registration are a profusion of white hairs in the mane or tail or the presence of white markings; also the formation of the teeth is looked at carefully. If a foal is borderline, it may be looked at again the next year. It may seem strange to reject Exmoor Ponies when they are so few in number yet this has been the key to ensuring the conservation of the race. It protects against accepting the offspring of accidental crosses which could occur if a non-Exmoor stallion broke into an enclosure and is the only way to manage a population as genetically restricted as the Exmoor.

Yet is it over-cautious? Certainly with regard to identifying the undesirable products of accident and inbreeding it remains appropriate but there are those who question whether there can be any lasting influence of non-Exmoor blood. It has long been viewed that white of any sort was not natural within the Exmoor race and that white patches of body hair or white marks in the horn of the hoof or on the sole are not legitimate. As these marks still appear very occasionally, the Exmoor Pony Society continues to purge the population of them through the inspection system. Can we be sure that they are such an offence? The answer is of course that no-one can be certain and we have to fall back upon the tradition and experience of the Exmoor breeders of earlier times who outlawed such features. It remains far better to be over-cautious in safeguarding the Exmoor purity than to risk undoing the efforts of many decades.

The task of the inspectors is therefore a very important one and consequently the Exmoor Pony Society runs a system of probationing which must be completed satisfactorily prior to appointment as an inspector. The autumn is a very busy time for the band of inspectors, for between them they must visit and assess Exmoor Pony foals anywhere in the British Isles. In 1990, 127 foals were put forward for inspection. Figure 10.01 shows the numbers of foals actually registered each year and well illustrates the increased breeding in recent years. Over the last six years, the numbers of failures have been recorded and have varied from 5.7% to 17.4% averaging at just over 11%.

Once a foal has passed its inspection, it is assigned an individual number in its owner's herd. This is then branded onto its left flank. The herd number plus the Exmoor Pony Society star is branded onto the left shoulder. The combination of marks means that an Exmoor Pony carries its stamp of legitimacy (the star) plus its breeding (the numbers) for life. Using the Stud Book, its breeding history can be identified at a glance. This is important both in distinguishing true Exmoor Ponies and in providing proof of individual identity. An unbranded Exmoor Pony is either one which has not been inspected or one which has been refused registration (or is perhaps not 100% Exmoor at all).

With all Exmoors being essentially identical, some form of marking which can be seen from a distance is vital in managing the free-living herds. Without this, there is no way to identify the parents of a foal or selectively extract an individual from the herd. While other marking techniques are available, most are only practical

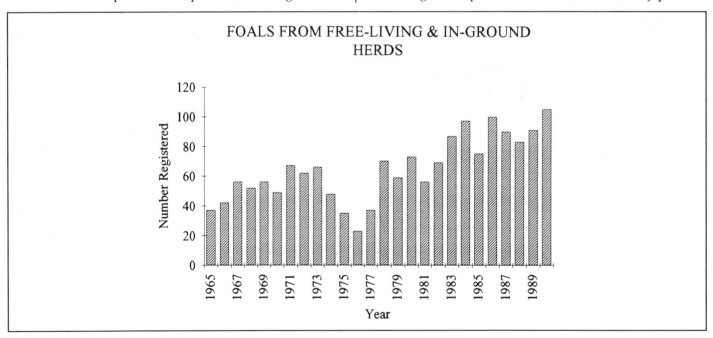

Figure 10.01 *Number of Exmoor foals registered annually*

Plate 115 *Newly branded foals at Knighton—H8/69 Knightoncombe Barred Sallow and H8/73 Knightoncombe Coronet*

Plate 116 *April's Gold (23/203) in summer coat showing the Exmoor Pony Society star and herd number on her shoulder and her individual number in herd 23 on her flank*

where the animals can be handled at close quarters and they would be useless for moorland ponies. Even brand marks have their limitations for when the winter coat is fully grown they are often quite difficult to make out.

Where more than one owner runs ponies on a single area of moorland, as on Withypool Common, it is helpful to have something which identifies the herd more easily for its owner. Herd 23 belonging to Mr Fred Milton therefore receives some additional attention while on the farm: the adult ponies have part of the lower portion of their tail cut out horizontally, which makes them readily distinguishable from those of Herd H8 with whom they live. This makes sorting the ponies at Weatherslade far simpler than if all the brands had to be read. Whilst it is certainly not a universal practise, one or two owners administer worm dosing to their ponies during this time on the farms.

Once inspection and marking are complete, the foals are separated from their mothers and the adults are released then or the next morning. For most of the foals, their liberty is at an end, although just a few may be kept to maintain the size of the herd and these return to the moor with their mothers. Inspection and marking

Plate 117 *The welcome re-release of the Winsford Hill ponies*

day is also a day for purchasing and people interested in buying foals from the moorland herds travel very long distances to attend, recognising the importance of incorporating the undomesticated blood in their breeding programmes.

Until fairly recently, the gathering and inspection days were planned for the week before Bampton Fair as this had been the traditional outlet for stock not sold directly from the farms since about 1856. Today, Bampton Fair no longer includes a pony sale but because of its long association with Exmoor Ponies it is perhaps right that we go back in time and see what used to happen.

Pony Sales

The sale of foals from the herds running on Exmoor Forest was carried out privately, direct from the estate, until about 1850 but then an annual auction was introduced at Simonsbath. The sale took place at Stony Plot where the church is now and Roger Burton records that in 1853 some 200 people attended the event. Perhaps the best description of the Simonsbath sales of the Knight ponies comes from an article included in *The Art of Taming Horses* by J. S. Rarey published in 1858; the unknown author of this piece wrote at length of his visit to Exmoor and the sale, including the following extract:

We crossed the stream – not by the narrow bridge, but by the ford; and passing through the straggling stone village of Simon's Bath, arrived in sight of the field where the Tattersall of the West was to sell the wild and tame horse stock bred on the moors. It was a field of some ten acres and a half, forming a very steep slope, with the upper path comparatively flat, the sloping side, broken by a stone quarry, and dotted over with huge blocks of granite. A substantial, but as the event proved, not sufficiently high stone fence bounded the whole field. On the upper part, a sort of double pound, united by a narrow neck, with a gate at each end, had been constructed of rails upwards of five feet in height. Into the first of these pounds, by ingenious management, all the ponies, wild and tame, had been driven.[96]

The ponies sold at Simonsbath were mainly cross-bred animals, the products of the Knight experiments. The above account goes on to relate how lively these sales were and H.H. Dixon (who wrote as "The Druid") recorded that at one sale Mr. Locke of Lynmouth once roasted an Exmoor Pony! Whether this equine barbecue was a crossed or true Exmoor seems somewhat academic! H.H. Dixon also wrote in 1860:

Thus the private sale at the Simon's Bath Inn gradually became a sort of rustic fete . . . . (There were) rude feats of wrestling not only with each other, but at the expense of their ponies, which they seized and dragged out of the fold with all a giant's thew. "Seventy years ago, sir" a bailiff said to us, "there were only five men and a woman and a little girl on Exmoor and my mother was that little girl. She drew beer at the Simon's Bath public house. They were a rough lot of customers there I promise you." [97]

Simonsbath church was built in 1856, so the pony sales were short-lived on this site. Subsequently, Bampton Fair became one of the outlets for the Knight ponies but Reading was also used. Roger Burton records that from 1861 to 1883 many ponies were sent to Reading to be sold.

It is not certain when the surplus from the Acland herd was first taken to Bampton but certainly it became the main focus for purchasers of both crossed and true Exmoor Ponies in the later eighteen-hundreds. Hence those with animals to sell favoured Bampton Fair and the prices obtained there. Ponies were also sold at Brendon Fair but this was a much smaller sale; interestingly though it is Brendon Fair which survives to this day though few true Exmoor Ponies are taken there now.

As with so many country fairs, Bampton's annual event was always more than just an animal auction. Whilst the main reason for attending was the buying and selling of stock, it became the major outing of the year for many inhabitants of remote Exmoor. Even in the first half of this century, there were many moorland folk for whom the annual trip to Bampton was the only occasion on which they left their immediate locality. Bampton Fair must have seemed an onslaught to their senses, with traders of all kinds selling their wares and more people than perhaps would be seen for the rest of the year in total. The aroma of food cooking intermixed with the animal smells, the noise from the milling throng of people, the colours of the materials and goods for sale, all this must have seemed like another world to those used to the tranquillity of an isolated hill farm.

Just when Bampton Fair began does not seem to be recorded; F. J. Snell commented in his *Book of Exmoor* that the first mention of it occurs in the reign of Henry VIII. Probably many centuries separate its actual birth as an animal sale and the final ending of this part of the Fair in 1985. Of all the descriptions of this lively day, the earliest appears to be in an article "An Exmoor Horse Fair" by an unknown author in Murrays Magazine of 1887. Its author required some 11 pages to describe all he saw but a few extracts convey the general scene:

As we reached the outskirts of the village we passed a field that was filled with every possible variety of the horse kind. From the smallest of ponies to the largest of cart-horses, there they were by the dozen and by the score . . . In the village itself, however, preparations for the important event of the morrow were in full swing on all sides . . . In the market-place men were busy fixing hurdles and forming sheep and cattle pens. Along the fronts of the houses barricades were being rapidly erected.

At one end of the main street hurdles are conspicuous by their absence. Here we learn the horse fair is held . . . We come upon the oldest inhabitant, and question him how far the fair nowadays falls short of the glories of the good old times. To our surprise he admits that the horse fair is as important and as largely attended today as it was fifty years ago.

Next morning, betimes, we were back at Bampton. From end to end the long village street was blocked with horses and with cattle, with sheep and men . . . Down the narrow passage in the middle surged, backwards and forwards, an endless stream of men on horseback, men on foot, droves of ponies, herds of cattle, flocks of sheep, all mixed together in inextricable confusion. How the drovers ever kept their own droves together was a mystery. At every moment some frightened beast would break loose from the mob that was being driven past, and thrust its way into the midst of a herd that was standing at its appointed station by the roadside.

The horse and pony sales did not begin till ten o'clock . . . From Holnicote, and the northern slopes of Exmoor close by Porlock, Sir Thomas Acland had sent a drove of thirty . . . The sale takes place in an inn-yard divided into two by a wall running down the middle, with an ordinary farm gate at either end. Against the outer side of the wall a rough platform of a few rough planks is erected for the auctioneer. In the inner yard the ponies are running loose. Lot No. 1, a well-grown two-year-old, is skilfully got away from its companions, and then driven by cries and flourishing of sticks to pass through the gate. The gate falls to again behind it, and the frightened little creature, looking more like a deer than a horse, with its startled eyes and springy step, finds itself in the centre of a ring of gazers. Too terrified to stir, it remains motionless, till it is driven to display its paces as well as possible in a few feet of space by the farm bailiff, who stands in the centre of the ring with a big whip, much like the master of ceremonies at a circus . . . After one's eye had got accustomed to the dimensions of the Exmoor pony, it was little short of startling to be asked to look at an ordinary horse again.

Leaving the fair, we climbed up through the orchards onto the hills above the village . . . By the time we got back, the business of the fair was nearly at an end. The men who had been going about all morning with bundles of halters for sale had well-nigh disposed of their stock. Only the few animals that had failed to find purchasers, and that were going back to their native hills, were still left at large. The rest had been caught and haltered, and handed over to the drovers . . . Their task seemed likely to be by no means a sinecure. Even with a halter on, an Exmoor pony does not always start, as an ostler would call it "sweetly and easily". As a rule each pony appeared to take, besides the man with the halter, one man grasping him round the neck, and a second man holding on by the tail for steerage purposes, in order to get him safely under weigh . . . as the animals were driven off, their places were at once taken by stalls and booths.[98]

Evelyn March-Phillips visited Bampton Fair in 1896 and observed a similar scene and wrote:

> Bampton is lively enough today. From end to end the street is a packed and seething mass of horses, ponies and humanity. Gentlemen, horsey persons on useful looking nags, tramps, touts, labouring men, large boned Devonshire farmers – some well to do and well mounted, others regular old West-country characters, in heavy blue or drab topcoats, grasping stout hazel sticks, tramping ankle deep in the churned up mud, or bestriding huge cart-horses with crazy saddles, greeting friends, exchanging good natured chaff with a sharp edge to it, or inspecting the stock with sagacious faces, drawing up the weather-beaten lines round their quiet, shrewd eyes.
>
> The cottage doors are "shored-up" half way with boards and hurdles, to guard against four-footed intruders, and groups of women and children lean over them laughing and chattering. Everything in the form of horse-flesh comes to try its luck at Bampton Fair; but, overflowing, as the street is, the real articles of the sale are not here, but penned up aside, waiting auction in yards and bartons.[99]

Another vivid description of the Fair is contained within F. J. Snell's book. Bampton Fair in the 1970s retained much of its earlier character but had changed somwhat. No longer were there animals milling about along the main street, the sheep and cattle sales were gone and the horses and ponies were all auctioned in the yard behind the Tiverton Inn. The stalls and traders, once a feature of the afternoon of Fair day, had taken over the main street from early morning; the bustle and throng of people "out for the day" remained but of course the ankle-deep mud and manure was a thing of the past.

The selling of the ponies was much as before, undoubtedly a stressful ordeal for animals unused to close contact with people. Exmoor farmers recall that in earlier days, the auctioneer's men would not go in with the wild Exmoor Ponies and their owners had to do this, but some of the handling in the '70s by those unfamiliar with the animals showed little skill or sensitivity. And so, attitudes changed, and what was once acceptable ceased to be so; the days of the pony sales were brought to an end.

In the era of motor transport, taking ponies from Exmoor down to Bampton has been a relatively easy task but it was not always so. Before the Second World War, the ponies to be sold had to be moved down to Bampton by mounted drovers. Often, farmers would join up with each other and drive their animals as a group down off the moor. F. J. Snell commented that there was no prettier sight than to see this pony "drift". Sadly, no photograph of Exmoor Ponies being drifted to Bampton has been found but Alfred Vowles captured the journey of a group of Porlock cross-bred ponies in the early 1930s; his photograph is reproduced here.

Bampton Fair was, of course, not the only outlet for selling the moorland ponies. We learnt from Mr Fred Milton in Chapter 6 how ponies were taken to Bridgwater sometimes but that the extra expense and effort outweighed the higher prices obtained. Also, No. 12 herd was started with ponies bought at the Minehead auction. Since the ending of the Bampton sale, the majority of Exmoor Ponies are sold privately. Most ponies are acquired now direct from the breeders and to assist both buyers and sellers, the Exmoor Pony Society Secretary maintains a list of ponies for sale throughout the country.

After the Gatherings

For those ponies sold away from the free-living herds, life takes on a wholly different character which we will explore shortly. The ponies which are returned to the moor re-establish their natural pattern of life very quickly and for them, contact with people is over for another year apart from the approaches of interested observers and visitors. Owners play no further part in the herds' lives unless some accident or exceptional situation arises.

However, as we discussed when looking at genetic aspects of the Exmoor Pony, the management of the herds has had more far-reaching effects than merely restricting the ponies in-ground for a day or two.

Plate 118 *A scene from the Bampton pony sales in the 1970s*

Choices will have been made; a colt may have been retained to grow up within a herd and be its future herd stallion. Some elderly ponies may have been kept back if they have begun to show signs of experiencing difficulty living unaided. Fillies may have been selected to take their place. All such judgements will have been by human eye, not according to the more ruthless selection of Nature. Yet the managers of the moorland herds have the accumulated experience of generations of making such choices and know the attributes they must look for. If they have chosen unwisely, the rigours of the free life will soon make this evident.

The rest of the moorland year is therefore a time for

Plate 119 *Cross-bred ponies from Porlock on their way to Bampton Fair, about 1936*

the ponies to live by their wits and call upon their own resources. Armed with their marvellous array of natural adaptations, the Exmoor Ponies tackle the winter challenges independently. Their tactics are to exploit whatever natural shelter they can find and to eat endlessly. The time spent resting is curtailed considerably for it is a luxury they cannot afford and their ancient instincts allow them to find adequate food from varied sources. Early spring is perhaps the most difficult time, for the ponies will have used up the fat laid down prior to winter and depend upon the arrival of the new growth of grass. And so we come round to the start of another foaling season.

Although the free-living Exmoor Ponies are owned and managed, their contact with people is minimal. The herds are cropped as a part of the hill-farming system but the essential policy for conserving the Exmoor Pony race is one of non-intervention.

Selection of Stallions

With any animal that lives in groups where one male breeds with a number of females, it is vital that the best males are selected. If we think of Red Deer, there is a complex hierarchy of males and much battling for dominance which ensures that the strongest, the most genetically fit stags, father the next generation. With truly wild horses and the feral horse populations where Man plays no part in managing the breeding activity, there is similar natural rivalry and fighting to test out the fitness of the males. A stallion has to be in optimum condition to win his place as herd stallion and he holds that position only as long as he can successfully counter the challenges of other males.

Free-living Exmoor Ponies live in relatively large herds compared to wild circumstances, with more mares per stallion than would be maintained if there were many males present. The only exception to this has been the group living on the island of Taero off Denmark where eventually there were seven stallions amongst a total of 17 ponies and much fighting as we saw in Chapter 7. For most of the free-living groups there is

just a single stallion present and only on Withypool Common and Winsford Hill are there two stallions living on the same area.

This means that very few stallions contribute to the continuance of the free-living Exmoor race and this is also true in domestic circumstances where success in the show-ring may determine that a disproportionate number of mares are taken to particular stallions. All this adds up to a situation where the role of Man in selecting which stallions are to be the chosen few is a heavy responsibility. Nature would carry out the task through ruthlessly subjecting every animal to intensive testing but in terms of management, people have to make judgements based upon outward appearance, suitability and previous performance of the bloodline.

For these reasons the Exmoor Pony Society rules demand that it must approve and licence all breeding stallions. This involves a further inspection at a minimum age of two years old. If a stallion fails this inspection then none of its former or subsequent progeny will be eligible for registration in the Stud Book. As with foal inspections, borderline animals may have one further re-inspection at a later date. Thus Exmoor foals can only be registered if they pass their own inspection and are by a registered and licensed stallion out of a registered mare. These restrictions are the level of protection which is crucial to conserving the race. The stallion inspection involves two of the Society's judges examining the animal and it must also pass a veterinary examination which checks for any physical abnormalities. Such stringent checks form an attempt to substitute for Nature as far as possible in selecting the prime specimens as sires. However, it has certain deficiencies as a conservation tool and we will examine these in the final chapter.

The Wild to Domestic Spectrum

Before we move on to domesticated Exmoor Ponies, we have a final task to complete with regards to the free-living ponies which have been the subject of most of this book. We began by asking the question "are they wild or domestic animals?" and speculated at the start that neither term would apply. Now, having explored their origins, history and the natural history of the moorland herds, we are in a better position to make a judgement as to just where they lie on the wild to domestic spectrum.

Perhaps we should remind ourselves of what wildness and domesticity involve in terms of the three factors – surviving, breeding and genetic character. A wild animal survives without any assistance from Man, and often in spite of what we do to the natural environments. In wild populations, Man is a total irrelevance when it comes to reproducing – people play no part in determining which animal will breed with which. Above all, wild animals have a genetic make-up which has been created by the forces of Natural Selection alone.

In contrast, we identified at the outset, that domestic animals depend upon Man for some if not all the resources they need for survival. Their breeding is controlled by people and their genes have been selected by humanly designed animal husbandry. We also saw that feral animals have this domesticated background but have returned to surviving and breeding without interference.

So, how can we classify the free-living Exmoor Ponies? Firstly, in terms of surviving, they have no need of us given a sufficient range of natural environment. They are fully adapted to finding their own food, making the most of natural shelter, withstanding the worst of the elements and participating in the varied competitive interactions with other animals. They are in fact survivors par excellence. For this factor then we must place them right at the wild extreme of the spectrum.

However, when we looked at their breeding, we found a blend of natural and artificial influences. The moorland herds retain a natural reproductive biology and cycle but Man interferes in the selection process. In so choosing which foals will remain in the herds and which colts will be allowed to become herd stallions, owners cannot possibly ensure that they select the genetically fittest animals; only Natural Selection can do this. Yet those ponies chosen by Man must be fit for

natural existence. If they are not genetically fit, then they will not survive living free on Exmoor. So in terms of breeding, the Exmoor is perhaps half-way between wild and domestic.

Finally, what is the genetic identity of the Exmoor Pony? Does it have a natural genetic blueprint, a direct inheritance from the British Hill Pony, or has Man re-designed Nature's original wild pony? The characteristics of the Exmoor show adaptive features on a par with truly wild animals and bear no hint of qualities artificially produced by selective breeding. The history of the Exmoor Ponies tells us that the influence of non-Exmoor blood upon the free-living population has been minimal and can be equated with the situation of Przewalski's Horse. Our examination of the Exmoor's origins has produced conflicting theories yet the case for an unbroken presence in Britain as a free-living animal is for me the more convincing. I would accept then that the Exmoor Pony is the surviving British Hill Pony and retains its genetic identity almost entirely. It therefore earns a place close to the wild end of the spectrum for this factor.

What of the possibility that the Exmoor was once domesticated and has resumed an independent life? Is it then a feral pony? It would seem that this is most unlikely for wherever Man truly domesticates animals, he leaves his enduring mark. The processes of altering the animal's environment and of replacing the forces of Natural Selection are surely too fundamental to allow an animal to retain its adaptations to a wild life to such a degree as in the Exmoor. Also, there is no hard evidence to tell us that the free-living herds have ever had a domesticated phase in their history. This is sometimes suggested as it is deemed by some so unlikely that free-living ponies survived the Mesolithic Age. Yet as we saw earlier in this book there is strong argument that it was not only quite possible but probably the case that they did. Thus, we have no basis upon which to classify the Exmoor Ponies as feral.

To summarise then, our scoring for the free-living Exmoor Ponies might be: Surviving – 100% wild; Breeding 50% wild 50% domestic; Genetic Character – 90%

wild. In terms of the spectrum then we would have to assess them as about 80% wild. Yet this is an unsatisfactory situation for we are most comfortable when we can use a single word to describe what we mean. Rejecting then wild, domestic and feral, as we must, there is no alternative to creating a totally different word for Exmoor Ponies and placing them in a separate location on our original diagram from Chapter 1 as shown in Figure 10.02. My solution to this matter has been to invent the word "econatural".

This means a genetically wild-type animal which has a natural relationship with its environment (a natural ecology) but is not fully wild due to Man's influence on its breeding. It actually proves quite useful to have such a definition and new word because the Exmoor Pony is not the only econatural animal. Many populations of Red Deer are now econatural rather than wild. Calling the free-living Exmoor Ponies econatural also rightly distinguishes them from the other free-living ponies in Britain. These have lost their original genetic identity through cross-breeding and are perhaps mid-way along the spectrum; semi-wild or semi-domestic is applicable to these.

The econatural Exmoor Ponies are therefore unique, probably the last survivors of Britain's original wild ponies, simply brought into the hill-farming system in a one-sided relationship. Man obtains a crop from them but they have received virtually nothing from Man. Their econatural status imposes considerable responsibility upon their owners, for their conservation in that state or even wilder becomes vital. We will consider the various challenges that must be met, if we are to effectively conserve the last of the British Hill Ponies, in our final chapter. The conservation issue is made more difficult by the very fact that the free-living Exmoor Ponies have proved hard to classify. When asked about their policy relating to free-living ponies, English Nature replied:

They are not strictly wild – our primary interest is in their effect on habitat as grazers.[100]

Where the Exmoors are concerned then, their conser-

vation is hampered by the fact that they are owned and have surrendered a small part of their wildness. Perhaps if the significance of the econatural state becomes appreciated, attitudes might become more positive.

For now, we will say farewell to the freedom and tranquillity of Exmoor's open spaces as we travel in search of all those Exmoor Ponies which are sold away from their moorland home.

Exmoors in the Service of Man

Having spent most of this book visiting free-living herds of Exmoor Ponies and emphasising their natural character and independence, it is now important to establish one of their most remarkable adaptive features – their ability to adapt to and form close, co-operative relationships with people. This natural trait in the true horses accounts for the existence of such vast numbers and of so many different forms today. Whilst tameness is an obvious attribute of domesticated horses and ponies it is perhaps less apparent that it lies within the make-up of members of free-living and wild herds. However, to remove an adult animal which has experienced some years of independence and tame such an individual is a long battle, sometimes never won. The flexibility to be tame or wild in character lies at the infant and juvenile stages.

This is certainly the case with Exmoor Ponies as with other free-living populations. If removed from the free life as foals at around six months and handled appropriately, they have a temperament and intelligence that well suits them for domestic life. Remove them as adults and the patterns of independent life may be far too set to permit the adjustment to close human contact. An example of this was my own mare, Daisy A/224.

Daisy was born on Winsford Hill and handled a little before joining Herd H8 on Withypool Common, where she lived until she was two years old. During her third year she spent some time living free and some time in-ground and then moved to the Cotswold Farm Park where she still lives today. Despite the limited early contact with people and the continual presence of visitors whilst the Park is open, Daisy has remained very

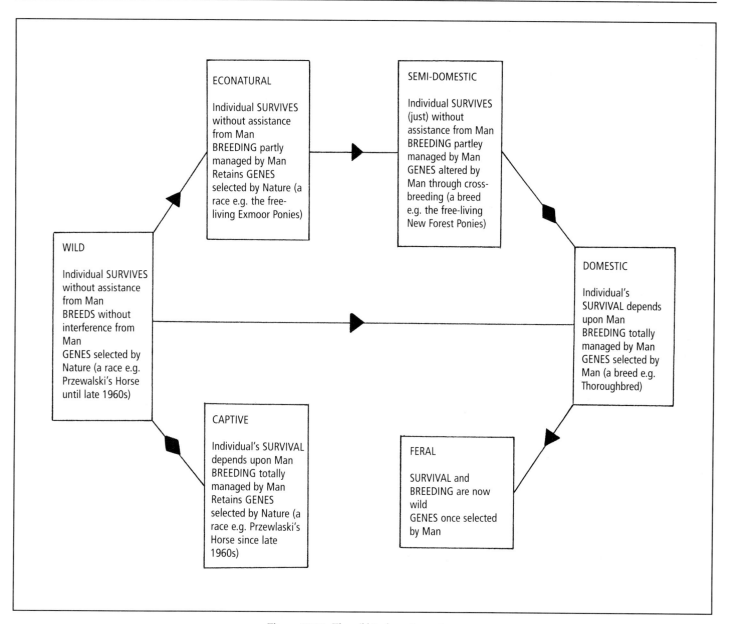

Figure 10.02 *The wild to domestic spectrum*

Plate 120 *Daisy (A/224) with her first foal, Meg (H27/1)*

aloof. Unlike her daughters born at the Park, Daisy will not socialise with the visitors and has shown on more than one occasion a distinct lack of co-operation when being moved to winter grazing. Certainly with this mare, the free-life during her first two years seems to have set the pattern of her behaviour. Of course, this is not to say that taming and breaking older Exmoor Ponies from free-living sources is impossible but the underlying resistance makes it generally inadvisable.

With foals, it is a quite different matter. Their responses have not yet been conditioned to avoiding people and can readily be trained in the opposite direction with patience and kindness. It is essential to establish the hierarchy in the relationship, for, living free, each foal would have to learn its place in the herd society and forge its own standing in the social order. Taken into domesticity, the humans who have close association with the animal become its herd; they must ensure that the young pony recognises the position of its human partner as leader. This means gaining the pony's trust and confidence through training based upon an understanding of the animal's natural fears and instincts. Anyone planning to undertake this task should read *Understanding Your Pony* by Lucy Rees, a book which looks at the equine-human partnership from the pony's point of view (and which, in my opinion, should be compulsory reading for anyone who rides).

With a foal from a free-living herd, it is important to establish that it can no longer simply run away as a response to humans. Remove that instinctive reaction from the Exmoor foal's mind and the rest will follow much more easily. The advice issued by those well-practised in taming Exmoor foals is to work regularly with each animal, making contact with humans pleasurable and unthreatening. Experience has shown that it does help to spend time handling (e.g. grooming) an Exmoor foal whilst it is tied up on a short rope to the head collar. After tugging against this restraint at first, foals quickly adapt to their loss of freedom without distress. Advice on how to do this can be obtained from the Secretary of the Exmoor Pony Society (see Useful Addresses).

Having re-programmed the young Exmoor, the normal processes of taming and eventually skilful breaking yield tremendous results; the Exmoor in domesticity is very impressive. This is perhaps the most significant aspect of the Exmoor Pony: tailored by Nature for natural existence yet so flexible that it will adapt to membership of a human herd. For those Exmoors born in-ground there is no early independence to overcome and obviously the more they are handled, the earlier they recognise that people are members of their society as well as other ponies.

Armed now with an understanding of just how and why Exmoor Ponies can be domesticated, we can begin our survey of the ways in which they have served Man in the past and how they do so today.

Driving

Exmoor Ponies are so suited to the sport of driving that it is surprising that it is only recently that this use for Exmoors began to flourish. Driven singly, their performance is impressive enough but find yourself a pair of Exmoors with matched stride and of course you have a perfectly matched pair in looks as they are virtually identical. Few sights can rival the impact of four Exmoors being driven, but sadly this has not been seen for some years now.

Driving is the modern descendant of much earlier

Plate 121 *Caractacus (1/9) being driven around 1935*

usage of Exmoors in harness. If we think back to times before the tractor or the car, then pony and cart were a means of transporting both people and goods and this must have been the case ever since humans realised the potential of the wheel and horse combined. Yet perhaps the most spectacular use ever for the British Hill Pony was as an animal of war, pulling chariots into battle. Dr Sandor Bokonyi wrote in 1968:

> *Chariot ponies of both eastern and western Europe in the Bronze Age (a period when riding was a rare occurrence outside central Asia) resemble the Exmoor Pony more than they do the European horses of the succeeding Iron Age.*[101]

If we think of Britain and chariots we come inevitably to a later time, to the battles fought against the Romans and unavoidably to Boadicea.

It has been suggested that Queen Boadicea faced her Roman enemies from a chariot drawn by Exmoor Ponies. On this basis, the 1979 Westward Television documentary on the Exmoor was entitled "Warhorse of the Britons". When interviewed on the subject as part of that programme, I used many "ifs" and qualifications because the simple truth is that we do not have a single piece of hard evidence that this was so. However, there are many hints that it may indeed have been this way.

Back in Chapter 4, we read that General Pitt Rivers, the noted archaeologist, stated that the Exmoor Pony was the nearest modern day animal to the ponies used by the Britons of Roman times. Thus, populations of British Hill Pony up on the moorlands and mountains probably were sources of foals taken into domesticity and trained in harness.

However, we also know that the Celtic tribes had a long history of horse-breeding and that other imported types and cross-bred animals have been identified from Celtic sites. So we cannot possibly be certain that the chariot ponies were all true British Hill Pony. It seems more likely that some were and some had other breeding. There is also the matter of Boadicea's status as Queen of the Iceni. If the brown and mealy British Hill Pony type was freely available, would such a common animal have suited her station? No-one can know, for there is no historical record and it would all have depended upon her character. If we visualise her as defiant throughout, then perhaps she would have chosen more distinctive chariot ponies. If she were concerned with her personal survival as leader of her people, she might have actively sought the anonymity of the native ponies.

Plate 122 *A Herd No. 2 Exmoor and veterinary student alias Celtic tribesman and pony*

We must leave the Exmoor and Boadicea as a wonderful image but one which is far from certain. That this race of ponies provided chariot-power for the ancient Britons generally, does seem an acceptable conclusion.

Anthony Dent's *The Pure-Bred Exmoor Pony* contains a photograph taken when students from the Royal Dick Veterinary College, Edinburgh made a chariot and harnessed two of their Exmoors to it for a BBC schools' programme. This was not an easy task but that is another story. The students also donned animal skins and impersonated their Celtic ancestors to collect for charity around Edinburgh one year, accompanied naturally by an Exmoor Pony.

In more recent times, in the late 1800s, many ponies were used to pull tradesmen's carts transporting all manner of goods. This took Exmoor Ponies into service and Evelyn March-Phillips wrote in 1896 of one working in London:

> *It is amusing to hear that one day last summer a carriage and fast-stepping pair of horses leaving the Imperial Institute was kept company by a costermonger's cart and sturdy pony, the shabby little follower refusing to be shaken off, till in Belgrave Square it passed the grand turn-out with a chaffing jeer at the smart coachman, – and on the flank of the plucky little steed the familiar anchor stood revealed.*

The advent of mechanisation brought to an end one of the saddest ways in which man has ever used ponies in harness, as labourers underground. It is impossible to imagine a greater contrast between the natural environment of ponies and the dark tunnels of a coal mine. It is a hard way of life for a human and, although they were well cared for, it must have been appalling for the pit ponies. The surplus from herds of free-living ponies around the country were all too often destined for this fate. The only happy fact to relate is that ponies are no longer shut away from the light of day underground.

When we see today's driving competitors racing around the intricate courses against the clock, we can be in no doubt that the native British pony must have been ideally suited to charioteering. Modern competitors no

Plate 123 *Exmoors belonging to Mr Ian MacDonald in Canada, providing transport in snowy weather*

longer have the spears and wheel scythes yet they still have to have courage and the determination to beat their rivals and the challenges of the courses.

The growing interest in driving Exmoors has also led to a driving teach-in being held by Bob and Melanie Wright on Exmoor in 1991. The response to this day's introduction has prompted the planning of a second event in 1993. It would be impracticable to review the successes of all the competitors in driving events and beyond the scope of this book as with riding and showing competitions. However, one or two more unusual events in harness deserve a mention.

Mrs Jemima Parry-Jones of the Falconry Centre, Newent gives displays of falconry at some of the major agricultural shows and is ably assisted by Merlin (78/49), a nineteen year old gelding, who pulls the exhibition cart. A totally different cargo was the responsibility of Mr and Mrs Wright's Knightoncombe Burnished Brass (H8/12) when he proudly drove Father Christmas into North Molton in December 1990.

Plate 124 *Merlin (78/49), a 19 year-old gelding assisting with the Falconry Centre's display at the Royal Bath & West Show in 1988*

Whether pulling chariots, carts or driving competitively, the Exmoor in harness is a wonderful sight. Exmoor Ponies have tremendous power and stamina which makes them ideal for driving. This use for the Exmoor will surely continue to grow.

Agricultural Usage

Farming today has a technology all of its own and it is sometimes hard to realise that before the arrival of motorised power, real horse-power was depended upon. On Exmoor, farmers bred a suitable work animal by crossing their native Exmoor Pony. The Devon Packhorse was probably part Exmoor part Draught Horse and the breeding of what is termed the Devon Cob is uncertain but again is thought to have been part Exmoor. However, on many hill farms, the living was insufficient to finance the use of an outside stallion and a number of farmers trained Exmoor Ponies to do their agricultural work.

Despite their relatively small size, Exmoor Ponies have enormous strength and staying-power. Mr Clifford Hooper, who farmed at Withypool, used two Exmoor Ponies side by side for ploughing his land in the 1930s.

Plate 125 *James Speed (right) seeing how Exmoors were being used for forestry work near Hanover, Germany in the 1950s*

Plate 126 *An Exmoor being used for shepherding in the 1940s*

The ponies were also highly suitable as general purpose transport and farmers rode them when shepherding and presumably for gatherings of all stock. Another local farmer recalls that where mares were used, they were also bred from. They would be allowed to foal and then, after a short time, resumed their duties being ridden with the young foal running freely alongside. Clifford Hooper used one of his Exmoors, Yo-Yo, for shepherding work and, armed with a shotgun, rode Yo-Yo when on Home Guard patrol on Withypool Hill. In 1947, he also undertook the postal deliveries mounted on an Exmoor. This one farmer's recollections provide us with a vivid testament to the versatility of the local pony. In Germany, Exmoors were also used to haul timber out of woodland.

Exmoors were also helpful as carriers particularly in taking food out to sheep or cattle through snowy conditions. There is also a story that the first lead

Plate 127 *In bygone days, mares would resume their agricultural work with their foal alongside*

accumulator battery used at Knighton Farm, Withypool was carried out there on the back of an Exmoor Pony. In the absence of roads, the cart was a late-comer to Exmoor and the transporting of loads in packs on ponies lasted longer than in most places.

The Exmoor Pony was then a multi-purpose animal for the hill farmer, carrying him at work or on home guard patrol as we saw earlier, conveying goods and in harness to work the land. Once the tractor came on the scene, the horse became obsolete in the farming context and the Exmoor Ponies were no exception. Today there is a growing band of farmers returning to using Shire Horses on their land, convinced of the economic sense as well as the benefit to the environment but Exmoor Ponies as farm workers remain a thing of the past, to date. Back in 1984 though, at their stud at Shaftesbury, Annie and Neville Dent turned the clock back and used their Exmoors for ploughing and harrowing. The ponies also accompanied them as pack animals walking the Ridgeway in Berkshire.

It seems unlikely that the Exmoor will ever resume its role in farming on Exmoor. Whilst some shepherding is still done on horse-back, the farmers favour larger mounts as they are often used for hunting as well. When

Plate 128 *Neville Dent harrowing with his Exmoor gelding, Rowanberry (23/139)*

riding an Exmoor out hunting, there is nothing lacking in strength and agility but there is a perceived deficiency in status. So, for Exmoors, use in agriculture is over. Or is it? When the Earth's fossil fuels run out, many may have good cause to be grateful to those who have conserved the Exmoor Pony.

Riding

Riding is perhaps the most fundamental use to which domesticated horses and ponies are put even though it is not known whether work in harness came before or after the start of riding. Riding as a means of travelling over long distances again declined with the advent of motor vehicles but has continued as an endless source of pleasure and competition for countless people.

In the past, the Exmoor Pony was highly praised both for riding for necessity and for pleasure. Evelyn March-Phillips wrote in 1896:

> *Exmoor ponies are noted for their endurance, their cleverness and their jumping powers. We know instances of their carrying men forty miles and running away the last mile. Dr Collyns, the veteran stag-hunter, and author of "The Chase of the Wild Red Deer" mentions having bought a two year old for twenty three shillings in 1816, which lived to twenty three years. A child learned to ride on it; and, twenty years after, when he was no light weight, the same pony, which was only eleven hands, carried him in a run in such a manner as to excite the surprise and envy of apparently better mounted sportsmen.*

Sir Walter Gilbey writing in 1900 quoted W. Youatt as having stated that an Exmoor Pony carried a 14 stone farmer from Bristol to South Molton, a distance of 86 miles, and arrived before the coach which was making the same journey. However, it is not certain whether this animal was a true Exmoor Pony or had been bred up through crossing. Generally, experience has shown that Exmoor Ponies will carry up to 12 stone for considerable distances without difficulty. It is for this reason that they are so suitable as a family pony, for parents as well as children may be able to ride them.

Plate 129 *Tom Summersgill riding Knightoncombe Royal Mantle (H8/6)*

Plate 130 *Royal Dick Veterinary College trekking ponies*

Today, Exmoor Ponies participate in many types of riding activity. Firstly, Britain offers every conceivable competitive possibility for almost anything that can be done on horse-back. There are long-distance rides, riding classes at shows, Pony Club competitions, even fancy dress contests and Exmoor Ponies take part in all these. In addition there are some specialised riding uses involving Exmoors.

Riding for the Disabled is a marvellous charity which provides disabled people around the country with a chance to experience the joys of riding and forming a bond with a pony. In Essex, one group, run by Miss A. Mitchell at Barrow Farm near Chelmsford, uses Exmoor Ponies most successfully, another testament to the sensitive temperament of the native pony.

North of the border, in Scotland, Exmoor Ponies have proved themselves as fine trekking ponies both for the Royal Dick Veterinary College students and until recently for Mr William Main at Dunbar. The Edinburgh students run a trekking establishment on a commercial basis at Snoot and have until recently bred their own ponies from the breeding group which originated from the Speed herd. Strangely, the Exmoor Pony has not been used for trekking to any extent on Exmoor itself;

what better way would there be to explore the wonderful moors and woods of Exmoor than mounted on its native pony?

The Exmoor's inherent jumping ability is less well-known than its stamina and power. There are accounts of the free-living Exmoors, when confined after gatherings, clearing five-barred gates in a bid for freedom, even jumping out of stables over the bottom doors from a standing start. Such abilities, there because naturally selected as yet another means of escaping threat, can be exploited for pleasure and in jumping competitions.

Exmoors are then extremely versatile and riding them can take on so many different aspects. In the era of "Moorland Mousie" they were very popular as children's ponies, perhaps because of the impact of the Mousie books but this did not last. The idea that as children grew in height they should move up to a larger pony was fostered and this highly questionable attitude came to be accepted. There are many people today who remember riding an Exmoor Pony in their childhood and who are stunned that they have become such a rare animal. Yet we cannot present Exmoors as the ideal child's pony without qualification; they are ideal for a competent young rider but not specifically as a child's first pony, as these ponies are blessed with considerable intelligence and their own firm opinions. They will readily enter into a relationship based upon common respect and respond best as partner to the rider.

Showing

Writing about showing Exmoor Ponies is hard because it is both good and bad for the Exmoor race. This use for the animals is undeniably a major part of why they survive – as with all uses it creates a market for the produce of the herds. Also showing, as with appearance of Exmoors in riding and driving competitions, increases public awareness of the ponies so further stimulating demand for them. Yet alongside these benefits are some very real threats to the natural genetic identity of the Exmoor, for the show-ring is a place where fashion and trends exert considerable influence.

We should always be proud of those first exhibitors of Exmoors who many decades ago decided that these ponies should always be shown in natural condition, not artificially presented in any way. Thus bathing and grooming are acceptable but no mane or tail pulling, plaiting or fancy patterns contrived on the coat are appropriate. For a long time, the Exmoor suffered competitively because of this when judged against the various pony breeds. They would sometimes be described as scruffy and woolly and were of course not as smart as the breeds which permitted "hair-dressing". There is still perhaps some of this attitude remaining for despite some notable successes in mixed mountain and moorland classes in recent years, generally the Exmoor continues to be passed over more than it deserves by judges who are unfamiliar with this race.

Thus people who show Exmoors need the understanding that their ponies have to be viewed differently because they are different and their primitive character has to be conserved at all costs. If ever the dictates of what pleases the eye of judges (attuned to the selectively bred pony types) is allowed to influence the development of the Exmoor population then the results may be very negative; we will return to this theme in the last chapter.

Yet despite all these reservations, showing is very important to the well-being of the Exmoor Ponies. The numbers of ponies would be far lower if the domestic markets were not boosted by the activities of the show-ring. Just when people started competing with each other on the basis of the quality of their stock can only be guessed at. Given how interested in horse-breeding the Celts were it may have had its birth as far back as then. Our first record of more modern Exmoors being shown are the photographs of Royal Oak and Gladys shown at the Royal Show at Islington Hall in 1897. The first Exmoor Pony Society Breed Show was held at South Molton in 1921 and it thrives today at Exford each year. There is also now a number of regional Exmoor Shows around the country which reflects the spread of the ponies away from Exmoor itself. Shows such as those held at Dunster, the county show of Devon and the Royal Bath and West Show, and a few others include classes specifically for Exmoor Ponies. In addition, most shows have mixed mountain and moorland classes.

So the showing of Exmoor Ponies is a high profile part of the Exmoor story. It is an activity which does tremendous work for the Exmoors but which could do harm as we will see. For those who show, as in any competitive sphere, it can bring the utter joy of winning or the despondency of losing; perhaps the wisest words ever spoken were "It doesn't matter who wins, you always take the best pony home with you".

A Source of Protein

If we are to consider all the ways in which Exmoor Ponies are used, we cannot avoid the subject of slaughtering for meat. At one time, particularly when Bampton Fair was in operation as a pony market, a high proportion of the foals and surplus adults sold out of the moorland herds found no buyer other than the "meat-man". Demand for Exmoor Ponies has at times been very low and, as with the Dartmoor and New Forest Ponies, many have been purchased to become food. Whilst the British traditionally reject the whole idea of eating horse-flesh, there is no such taboo on the Continent and so much is exported. However, with the growth of a multi-cultural society in Britain, there is also some demand here.

It is inevitable that with free-living populations of any kind, where more foals are born than are wanted for domestic activities, the remainder cannot be returned to their birthplace; the numbers would soon damage the land and eventually none would be sustainable. Thus, a small proportion will sometimes have to be utilised for food. Where Exmoor Ponies are concerned, the numbers of foals born each year are relatively small. However, despite every effort to publicise their rarity and importance, there are times when supply exceeds demand and the inevitable results.

We tend to be enormously uncomfortable about the use of horses and ponies for food, no doubt a legacy from our early Christian times when eating horse-meat was forbidden. Yet despite a growing commitment to vegetarianism, most people still accept the production of livestock such as cattle, sheep and pigs for the sole purpose of eating them. Perhaps we should be more caring about the way in which all animals are kept during their lifetime and totally intolerant of any inhumane practice when it comes to ending their lives. If the animals, including our wonderful ponies, have a good quality of existence and then a rapid and humane dispatch this is the best that can be done within a meat-eating culture. With regard to ponies, every effort must surely be made though to oppose any changes in regulations which would permit their live export for eventual slaughter. Britain should be proud of its protective measures which have made this impossible for so long and must ensure they persist.

The most ironic aspect of Exmoor Ponies being used for food is that if pony meat were a regular part of the traditional British diet, the demand would mean that they would exist in far greater numbers and probably be more secure. Conservation would be a much easier proposition. However, this is too high a price to pay.

Any healthy Exmoor Pony which ends up as meat is surely the ultimate waste – equivalent to the ludicrous idea of eating Giant Pandas, which are actually more numerous than Exmoor Ponies. It is a reflection of this country's lack of appreciation of how valuable these ponies are; an Exmoor Pony carcass is a lost opportunity for conservation.

Exmoor Ponies as Conservationists

The subject of conserving the Exmoor Ponies underlies much of this book but they can be conservationists themselves. In assessing their uses we come to the latest task for which they have been selected – as assistants in the process of conserving other natural species.

In 1990, both the National Trust and English Nature (then the Nature Conservancy Council) purchased youngstock from the Exmoor National Park Authority's free-living herds. Those bought by the National Trust were taken to the Purbeck Hills of Dorset while the others have a new home in Cornwall.

The group bought by the National Trust consisted of one eight year-old mare, two six month-old fillies and three six month-old colts. All were from Herd H42 which runs on Haddon Hill on Exmoor. Their new home is in Seacombe Valley on the Purbecks where they graze alongside sheep and cattle on 270 acres of limestone grassland. Mrs G. J. Hann of the Trust explained their reasons for introducing Exmoor Ponies:

> One of the main objectives of the National Trust is Conservation – with the use of Exmoor Ponies as a management tool, we not only produce a better sward to allow more interesting flora to establish, we are also preserving a Rare Breed.
>
> We decided to use Exmoors as they are a Rare Breed and also because of their ability to exist with very little management. The National Trust has an 8,000 acre holding on the Isle of Purbeck and if the ponies are successful, there is no doubt with the decline in Agriculture and the difficulty in finding animals to graze these important areas, we shall use them elsewhere on the Estate.[102]

This is an exciting new application for the Exmoor and one to which it is ideally suited. Most importantly, it represents new groups being established under free-living conditions and is therefore doubly welcome. The principle of the ponies generating improvements in the vegetation is a sound one for their grazing habits are varied and in balance with the environment. In Cumbria, Veronica Watkins has kept Exmoor Ponies on a remote fell for many years and living close to them has observed their habits in great detail. In a letter to me she described their relationship to their habitat:

> *The herd fit my grounds, so I have a flower conservation area which requires no labour. The herd do all that and it improves every year. After the twenty-three years I've been here, the variety of plants that flower has increased and continues to do so every year. The Botanists find new species each year. You see ponies don't eat flowers, they weed round them, letting in the light and keeping down the coarse plants like rushes and bracken and grasses.*[103]

So the Exmoor Ponies come well recommended as conservation workers. If the Cumbrian experience is anything to go by, the National Trust and English Nature should see beneficial results from these experiments and it is hoped that the use of Exmoor Ponies in this way will increase. It aids in the conservation of habitats and the free-living characteristics of the ponies themselves.

Public Relations Work

The work undertaken by a small number of Exmoor Ponies is in the area of Public Relations, in encouraging public awareness of the importance of their race and the need for active conservation measures. We have already seen that a few live in Sababurg Zoo in Germany but no British zoos include Exmoors – yet. However, as their population is classified as Category 1 – Critical by the Rare Breeds Survival Trust (R.B.S.T.), Exmoor Ponies are exhibited in a number of Rare Breeds Parks as we saw with my mare Daisy at the Cotswold Farm Park.

In addition, a mare and foal on show in a corral has proved to be a most successful means of attracting interest in displays at both County and local events. The R.B.S.T. usually include an Exmoor representative at the Royal Cornwall, the Devon County and the Royal Bath and West Show at Shepton Mallet. The Exmoor Pony Society has a mare and foal for visitors to Exford Show

to meet each year and Exmoor National Park Authority has followed suit at some of its public occasions.

From time to time there are also equestrian events of a national scale in which the Exmoor is represented, such as the 300th anniversary of Rotten Row in 1990 and the display at the Royal Agricultural Society of England's British Equine Event in November 1991 and 1992.

These examples of publicity work illustrate the promotional role which every Exmoor Pony and its owner undertakes. The best possible way to increase awareness and appreciation of the domestic suitability of the Exmoor is by exploiting situations where people may come face to face with the ponies themselves. Whether in permanent exhibitions or at shows and events, the Exmoor Ponies involved are ambassadors for their race.

Scientific Studies

The Exmoor Ponies owned by the students at the Royal Dick Veterinary College, Edinburgh are not only useful as the mounts for trekkers, they also aid in the veterinary training of the students involved. Through their close relationship and involvement with the Exmoors, these students have a rare opportunity for regular experience of handling and managing ponies.

Exmoor Ponies have also been included in a few scientific research projects. Chapters 7 to 9 of this book are based upon my own research which focused upon the relationship of the free-living herds to their environment on Exmoor. This concentrated mainly on the ponies on Withypool Common (hence referring to it in this book as "The Withypool Study") but included all the Exmoor locations to some degree.

Ten years after this was completed, Dr Elaine Gill included regular visits to Exmoor to study ponies' condition and diet as part of her comparative research to identify ways of improving the condition of free-living New Forest Ponies.

At various times, Exmoors have provided blood samples for blood-typing studies, genetic research and investigations into sweet-itch. It seems certain that studies of blood may hold valuable information which may clarify in the future some of the debatable aspects of equine history. Also, studies of bloodlines by the RBST and private individuals need further development.

Yet long before all the investigations listed here, Exmoors were studied by those trying to unravel the development of the horse family through comparative bone studies and breeding experiments. This began with Professor Alfred Nehring who selected the Exmoor as a standard type to which he compared German fossil horses in 1884. Similarly, Professor J. Cossar Ewart used Exmoors significantly in his breeding research at Penicuik at the turn of the century. Finally, the work of James and Mary Speed built upon these early foundations.

All these examples seem to convey a rich usage of the Exmoor as a subject for scientific interest, yet, in truth, we have only scratched the surface. There is still so much to understand and potential for many more research projects.

Exmoor Travellers

The ancestors of Exmoor Ponies travelled thousands of miles seeking out new lands and finally came to be isolated from continental Europe by the English Channel. Thus, the British Hill Pony and subsequently the Exmoor could not resume its wandering habits until Man interfered. Through human intervention, small numbers of Exmoors have been exported and returned to countries where perhaps once their ancestors roamed. Others have been sent to totally new lands.

We have made many journeys in this book but to undertake visits to all the Exmoors outside Britain, though they total just 40, would delay us too long. It must be left perhaps for another time. It is interesting to note though that Exmoors now live in Canada, the United States of America, the Falkland Islands, France, Germany, Sweden, Holland and Denmark and there are records of them having been sent in the past to India, Australia, New Zealand and even one to Corfu!

The most active group abroad at present is in Sweden where the owners have formed their own Society and are in close contact with the British Exmoor Pony

Society. Yet even here, the numbers are very small as yet. It is a sobering statistic that there were 777 Exmoor Ponies world-wide at the last census while, for example, there are around 7,000 Connemara Ponies in France alone!

The opening of the European market in 1992 must surely present a real opportunity. The Exmoor Pony may find new homes where once its fore-runners lived on the hills and mountains of many countries – if it is marketed appropriately and enthusiastically.

The Exmoor Pony Society

No exploration of the association between Exmoor Ponies and Man could end without a further visit to the Exmoor Pony Society. We reviewed its founding and early history in Chapter 6. Today, the Society continues as a body committed to encouraging the breeding and use of Exmoors. Where once its membership was almost totally of Exmoor residents, today there are members nation-wide and abroad.

We have already seen how the Society undertakes the inspecting and registering of foals, the licensing of stallions and the maintenance of the British Stud Book. It also administers an annual grant from the Horse Race Betting and Levy Board, in common with all the pony breed societies for each mountain and moorland type. This grant, and a proportion of the Society's other income, is devoted to awarding premiums aimed at encouraging the breeding of Exmoors. Foal premiums are included in this and awarded in the autumn.

The Stallion Parade

There are separate premiums for stallions which receive mares in addition to their own, mostly in-ground and for those which run with their own free-living herds. In theory, any stallion can be brought to the annual Stallion Parade held on the first Wednesday of May on Exmoor but in practice few of the moorland stallions can be handled. The Parade is held at Exford and members and ponies travel considerable distances to attend. For the human contingent, the Society's Annual General Meeting follows in the afternoon.

Plate 131 *Exmoor Pony Society stallion parade in 1991 (ponies L–R: Waltersgay Sundew H29/7, Knightoncombe Clouded Silver H8/22, Knightoncombe Lackey H8/61, Winged Bowman H56/1, Jiminy Cricket H29/1).*

willing stallions often involved two or three men to each animal, hanging on to ropes with all their strength. By comparison, the modern event is a tame affair. However, it still involves bringing mature stallions in relative close proximity to each other at a time when all their instincts of rivalry are stimulated. Despite this, they are usually very well-behaved but their exhibitors still require a strong arm.

Plate 132 *Exford Show 1972—this yearling colt from Winsford Hill had been haltered for the first time the day before the show*

It has sometimes been suggested that the Stallion Parade being held at the beginning of May is a legacy from pagan festivals involving ponies. This may well be true although I know of no firm evidence with which to support the idea. However, it would again be quite reasonable to assume that those great pony-breeders, the Celts, would have held some similar event to compare their stock.

In the early days of the Exmoor Pony Society, the Parade was as it sounds, a chance to display the stallions which were being used in breeding and for any which met the necessary standards of quality to be awarded premiums. Over the last few decades, it has become more of a competition, with classes for stallions and colts which are judged and placed in an order of merit, as well as the awarding of the premiums. This has perhaps detracted from what it once was, a celebration of Exmoor sires where all could be their own judge and assess which they preferred and would try to use.

In the past, when most ponies were living in the Exmoor locality, stallions were brought straight off the moor to the Parade. These were unhandled stallions, wild by nature and totally resentful of the disturbance at the start of the breeding season. Parading such un-

Occasionally we do see stallions which successfully combine tame behaviour with a free-living existence, if they have been handled when young. For example, Knightoncombe Lackey H8/61 is the herd stallion running with National Park Authority mares beyond Warren Farm. He lives a free life with little human contact throughout the year except for two outings and the gathering. Just as he is fulfilling his purpose in early summer, he is removed from his harem for a day or two, to be paraded at Exford. Lackey offers no resistance to being taken from his herd, behaves impeccably at the Parade and then returns to the more important business at Warren. In August the process is repeated for the Exmoor Pony Society Show.

How well this illustrates the incredible flexibility of Exmoor Ponies. Lackey was handled and trained to showing as a foal in 1986 and as a yearling and continued with regular human contact until he was two and a half years old. He then took up his natural role out on Exmoor Forest. He retains this wonderful tolerance of people, developed in his youth, yet out on the moorland he has to be totally fit to survive in every way. It is surely this potential for relationships with people, in combination with the natural hardiness, that makes the adaptive repertoire of the Exmoor the ultimate survival package.

Other stallion and brood mare premiums are awarded at various shows around the country. However, with the geographical spread of ponies, perhaps a second Stallion Parade will be introduced in another location before too long.

The Annual Show

The Exmoor Pony Show is held on the second Wednesday of August each year at a location between Exford and Withypool. Blessed with a clear and sunny day, this high point provides a perfect setting but is not so kind in inclement weather. The Exmoor Pony event is part of Exford Show and is a great meeting place for Exmoor Pony enthusiasts as well as exhibitors. Many set off in the early hours and cover many miles of motorway before arriving at the showground.

The day is filled with in-hand, ridden and sometimes driving classes and culminates with the presentation of many cups and trophies. It is a time of great camaraderie alongside tremendous rivalry, a time to revel in all things Exmoor with people of like mind. There is the comfort of knowing your neighbour around the ring shares your love for these wonderful ponies. It is also an

Plate 133 *Exford Show*

ideal place for anyone interested in finding out about Exmoor Ponies to come. Concentrated there are the ponies themselves plus a wealth of experience of owning and breeding ponies and the officials of the Exmoor Pony Society only too willing to answer questions and cultivate new interest.

A Treasured Friendship

Having surveyed how Exmoor Ponies live and work in domesticity, we have a picture of adaptability yet again. Whether being ridden, driven, or in any of the other varied occupations in which we have found them, Exmoors prove to be both willing and able partners for humans. Also, breeding is an important role for some of the domestic population too.

Perhaps though in looking at all the separate ways in which we use Exmoors we are in danger of over-looking the most important purpose so many domestic ponies, including Exmoors, fulfil: they are companions to Man. Particularly in these modern times, where pressure and stress is the human condition in developed countries, horses and ponies are part of the counter-balance to such negative influences. Associating with ponies is a healing relaxation for the tired human mind. Who can fail to forget their problems when galloping across beautiful countryside or driving down quiet woodland rides. Even simply grooming and handling ponies can bring a peace to the soul which we all need so badly amidst modern chaos.

The domestic horses and ponies of history have been primarily food, beasts of burden and weapons of war. Now they have also become our friends and this is perhaps the most important aspect of the human-equine relationship there has ever been.

CHAPTER 11

FIT FOR THE FUTURE?

Having journeyed together across thousands of miles and millions of years to investigate the natural history of the Exmoor Pony, we have reached our destination. We have shared a marvellous voyage through time and space and found the Exmoor Pony to be as wild as can be without actually being wild. We have seen a pony which is part of the natural fauna of Exmoor yet can become so much a part of family life. We have encountered different interpretations of its ancestry yet, even the least exciting of these means we are left with a very ancient breed if not, as seems more logical, the natural British race itself. So, at the end of this exploration, the Exmoor Pony emerges as a very special animal which deserves every effort on our part to provide it with a secure future.

In assessing the problems faced in conserving Exmoor Ponies and in seeking solutions, I will express opinions in this final chapter which should clearly be recognised as my own personal views. I am conscious that on occasions my words may be unpalatable to some and may ruffle a few feathers. My object is not to cause discomfort but to clarify just what needs to be done to safeguard the Exmoor Pony.

Most of this look to the future will apply to conserving the free-living population. This is not to ignore domesticated Exmoors or to present them as a somehow inferior group. If a sound future can be achieved for the econatural ponies, then the domesticated Exmoors will thrive for as long as there are people interested in owning them. Conserving animals in their natural habitat though is a much more complicated business.

This final chapter is not going to be a prediction of doom and extinction for the Exmoor Ponies although the challenges faced are fairly daunting. I believe wholeheartedly that, given commitment and co-operation, a healthy future can be ensured. Failure is just too awful to consider. Although the title of this section is "Fit for the Future", it is as much a question of creating future conditions that are fit for the Exmoor Ponies as making sure that we do not alter their biological fitness.

Home Insurance

Conservationists throughout the world have come to realise that the key to conserving any species is to ensure that its home is protected and survives. How often there are television documentaries which tell the sad story of animals facing extinction because too much of their natural home has been destroyed. Usually, the main threat to the environment is Man and his need to utilise land for other purposes.

Exmoor is a recognised area of outstanding natural value as evidenced by its designation as a National Park but it is also a place where generation upon generation have tackled the hard life of farming its unkind hills and moors. Thus farmers need land for cultivation and for stock grazing alongside visitors who need its open spaces for an array of leisure uses and for enrichment of the soul. Into this competitive arena comes the question of conserving some land as suitable homes for the Exmoor Ponies.

Exmoor herds live on just a few enclosures within the National Park amounting to a total of just over 8,000 acres. They share these homes with cattle, sheep and deer and in some cases with visitors. What impact do these other species have upon the ponies' habitats?

Firstly, and most obvious, there is the degree of overlap in the diets of grazing animals which means that some competition exists for the natural resources. Graze too many stock through the summer and the remaining resources for the ponies which winter out are reduced. Keep the sheep and cattle out during the winter and the competition is intensified. So stocking levels have a direct impact upon the amount of food available to the Exmoor Ponies.

People visiting the moors and commons create different pressures. Although the ponies have adapted their behaviour to minimise contact, the approach of people is a disturbance. More importantly, they can cause damage to the vegetation and to the ponies. Vehicles are often driven considerable distances off the roads, wearing away the grass and deepening rutted tracks. Most distressingly, ponies are from time to time killed in road accidents. The recent death of the stallion, Prince Arthur, on Molland Moor brings home the devastating effect of careless driving by visitor or local resident.

A further threat to the moorland enclosures comes from the deterioration of the vegetation itself. As heather ages, the plants become very woody and cease to offer the amount of food that younger plants do. The management of moorland by controlled burning is necessary to maintain the quality of the vegetation. This has to be carefully judged for whilst burning at suitable intervals stimulates new growth of the heather and grasses and improves the grazing, burning too often can cause even

Plate 134 *Gorse is a very important source of food in winter*

worse deterioration of the grazing. So conserving the moorland habitat requires careful monitoring of the state of the vegetation and a balanced management plan.

Gorse represents an important winter food plant for the Exmoor Ponies but the amount available has noticeably declined on both Winsford Hill and Withypool Common. This is perhaps due to severe frosting of the mature gorse some years ago and then the lack of replacement bushes developing. It may be that the young gorse shoots have not had a chance to mature due to the pressure of continual grazing by sheep. Perhaps it would be timely to have previous surveys of the vegetation in these areas updated to assess just what changes are taking place and to identify how to arrest any further deterioration.

This limited review shows that conserving the moorland as homes for Exmoor Ponies is not simply about ensuring no acreage is lost. There is a need for active management of the vegetation, establishment of controls on stocking with other animals and education of visitors to take care of the environment.

I would like to see the establishment of the enclosures where the free-living herds run as designated Exmoor

Pony conservation areas. These "reserves" would have to be managed primarily as pony habitats which would of necessity mean that the farmers involved would have their agricultural freedom restricted. However, more and more, farmers are finding that traditional farming is less profitable and are being encouraged to undertake conservation projects. If managing land for Exmoor Ponies involves reducing stocking levels of sheep and cattle and increasing time spent on vegetation management, there would have to be suitable financial compensation and inducements. The key element would be to obtain the farmers' commitment to such a scheme and this is impossible if success for the ponies is at the farmers' expense.

The management of these conservation areas would have to be a joint venture involving the local farmers, the National Park Authority and perhaps even English Nature. This should ensure that expertise on all aspects of the moorland use and needs is harnessed. Expert research could then determine how best to maintain the health of the vegetation, including what levels of sheep and cattle can safely be combined with the ponies and over what periods of the year. Such pony reserves could be protected by introducing speed limits on any roads across them. Motorists could be warned by the use of signs that they are entering a conservation area and asked to drive carefully. Whilst no scheme will deter the determined lunatic, I am sure many people would respond appropriately. Publicity could be given to the special designation of these areas and both Exmoor residents and visitors educated towards more thoughtful behaviour in these locations.

A wonderful day-dream? I hope not – for having observed these pony habitats over the last seventeen years, I am well aware of deterioration and needless accidents. I feel sure that drastic measures are needed to safeguard the quality of the ponies' environment. I also believe this scheme could be a practical reality. With such a small area involved, the financial implications are of a manageable scale. The biggest hurdle, as ever, is obtaining the co-operation of all those involved. The importance of the Exmoor Pony is not widely appreci-ated on Exmoor itself. Skilled explanation of the reasons why they should receive such special treatment would be a necessary prerequisite to the presenting of such a scheme.

The moorland is the key to the survival of the natural characteristics of the Exmoor Pony; alter the habitat and the ponies will alter. Allow it to deteriorate and the future for free-living herds becomes doubtful. Actively and positively conserve the land and the ponies will have a firm foundation for a successful future.

The Agricultural Dimension

The existence of free-living ponies throughout Britain is precarious because, quite simply, it is usually more profitable to run sheep or cattle. Generally, those who maintain herds of ponies on open grazing do so because of a sense of tradition rather than for reasons of agricultural economics.

If cattle or sheep were run where the Exmoor Ponies currently live, they would yield a higher income than the ponies for, being designated as agricultural animals, they attract subsidies. The ponies are not recognised as part of the hill-farming system in this way and so their owners receive no encouragement to carry on breeding ponies. In fact, this situation acts as an inducement to abandon keeping hill ponies at all. Added to this is the stark fact that often a cross-bred pony, being larger, will fetch a higher price. So the odds are fairly well stacked against the true Exmoor Pony when its existence is assessed in economic terms.

The importance of family heritage in the story of the Exmoor remains evident today. Those few people who keep free-living herds on Exmoor have kept faith with the beliefs of those before them, that the local pony deserved to be conserved. The days of earning a reasonable living from rearing the ponies are now long gone, a feature of the pre-mechanised era. Therefore, most hill farmers who retain herds do so because of their ties with that past. A few herds have been established more recently in response to the growing awareness of their scarcity in free-living conditions. Whatever motivates the private owners of herds to continue keeping their

Plate 135 *Mare and foal on Haddon Hill, members of the Exmoor National Park Herd H42*

Exmoor Ponies, they should be saluted for their efforts. The future of their Exmoor Ponies depends upon that motivation being inherited by whoever is next to farm the land with grazing rights.

This is hardly a secure situation. Even assuming that the farms in question stay within the families of the present owners, there is no guarantee that new generations will feel as committed to the old ways. The rest of social evolution suggests that such traditional affinities are weakened steadily. Future generations face an uncertain future themselves with farming and who can say when they will have to abandon sentiment and be driven totally by economics. In order to ensure a future fit for the Exmoors there is a need to make the breeding of ponies more viable within hill farming and this requires government involvement.

I believe the time has come for the nation to play an active part and for hill ponies to be looked upon as part of the hill-farming system in a conservation context. The state is beginning to pay farmers to set aside land and become involved in "green" projects. As a development of this concept, I would suggest that subsidies should be awarded to encourage the breeding of native ponies living free in their natural habitats.

Such a scheme could be designed to benefit all types of British pony for the subsidy could be applicable where the owner ran registered animals of a native breed. This would swing the pendulum away from cross-breeding and in favour of conserving the true types. Some effort on these lines has already been started within Dartmoor National Park in trying to encourage the breeding of the true Dartmoor Pony type rather than mongrelised ponies. This is to be admired but a nation-wide initiative, not dependent upon the available budget locally, would be a more stable arrangement. A national commitment to our wonderful equine heritage is long overdue.

The level of subsidy would have to be carefully calculated for it would be undesirable if this prompted increases in pony breeding on a massive scale. The market for ponies in Britain would not support significantly higher levels of production. However, there are the other European countries to consider. With the markets for horse-meat on the continent and the freeing of trade after 1992, I for one would not wish to see British farmers deliberately turning to pony rearing to satisfy that demand. Few can be unaware by now of the proposals to lift the minimum value export restrictions for live ponies. If this comes to pass it will create conditions where ponies will be transported to the continent for slaughter. The fight against this must continue and be won. If it is not, subsidising pony breeding without qualification could have unsought results.

Any subsidy scheme would therefore have to apply to the breeding group, not their progeny. It would only be applicable if the stallion and all of the mares run by the owner are registered animals of one native breed, not to mixed herds. This would ensure little impact upon the market economics but would offer some extra inducement to breed pure and conserve the native types. Formulated thus, it would not favour the cross-breeder or anyone who is willing to earn their living from exporting for slaughter.

In this way, the Ministry of Agriculture could play an important role in conserving the Exmoor Pony and the other native breeds where it matters most, in natural circumstances. By introducing a scheme on these lines, it would contribute to the security of the Exmoor. For if family tradition ever wanes, if there is no following generation to take over and herds pass into new ownership, more commercial judgements may be made. The existence of a financial reward for breeding the true local pony might just sway the decision in favour of the Exmoor.

Can it be done? The answer must be positive for there is no obvious practical reason why such a scheme could not be introduced. Again, in relative terms, the financial implication is not unmanageable. It should be done as part of the nation's protection of its heritage and as some measure of support for the beleaguered hill farmers.

I wrote recently to the Ministry of Agriculture requesting a statement of their existing policy pertaining to free-living British ponies and received the following answer:

> *The Ministry, in fact, has very little to do with free-living or confined horses or ponies, on Exmoor or elsewhere. They are not now generally kept for agricultural purposes. We do not, for example, provide any grants or subsidies which help farmers to keep them. We recognise that on Exmoor, Dartmoor and in the New Forest the keeping of free-living ponies is a traditional practice and part of the rural landscape. Local Agricultural Development & Advisory Service (A.D.A.S.) officers do have some knowledge of this practice and can provide advice on various matters. Our main concern is with the welfare of these ponies. Officers of our State Veterinary Service are prepared to offer advice, and have done so, in the general interest of animal welfare in the countryside.*[104]

So a totally new approach would have to be added within the agricultural context. The Ministry of Agriculture is however taking steps which ought to benefit free-living ponies through conserving their habitats, as reported in the Daily Telegraph (14/11/91):

> *Plans for "greener" subsidies for hill farmers, to help them survive and protect Britain's most rugged landscapes, were published by the Ministry of Agriculture yesterday.*

> *New Environmentally Sensitive Areas would be set up, where farmers would be paid to regenerate damaged heather and other upland vegetation and avoid overgrazing.*

However, in practice, the M.A.F.F. proposals for Environmentally Sensitive Areas as originally presented in 1992 actually constituted a potential threat to free-living Exmoors. Farmers joining the voluntary scheme for maximum protection of the habitat have to remove all grazing stock over the winter months. Unfortunately, the original proposals included the free-living Exmoor Ponies within the definition of "stock". If this had been implemented, the survival of the environment would have been at the expense of the ponies. Regular removal from the natural life, even if feasible, would destroy their survival capabilities. Strong representations were made for the Exmoor Ponies to be exempt from the removal regulations. As this book goes to print, the final Ministry decision on the ponies' fate within the E.S.A. scheme has just been announced. Happily, the revised scheme permits registered, pure-bred Exmoors to remain on the E.S.A.s throughout the year.

With this exemption for free-living ponies now part of the E.S.A. system on Exmoor, then perhaps that scheme might provide the basis upon which further measures to actively conserve the ponies can be built.

Another Rare Breed

I have touched upon the importance of family continuity to the future security of the free-living herds and this needs some further comment. The reason that Exmoor Ponies are still found on Exmoor today is that grandfathers and fathers passed on their admiration for the ponies and the skills needed to manage them. Sometimes, this education was of members of their own family and, in other cases, the moorland farmers have passed their knowledge and understanding on when new families have become involved. The involvement of the farmers in the Exmoor Pony Society has to some degree spread the expertise needed.

Yet those steeped in the customs of owning and managing Exmoor Ponies and their "students" are themselves a very rare breed. With the spread of families away from the moor and the accelerated rate of new ideas reaching Exmoor at last, there are few young people to take over in the future. Gathering, handling and branding wild ponies are skills which take time and experience to acquire.

There is no way to force new generations into enthusiastic guardianship of Exmoor Ponies – this can only be encouraged. Perhaps if Britain recognised the value and importance of its native ponies, and public bodies actively promoted the conservation message, young individuals would be more likely to see a role for themselves in carrying on the family traditions. The Exmoor Pony Society positively tries to foster the involvement of young members and needs to continue such an approach. Every opportunity to train others in the management skills of the moorland breeders will have to be taken.

Back in the late 1800s and earlier part of this century, there was enormous pride in the Exmoor breed. The breeders believed that the Exmoor was the best of all British ponies – remember Mr Tapp's words and the applause at the first ever meeting of the Exmoor Pony Society. That pride produced owners who were firmly committed to ensuring a safe future for the ponies. Whoever takes up the ownership of moorland herds in the future, whether old or new families, people born on Exmoor or new settlers, everything must be done to make them feel proud to breed Exmoor Ponies.

Both the Exmoor National Park Authority and the Exmoor Pony Society can help to create such conditions. Also, combining recognition with some financial incentives would make a powerful force for encouraging Exmoor people to hold true to the old ways. Conservation measures are needed for this other rare species, the enthusiastic, skilled moorland breeder who is dedicated to the Exmoor Pony. They are possibly under even greater threat than the ponies themselves.

Security Measures

The majority of econatural Exmoor Ponies live on Exmoor itself. Although there are other herds in Cornwall, Dorset, Cumbria and in Scotland, they repre-

sent just 60 animals out of the total free-living population of 197. If the herds on Exmoor were ever lost, rebuilding from such a small surviving group would be possible but difficult. Again there would have been drastic depletion of genetic variation. A sound conservation approach would therefore involve both measures to ensure the continuance of the herds on Exmoor and increase the free-living population in other locations.

I have already explored some of the problems relating to the situation on Exmoor. The privately owned herds cannot be considered as totally secure. It is not impossible that where a farm changes ownership in the future, the new owner might not be sympathetic to the Exmoor Pony and decide to sell off the stock. Rather than wait until such an undesirable situation arises, it might be prudent to explore some form of "safety net" now. The 1992 Exmoor National Park Plan includes the following statement relating to Exmoor Ponies:

> The National Park Authority will maintain its breeding herd of Exmoor Ponies and support other privately owned herds.[105]

I hope that this may be the basis for some discussion between the Authority and the Exmoor Pony Society aimed at formulating contingency plans in case private moorland herds ever face dispersal.

There will always be the need to have a healthy free-living population away from Exmoor itself. This is basic insurance against disease or other catastrophe hitting a concentrated population of a rare animal. It was on this basis that the Rare Breeds Survival Trust established a population of North Ronaldsay Sheep on a second island. The danger lies in that old cliche of having all your eggs in one basket. To arrive at a more secure position for the Exmoor, it is necessary to establish more groups living in free conditions around the country.

The involvement of the National Trust and English Nature presents a real opportunity for progress. If the experiments with using Exmoors to maintain vegetation on nature reserves prove successful then this may prompt those bodies to extend the project. It is only organisations or individuals which have access to extensive areas of natural habitat that can enlarge the econatural population.

The establishment of any new free-living herd presents an opportunity to add to the security of the race. If the maximum benefit is to be obtained, then careful selection of ponies is necessary. The ideal situation would be to create free-living herds which essentially duplicate the breeding programmes which exist on Exmoor. Additional herds elsewhere, mirroring those on Winsford Hill, Withypool Common and Codsend Moor, the three parent populations, would safeguard the breeding of the recognisable local types. This could be complemented by other free-living herds in which lines are blended. The combination of both approaches would create a far more secure situation. Although there is a considerable reserve within the domestic population, we cannot look upon these for absolute guarantees of the future.

Conserving Wildness

Perhaps the biggest challenge in the future will be to ensure that the free-living ponies retain their econatural state and do not drift towards domesticity. There are a number of potential causes of a dilution to their wild side.

Management Practices

The traditional way of managing a free-living herd on Exmoor has been according to a policy of minimum intervention in the lives of the ponies. The hill farmers knew that their animals had inherent survival capabilities and relied upon these. The few occasions on which owners assisted their Exmoor Ponies were rare exceptions. Ponies within the hill-farming activity had to be sufficiently tough to survive without help or they could be no part of the system. This was why cross-breeding was rejected by the traditionalists.

Today, this approach survives with those families and herds which have a long history. However, with the establishment of newer herds there has been some change and a higher level of intervention. While un-questionably well-intentioned, this may begin to lessen the ponies' biological fitness.

Some owners now administer anti-worm treatments when the ponies are brought onto the farms following the autumn gathering. The outward effect of this is noticeable and the individuals concerned do look sleeker and in better condition than those ponies which are not wormed. I am sure that those who worm their ponies believe it is kinder than leaving them to cope with the worm burden alone.

However, coping with the stresses of internal and external parasites is part of life in the wild. Fitness means having sufficient natural hardiness to establish a balanced relationship with parasites. The strongest and therefore fittest animals achieve this and survive to breed. Whenever a free-living Exmoor Pony is given anti-parasitic treatment it is being cushioned from one of the natural pressures which have shaped it in the past. Treating all members of a herd means that some individuals which ruthless Nature would not have permitted to breed, survive to do so. Their weaker genes will therefore be part of the next generation. As the process continues, so the overall strength of the population may be reduced and ultimately it may become a case of having to worm the ponies if they are to survive. Then they would have become domestic animals.

The non-intervention approach is only sound if the free-living herds are running on habitats with suitable vegetation mix and of sufficiently large acreage with appropriate stocking levels of grazing animals. If they are not in such conditions then rather than artificially compensate, the question must surely be asked as to whether they should be there at all. Should an entire herd in apparently suitable circumstances exhibit serious worm problems, then this would indicate that there was in fact something wrong environmentally or that perhaps an unusual illness had struck. Such a situation would warrant careful investigation and justify inter-vention and treatment.

For those herds which do have the right environment then the traditional management system is far more likely to ensure their conservation than administering drugs routinely. It does not have to be an inhumane practice and I would not wish readers to think I am advocating leaving weaker ponies to suffer. Rejecting routine worming has to be allied with careful culling of the herd and monitoring of worm levels through periodic analysis of dung samples. Culling does not have to be the same as killing: it is the selective removal of individuals from the herd when they are identified as poor-doers. These can be sold away from free life into domestic circumstances although sometimes, if the individual is older, it is kinder to destroy them.

By observing which animals thrive and which cannot maintain condition,
the owner can determine which are the weak ponies which should not breed. In removing these animals, the natural outcome is mirrored, for in the wild, they would be unlikely to reproduce even if they managed to survive. This would be management accord- ing to the principles of natural selection which has preserved the wild blueprint for so long in the Exmoor Pony.

The price of making this commitment to natural management is that the ponies in the free herds may not rival their domestic counterparts in the show-ring. In unusual years, such as with mild winters, even the strongest ponies may lose some condition temporarily. In normal circumstances, they are unlikely to attain the appearance of domestically reared animals. If owners of moorland herds wish to show ponies competitively, then it is perhaps better to manage their free-living breeding stock and their show ponies in different ways. The former can be managed naturally and any individuals of show potential can be given domestic assistance. By trying to combine the two activities and using "blanket worming" the long-term hardiness of the ponies is being jeopardised.

All these arguments apply equally to providing additional food in winter. Given the right environment, the ponies' natural flexibility of diet and impressive digestive system will see them through. They have hundreds of thousands of years of heritage which has conferred these survival capabilities upon them. Unless totally abnormal conditions prevailed where there was a real danger of losing every pony, intervention is unwise. Certainly such difficulties have not been experienced in our lifetimes; remember how the ponies came through the winters of 1947/48 and 1962/63 with no assistance. Experience has shown them to be hardier than sheep or even deer.

A few owners provide some winter provisions in what is deemed bad weather and do so I am sure with the same compassionate intentions that apply to worming. Yet again the effect is to suspend the influence of natural selection and ultimately this will weaken the ponies. The principle of no aid but removal of individuals which cannot cope is needed to keep the Exmoor Pony hardy.

I must make clear that all this applies purely to herds of true Exmoor Ponies which are living in sufficiently natural conditions. Where they cannot free-range then Exmoors cannot be expected to cope with parasites or obtain enough food without assistance. We have to be very clear on the difference between free-living and domesticity. This makes the selection of new locations for free-living herds very important. They have to be carefully assessed in terms of size and the proportions of plant species present. Hopefully, the publication of the diet information in this book will assist in the process of choosing suitable habitats. Yet if we are to fully under-stand all the natural requirements the Exmoor Ponies have then far more research is needed.

Once again throughout this analysis of management practices the importance of the environment has been paramount. If the quality of the vegetation is allowed to deteriorate then, eventually, all chance of conservation as essentially wild animals may be lost, for owners may have no alternative to worming and feeding. Protecting their home is vital to conserving the Exmoor.

Fit to Breed

The reason why Exmoors are not fully wild is that despite a natural identity and independent survival ability, their breeding is influenced by Man. Each time an owner of the free-living herds makes a choice of which foal to keep and which to sell, it is a gamble. He or she can only judge by outward appearance and pedigree but there is no guarantee that this will identify the most biologically fit. Family history is probably a sounder guide than appearance but the latter is probably most influential in practice.

Accepting then that human choice can never be as callously efficient as natural selection, the individuals which are returned to grow up within a free herd may or may not be the best choice. This makes it doubly important to remove any which do not perform well. Generally, the experienced eye of those who have bred Exmoors for many years seems to pick sound animals. But can we be sure? The time during which Man has managed herd breeding is just an instant on the evolutionary clock.

So selection has to be followed by careful scrutiny of how the individual fares and removal of those ponies which prove to have been doubtful choices. This applies to all the ponies but is particularly significant with stallions. A stallion will contribute to the next generation far more than any one mare.

Potential stallions have to pass rigorous inspection and veterinary assessment as we have seen. Yet, again, this is on outward characteristics and cannot possibly cover all the attributes that would be tested by Nature. For the good of the race, it is desirable that the males with the fittest and hardiest genes succeed in becoming sires.

In the wild, young colts form bachelor groups in which they establish a hierarchy. Eventually, the dominant animals will challenge existing herd stallions. This is true "performance testing". Only animals with strength and stamina and with the ability to dominate stand any chance and these are the very characteristics that need to be conferred upon a new generation. Through confrontations ranging from competing for the same place to rest, with one pony displacing another, through to actual fights, the young males are continually tested. In this way natural selection ensures only the fittest will breed.

With the restricted homes Exmoor Ponies now occupy it would be difficult, but not impossible, to create conditions similar to the wild state. However, limited grazing rights and the need to maximise the crop of foals to sell make it unlikely that owners would allow several colt foals to remain with a herd, to establish the best new stallion naturally. Also, such a situation would demand careful observation to be sure which males were actively breeding with which females and this is far from easy. With any uncertainty there would be problems obtaining registration of the progeny under current Exmoor Pony Society rules. However, it has to be said that where even just two stallions share some enclosures, identifying which the mare mated with is not 100% fool-proof. One mare was observed living regularly in one herd yet actually mated with the stallion of the other herd.

If there were a real desire to ensure that the best stallions in biological terms were chosen, then establishing a herd where several colts were present would require special consideration by the Exmoor Pony Society. It would require the recognition that with moorland herds the foals might have to be registered as by one of perhaps two or three contenders. Colts approaching the point of challenging for the herd can sometimes cover a stray mare or two. Alternatively, young colts would have to be tested out elsewhere running free with a small herd and resident stallion, in a situation where it is accepted that the foals can never be registered.

Although re-establishing natural selection in this way would aid in conserving the Exmoor Pony, I cannot foresee either of these two scenarios actually occurring. The difficulties seem too great given that the benefits are so long-term and intangible. The possible lower productivity and registration problems would seem insurmountable problems. Perhaps this might only be undertaken in a research situation. If the outcome challenged the accepted judgements made today then it might have to be given further thought.

This means we rely upon our present system of judgements by two Exmoor Pony Society inspectors/judges and a veterinary surgeon. The task of the latter is clear, to certify the potential stallion as free from physical deformity. The harder role is played by those who assess the animal for "suitability". A heavy responsibility rests upon their shoulders.

With such a small total population and low number of breeding stallions, it is in the best interests of the

Exmoor to ensure that all stallions are suitable for running with the free-living herds if they are needed. Controlling in-breeding often requires moving stallions around between different locations. Ideally, every stallion which is allowed to influence the future of the race should have to prove itself by successfully living free. Yet this is again difficult to arrange. There are the practical problems of where to run young males and even more the difficulty of controlling stallions that have tasted the free life when young. I see no easy way to accomplish this natural testing for all stallions, however desirable it might be.

So again we have to look to the criteria on which the stallions are assessed at inspection. The adaptive features needed for survival have to be rigorously checked even if the animal is destined immediately for domestic service. Having greater survival powers than they need is of no disadvantage to an animal in domestic surroundings. Lacking sufficient hardiness and passing this on to offspring could irreparably damage the free-living population. So weighting the judgements towards the demands of the free life is justifiable.

This means that the Exmoor Pony Society must always have a panel of inspectors who fully appreciate the need to select for stallions well endowed with the full range of natural characteristics. This is not as easy a task as it sounds because of the changing character of the Society itself.

As Exmoors spread throughout the country, happily membership of the Society is growing. However, the proportion of people who have intimate knowledge of the way of life of free-living Exmoors is declining. Added to this is the fact that many of the experienced moorland farmers are reaching the time for retiring from active duties. Recognising stallions which are best equipped to live and breed with free herds depends upon fully understanding the natural animal and its life-style.

The Society is careful to train inspectors and they have to undergo a probationary period. All have to attend some moorland brandings and in the past most have had the chance to train alongside experienced moorland breeders. In this way, the understanding of the Exmoor's natural characteristics has been passed on. In the future, this will become less easy to accomplish. It may be necessary to arrange formal teach-ins. Perhaps now, those moorland inspectors near retirement might be persuaded to assist in preparing material for use in future training.

If some such initiative is not taken then there is every possibility that judgements may gradually alter. If the influence of the moorland requirement is allowed to diminish we may come to a point where stallions (and foals) may be assessed in a less demanding way. Possibly, evaluation may shift towards what is needed in domestic conditions. Once this happens, the days of the free-living herds are numbered.

I do not believe this is being overly alarmist. The understanding of the natural dimension of Exmoors has been crucial to its survival to this point. If we are to conserve the free-living population then we have to preserve that understanding. That involves developing a Society in which all members are committed to the conservation approach.

Two Types of Exmoor Pony?

If there is a move away from the traditional, moorland type of Exmoor Pony then, at best, the result may be a distinct split into two sub-populations. It might become necessary for the Exmoor Pony Society to recognise the two types of pony, the econatural population living free and the domesticated population. Different rules and assessments might then have to apply to each. Genetic interchange between them would have to be restricted to a flow from econatural to domestic but the reverse prevented.

I sincerely hope this point is never reached for I believe each sub-population and the owners involved would be disadvantaged. I also foresee that such a split would probably lead to the demise of the free-living group. It is the partnership between the two groups which is surely the greatest strength of the Society.

What a gloomy scenario. Is this really a distinct

possibility or is this an over-dramatised view? Consider the statistics. In 1991 the total population was counted at 777 registered ponies of which just 197 are in free-living herds. The remainder are used in a variety of domestic activities as we saw in the last chapter. I hinted then that with regard to showing Exmoors there might be certain negative pressures arising. It is these influences which could inadvertently lead to a divergence into two types.

I should make quite clear that I am not against the idea of showing the ponies. I thoroughly enjoy going to shows, trying to judge for myself which seems best in my eyes, taking pleasure when favourite ponies do well. As I have said before, showing is an important part of marketing the ponies as well as enjoyable. So I am in no way suggesting that showing itself is a bad thing.

However, judgements made in the show-ring can act as agents of change. Exhibitors begin to recognise what impresses the judges and the inevitable result is to try to meet those demands. Thus breeding can become directed towards producing a pony which conforms to the fashions of the show-ring.

In more recent years, and in a variety of situations, I have increasingly heard Exmoors described in terms of being pretty or coarse – judgements which in my opinion are irrelevant. I have also seen, much as it is hotly denied by many, the emergence of Exmoor Ponies which are much less stocky and which seem to have less well developed adaptive features. A trend towards a domesticated Exmoor is recognisable to me, albeit in its infancy.

The danger in all this is that we arrive at an image of "the ideal Exmoor Pony" and this comes to influence judgements of all Exmoors. It is easy to see how the moorland population might then begin to be affected, particularly if such criteria were applied to stallion approval. Those very survival characteristics might become compromised by the fixation upon a pony fitted for another purpose altogether.

There are grounds for thinking we may have already embarked upon this focusing in on a type. Surveying collections of photographs taken over the decades it is impossible to avoid the conclusion that we are losing variation. Certainly all Exmoors are essentially identical but there used to be far more variety. There were undoubtedly ponies which today would be described by some as plain or coarse. I wonder if some of the stallions from earlier years would find favour in the show-ring today. Yet they had the hardiness required and passed the true tests of performance.

Maintaining naturally produced genetic variation is so important. I believe the Exmoor stands at a crossroads in the 1990s. If the trends I have outlined were to continue then divergence into econatural and domestic ecotypes would be on the horizon. This would surely make the future for the free-living ponies very doubtful.

Yet there are ways to safeguard against this undesirable outcome. There is an alternative route which leads to a successful future for all Exmoors through the continuity of a single race. However, taking that path requires the adoption of a Society-wide approach.

Firstly, all breeding programmes in domestic circumstances would need to include regular infusions of moorland genes. Secondly, all breeders, inspectors and judges would have to be committed to conserving the natural types and be vigilant in selecting against loss of original characteristics. Such a conservationist approach would mean exhibitors of Exmoors continuing to accept the difficulties of competing in mixed classes.

Yet this is no radical programme of change for the Exmoor Pony Society. It is simply a re-stating of the policies which have served the ponies well through the seventy years of the Society's existence. All that is needed to avert the possible problems of divergence which lie ahead is a re-affirmation of the basic principles upon which the Society was founded.

I do not wish to see two distinct forms of Exmoor Pony emerge. I am sure this would be the beginning of the end for the ponies. This issue has to be faced now before it is too late to reverse any unintentional drift away from the true Exmoor Pony.

Managing the Gene Pool

The 1991 census of Exmoor Ponies produced some encouraging figures. The total population was 777 individuals compared to 507 located in the previous count five years earlier. Yet the Exmoor Pony remains an extremely rare animal. Even this size of population is extremely small and the overall total conceals the true picture in breeding terms. There are just 274 mares in breeding situations – 121 free-living, 153 in-ground. There are just over 40 licensed stallions but not all are breeding to any great extent. Therefore the real situation is that the future of the Exmoor race is based upon about three hundred animals only.

Genetically this is a very small number and there are a number of very real problems associated with such a limited gene pool. This term has a literal meaning of the pool or combined total of all the individual ponies' genetic material. It is the full array of all the variation which exists in the race. Every individual animal has genetic material which is slightly different to its fellows. Thus while Exmoors (or any wild animal) are essentially uniform in appearance, they are all individually unique. So the larger the number of animals actually breeding, the greater the amount of natural variety at the genetic level. The greater the natural variation, the healthier the population. The need to increase the size of the breeding group continues. At the existing level it is appropriate that the Rare Breeds Survival Trust continue to include the Exmoor within Category 1 – Critical.

Keeping the Exmoor population fit is not just a matter of numbers. This all important genetic variation is also affected by which animals are being bred from. In Chapter 9, I reviewed the situation on stallion bloodlines and the picture was far from encouraging. Whilst some branches of the three male lines left in the Exmoor race are well represented in new generations, there are others which have just a single stallion left. In some cases, the last of the line is not actively breeding. The mare situation may also prove to have a highly unbalanced profile.

The importance of making the most of what limited variation the Exmoor race has cannot be over-emphasised. Their near-extinction back in the 1940s meant that their gene pool was reduced dramatically. Subsequently, all variation has to be different combin-

Plate 136 *Herd No. 44 mares, one of the rarer female lines*

ations of that very small number of surviving genes. A lack of co-ordinated breeding means that the foals born each year can have a very restricted representation of all the possible genes.

This can be a rather complicated picture to visualise so perhaps an example might help. Consider the primary colours of paint. By mixing different combinations of those colours we can produced yet more tones and shades, so arriving at a full artist's palette. The final quality of a great painting depends upon the artist's ability to blend and vary the basic ingredients. If the artist stops using some of the base colours, then the picture inevitably becomes less varied.

So whenever the breeding of Exmoor Ponies becomes unbalanced in terms of using the basic ingredients, the different bloodlines, the net result has to be more limited than if all were included. Limiting the variation in a new generation decreases its overall fitness. In-breeding is this process taken to an extreme where very closely related individuals are mated and I have already out-lined how the genetic problems can give rise to noticeable degeneration.

The key message in all this is that to produce the

healthiest population, the one fittest for survival now and in the future, a balanced breeding programme is essential. This can only be achieved if it is a co-operative Society scheme. It also requires careful planning and monitoring. Breeders seeing the unbalanced stallion line input might well be prompted to individually try to remedy the situation. If all move from breeding with one well-represented line to a rare line, the outcome can be just as unbalanced. The rare becomes common but vice versa. I suspect this has happened to some degree in the past.

I am sure that the establishment of a balanced breeding programme within the Society is absolutely crucial to the future of the Exmoor Pony. Each year that goes by with some lines dominating and some under-used damages the long-term genetic fitness of the population. Yet I also recognise this is a highly ambitious project and one which will not be easy to arrange. It can only work if it has the full enthusiasm and support of those who breed Exmoor Ponies. However, if just some of the owners entered into such a joint scheme then improvements could be achieved. So if a full collaboration is unrealistic, it is still worth trying to work towards some level of Society breeding programme.

What would this entail in practice? Firstly, the full computer analysis of the contribution rates in foals of both male and female lines is needed before policy can be agreed. That will more clearly identify where breeding can be safely reduced to some extent and where it needs to be increased. The key animals involved can then be highlighted. The outcome could be, with the assistance of the Rare Breeds Survival Trust, a programme of the desirable breeding levels from different stallions and the optimum sire/dam combinations. This could be prioritised according to the degree of under-representation.

The advice of a professional geneticist would have to be sought as to the degree of line-breeding which could healthily be incorporated. Many breeders have particular loyalties to certain lines and wherever possible this would have to be accommodated within the breeding plan.

This would certainly not be an easy undertaking but can the Exmoor Pony Society afford not to adopt such a scheme? If the current uncoordinated system continues then the loss of certain branches of the basic lines looks inevitable. Consider that in terms of males, five of the nine bloodline branches identified in Chapter 9 are represented by only one or two licensed stallions (in 1991).

The only way to succeed with a Society breeding programme is through the willing and enthusiastic involvement of members. Some animal breeding societies actually control breeding in a dictatorial way, some through ownership of all breeding males. That is not the Exmoor way and I hope never will be. I know that there are many breeders who have the long-term interest of the ponies at heart. There is the potential for recruiting such-minded people into a co-ordinated breeding programme. What is required is the framework in which to operate.

Outside Influences

The opening up of trade between members of the European Community from 1992 onwards brings new complications for many aspects of life. Animal breeding is no exception and there are many implications for breed societies. The Community, rightly or wrongly, is to try to operate generalised regulations to which all member countries must conform. It is the all-embracing nature of the approach which may produce difficulties for animal breeds which are not managed in the domestic way.

Where horses and ponies are concerned, the regulations being drafted are supposed to sensibly cover all situations. Yet within the Community there is every possible system of management practised. The requirements for Thoroughbreds worth many thousands of pounds, bred in stud conditions, are a world away from those relating to free-living ponies worth very little financially. I fear it is all too obvious which will be the greater consideration in formulating the controlling system.

Britain is unique within the European Community in its richness of free-living ponies. There are a few populations which free-range elsewhere, but no one country has a comparable situation. Thus, Britain may once again be a lone voice in trying to ensure an outcome which does not seriously disadvantage its free-living ponies. In 1990, each pony Society was asked to contribute their observations, on what was known of the likely European proposals, to the Ministry of Agriculture. These were to be taken account of in preparing the British approach to the discussions. The Exmoor Pony Society submitted a document entitled "The Way Forward" and explored the effects of likely regulations.

This report expressed some deep concerns. Certain proposals might lead to higher costs for registering animals which would seriously deter breeders of relatively low-value ponies. Any move which discouraged registration of Exmoor Ponies would damage the conservation effort. The idea of making stud books open to registrations from any member country might prove harmful unless controlled. It is fundamentally important that for each breed the requirements of the country of origin are adopted by all. The possibility that marking by branding might not be permitted would cause insoluble problems for any breeder of free-living ponies. The need to identify individuals is vital to practical management and registration and no other marking method would be realistic for free-living ponies.

The discussions at European level continue and so far the signs are encouraging. The principle has been agreed whereby the country of origin holds the parent stud book and determines the criteria for registration. The other member countries will then adopt those same criteria and operate "daughter" stud books. The full set of regulations are due to be finalised in 1993.

Full advantage has been taken of the opportunity to influence the deliberations through the official channels within the European Community. Hopefully the regulations which emerge will not obstruct the conservation of the Exmoor Pony. If they do, then a campaign to have Exmoors (and perhaps others) considered as a special case would have to be put to the European Parliament. Whilst I am fairly optimistic this will not prove to

be needed, some contingency planning by the Societies would be a sensible approach.

It is a hard enough challenge to ensure a future fit for the Exmoor Pony simply within the British context. The European dimension complicates this further.

Problems in Perspective

At the outset of this chapter I stated that doom and despondency would not characterise the end of this book. It can feel very negative exploring the varied problems which may occur in the future but preventative and remedial steps can be taken. In some cases, the solutions I have put forward are highly ambitious and far-reaching. I have suggested that conserving the Exmoor Ponies requires initiatives at both local and national level.

When I consider all the problems which must be overcome if the Exmoor is to be conserved, I am not pessimistic. There are some very high hurdles to get over but none is unassailable. Conservation is becoming rather a well-worn word but really just means preserving through active management. Management comes down to making things happen.

So much can be achieved by a combined approach from the Exmoor Pony Society, the Exmoor National Park Authority and the Exmoor farming community. Other bodies such as the Rare Breeds Survival Trust, English Nature and the National Trust can also help. Yet how can such co-operation be achieved? Each individual body if not person has his or her own priorities.

I suggest that the first step could be a day's conference on the subject of "Conserving the Exmoor Pony" to which all interested parties are invited and at which perhaps just two items are tackled. Firstly, the establishing of a defined objective which clearly states what all concerned wish to achieve on behalf of the free-living Exmoor Ponies. Once formulated, the rest of this first conference could be spent defining the problems which have to be overcome to meet the objective. The tendency is always to rush into finding solutions but the time spent in really understanding the problems, from everyone's viewpoint, is a sound investment. If at the end of this first meeting, all parties were agreed on what they want the future to hold and what hinders progress towards that, it would be a marvellous basis for the next stage.

Each party could then take time to independently examine the issues and discuss options for how to overcome the difficulties identified. For example, a special day could be arranged by the Exmoor Pony Society inviting all members interested in the conservation issue to attend and debate the conference points. Subsequently, a second joint conference of all parties would allow solutions to be thrashed out. I use those words deliberately because finding a consensus is never an easy task. Yet debating solutions in an arena where all viewpoints are represented is the only way to produce plans which are accepted by all involved. Ideals are rarely achieved but effective compromises are far better than no action at all. The combined knowledge and expertise of all the relevant groups is more than

adequate to the task. All that is needed is the desire to succeed.

I hope that this book will help in kindling the flames of that desire. These are terms of passion but that is what drives every successful attempt to safeguard part of our natural heritage. These pages have told the story of a great survivor and shown how important it is to perpetuate the wildness that persists in the Exmoor Pony. Let us now return to Exmoor to take a last look at the treasure we have to guard.

It is a beautiful summer morning and high above us a buzzard is calling to her young which have joined her in the skies. The last deer quietly move down into the woods to lie up during the day. A rare high brown fritillary butterfly flits over the vegetation. Across the valley, visitors are starting to arrive and children head straight for the stream. There before us is a herd of Exmoor Ponies. While some graze, others are at rest and beside several of the mares are sleeping foals.

These remarkable creatures are the descendants of

Plate 137 *Mares and foals on Winsford Hill*

Plate 138 *Tortoise Shell, A/257 on East Anstey Common, Winter 1991*

ponies that staked a claim on Britain long before we did. Their race has seen the evolution of Man from a primitive animal subject to Nature into one which now controls the destinies of others. The ponies have survived through all this time benefiting Man at all points along the way. Nature has blended in these beautiful animals an incredible talent for survival with a ready acceptance of the partnership with people. We owe it to the Exmoor Ponies to ensure that their heritage as natural animals is not sacrificed in the future.

We have travelled back in time to look at the origins and history of the Exmoor Pony. We have explored the present to find out how they live now. We must undertake a final journey and this time into the future. We arrive at the year 2053 and have come to read an article about the Exmoor Ponies published in the popular newspaper of the day. What will it say?

Will it be this version?

ENVIRONMENTAL DAILY
Monday April 25th 2053

EXMOOR NATIONAL PARK ABANDONS ATTEMPT TO RE-INTRODUCE EXMOOR PONIES

The Exmoor National Park Authority has formally announced an end to the project to try to re-establish independent free-living herds of the Exmoor Pony. Back in the late 1900s there were over a 100 of these ponies living on enclosed moors and commons. They were the remnant of a race of ponies thought to have existed in Britain since before Man.

The Exmoor survives in domestic circumstances and is still shown competitively. However, it dwindled and eventually disappeared from the open moorlands. This was in part due to problems of habitat deterioration but also to the decline of the traditional way of life on Exmoor. The herds owned by the National Park Authority proved too small a genetic base to continue independently. The introduction of domesticated Exmoor genes is thought to account for why the experiments to re-stock parts of Exmoor have failed. The ponies have apparently lost some of the hardiness which less than a century ago allowed Exmoor Ponies to live an econatural life. The National Park Authority will continue to keep its ponies on open moorland. The programme of winter feeding and regular worming will have to be maintained.

Or will this article greet us?

Which will it be? The choice is ours.

ENVIRONMENTAL DAILY
Monday April 25th 2053

EXMOOR PONY CONSERVATION SCHEME HAILED AS GREAT SUCCESS

In a joint report published today, the Exmoor National Park Authority and the Exmoor Pony Society announced that the free-living population of Exmoor Ponies in Britain passed the 500 level this year. They state that the population is in fine condition with all bloodlines well-represented. In the sixty years since the Exmoor Pony Conservation Plan was formulated, there have been many positive achievements. The moorland habitats on Exmoor have been protected and herds have also been established on suitable land elsewhere in Britain. Numbers have grown steadily and although still rare, the Exmoor Pony is no longer assessed as in critical state by the Rare Breeds Survival Trust.

The schemes run within the Exmoor Pony Society for training in traditional management methods have proved a great success. Also the coordinated breeding programme which gathered strength after a hesitant start has yielded good results. Those bloodlines once so threatened are now secure and the domestic population shows no signs of losing the natural characterisitcs of the free-living Exmoor.

The report emphasises that the conservation measures taken will have to be maintained as the Exmoor Pony is still a rare animal. The Secretary of the Exmoor Pony Society expressed delight at progress to date, saying "It just shows what can be done if enought people care and keep trying."

The coming generations will have good reason to call us unfaithful stewards if when we are gone there are no little horses on the Exmoor hills.

Mary Etherington, 1947

GLOSSARY
OF SCIENTIFIC TERMS

ADAPTIVE RADIATION
The development of animals of allied stock along different evolutionary paths in response to differing environments.

AFFORESTATION
Designation of area of land as a Forest subject to Forest Law.

AGISTER
An official of a Royal Forest responsible for livestock management (a term still used in the New Forest).

AMNIOTIC FLUID
Liquid filling the space between the embryo and the foetal membranes.

ANOESTRUS
In female mammals, the resting period(s) between periods of oestrous.

BLOODLINE
A line of direct relationship between a sequence of generations.

BOREAL PHASE
Period in history of British vegetation when trees were dominant.

BREED
A group of domesticated animals with the same ancestry.

BRONZE AGE
A period of human culture, in Britain dated about 3,700–2,650 B.P.

BROWSER
Animal which feeds on leaves, twigs and young shoots of trees and/or shrubs.

B.P.
Before present – relating to dates.

CHASE
A royal hunting ground.

CHESTNUT
A horny growth (callosity) near the knee or hock of horses and ponies.

CHROMOSOMES
Microscopic thread-like structures within the nucleus of each cell, made up of genes.

DISAFFORESTATION
Changing the status of land from that of a Forest (subject to Forest Law) to that of ordinary land.

DNA
Deoxyribose-nucleic Acid – a complex molecule containing genetic information of which genes are comprised.

DOMINANT GENE
One of a pair of alternative forms of a gene, which will mask the alternative and manifest itself.

DRIFT
Gathering or round-up of animals (a term still used in the New Forest).

ECOLOGY
Scientific study of the interrelations between living organisms and their environment.

ECONATURAL
A genetically wild-type animal which has a natural relationship with its environment but is not fully wild due to Man's influence on its breeding.

ECOSYSTEM
Any area of nature in which living organisms and non-living substances interact – the basic functional unit of Ecology.

ECOTYPE
A sub-population that has become genetically distinct through adapting to a localised habitat.

EOHIPPUS
Small fox-like animal, ancestor of the horse, which lived about 50 million years ago (also called *Hyracotherium*).

EQUID
A member of the family *Equus*.

EQUINE
Pertaining to a horse.

EQUUS
The latin name for the family of animals including the horses, asses and zebras.

ERGOT
A horny growth (callosity) under the fetlocks of horses and ponies.

FAUNA
The animals of a specified region or time.

FERAL
Animals which though living in the wild state now, have been domesticated at some time in their history.

FLUME/FLUMINA
Arrangement of body hair in a directed stream.

FOETAL MEMBRANES
Outgrowths from the foetus which surround and protect it.

FOETUS
Fully developed egg/embryo.

FREE SUITOR
Resident of the parishes of Withypool or Hawkridge on Exmoor, who carried out duties (mostly related to stock management) on the Royal Forest in return for grazing rights.

GATHERING
Local Exmoor term for the round-up of the ponies.

GENE
Unit of DNA having a specific effect on the structure or function of cells.

GENE POOL
The pool or combined total of all individuals' genes.

GLACIAL
Pertaining to a period of ice-cover.

GRAZER
Animal which feeds on grass and herbage.

HAND
Unit of measurement used for heights of horses and ponies – 1 hand = 4 inches or 10.16 cms.

HIPPOLOGIST
One who studies horses and ponies.

HOME RANGE
A definite area to which individuals, pairs, families or herds restrict their normal activities.

HUSBANDRY
Management of breeding.

HYPSODONTY
The features of high crowns and deep sockets in mammalian teeth.

HYRACOTHERIUM
See *Eohippus*

INBREEDING
Breeding with closely related individuals – the degree of inbreeding is the closeness of the relationship between the egg and sperm.

INCISOR
Front, cutting teeth between the canine teeth in mammals.

INDIGENOUS
Native to (not imported into) a region or country.

INTER-GLACIAL
Between periods of ice-cover.

IRON AGE
Period of human culture, in Britain dated about 2,650–1,900 B.P.

LINE-BREEDING
A breeding programme which uses individuals which belong to the same bloodline.

MERYCHIPPUS
Descendants of *Mesohippus* on the evolutionary path which gave rise to the horses, living about 26 million years ago.

MESOHIPPUS
Descendants of *Eohippus* on the evolutionary path which gave rise to the horses, living about 38 million years ago.

MESOLITHIC PERIOD
A period of human culture, in Britain dated about 10,000–5,300 B.P.

METABOLISM
The sum total of the chemical and physical changes constantly taking place in living matter.

MIOCENE PERIOD
A geological period, in Britain dated about 28 million–12 million B.P.

MOLARS
The posterior grinding or cheek teeth of mammals.

MONGREL
The offspring of a cross between varieties or races of a species.

MUTATION
A change in the characteristics of an organism produced by an alteration of the hereditary material.

NATURAL SELECTION
A theory of the mechanism of evolution which postulates the survival of the best adapted forms and the elimination of insufficiently adapted characteristics.

NEOLITHIC PERIOD
A period of human culture, in Britain dated about 5,700–3,700 B.P.

NICHE
Position or status of an organism within its community or ecosystem.

OESTRUS
In female mammals, the period of sexual excitement or "heat".

ORGANISM
A living entity.

PALAEOLITHIC PERIOD
Period of human culture, in Britain dated about 400,000–10,000 B.P. (Lower Palaeolithic 400,000–200,000; middle 200,000–35,000; upper/late 35,000–10,000).

PASTURAGE (RIGHT OF)
Right to put stock out to graze on a pasture.

PERAMBULATION
Official survey to define the boundaries of the Royal Forest of Exmoor (an actual walk around the perimeter of the Forest which established the route of the boundary).

PHYSIOLOGICAL
Relating to the functions of plant or animal as a living organism.

PLEISTOCENE PERIOD
Geological period which began about one million years ago and lasted until about 10,000 B.P.

PLIOCENE PERIOD
Geological period about 12 million to 1 million years ago.

PLIOHIPPUS
Descendant of *Merychippus* on the evolutionary path which gave rise to the horses – *Pliohippus* lived around 7 million years ago.

PONY-HERD
Term once used to denote the manager of the Acland Exmoor Pony population.

POPULATION DYNAMICS
Statistical characteristics of a population and the changes in those characteristics.

PREALBUMIN SYSTEM
Varieties of the protein prealbumin, found in the blood.

PREMOLAR
The anterior grinding or cheek teeth of mammals.

PROTOTYPE
An ancestral form – an original type or specimen.

RACE
A population occurring within a species which exhibits distinctive characteristics and has a natural ancestry.

RECESSIVE GENE
One of a pair of alternative forms of a gene, which will not be manifested if both are present since it is masked by the alternative (the dominant gene).

RHIZOME
An underground stem.

SPECIES
A group of closely-allied, mutually fertile individuals showing constant differences from allied groups.

SUB-ARCTIC
Almost Arctic.

SUCKER
Unweaned foal.

SUITORS AT LARGE
Residents of parishes bordering the Royal Forest of Exmoor, who had to duties to and privileges from the Warden (but less than for the Free Suitors).

TARPAN
An extinct type of wild horse once found in central and eastern Europe.

TERRITORY
A home range which is partly or wholly defended by an individual.

TUNDRA
Nearly level, tree-less plains associated with sub-Arctic environments.

VORTEX/WHIRL
Arrangement of body hair in a circular pattern.

WITHERS
Ridge between a horse or pony's shoulder-blades.

ZOOGEOGRAPHY
The study of animal distribution.

(Glossary compiled with the aid of Chambers Dictionary of Science and Collins Concise English Dictionary)

BIBLIOGRAPHY A

(Books which have been quoted from). Quotes reproduced with the kind permission of the authors (or other copyright holders) and publishers. Books in quoted order.

CHAPTER 1:
1. Munnings, Sir Alfred, *An Artist's Life* (The Museum Press, 1955 & courtesy of The Sir Alfred Munnings Art Museum)
2. Youatt, W., *The Horse* (Baldwin, 1851)
3. Snell, F.J., *A Book of Exmoor* (Methuen & Co, 1903)

CHAPTER 2:
4. Michener, J., *Alaska* (Martin Secker & Warburg Ltd., 1988)
5. Ebhardt, H., "The Origin of the Exmoor Pony" (*The Exmoor Pony Society Newsletter*, 1975)
6. Bokonyi, S., *The Przevalsky Horse* (Souvenir Press, 1974)
7. Speed, J.G., *The Natural History of the Horse* (Unpublished)

CHAPTER 3:
8. Balch, H.E., *Mendip – its Swallet Caves & Rock Shelters* (Simpkin Marshall/J. Wright & Sons, 1948)
9. Speed, J.G. – as for (7)
10. Evans, J.G., *The Environment of Early Man in the British Isles* (Book Club Associates, 1975)
11. Childe, G., *Prehistoric Communities of the British Isles* (London & Edinburgh, 1947)
12. Donovan, D.T., (Personal communication)
13. Dent, A.A., (Personal communication)
14. Piggott, S., *Ancient Europe* (Edinburgh University Press, 1965)
15. Dent, A.A. & Machin Goodall, D., *The Foals of Epona* (Galley Press, 1962). Reprinted as *A History of British Native Ponies* (J.A. Allen, 1988)
16. Clutton-Brock, J., *A Natural History of Domesticated Animals* (Cambridge University Press for the British Museum of Natural History, 1987)
17. Speed, J.G. & Etherington, M.G., "The Origins of British Ponies" (1953; included in *The Exmoor Pony – its origins and characteristics* by Speed & Etherington, Countrywide Livestock, 1977)
18. Ebhardt, H., "Ponies und Pferde im Rontgenbild nebst einigen stammesgeschichtlichen Bemerkungen dazu" (in *Saugetierkundliche Mitteilungen* 1.11.1962)

CHAPTER 4:
19. Marshall, W., *The Rural Economy of the West of England* (G. Nicol, London , 1796)
20. Introduction to *The Polo Pony Society Stud Book*, 1899.
21. Cecil, Lord Arthur, Article (in the Introduction to *The Polo Pony Society Stud Book*, 1899)
22. Dykes, T., "The Highland Pony" (in *Transactions of the Highland and Agricultural Society of Scotland*, 1905)
23. Cossar Ewart, J., "The Multiple Origins of Horses and Ponies" (in *Transactions of the Highland and Agricultural Society of Scotland*, 1904)
24. Gilbey, Sir Walter, *Thoroughbreds and other Ponies* (Vinton, 1903)

25. Hayes, M.H., *Points of the Horse* (Hurst & Blackett,1904)
26. Speed, J.G., "The Iceland Connection" (*The Exmoor Pony Society Newsletter*, Autumn 1981)
27. Bjarnason, G., *The Horse in the Sagas* (Notes of lecture given at Bergen, Norway, 1958)
28. Leivsson, T., (Personal communication)
29. Speed, J.G. and Etherington, M.G., "An Aspect of the Evolution of British Horses" (*The British Veterinary Journal*, Vol. 108 No. 5, published by Balliere, Tindall & Cox,1952)
30. Snell, F.J. (as in (3))
31. March-Phillips, E., "Exmoor Ponies" (*Pall Mall Magazine*, pages 267–274, October 1896)
32. Scott, M., *Blood-typing of Mr.R.C.Western's Exmoor Pony Herd* (Report to the Exmoor Pony Society, 1976)
33. Ryder, O., (Personal communication)
34. Whyte-Melville,G.J., *Katerfelto – A Tale of Exmoor* (Chapman and Hall, 1876)
35. Daniel, G., *150 Years of Archaeology* (Duckworth, 1975)
36. Pitt Rivers, A.H.L., *Current Excavations in Cranborne Chase Vol. 2, p. 217* (Harrison & Sons, 1888–98)
37. Encyclopaedia of Rural Sports (1840)
38. Dent, A.A., *The Pure-bred Exmoor Pony* (The Exmoor Press, 1970)

CHAPTER 5:

39. Carlyle, T., *On Heroes, Hero-Worship and the Heroic in History* (Chapman and Hall, 1840)
40. Dent, A.A. & Machin Goodall, D., (as in (15))
41. Morris, J., Thorn, C. & Thorn, F., *Domesday Book Part 8 (Somerset)* (Phillimore, 1980)
42. Defoe, D., *A Tour Through the Whole Island of Great Britain* (Rivington, 1769)
43. Morris, J.,Thorn, C. & Thorn, F., *Domesday Book Part 9 (Devon)* (Phillimore, 1985)
44. Snell, F.J. (as in (3)).
45. MacDermot, E.T., *A History of the Forest of Exmoor* (David & Charles, 1973)

46. Meynell, L., *Exmoor* (Robert Hale, 1953)
47. Burton, R.A., *The Heritage of Exmoor* (R.A. Burton, 1989)
48. Thorne, J., *Personal Diary* (Unpublished, 1790)
49. Collinson, J., *The History and Antiquities of the County of Somerset* (R.Crutwell,Bath, 1791)
50. Billingsley, J., *General View of the Agriculture of the County of Somerset* (1798)
51. Reeks, F.H., "The Acland Herd of Exmoor Ponies" (Draft of article, 1960, extracts later published in *The Exmoor Review*,1970)

CHAPTER 6:

52. Acland, Sir Thomas, (*Livestock Journal*, 28th May 1886)
53. March-Phillips, E., (as in (31)).
54. Acland, T.D., "On the Farming of Somerset" (*Journal of the Royal Agricultural Society of England*, p 688, 1850)
55. Hancock, F., *The Parish of Selworthy* (Barnicott & Pearce, 1897)
56. Gilbey, Sir Walter, *Ponies Past and Present* (Vinton, 1900)
57. Reeks, F., (as in (51))
58. Acland, Sir Charles, (Quoted in Snell,F.J. as in (3))
59. Calmady-Hamlyn, S., (Letter, 1955 to Alice Sanders in Exmoor Pony Society archive)
60. Tapp, D., (Text of 1946 talk – included in Best, M.G.S. & Etherington, M.G. *The Little Horses of Exmoor* (The Favil Press, 1947))
61. Acland, M., (Letter to Alice Sanders, 1960 in Exmoor Pony Society archive)
62. Lycett-Green, S., "History of the Anchor Herd 1928–1953" (Written for the Green family stud book, 1953, reprinted in the *Exmoor Pony Society Newsletter*, 1990)
63. MacDermot, E.T., (as in (45))
64. Burton, R.A., (as in (47))
65. Snell, F.J. (as in (3))
66. Hayes, M.H., (as in (25))
67. Milton, F.C.J., "The Miltons of Withypool" (in *The Exmoor Review*, 1968)

68. Thorne, W.G., (Text of talk – included in Best, M.G.S. & Etherington, M.G. *The Little Horses of Exmoor* (The Favil Press, 1947))
69. Thorne, L., "Bampton Fair" (in *The Exmoor Pony Society Newsletter*, 1974)
70. Crockford, W., "My Exmoor Ponies" (included in Best, M.G.S. & Etherington, M.G. *The Little Horses of Exmoor* (The Favil Press, 1947))
71. Pring, T., "From Mr. Tom Pring" (included in Best, M.G.S. & Etherington, M.G. *The Little Horses of Exmoor* (The Favil Press, 1947))
72. Ministry of Agriculture, Fisheries & Food, *The Improvement of the Mountain and Moorland Breeds* (Ministry of Agriculture, Fisheries & Food Report, 1912)
73. West Somerset Free Press & North Devon Journal – items on the formation of the Exmoor Pony Society, 1921.
74. The Exmoor Pony Society, "Annual Report" (*Polo Pony Society Stud Book*, 1927)
75. Hurley, J., *Exmoor in Wartime* (The Exmoor Press, 1978)
76. Best, M.G.S. & Etherington, M.G. *The Little Horses of Exmoor* (The Favil Press, 1947))
77. Speed, J.G., (as in (26))
78. Morgan, E., *The Descent of Woman* (Souvenir Press, 1973)

CHAPTER 7:
79. Burton, S.H., *Exmoor* (Robert Hale, 1969)
80. Poulsen, H., (Personal communication, 1991)
81. Davy, D., (Personal communication, 1991)
82. March-Phillips, E., (as in (31)

CHAPTER 8:
83. Thorne, J., (as in (48))
84. Slader, J.M., "The Great Freeze" (in *The Exmoor Review*, 1963)
85. Blackmore, R.D., *Lorna Doone* (1869, reprinted Collins, 1952)
86. Bourne, H.L., *Living on Exmoor* (Galley Press, 1963, reprinted The Exmoor Press, 1991)

87. Watkins, V., (personal communication, 1991)
88. Speed, J.G., "Ponies' Coats" (*The Centaur*, date unknown)
89. Speed, J.G., (personal communication, 1978)

CHAPTER 9:
90. Wilson, W., (personal communication, 1991)
91. O'Connell, F., (personal communication, 1991)
92. Darwin, C., *The Origin of Species* (1859)
93. Alderson, L., *Exmoor Pony Breed Structure – Analysis of Male Lines based upon 1981 registrations* (Report to The Exmoor Pony Society, 1984)
94. Munnings, Sir Alfred, (as in (1))

CHAPTER 10:
95. Painter, E., "Exmoor Round-up" (in *The Exmoor Review*, 1989)
96. Anonymous, "The Wild Ponies of Exmoor" (in Rarey, J.S., *The Art of Taming Horses* (George Routledge, 1858))
97. Dixon, H.H. "The Exmoor Ponies" (in *The New Sporting Magazine*, Vol. 40, October 1860)
98. Author Unknown, "An Exmoor Horse Fair" (*Murrays Magazine*, p811 –821, Jul–Dec, 1887)
99. March-Phillips, E., (as in (31))
100. English Nature, (personal communication, 1991)
101. Bokonyi, S., *Mecklenburg Collection Part II* (Cambridge, Massachusets, 1968)
102. Hann, G.J., (personal communication, 1991)
103. Watkins, V., (as in (87))

CHAPTER 11:
104. Ministry of Agriculture, Fisheries & Food, (personal communication, 1991)
105. Exmoor National Park Authority, *Exmoor National Park Plan 1992*
106. Etherington, M.G., "What is an Exmoor Pony?" (included in Best, M.G.S. & Etherington, M.G. *The Little Horses of Exmoor* (The Favil Press, 1947).

BIBLIOGRAPHY B
(Additional Sources)

Acland, Lady Anne, *A Devon Family – The Story of the Aclands* (Phillimore & Co., 1981)

Allen, N.V., *The Exmoor Handbook and Gazetteer* (The Exmoor Press, 1972)

Annandale, Nelson, *The Faroes & Iceland – Studies in Island Life* (Clarendon Press, 1905)

Archer, C.H., "The Winter of 1962–63" (*The Exmoor Review*, published by the Exmoor Society, 1963)

Baker, Susan, "The Gathering" (in *Somerset & Avon Life*, September 1990)

Baker, Susan, "Katerfelto Unmasked" (*Exmoor Pony Society Newsletter* 1992)

Berger, Joel, "Organizational Systems and Dominance in Feral Horses in the Grand Canyon" (*Behavioural Ecology & Sociobiology* 2, 131–146, 1977)

Binding, Hilary & Bonham-Carter, Victor, *Old Dulverton and Around* (The Exmoor Press, 1986)

Blokhuis, H.J. & Buis, R.C., "Genetic relationships between breeds of horses and ponies in the Netherlands" (*Animal Blood Groups Biochemistry, Genetics*, 10, pp. 27–38, 1979)

Bokonyi, Sandor, *The History of Domestic Animals in Central and Eastern Europe* (Budapest, 1974)

Bonham-Carter, Victor, "Withypool Common – the Historical Background" (*The Exmoor Review*, 1968)

Bourne, Hope, "Exmoor Ponies" (*The Exmoor Review*, published by the Exmoor Society, 1960)

Bourne, Hope, *A Little History of Exmoor* (J.M. Dent & Sons, 1968)

Bruemmer, Fred, "The Wild Horses of Sable Island" (*Animals* Vol. 10, 1967)

Clabby, John, *The Natural History of the Horse* (Weidenfield & Nicolson, 1976)

Codrington, W.S., *Know Your Horse* (J.A. Allen, 1966)

Dean, Peter, "Exmoors in Cumbria" (*The Ark*, published by the Rare Breeds Survival Trust, Vol. XV, No. 10, 1988)

Dixon, H.H. (The Druid), "The Exmoor Ponies" (*The New Sporting Magazine* Vol. 40, pp. 231–240, 1860)

Feist, J.D. & McCullough, D.R., "Reproduction in Feral Horses" (*Journal of Reproduction and Fertility*, 23, 13–18, 1975)

Forsten, Ann, "Equus Lambei (Hay), the Yukon Wild Horse, not Ass" (*Journal of Mammalogy*, 67(2), pp. 422–423, 1986)

Forsten, Ann, "The Small Caballoid Horse of the Upper Pleistocene and Holocene" (*Journal of Animal Breeding, Genetics*, 105,1988)

Frick, Charles, *Alaska's Frozen Fauna* (American Museum Natural History, 30, pp. 70–80, 1930)

Gates, Susan, "The Exmoor Pony – a Wild Animal?" (*Nature in Devon*, published by Devon Trust for Nature Conservation, No. 2, 1981)

Gates, Susan, "A Study of the Home Ranges of Exmoor Ponies" (*Mammal Review*, Vol. 9, No. 1, pp. 2–18, 1979)

Gates, Susan, *Studies of the Ecology of Free-Ranging Exmoor Ponies* (Ph.D. Thesis, University of Exeter, 1979)

Gill, Elaine, *Factors Affecting Body Condition of New Forest Ponies* (Ph.D. Thesis, University of Southampton, 1988)

Grinsell, L.V., *The Archaeology of Exmoor* (David & Charles, 1970)

Groves, Colin, *Horses, Asses and Zebras in the Wild* (David & Charles, 1974)

Hagedoorn, A.L., *Animal Breeding* (Crosby Lockwood, 1954)

Harrington, C.R., "Pleistocene Vertebrate Localities in the Yukon" (*US Geological Survey Circular* 1026)

Harrington, C.R., "Ice Age Mammal Research in the Yukon Territory and Alaska" (in *Early Man and Environments in Northwest America*, University of Calgary Students Press, 1970)

Harrington, C.R. & Clulow, F.V., "Pleistocene Mammals from Gold Run Creek, Yukon Territory" (*Canadian Journal of Earth Sciences* Vol. 10, No. 5, 1973)

Harrington, C.R., "Quaternary Vertebrate Faunas of Canada and Alaska" (*National Museums of Canada*, Syllogeus No. 15, 1978)

Harrington, C.R., "Pleistocene Mammals of Lost Chicken Creek, Alaska" (*Canadian Journal of Earth Sciences*, Vol. 17, No. 2, 1980)

Hinton, Phyllis, *British Native Ponies and their Crosses* (Thomas Nelson, 1971)

H.W.K., "Katerfelto – the Wonder Horse" (*The Exmoor Review*, published by the Exmoor Society, 1960)

Joyce, Walter, *Moorside Tales and Talk* (George Allen & Unwin, 1935)

MacDonald, J., *Highland Ponies* (Eneas Mackay, 1937)

Ministry of Agriculture, Fisheries and Food, *British Breeds of Livestock* (Report, 1920)

Mohr, Erna, *The Asiatic Wild Horse* (J.A. Allen, 1971)

Orwin, C.S., *The Reclamation of Exmoor Forest* (David & Charles, 1970)

Pennington, Winifred, *The History of the British Vegetation* (English Universities Press, 1969)

Pewe, Troy, *Quaternary Geology of Alaska* (US Government Printing Office, Washington, Geological Survey Professional Paper 835, 1975)

Polling, Elizabeth, "The Exmoor Pony" (*Exmoor Pony Society Handbook*) (The Exmoor Pony Society, 1986)

Rathbone, George, "The Native British Foundation of the Thorough-bred Horse" (*The British Racehorse*, October 1966)

Rees, Lucy, *Understanding Your Pony* (Stanley Paul, 1991)

Rubenstein, Daniel, "Ecology and Sociality in Horses and Zebras" (In *Ecological Aspects of Social Evolution*, Princeton University Press)

Russell, Valerie, *The New Forest Ponies* (David & Charles, 1976)

Salter, R.E. & Hudson, R.J., "Feeding Ecology of Feral Horses in Western Alberta" (*Journal of Range Management*, Vol. 32, No. 3, pp. 221–225, 1979)

Sanders, E.A., "Exmoor Ponies" (*The Exmoor Review*, published by The Exmoor Society, 1963)

Simpson, George, *Horses* (Oxford University Press, 1951)

Sinclair, Geoffrey, "Withypool Common – Present and Future Use" (*The Exmoor Review*, published by The Exmoor Society, 1968)

Slader, J.M., "The Knights of Exmoor" (*The Exmoor Review*, published by The Exmoor Society, 1964)

Snell, F.J., *The Blackmore Country* (Adam & Charles Black, 1911)

Speed, J.G., "The Natural History of Horse Breeding Parts I and II" (in *Light Horse* – Part II August 20th 1952)

Speed, J.G., *The Origins of Native Ponies and their Practical Importance* (Unpublished, 1953)

Speed, J.G., "A Note on the History of British Horses in the Light of recent Investigations" (*The Veterinary Record*, 62, 1950)

Speed, J.G., *The Natural History of Ponies in Relation to their Anatomical Variations* (Unpublished, date unknown)

Speed, J.G., "Ancient Mendip Horses and Modern Exmoor Ponies" (in *Fourteen Years at the Badger Hole/Diaries of H.E. Balch*, published by Mendip Nature Reserve Committee, 1950s)

Speed, M.G., *The Pony Folk* (Unpublished)

Tyler, Stephanie, *The Behaviour and Social Organisation of the New Forest Ponies* (Animal Behaviour Monographs, 5, 1972)

Vesey-Fitzgerald, Brian, *The Book of the Horse* (Nicholson & Watson, 1946)

Wace, M.A., "The Exmoor Pony" (in *Vesey-Fitzgerald*, 1946)

Wallace, Robert, *Farm Livestock of Great Britain* (Edinburgh, 1907)

AUTHOR'S NOTES

CONVERSION OF
IMPERIAL MEASUREMENTS
TO METRIC EQUIVALENTS

LOCATION	IMPERIAL		METRIC		LOCATION	IMPERIAL		METRIC	
Chapter 2					**Chapter 5**				
	2.5	hands	25.40	cms		30	acres	12.14	hectares
	6	hands	60.96	cms		300	acres	121.41	hectares
	10	hands	101.60	cms		120	acres	48.56	hectares
	13–14	hands	132–42	cms		20000	acres	8094.00	hectares
Chapter 3						30	miles	48.27	kms
	100	sq miles	259.00	sq. kms		18927	acres	7659.76	hectares
	200	sq. miles	518.00	sq. kms		3021	acres	1295.44	hectares
	2500	feet	762.00	metres		31	acres	12.55	hectares
	1000	feet	304.80	metres		4700	acres	1902.09	hectares
	11	hands	111.76	cms		10262	acres	4153.03	hectares
	10	hands	101.60	cms		14	acres	5.67	hectares
	11.3	hands	114.81	cms		16000	acres	6475.20	hectares
	12.3	hands	124.97	cms	**Chapter 6**				
	12	hands	121.92	cms		3000	acres	1214.10	hectares
	6.3–7.1	inches	16–18	cms		11.2	hands	113.79	cms
Chapter 4						12.2	hands	123.95	cms
	10.2	hands	103.63	cms		30	miles	48.27	kms
	14.2	hands	144.27	cms		48	acres	19.43	hectares
	12	hands	121.92	cms		8	miles	12.87	kms
	11	hands	111.76	cms		10	miles	16.09	kms
	12.2	hands	123.95	cms		13.2	hands	134.11	cms
	12.3	hands	124.97	cms		12.3	hands	124.97	cms
	13.2	hands	134.11	cms		13	hands	132.08	cms
	14	hands	142.24	cms		11	hands	111.76	cms
						12	hands	121.92	cms

LOCATION	IMPERIAL		METRIC		LOCATION	IMPERIAL		METRIC	
Chapter 7						60	inches	152.40	cms
	1700	feet	518.16	metres		2000	feet	609.60	metres
	20	miles	32.18	kms		3	feet	0.91	metres
	35	miles	56.32	kms		6	feet	1.83	metres
	265	sq. miles	686.35	sq. kms		400	acres	161.88	hectares
	1395	feet	425.20	metres		20	miles	32.18	kms
	1760	acres	712.27	hectares		2	miles	3.22	kms
	1398	feet	426.11	metres		2500	acres	1011.75	hectares
	1923	acres	778.24	hectares		6000	acres	2428.20	hectares
	2000	acres	809.40	hectares		100	yards	91.44	metres
	1000	feet	304.80	metres		400	yards	365.76	metres
	1500	feet	457.20	metres	**Chapter 8**				
	100	acres	40.47	hectares		2	inches	5.08	cms
	111	acres	44.92	hectares		3	inches	7.62	cms
	2000	acres	809.40	hectares		30	feet	9.14	metres
	2138	acres	865.25	hectares		10	acres	4.05	hectares
	1500	feet	457.20	metres	**Chapter 9**				
	1160	acres	469.45	hectares		30	feet	9.14	metres
	400	acres	161.88	hectares		7.3	hands	74.17	cms
	100	acres	40.47	hectares		2000	acres	809.40	hectares
	50	acres	20.24	hectares	**Chapter 10**				
	1000	feet	304.80	metres		5	feet	1.52	metres
	6000	acres	2428.20	hectares		10.5	acres	4.25	hectares
	150	acres	60.71	hectares		11	hands	111.76	cms
	112	acres	45.33	hectares		40	miles	64.36	kilometres
	100	acres	40.47	hectares		86	miles	138.37	kilometres
	2053	feet	625.75	metres		270	acres	109.27	hectares
	70	miles	112.63	kms		8000	acres	3237.60	hectares
	5	miles	8.05	kms	**Chapter 11**				
	4000	acres	1618.80	hectares		8000	acres	3237.60	hectares

(NOTE: 1 hand=4 inches)

Index

(Individual Ponies & Herd Numbers follow Main Index)

Acland
family, 74, 76, 78–82, 87, 96
herd, 49–51, 74, 76, 78k–82,
84–89, 94, 97, 99, 106–107, 116,
156, 180, 196 Sir Thomas, 54,
71, 73, 75–76, 78–80, 85, 87,
91–93, 98, 197
Adaptations, 3, 8, 10, 12, 14,
18–19, 31, 45, 51, 55, 141, 147,
154, 157, 164
Agricultural Use, 90, 92, 207–209
Alaska, 10–13, 17, 19–20
Arab Horse, 13, 18, 36, 41, 52, 54,
55
Ashway Farm/Side, 75–76,
79–82, 84, 87, 89, 92, 95, 107
Asses, 9–10, 15, 34, 123

Bampton Fair, 73, 80–81, 87,
90–91, 93, 167, 196–198, 211
Bawden, Gladys, 81–82
Beard, 46, 142, 145, 147
Behaviour, 160, 163, 204
aggression, 123–125, 200, 226
defensive, 163–164, fear, 120,
122, 204 feeding, 136, 153
herding, 175–176 play, 123,
172–173 shyness, 112, 135–136,
139

Blood-typing, 41, 52–53, 56, 179,
213
Bloodlines, 116, 180, 182–184,
186, 214, 229–230, 234
Boadicea, 205–206
Boevey, James, 66–68
Body condition, 159–161, 164,
173–174, 200, 213,224–225
Bones
Alaskan, 11–12, 17, 28, 33, 45,
51, bone record, 9,. 12, 17,
19–20, 24–25,28,34, 43, 55
comparisons, 17., 28, 33, 45,
47, 51–52, 55, 100, 214 studies
of, 5–7, 9, 12, 16–20, 32–34,
51–53, 55
Bradymoor, 108, 122–123, 126,
133, 136, 139, 151, 156, 167,
176, 189
Brand-marks, 66, 78, 80, 82, 91,
94–96, 107, 172, 194–195
Branding, 65, 71, 79–80, 82, 84,
96, 194, 223, 227, 231
Breeding, 3, 10, 36, 45, 50, 52, 54,
57, 71–72, 75–76, 79, 86, 89–90,
94, 125–126, 147–148, 167–168,
180, 186, 210–202, 217, 220, 224
breeding-back, 101
conception, 168–169 effects on

health, 155, 160 emergence of
breeds, 36-37, 41 gestation, 169
life-span, 174, line-breeding,
179, 182, 186, 230, policy, 89,
182, 184 programmes, 36, 48,
94, 182, 184, 224,230, 234 pure-
breeding, 78, 92–93
season/seasonality, 3, 122, 125,
144, 154, 168, 175, 215
statistics, 174 unnatural
influences, 186, 225, 228
Brendon, 58–59, 87, 89, 92, 98,
106, 115, 196
Brendon Common, 97, 106,
115–115, 157
Brightworthy Farm, 91, 148
British Hill Pony, 23, 31–42, 45,
47, 49, 51–53, 56–57, 74, 93,
101–104, 118, 179, 180,192,
201–202, 205–206, 214
Bronze Age, 32–33, 205

Camouflage, 10, 18, 21, 34, 45,
164
Caves, 17, 19, 26, 28
Mendip, 24, 27–28, 32
painting, 34, 42
Cecil, Lord Arthur, 37, 39, 56, 94
Celtic Era, 32–33, 40, 59, 100,

163, 205–206, 211, 215
Census, 19, 43, 75, 119, 214, 228
Chains, 106, 115, 135, 156
Characteristics, 36–37, 45, 48, 51,
57, 74, 78, 101–102, 141, 147,
154, 178, 201, 213, 220,
226–228, 234
Chariots, 205, 207
Chromosomes, 9, 15, 179
Climate, 11, 13, 17, 26, 28, 30–31,
35, 78–79, 140–144, 147
Coat, 10, 14, 20–21, 34–35, 41–42,
46, 49, 51, 54, 66, 73–75, 80,
107, 142–144, 147–148, 154,
163, 172, 195, 198, 211
Codsend Moor, 91, 106, 110, 112,
120, 126, 129, 135, 149, 169,
174, 179, 185, 190, 224
Colouring, 15, 17, 20–21, 34,
36–37, 41–42, 45, 50–51, 54, 56,
66, 73–74, 78, 95–96, 146, 164,
172
Commoners, 56, 62, 66, 69, 108,
158
rights, 65, 88, 108, 158, 178
Competition, 10, 14, 18, 20, 96,
120, 124, 126, 141, 156–159,
161, 177–1768, 201,
206–207,209–211, 215, 219,

225–226, 228, 233
Connemara Pony, 36, 214
Conservation, 41, 57, 78, 82, 87, 92–94, 99–102, 112, 159, 161–162, 177, 184, 187, 193, 200, 202, 211–213, 218–228
Crockford, William, 81, 91, 96, 99
Cross-bred ponies, 41, 50–51, 55, 68, 74, 86, 94–95, 112, 114–115, 126, 141, 147, 155, 157, 192, 196, 198, 205, 220
Cross-breeding, 19, 32–33, 37, 41, 45, 49, 74, 78, 86, 90, 92–94, 100-101, 108, 141, 155, 179, 192, 202, 221, 224
culling, 55, 75, 78, 81, 84, 86, 102, 155, 184, 186, 225
Cumbria, 101, 116–117, 124, 129, 142, 213,223
Dales Pony, 28, 36
Dart family, 110
Dartmoor, 30, 61, 94, 104, 110, 155, 158, 221–222
Dartmoor Pony, 36, 56, 80, 136, 153, 156, 211
Darwin, Charles, 6, 10, 178
Davy, Debbie, 117, 133
Dawn Horse (see Eohippus)
Dean, Peter, 101, 116–117
Death, 87, 108, 110, 114, 119, 125–126, 141, 147-149, 152, 159, 161–162, 164–165, 196, 219
Deer (see Red Deer)
Dent, Anthony, 29–30, 32-33, 56, 58, 68, 162–163, 206
Devon Cob & Packhorse, 207
Diet, 12, 18, 21, 24, 30–31, 46, 54, 74, 112, 118–119, 151–157, 160, 168, 213, 219, 225
Digestive System, 154, 159, 161, 225
Domesday Book, 58–59, 61-62, 72
domestic classification, 201–202, 224, 227–228, 234
domestic equids, 16–18, 20, 102, 119, 159, 164, 200, 209, 217-218, 225 process, 120, 178, 187, 201, 204, 223 state, 101, 120, 126, 148–149, 156, 159–160, 163, 167, 169, 188, 200–202, 204–205, 213, 217,

224–225, 227–228, 230, 233
Dongola Barb, 86, 93
Driving, 204, 206–207, 211, 216–217
Dulverton, 78, 81, 88, 90, 94–95, 106, 115
Dung, 123–124, 136, 149, 154, 159–161, 225
Dunkery Beacon, 80, 91, 104, 112, 190

Ears, 1, 35, 37, 46, 91, 147, 171–172
Eating ponies, 40, 99, 163–164, 188, 196, 211–212, 217, 221
Ebhardt, Hermann, 12, 19, 33–34, 48, 52, 56, 155
Econatural, 202, 218, 223–224, 227–228, 234
English Nature, 119, 202, 212–213, 220, 223, 231
Eohippus, 5–9
Equus
  caballus, 15 family, 6, 8–10
  przewalskii, 15
Eriskay Pony, 36
Etherington, Mary (see Mary Speed), 41, 45, 51, 89, 91, 98–100, 234
Evans, Daniel, 80, 87–88
Ewart, Professor J. Cossar, 14, 39, 214
Exford, 72, 95, 106, 110, 114, 136, 214
Exford Show, 211, 213, 216
Exmoor Forest (see Royal Forest of Exmoor)
Exmoor National Park, 104, 106, 110, 112, 114–116, 212–213, 215, 218–220, 223, 231, 233–234
Exmoor Pony Society, 41, 66, 90, 96–98, 101, 184, 194, 198, 204, 214, 217, 222–223, 227, 231–232, 234
  breed standard, 42 breeding programme, 184, 228, 230 committee, 96 formation of, 82, 88, 93–97, 192, 223 herd numbers, 89 inspections, 82, 84, 95–96, 102, 119, 167, 175, 192–196, 200, 214, 226–228

objects of, 95, 192, 214, 223, 228 registrations, 96, 226 rules, 43, 95–96, 200, 226–227
Eyes, 7, 15, 18, 34–35, 37, 39, 41–42, 45, 56, 80, 142, 145–147, 172

Faroe Pony, 39–40, 53, 56
Feet, 1, 5, 7–8, 11, 18–19, 34, 38, 45–46, 78, 90–91, 148, 163–164, 171–173, 190, 192–193
Fell Pony, 28, 36, 94
Feral: classification, 4, 32, 200–202 populations, 32, 101, 118, 124, 163 Foals, 2–3, 29, 48, 55, 68, 71, 75, 78–81, 86, 98, 107, 117, 119, 125, 133–135, 144, 147, 161–165, 167–169, 171–173, 190, 192–194, 202, 204
Foaling, 2, 48, 51, 69, 98, 122, 125, 144, 147, 164–165, 167–174, 176, 182, 186, 188, 202, 204, 212, 229, Foaling season, 168–169, 200
Food, 2–3, 5, 7–8, 10, 12–13, 15–18, 23, 30, 34, 46, 48, 101, 107, 112, 120, 124–126, 129, 133, 135, 141, 148–149, 151-160, 164, 168–169, 177, 200–201, 219, 225
Ford, G., 115
Forelock, 15, 20, 35, 145, 172
Fortescue, Lord, 75, 81–82, 87, 94–96
Free Suitors, 64–66, 68–69, 71–72, 75, 88, 90, 93
Gatherings, 63–66, 78–80, 89, 122–123, 134–135, 161, 167, 189–190, 192, 196, 198, 208, 210, 215, 223–224
Gene pool, 179–180, 186, 228–229, 234
Genes, 9–10, 14, 48–49, 51, 55, 120, 155, 178–180, 184, 186–187, 192, 198, 201–202, 211, 213, 224, 226–230, 234
Genetic fingerprinting, 52–53
Genetic variation, 10, 15, 48–49, 51, 179, 182, 193, 223, 228–229
Girdler family, 116
Grazing rights, 62, 64–65, 68, 82,

88, 178, 188, 221
  family, 84, 106 Frank, 82, 84, 88
  Lycett-Green, Col. Simon, 82, 84–85
  Rose (see Rose Wallace)
Grey Exmoors
  Acland, 49, 51

Habitat
  preferences, 129 types, 139
  use, 129, 139
Haddon Hill, 106, 115–116, 212
Hardiness, 37, 93, 101, 141, 147, 149, 154, 160–161, 216, 224–225, 227–228, 234
Harems, 54, 176, 178, 186, 215
Hawkridge, 61, 64
Hebridean ponies, 38–39
Height, 7, 19, 33–34, 38, 42–43, 45, 51, 63, 74, 80, 91, 95–96, 172
Helman Tor, 116
Herds
  locations of, 104 purpose of, 7, 158, 166, 204 structure, 30, 104, 107–108, 120, 124, 158, 162, 173, 204, 226
Highland Pony, 36–39
Holnicote Estate, 75–76, 78–81, 197
Home ranges, 117–118, 120, 122–126, 129, 133, 135–136, 139, 148, 151, 158, 160, 192
Hunting, 17, 20, 24–25, 28–30, 34, 59, 61–62, 67, 86, 94, 123, 134–135, 141, 163–164, 209 of ponies, 31, 120, 135, 162–163
Hyracotherium (see Eohippus)

Ice
  ages, 23–26, 28 barriers, 11–12 caps, 11, 13, 23–24, 31
Icelandic Horse, 40, 53, 56
Improvement, 41, 86, 93–94, 192
Inbreeding, 184–186, 192, 227, 229
Iron Age, 33, 157, 205

Jaw, 7, 18–19, 28, 34, 47, 154–155

Katerfelto, 53–55
Killerton, 78–81
King Henry VIII, 62–63, 197

Knight
  John, 75–76, 78, 85–86, 93
  ponies, 85–87, 93, 102, 196 Sir
  Frederic, 76, 86–87, 114
Knighton/Knightoncombe, 108,
  148, 209
Konik Pony, 17

Lanacre Farm, 64, 90, 108
Landacre Bridge, 108, 110, 125,
  136, 170
Le Bas, Reginald, 95–96
Life-span, 47
Lock, William, 73, 75
Luckwell Bridge, 91, 112, 191
Lydons Moor, 91, 110

Management of herds, 115, 188,
  193–194, 198–200, 212,
  222–226, 231, 234
Mane, 15–17, 20–21, 34–35, 41,
  80, 145, 147, 172, 193, 211
Markings
  Exmoor, 41–42, 45, 74, 164
  Przewalski Horse, 42,
  primitive, 34, 42, 45, uniform,
  1, 42, 167, 172, 229 variety of,
  36 white, 49, 96, 193
Mating, 55, 115, 134, 173, 176, 182
  season, 122, 168, 186
Mendips, 24–25, 27–28, 32
Merychippus, 7
Mesohippus, 6–7
Mesolithic Period, 26, 28–32,
  201
Metabolism, 154, 161
Milton,
  family, 90, 92, 148, 165 Fred,
  90, 108, 165, 167, 195, 198
Ministry of Agriculture, 41,
  221–222, 231
Miocene Period, 7
Mitchell, Creenagh, 108
Molland, 61, 66, 110 Moor, 106,
  110, 126, 129, 136, 157, 164,
  183, 219
Mongolian Wild Horse (see
  Przewalski's Horse)
Mongrel Ponies, 32, 92, 106–108,
  114, 126, 147, 176, 221
Mountain & Moorland Ponies,

33, 35–36, 41, 93–94, 147, 211,
  214
Movement, 18–19, 133–136, 164,
  189
Mucklow, Edward, 88
Munnings, Sir Alfred, 1, 186
Mustangs, 4, 168–169, 175, 178,
  189
Muzzle, 5–7, 15, 34–35, 39, 41–42,
  45, 51, 56, 78, 90, 102, 172

National Pony Society (N.P.S.), 96
National Trust, 106, 119, 212–213,
  223, 231
Nature reserves, 119, 223
Neolithic Period, 28–29, 32
New Forest Pony, 36, 39, 56, 94,
  123, 136, 153, 155–156, 160,
  168–169, 172–174, 211, 213, 222
North Molton, 61, 65–66, 72, 86,
  206
North Radworthy Farm, 72, 91,
  140
Norwegian Ponies, 36, 40, 56

Oestrus, 168–169, 173
  anoestrus, 168 monoestrus,
  168, 186
Origins, 4, 9, 12, 20, 32, 41–42,
  53, 56, 201
Over-grazing, 151, 155, 222

Palaeolithic Period, 17, 25–28, 30,
  32, 34
Parasites (see also Worms), 10,
  141, 155, 159–161, 224–225
Parkman, Tom, 80–82, 88, 95–96
Pedigrees, 52, 79, 96, 184, 186, 225
Phoenicians, 53
Physiology, 102, 144, 154–155
Pit ponies, 90, 206
Pitt Rivers, General, 55, 205
Pleistocene Period, 15, 17, 20–21,
  23, 25
Pliocene Period, 7–8
Pliohippus, 7–9
Polo Pony Society, 37 stud book,
  37, 43, 50, 81–82, 94, 180
Polo Ponies, 37,, 88, 94
Poltimore, Lord, 91, 94–95
Pony-herd (manager of Acland

herd), 76, 78–82, 88
Population
  age structure, 177 sex ratio,
  125, 175, 178, 200 size, 30–31,
  68–69, 71, 97–98, 119, 226
Porlock, 65–66, 88, 95, 197–198
Porlock Common, 92, 112
Pounds
  Lanacre, 64, 66 Simonsbath,
  66–67, 196
Prealbumin, 52–53
Predators, 5, 7, 10, 13, 18–19, 30,
  34, 46, 135, 139, 141, 147,
  162–164, 172, 188
Prehistoric Art, 17,. 34, 42
Pring
  family, 95–96 Tom, 92, 99
Productivity, 3, 158, 176–177,
  185, 226
Prototypes, 12–14, 1'6, 18, 20, 41,
  57, 101 forest horses, 18, 20
  mountain ponies, 19–20, 24,
  28, 30, 32–34 steppe horses, 13,
  15–17, 19–20, 24, 28, 30, 34
Przewalski's Horse, 13, 15–17,
  28, 34, 42, 53, 57, 101–102, 120,
  159, 201
Przewalsky, Col. N. M., 15

Rare Breeds Survival Trust, 181,
  213, 223, 229–231, 234
Rawle, John, 76, 78–79 Richard,
  79, 80, 82
Red Deer, 24, 29–31, 61–63, 91,
  96, 99, 102, 104, 107–108, 110,
  114–116, 118, 149, 155, 157–158,
  200, 202, 209, 219, 225, 232
Reeks, Col. F. H., 74, 78, 82
Reproduction (see Breeding)
Riding, 209–211, 213
Roman
  cities, 102 contact with
  Exmoor, 102 era, 36, 162, 205
Routes, 120, 133, 135, 189
Royal Dick Veterinary College,
  14, 45, 53, 89, 206, 210, 213
Royal Forest of Exmoor, 49, 54,
  58–59, 61–64, 67–68, 74–75,
  85–86, 112, 114, 216
  courts, 65–66 Forester/Deputy
  Forester, 62–64, 66–67, 71–74

dwellings, 67, 73, 86 grazing
  system, 61, 63, 65, 68–69,
  71–72, 74 income, 67, 69, 71,
  73, laws, 61–62, 64, 75 sale of,
  65–67, 71, 75–76, 85, 88, 92
  stock levels, 68–69, 71, 74, 88
  wardens, 54, 61–69, 71–75, 88,
  93, 114

Sales, 67, 71–72, 76, 78–79, 85,
  88–91, 114, 188, 196–197
  (see also Bampton Fair) prices,
  68–69, 90
Scandinavian Ponies, 40, 53, 56
Scientific Studies, 110, 123–125,
  136, 149, 153, 158–160, 164,
  168–169, 172–174, 176, 189, 213
Scoraig, 117–119, 133, 153
Sea levels, 11, 31–32, 214
Second World War, 180, 184, 198
  Acland herd theft, 84, 97
  Exmoor Mounties, 98, 208 lack
  of herd management, 98 loss
  of moorland gates, 98–99
  ponies as targets, 98
Selection
  artificial, 3, 14, 23, 32, 48, 57,
  101–102, 178, 180, 186,
  199–201, 224 natural, 2, 9–10,
  12–14, 19–21, 30, 101, 147, 155,
  161, 178, 199, 201, 225–226
Shelter, 2–3, 10, 23–24, 28, 72,
  106, 114, 116, 118, 120, 126,
  129, 133, 135, 142, 148–149,
  153, 156, 159, 164, 168, 200–201
Shetland pony, 36, 40, 99
Shows/Showing, 90–91, 95–96,
  170, 183, 206, 210–211,
  213–216, 225, 228
Siberia, 17, 20, 27, 33
Simonsbath, 66–67, 72–73, 75, 86,
  95, 106, 114, 196
Snow, 72, 107, 129, 133, 140–141,
  143–145, 148–149, 156, 165,
  feeding in, 107, 148, 153, 155,
  208 snow-chute, 146
  snow-thatching, 143
Social
  life, 18, 185, 204 organisation,
  3, 21, 75, 126, 175 structure, 2,
  30, 74, 126, 204

South, Len, 115
South Molton, 65, 90, 96, 108, 209, 211
Speed, James, 14, 18–20, 24, 27–28, 32–33, 40–41, 45, 51–52, 55–56, 100–101, 142, 147, 149, 153–154, 210, 214
Speed, Mary (see Mary Etherington), 52, 89, 147, 180, 214
Stallion Parade, 214–216
Stallions
  dominance, 54, 74, 84, 139
  exchange of, 81–82, 94, 96, 174, 227 Exmoor herds (1991), 106 on Royal Forest, 54, 68, 71, 73–74 rivalry, 120, 122–126, 134, 175, 200, 215, 226 selection of, 3, 74–75, 199–200, 226–227
Stone Age, 17, 24
Stud books
  Acland, 81–82 Exmoor Pony Society, 91, 95–96, 174, 180, 186, 192, N.P.S., 96 (see also Polo Pony society)
Suckers, 71, 78, 81–82, 87, 91, 96, 190, 192
Suitors at Large, 65–66, 68–69, 75, 93
Swainmote Courts, 64–66, 73

Taero Island, 118–119, 124–125, 153, 200
Tail, 5, 15, 19–21, 34–35, 41, 46, 74, 79, 84, 102, 141–142, 145–148, 161, 165, 170–172, 193, 195, 197, 211
Tameness, 2–3, 32, 135, 142, 196, 202, 215
Tapp, David, 81, 88, 92, 94–96, 99, 223
Tarpans, 13, 17, 101
Teeth, 5, 7–9, 18–19, 21, 34, 46–47, 54, 84, 154–155, 163, 173, 193
Territories, 119, 123, 125
Thorne
  family, 91–92, 96 John, 73, 91, 140, 156 Leo, 91
Thoroughbred Horse, 3, 36, 39, 52, 86, 88, 93, 154, 230

Toad eye, 45, 146–147
Tourists, 104, 114, 116, 129, 135–136, 139, 159, 198, 219
Trading Routes, 18, 59, 86, 93, 102
Twins, 167, 179
Twitchen, 91, 110

Varle Hill, 82
Vehicles, 99, 124–125, 136, 165, 205, 209, 219
Vikings, 36
Vocalisations, 123, 176

Wallace, Rose (see also Green, Rose), 84–85, 106
Warren Farm, 106, 114–115, 215
Water, 2–3, 10, 119–120, 124–126, 129, 135, 149, 152, 159, 165 dispersal, 35, 45–46, 142, 145–148 holes, 16, 107, 120, 124, 149, 159 proofing, 20, 35, 142–143
Watkins, Veronica, 117, 142, 154, 213
Weather, 13–15, 20, 35, 48, 54, 116, 118, 129, 133, 140–149, 159, 161, 169, 177, 189, 225
Weatherslade, 90, 108, 148, 167, 190, 195
Welsh Pony/Cob, 36–38, 136, 154, 168
Werner, Mary, 110
West Hawkwell Farm, 81, 91, 112
Westcott
  Bob/Charlie/Sidney, 89
  Family, 81–82, 88–92, 95–96, 99
Western
  Bill, 91 family, 92, 112, 190
Wild
  race, 3–4, 16–17, 35, 49 type 41, 48, 51, 57, 74, 101–102, 202
Wild to Domestic Spectrum, 3–4, 141, 178, 200–202
Williams
  family, 93, 96 Harry, 82
Winsford, 78, 87, 106
  Hill, 73, 76, 79–85, 88, 92, 94, 106–108, 110, 112, 123–124, 126, 129, 136, 139, 157, 165, 176, 190, 200, 202, 219, 224
Winter, 12–13, 26, 28, 31, 35, 37,

46, 54–55, 64–65, 67, 71–72, 74, 79, 86–87, 91, 93, 101, 104, 108, 116, 118–119, 126, 139–141, 145, 147–149, 152–158, 161–165, 168–169, 172, 174, 176, 178, 186, 188, 195, 200, 204, 219, 222, 225, 234
Withypool, 1, 61, 63–64, 66, 68, 72–73, 88, 90–91, 93, 98, 107–108, 110, 125, 139, 144, 149, 158, 163–164, 168–169, 172–176, 179, 189–190, 207, 209, 213, 216
  common, 74, 90–91, 106–108, 110, 114–116, 120, 123–126, 129, 133–136, 139, 151, 153, 156, 158, 165, 167, 169–170, 174–177, 185, 189, 192, 195, 200, 202, 213, 219, 224, Hill, 108, 125-126, 141, 148, 208
Wolves, 58, 141, 162–163
Worms (see also Parasites), 10, 159–161, 164, 195, 224–225, 234
Worship, 40, 51

Zeal Farm, 81, 88, 91
Zebras, 7, 9–10, 123, 135
Zoos, 15, 17, 28, 53, 57, 99, 102, 120, 163, 213

INDIVIDUAL PONIES & HERD NUMBERS

Aclander, 174, 181–182
Aga, 125, 165
Bracken Sundown, 165
Bright Bay, 172
Caractacus, 89, 99, 180, 183
Colonel, 80
Cracker, 107
Crackshot I, 89, 180
Crackshot II, 89
Crasus, 117
Daisy, 202, 204, 213
Dazzling Boy, 107, 113, 124–125
Domitian, 116
Don Quixote, 183
Duke, 79
Dunckery, 81
Forest, 174, 181
Foxglove, 99
Gladys, 88, 211

Golden Gorse, 108, 120, 122–126, 129, 136, 139, 149, 151, 164, 170, 174–176, 185
Hannibal, 123
Hawkwell Caligula, 112
Hawkwell Codsend, 185
Heatherman, 181–182
Jan Ridd, 91
Knightoncombe Burnished Brass, 206
Knightoncombe Lackey, 144, 215
Ladybird, 91
Loganberry, 107
Merlin, 206
Mounsey Hill, 123
Octavius, 117
Prince Arthur, 110, 126, 165, 183, 219
Prince Harry II, 108, 126
Prince of Wales, 80
Red Bay, 167
Red Boy II, 167
Red King II, 167
Royal Duke, 119, 121–122, 124–125, 128, 135, 138, 160, 165, 167, 175–176, 185
Royal Oak, 88, 211
Snoopy, 115
South Hill, 87
South Hill II, 80
Tawbitts Mr Toff, 116, 190
Tommy, 174 Yo-Yo, 208

Herds
  Acland/Anchor (see main index)
  No. 12, 91, 112, 190, 198
  No. 14, 115–116, 184
  No. 21, 116
  No. 23, 89, 107, 168, 173, 194
  No. 37, 116
  No. 44, 90, 109
  No. 99, 109
  No. H8, 107, 194, 201
  No. H23, 114
  No. H42, 115, 211
  No. H52, 113
  No. H67, 114
  Taero (see main index)